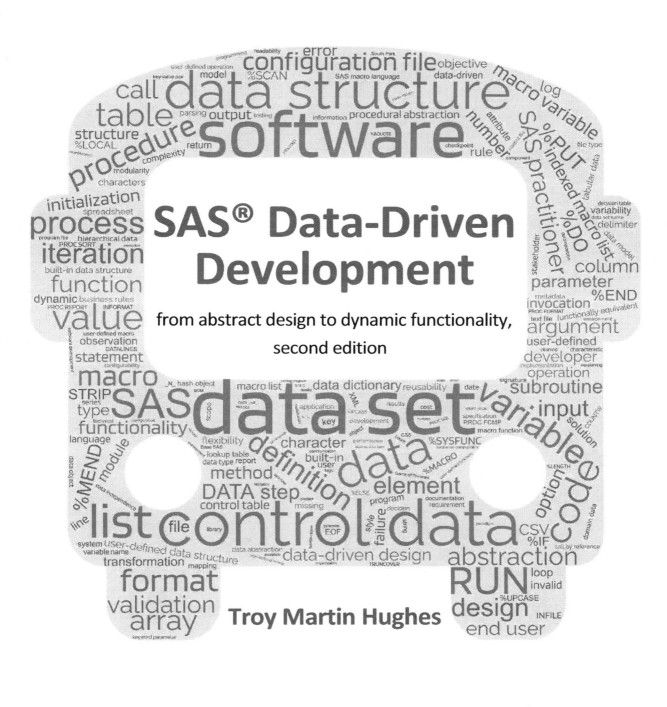

SAS® Data-Driven Development

from abstract design to dynamic functionality,

second edition

Troy Martin Hughes

SAS® Data-Driven Development

Library of Congress Cataloging-in-Publication Data

Names: Hughes, Troy Martin, 1976- author.
Title: SAS data-driven development : from abstract design to dynamic functionality, second edition / Troy Martin Hughes.
Subjects: SAS (Computer file) | Computers / Data Modeling and Design

Cover Design: Troy Martin Hughes
Cover Image: © Data-Driven Dude

Printed in the United States of America

10 9 8 7 6 5

In Memoriam

Ray Martin Hughes
1932 – 2017

Beloved Husband, Father, Grandfather,
Brother, Uncle, and U.S. Airman

Contents

Preface

That data lie at the heart of SAS software is incontrovertible. The SAS application, through the SAS language, transforms data into information, intelligence, decision-making, and ultimately, into business value. Even outside of the SAS microcosm, it is often touted that software exists only to transform data.

As developers, we are taught that *data* include 0s, 1s, and character strings whereas *code* includes IF statements, DO loops, DATA steps, and SORT procedures. We aptly distinguish between *code* and *data* yet often misconstrue that *software* includes only code but not data; this is false.

Data-driven programming eschews this outmoded interpretation of "software" and espouses the more inclusive reality that software contains both code and *control data*—a class of data comprising data mappings, formats, hierarchical data models, data quality rules, business rules, decision tables, configuration files, conditional logic, and other dynamic elements.

Data-driven methods maintain these dynamic elements in external data structures rather than in code, whose role (in data-driven programming) shifts from *executing concrete instructions* to *interpreting and following abstract instructions* that are derived from control data. In this new paradigm, dynamic functionality can be achieved by altering only control data while leaving the underlying code untouched.

To end users, data-driven programming delivers highly configurable, "codeless" software. To developers, it maximizes the flexibility of software, which adapts adroitly in response to dynamic inputs. And to key stakeholders funding software development, data-driven programming improves productivity through increased maintainability, reusability, and extensibility of both code modules and data structures.

Understanding and application of the SAS macro language often signify the first milestone in a SAS practitioner's career—because macros facilitate building more dynamic, flexible, reusable software. Embracing data-driven design pillars, principles, constructs, and best practices should be the next milestone, and this text provides the guidebook for that incredible journey.

Objective

SAS® Data-Driven Development instructs SAS practitioners how to build more flexible, configurable, reusable, and maintainable software— performance objectives that increase software quality. Chapters explore how specific SAS development tasks (e.g., data ingestion, data governance, data transformation, data analysis, data reporting, dynamic program control) can be achieved through data-driven programming.

But the title intimates a higher truth—that data-driven *development* objectives must be achieved through data-driven *design*, including concepts, constructs, and principles that redefine how we conceptualize and build software. As data-driven programming lies at the nexus of code and control data, its adoption changes not only how we write programs but also how we build, interpret, and utilize data structures.

The primary objective of this text is to introduce SAS practitioners to data-driven programming while bridging the gap that too often exists between the instruction of software design and the instruction of software development. Readers will gain an understanding of high-level, software-agnostic design concepts—abstraction, software modularity, and data independence—that underpin data-driven programming. Interwoven throughout these concepts are SAS language techniques that support data-driven design, with examples that contrast undesirable, code-driven (i.e., hardcoded) design patterns and practices.

Audience

The intended audience includes *SAS practitioners*—the developers, testers, quality assurance engineers, data scientists, researchers, students, financial analysts, biostatisticians, and anyone who writes software using the SAS language. In other words, to those like-minded professionals who code to explore data, find answers, create data products, and support data-driven decision-making, this book is for you!

Because software abstraction is so central to data-driven programming, and because it is commonly operationalized through SAS macro statements, a solid foundation in the SAS macro language is a recommended prerequisite for this text. I unapologetically endorse *Carpenter's Complete Guide to the SAS® Macro Language, Third Edition* to anyone seeking this foundation.

Organization

This text is intended to be read cover to cover or to be used as a reference. It comprises two parts, including:

- **Part I. Data-Driven Design** – High-level software design concepts are introduced, including abstraction, software modularity, and data independence. Abstraction—including data abstraction, procedural abstraction, and iteration abstraction—is the focus of four chapters. Later chapters explore the intersections between data-driven design and various stakeholders, the software development life cycle (SDLC) phases, and related disciplines, including table-driven design, object-oriented programming (OOP), master data management (MDM), and business rules interpretation and application.

- **Part II. Control Data** – Control data provide the malleable instructions that facilitate flexible software functionality. Chapters explore various control data classifications and the data structures (both built-in and user-defined) that containerize control data. Parameters, lists, macro lists, control tables, hierarchical data models, configuration files, and other control files are introduced, as well as software operations that interact with these diverse data structures.

More than 270 marginal annotations (which appear as active URLs in the electronic version of this text) facilitate immediate exploration of related topics elsewhere within the text and help straddle the design-development gap. For example, data independence is introduced in Chapter 1, although readers can follow an annotation to the "Data Independence" section in Chapter 4, or to an example in Chapter 16 in which data independence is achieved through CSS files.

> Data independence is defined in Section 1.3.3, is discussed in Section 4.6, and is demonstrated through CSS files in Section 16.5.2

Each chapter is intended to be read separately to facilitate freedom of movement among readers. However, as examples often build incrementally within a chapter, readers are cautioned that the first, facile solution they encounter in a chapter will often be improved in subsequent sections. Thus, many sections introduce a hardcoded solution that, albeit functional, is replaced with more desirable data-driven methods.

"Data-Driven" Disambiguation

A prospective employer commits to pay you "biweekly"—but are you certain how often that paycheck will arrive? Twice a week? Once every two weeks? Or would that be *bi-monthly*? If ever there were just cause to resurrect *fortnightly* from obscurity, this ambiguity is it!

Even Merriam-Webster refuses to arbitrate the *biweekly* conflict, citing "This ambiguity has been in existence for nearly a century and a half and cannot be eliminated by the dictionary."[1] So, you'll probably want to clarify those *biweekly* logistics before signing that job offer.

The same confusion can erupt when "data-driven" is bandied about in software circles and literature. *Data-driven design*, *data-driven software design*, *data-driven development*, and *data-driven software development* each should be considered to be ambiguous until proven otherwise. In all cases, it is clear that "data" are in the driver's seat, but whom or what are those data driving?

Data-driven design can be interpreted more formally as *data-driven software design*—but does this represent "the design of data-driven software" or "the data-driven design of software?" In other words, is the *software* data-driven or is the *design* data-driven? Both interpretations are common throughout literature, but to facilitate clarity and consistency, within this text only *software* is driven by data.

Thus, in this context, *data-driven design* refers to the design of software in which that software's execution is driven by control data. Similarly, *data-driven development* refers to the development of software in which that software's execution is driven by control data. Finally, *data-driven programming* broadly refers to all phases of the SDLC—including planning, design, development, testing, release, and operations and maintenance (O&M)—in which the software's execution is driven by control data.

> The importance of data-driven programming throughout the SDLC is the focus of Chapter 7

Several authors support this common "data-driven" usage. For example, Eric Steven Raymond notes that in "*data driven programming*, one clearly distinguishes code from data structures on which it acts, and designs both so that one can make changes to the logic of the program by editing not the code but the data structure."[2] In SDL Game Development, Shaun Mitchell takes an object-oriented programming (OOP) approach, and describes *data-driven design* as "keeping classes generic…and loading external data to determine their state."[3]

On the other hand, some texts reference *data-driven design* as software design that is driven (i.e., informed) by data. Those data could be metrics that describe software attributes (e.g., lines of code per program, number of times a user-defined function is reused), metrics that describe the development experience (e.g., average number of defects discovered per software testing iteration), or metrics derived from end user experience (e.g., number of users requesting some new functionality).

For example, if software modularity is prioritized within a team or organization, the team could collect metrics on the number of lines of code that each program or module contains. In so doing, a developer could analyze trends in module length and subsequently refactor programs to improve their modularity. Similarly, development teams commonly track new defects and utilize these metrics to help evaluate both the strength of their developers and the success of their quality assurance testers.

One text that supports this alternative usage of *data-driven design* is *Designing with Data: Improving the User Experience with A/B Testing*. It argues that software design should be driven by data rather than "instincts and intuition," and describes *data-driven design* as "data that is collected determines (in other words, drives) design decisions."[4] Despite an altogether separate focus, *Designing with Data* is a phenomenal read that demonstrates how data collected and derived from user experiences should "drive" software development and refactoring.

Notwithstanding, throughout this text, *data-driven design*, *development*, and *programming* always refer to software whose flexibility, reusability, configurability, and other dynamic functionality is facilitated by the interpretation of control data. And with control data behind the wheel, the road trip to higher-quality software can commence!

Acknowledgements

So many people, through contributions to my life as well as endurance and encouragement throughout this journey, have contributed directly and indirectly and made this project possible.

To the family and friends grown weary of hearing "I can't—I'm writing," thank you for your love, patience, understanding, and the fleeting moments of sanity you provided.

To my English teachers who instilled a love of writing, thank you for years of red ink and encouragement: Estelle McCarthy, Lorinne McKnight, Dolores Cummings, Millie Bizzini, Patty Ely, Jo Berry, Liana Hachiya, Audrey Musson, Dana Trevethan, Cheri Rowton, Annette Simmons, and Dr. Robyn Bell.

To the mentors whose words continue to guide me, thank you for your leadership and friendship: Dr. Cathy Schuman, Dr. Barton Palmer, Dr. Kiko Gladsjo, Dr. Mina Chang, Dean Kauffman, Rich Nagy, Jim Martin, and Jeff Stillman.

To my SAS spirit guides, thank you for your continued inspiration: Art Carpenter, Frank DiIorio, Linda Jolley, Ron Cody, Dr. Gerhard Svolba, Kirk Paul Lafler, Louise Hadden, Richann Watson, Ronald Fehd, Lex Jansen, Mark Jordan, Susan Slaughter, Lora Delwiche, Thomas Billings, Peter Eberhardt, Michael Raithel, and Charlie Shipp.

To SAS Institute, thank you for providing free software, without which this endeavor would have been impossible.

About the Author

Troy Martin Hughes has been a SAS practitioner for more than 20 years, has managed SAS projects in support of federal, state, and local government initiatives, and is a SAS Certified Advanced Programmer, SAS Certified Base Programmer, SAS Certified Clinical Trials Programmer, and SAS Professional V8. He has an MBA in information systems management and additional credentials, including: PMP, PMI-ACP, PMI-PBA, PMI-RMP, SSCP, CSSLP, CISSP, CRISC, CISM, CISA, CGEIT, Network+, Security+, CySA+, CASP+, Cloud+, CSM, CSP-SM, CSD, A-CSD, CSP-D, CSPO, CSP-PO, CSP, SAFe Government Practitioner, and ITIL Foundation. He has given more than 100 trainings, hands-on workshops, and presentations at SAS conferences, including SAS Global Forum, SAS Analytics Experience, WUSS, MWSUG, SCSUG, SESUG, PharmaSUG, BASAS, and BASUG. He is the author of the 2016 John Wiley & Sons text: *SAS® Data Analytic Development: Dimensions of Software Quality*. Troy is a U.S. Navy veteran with two tours of duty in Afghanistan.

Part I
Data-Driven Design

Chapter 1.

INTRODUCTION

This chapter has the following objectives:

- ❖ Define and introduce *data-driven design*.

- ❖ Contrast concrete *code-driven design* with abstract *data-driven design*.

- ❖ Differentiate *data*, *domain data*, and *control data*.

- ❖ Introduce the data-driven design pillars of *abstraction*, *software modularity*, and *control data independence*.

- ❖ Introduce data-driven design principles that guide software development best practices.

- ❖ Demonstrate that within a data-driven design paradigm, *software* comprises not only code but also control data.

Data-Driven Design

Software design in which the control logic, program flow, data rules, business rules, data models, data mappings, and other dynamic and configurable elements are abstracted to control data, and are interpreted by (rather than contained within) code.

Data-driven design enables software to be controlled remotely so that data products, output, and functionality can be altered without the need to modify underlying code. Rather than containing explicit instructions that perform some action, data-driven software instead interprets control data and transforms them into abstract instructions and, ultimately, action. Data-driven design maximizes software flexibility, facilitating processes that respond dynamically to malleable inputs, and enabling developers, analysts, system administrators, and end users to configure software with ease by interacting only with control data.

At the heart of data-driven design lie *control data*—data that are interpreted and transformed into software instructions that are executed. The simplest control data include primitive data types (e.g., integers, strings) that are passed as parameters to software or software modules. More complex control data include linear data structures such as lists, sets, and arrays that can be parameterized or maintained in external control files. Even more complex control data include hierarchical data models (e.g., trees), control tables, configuration files, and other control files.

Regardless of their complexity, format, and method of access, *control data* are distinguished as the subset of *data* that provide instruction to software. That is, rather than comprising the domain data that are principally analyzed or transformed by software, control data effect flexibility, with variable control data (input) delivering variable functionality (output).

For example, parameters that are passed to a function or procedure represent *control data*, whereas the pharmaceutical patient records being analyzed represent *domain data*—the data of principal business focus. The International Organization for Standardization (ISO) defines *control data* as "data that select an operating mode, direct the sequential flow of a program, or otherwise directly influence the operation of software."[5] Because data-driven design focuses on *control data* rather than *domain data*, its methods are applicable across industries and organizations.

The role of control data in software is introduced in Section 1.5, and control data classes are differentiated in Chapter 9

4

Control data are central to data-driven design, yet rely on the underlying code that validates, interprets, and operationalizes them; neither can exist without the other. Thus, successful data-driven programming requires the marriage of code and control data, guided by the data-driven design pillars of abstraction, modularity, and data independence, and supported by overarching data-driven design principles that prescribe best practices. This chapter introduces data-driven design pillars and principles, and lays a foundation for the text.

1.1   ALL THE WORLD'S A STAGE

The sometimes subtle distinction between *domain data* and *control data*, as well as the respective roles these components play in data-driven design, can be likened to a marionette show, as depicted on the book cover. A marionette's actions are controlled principally by the content of the show (being performed) and by the puppeteer (or marionettist) pulling the strings (or wires). The narration, dialogue, scenes, songs, and costumes comprise the content of the show. It is this content that differentiates one puppet show from another; it signals whether you are laughing out loud through *Team America: World Police* or painfully enduring (as an adult) Jim Henson's *The Dark Crystal*.

Content is key, but content alone does not make the show. An expert script performed by lifeless, emotionless puppets will not dazzle anyone. Movement adds the humanity, vibrance, warmth, and depth that an audience expects, but requires nuanced complexity—joints and "articulated" features that can kneel, run, grimace, smile, or subtly raise a concerned eyebrow. Without these articulations, you would have only mannequins suspended by strings, and a show not worth watching.

> Software articulation is discussed and contrasted with software abstraction in Section 2.2.1

The marionette *operator* is focused on the seamless synchronization of this movement and the script, but the marionette *builder* (think Geppetto of Disney's *Pinocchio*) must first determine which articulations to create, how they will be independently controlled from above, and the breadth of actions that a puppet should be able to perform. The more flexible a marionette can be built, the more actions it can perform in a single show and the more lifelike it will appear. Moreover, this flexibility also represents an investment, because more versatile marionettes are better suited to perform in future, unrelated shows.

Data-driven design, in many ways, mirrors marionettes and their performances. A software's core functionality, like the content of a show, is the reason software exists; it differentiates one software product from another. But just as mannequins make poor performers, rigid software cannot be controlled or configured without often painful maintenance and modifications. You don't want to stop mid-performance to paint a smile on your dummy's face just so he can convey a moment of glee—or stop to contort his body in some new way that a scene demands. But these unnecessary interludes result when developers build rigid software that cannot flex to customer needs or to the dynamic elements that abound within the software environment.

To overcome rigidity, developers, too, can add "joints" to our code that enable software to flex in prescribed ways. In some cases, a user holds (and controls) the strings by interacting directly with control data through some interface. This occurs when a user runs software and supplies runtime arguments, or modifies a configuration file to alter software functionality. In other cases, the strings are held by other processes or programs that supply dynamic inputs that represent environmental states, analytic results, process output, or other control data. For example, this occurs when the FREQ procedure is used to find the most commonly occurring value in some variable, and that value—encoded as a macro variable—is subsequently parameterized and supplied to alter the functionality of a separate macro or module.

Regardless of who (or what) is holding the strings, it is critical that operators remain out of sight. After all, it would be a distraction to see the marionettist pulling the strings—recall the infamous, untimely exposure of the Wizard of Oz to Dorothy and her companions! This separation is central to data-driven methods as well, in which the control data driving software always must be external to the code interpreting and implementing those abstract instructions. Software modularity and data independence facilitate the flexibility, configurability, and reusability of both code and the data structures in which control data reside.

So why are not all puppets lifelike and not all software products driven by data? First, flexibility and configurability are not always required, or are required only in specific areas. Some marionettes do not need to be able to run around and contort their legs, so providing these abilities would add no value while making the marionettes needlessly more difficult to control. Software, too, might contain few elements requiring end user configuration or dynamic input. For example, a data-driven process might be primarily static and require only a single parameter through which end users specify the data set name upon which the process acts.

Second, reusability and *extensibility*—flexibility with an eye toward the future—are not always required. If a marionette is intended for use in a single show and will not be reused in subsequent, unrelated performances, it can be designed to the specifications of that single show. Gorilla-Glue the King's crown and robes to his woody undercarriage because he'll forever be royalty! Software, too, might be constructed for a specific objective that does not lend itself to reuse. For example, extract-transform-load (ETL) software might contain a complex sequence of operations whose uniqueness dictates that the code should not be reused and would not benefit from data-driven design.

Third, flexibility can be expensive; the added work to build joints, attach strings, and construct controls creates a superior work of art, but this quality is only appreciated where it adds purpose and value. Data-driven design similarly should be implemented where its benefits to a specific software product are clear and where technical requirements demand a higher level of abstraction and flexibility. It is this potential expense—of increased scope, schedule, and cost—that dictates why data-driven programming is principally a *design* rather than a *development* consideration.

> Data-driven design can help *reduce* scope, schedule, and cost when consistently applied throughout the SDLC, as discussed in Sections 7.1 and 7.2

Baking data-driven methods into software design is preferred to sprinkling them on top after software has been developed and deployed. The design and implementation of data structures that facilitate data-driven design should be one of the first considerations in planning a software product, for although it is never impossible to refactor hardcoded software with data-driven design methods, this post hoc undertaking is neither efficient nor ideal.

1.2   DATA-DRIVEN VS. CODE-DRIVEN

When someone speaks of *data-driven decisions*, this not only distinguishes that certain decisions purport to be rooted in fact or data, but also intimates that other decisions are *not* driven by data; perhaps they are instead driven by intuition, instinct, or whimsy. Accordingly, when Rick Warren penned *The Purpose Driven Life*, he was as much providing commentary on lives that *lack* purpose as those that *have* purpose. In fact, whenever "driven" is used as a modifier, the audience or reader is immediately alerted that an inherent comparison is being made. So, a title like *Data-Driven Development* begs the question, "What development or design is *not* driven by data?"

The unmistakable allure of abstraction is explored in Chapter 2, The Abstraction Attraction

Code-driven design, although seldom referenced as such, describes a paradigm in which dynamic elements or instructions are hardcoded within (rather than interpreted by) a software module's code. These concepts are differentiated in that data-driven design is more abstract whereas code-driven design is more concrete. Code-driven processes can still behave dynamically—based on domain data, the operating system (OS), environmental states, runtime errors or exceptions, and other sources of variability—but this dynamic functionality is hardcoded within the program itself, rather than spawned from control data. Data-driven and code-driven methods must be distinguished so that developers can select the right tool for the task.

A common first objective in many programming textbooks instructs would-be developers to print "Hello World!" The %PUT statement accomplishes this task in the SAS macro language:

```
%put Hello World!;
```

Yet even this primal task, despite its simplicity, can be made more dynamic by using data-driven concepts. For example, rather than always printing "Hello World!," the code could be rewritten so that any message—passed in an argument, or specified within a configuration file or other external data structure—could be printed. In the following data-driven alternative, "Hello World!" no longer appears in the code, having been replaced by an abstraction—the MSG parameter and associated &MSG macro variable:

```
%macro message(msg= /* message */);
%put &msg;
%mend;
```

For example, the MESSAGE macro can produce varying output:

```
%message(msg=Hello World!);


Hello World!


%message(msg=Hi World!);
```

Hi World!

Both the data-driven and code-driven methods demonstrate equivalent basic functionality (i.e., printing "Hello World!"), yet the data-driven solution extends this functionality because it can print other user-specified messages. Dynamic messages can be changed over time based on current business need (i.e., flexibility), or can be specified by various end users (i.e., configurability), providing each user a different message. These objectives—flexibility and configurability—are two of the primary software performance characteristics that data-driven design delivers.

Thus, end users, who may themselves not be developers, are empowered to configure software, thereby reducing unnecessary software maintenance and modification that developers would otherwise have had to perform. Moreover, developers can often reuse flexible software modules to solve subsequent challenges.

The previous example demonstrates *substitution*, a form of abstraction in which a parameter, pointer, reference, or other object is replaced before or during software execution. More complex abstraction can be implemented to interpret and apply business rules and other conditional logic. For example, the TIME_MESSAGE macro includes static business rules that print a time-sensitive welcome message before the user-specified message:

End users represent any user of software (including SAS practitioners), and are discussed in Section 7.1.3

Section 2.2.2 demonstrates how substitution is used to traverse levels of data abstraction

Business rules are defined and discussed in Section 8.3

Data structure rules are discussed in relation to data independence objectives in Section 4.6

```
%macro time_message(msg= /* message */);
%local timesec timemsg;
%let timesec=%sysfunc(time());
%if &timesec<21600
   %then %let timemsg=Go back to sleep!;
%else %if &timesec<43200
   %then %let timemsg=Good morning!;
%else %if &timesec<64800
   %then %let timemsg=Good afternoon!;
%else %let timemsg=Good night!;
%put &timemsg;
%put &msg;
%mend;


%time_message(msg=Hey there!);
```

SAS maintains time values as the number of seconds (in decimal notation) since midnight; thus, 21,600 seconds corresponds to 6 am, 43,200 seconds to noon, and 64,800 seconds to 6 pm. In the TIME_MESSAGE macro, users are kindly told "Go back to sleep!" between the hours of midnight and 6 am, "Good morning!" between the hours of 6 am and noon, "Good afternoon!" between noon and 6 pm, and "Good night!" between 6 pm and midnight.

The importance of establishing which stakeholders will interact with which control data is discussed in Section 2.2.3

The program represents code-driven, concrete logic in which the business rules are hardcoded as literal values that correspond to time ranges and their respective messages. But what if a user wanted to change a time range, alter a time-sensitive message, or add or remove a time range entirely? Each of these modifications would unfortunately (and unnecessarily) require altering the code—because the business rules are maintained in the program itself.

A data-driven approach would instead abstract these business rules to an external data structure so they could be modified independently while the code remained unchanged. The cfg.txt comma-separated values (CSV) file now represents these business rules:

```
21600,Go back to sleep!
43200,Good morning!
64800,Good afternoon!
0,Good night!
```

Data structure rules should be defined to ensure that the data they contain are valid and are formatted, structured, and interpreted correctly. Especially where user-defined data structures are shared among developers, or maintained by nontechnical end users, the formal definition and documentation of data structure rules becomes increasingly important. From the preceding CSV file, the following rules can be inferred:

Configuration files often include data structure rules within file comments, as demonstrated in Section 16.3.2

- Time values are displayed in seconds (since midnight).
- Messages cannot contain commas.
- A line lists a time value and a message, separated by a comma.
- Lines are read and processed in order.
- Each message is applied to a time value *less than* (i.e., exclusive of) the corresponding time value.
- The final line contains the time "0" and the message that will be applied to any remaining, unassigned time values.

Data structure rules can also speak to how a data structure is intended to be maintained or modified—in other words, manually by an end user, or automatically by a program or process. In this scenario, only one operation—reading the data structure—is conceptualized. Thus, the control table is intended to be edited by end users and interpreted by an underlying program, but the program will not write to (or otherwise modify) the data structure or its contents.

Section 14.2 demonstrates checkpoint tables— *control tables with which processes (rather than people) interact*

The TIME_MSG_CFG macro is functionally equivalent to TIME_MESSAGE but now relies on data-driven techniques to read the control table (via the INFILE statement), interpret its business rules, and dynamically apply those rules:

```
%let loc=d:\sas\; * USER MUST CHANGE LOCATION *;
%macro time_msg_cfg(msg= /* message */,
   cfg= /* configuration folder and file */);
%local timesec timemsg syntax;
filename cfgfile "&cfg";
data _null_;
   infile cfgfile dsd dlm=',' lrecl=1024 end=eof;
   input timesec :8. timemsg :$100.;
   length dtg 8;
   dtg=time();
   if dtg < timesec or timesec=0 then do;
      put timemsg;
      stop;
      end;
run;
%put &msg;
%mend;


%time_msg_cfg(msg=Hi there!, cfg=&loc.cfg.txt);
```

The refactored macro (TIME_MSG_CFG) is more complex but only slightly longer than the code-driven alternative (TIME_MESSAGE). Rather than containing explicit instructions (i.e., conditional logic that assigns the time-dependent messages), the data-driven solution contains a DATA step that interprets the external control table in which the business rules are maintained. When a time range is identified that corresponds to the current time, the Timemsg variable is printed to the log, and STOP terminates the DATA step so that subsequent conditional logic statements will not be evaluated.

The data-driven alternative delivers tremendous benefits—software modularity and data independence that enable business rules to be modified without changing the underlying code that interprets them. Subtly more complex but with a huge payout!

For example, if a user wanted to further differentiate the times of day, he could modify the business rules to include a "Good evening!" message by altering only the control table (cfg.txt):

```
21600,Go back to sleep!
43200,Good morning!
61200,Good afternoon!
72000,Good evening!
0,Good night!
```

The revised business rules, with no modification to the underlying code, now prescribe the "Good afternoon!" messages until only 5 pm, the "Good evening!" messages until 8 pm, and the "Good night!" message thereafter. When the TIME_MSG_CFG macro is run, the new business rules (within the control table) are parsed until a match is found and the associated time-sensitive message is printed to the log.

Note the unnecessary step, however, that a developer had to first transform 5 pm into the corresponding SAS time value of 72000. This manual transformation can be avoided if the macro is refactored again to recognize timestamps in a more readable HH:MM 24-hour notation.

First, a new configuration file (cfg_24.txt) should be created:

```
06:00,Go back to sleep!
12:00,Good morning!
17:00,Good afternoon!
20:00,Good evening!
00:00,Good night!
```

Next, the macro is refactored to read and transform 24-hour notation, and the invocation is pointed to the new configuration file:

```
%let loc=d:\sas\; * USER MUST CHANGE LOCATION *;
%macro time_msg_cfg(msg= /* message */,
```

```
        cfg= /* configuration folder and file */);
%local timesec timemsg syntax;
filename cfgfile "&cfg";
data _null_;
    infile cfgfile dsd dlm=',' lrecl=1024 end=eof;
        input timesec_hhmm :$8. timemsg :$100.;
    length dtg timesec 8;
    dtg=time();
    timesec=(input(scan(timesec_hhmm,1,':'),8.) * 3600)
        + (input(scan(timesec_hhmm,2,':'),8.) * 60);
    if dtg < timesec or timesec=0 then do;
        put timemsg;
        stop;
        end;
run;
%put &msg;
%mend;


%time_msg_cfg(msg=Hi there!, cfg=&loc.cfg_24.txt);
```

With these subtle modifications, SAS practitioners are no longer required to transform dates to SAS date values; this complexity is not only automated but also hidden within the macro.

In addition to supporting ease of software maintenance, this data-driven design also maximizes software configurability for end users. For example, Bill might prefer the initial business rules (without "Good evening") whereas Jane might prefer the revised business rules. Both analysts can be accommodated by data-driven design because they can save their respective business rules to separate configuration files. By changing only the configuration file name (specified in the CFG parameter), both users can continue to run the identical TIME_MSG_CFG macro, thus reusing software while implementing their preferred business rules.

The alternative code-driven solution (TIME_MESSAGE macro) would have required each analyst to maintain a separate program because business rules would have been maintained *inside* the code, not within a remote data structure. Throughout this text, data-driven methods demonstrate these software configurability objectives, providing an interface through which end users can interact with software to meet their unique business needs.

Although *data-driven* and *code-driven* design are contrasted here as protagonist and archvillain, all software in fact lies on a continuum that can include varying degrees of abstraction, modularity, and data independence. Just as no software is ever fully abstract, no software is ever fully data-driven; concrete components are always required, so explicit instructions will always exist. But where additional flexibility is desired, software can be built (or refactored) to replace concrete with abstract design. These "joints" provide flexibility and configurability, and spur dynamic functionality.

Data-driven design is not a new design pattern, but rather an amalgam of concepts and techniques, as discussed in Chapter 8

1.3   DATA-DRIVEN DESIGN PILLARS

The variability and versatility of data-driven programming are limited only by the creativity of developers. But when you step back, common language-agnostic pillars undergird data-driven design, and common principles and patterns can be relied upon to guide data-driven development.

Data-Driven Design Pillars

Abstraction simplifies and focuses aspects of software. Procedural abstraction, data abstraction, and iteration abstraction are three flavors of abstraction that are discussed and demonstrated throughout this text. Abstraction is critical to data-driven design because it enables program logic (and other dynamic elements) to be represented abstractly as control data, rather than concretely as code. Moreover, abstraction is fundamental to building flexible, configurable, reusable chunks of code—user-defined procedures, functions, subroutines, and other processes.

Abstraction is further explored in Chapter 2, and is the focus of the next four chapters

(Software) Modularity typically describes the separation of software into distinct modules that are "loosely coupled and functionally discrete." *Loose coupling* requires that where procedures, functions, and other modules are defined, associated control data should be parameterized and passed through predefined channels. *Functionally discrete* modules require that a process "do one and only one thing" and support data-driven design by not commingling operations that interact with control data.

Modularity is demonstrated in Section 1.3.2, and is defined from an OOP perspective in Section 8.4.2

(Control) Data Independence separates control data from functionality. It requires that control data and their underlying code (that validates, interprets, and operationalizes them) be independently maintained, including in separate files (when control data are stored). Both control data and code should be sufficiently abstract and flexible, such that modifications made to one (in prescribed ways) will not cause failure or require redesign in the other. Finally, data independence requires that control data must be able to be readily, reliably, and securely accessed by the end user, developer, administrator, process, or program intended to view, maintain, and modify them.

Data independence is discussed in Sections 1.3.3 and 4.6, and is contrasted with modularity in Section 4.7

1.3.1   Abstraction

Abstraction, the first pillar of data-driven design, is so fundamental to data-driven design that the concepts can seem indistinguishable at times. If you're controlling a marionette and move a wooden control block up and to the right to effect a corresponding movement in the puppet's foot, your movement is an abstraction—a simplified representation of the action to be performed by the puppet. In software, similarly, control data (and the interpretation thereof) convey abstraction. For example, modifying a business rule in a configuration file can be used to effect a representative change in the software processes that evaluate or implement those rules.

Abstraction is so ubiquitous throughout software that it is difficult to find code lacking it. Variables themselves, in fact, represent abstraction in which a symbolic name is substituted for some value that may be unknown at the time of software development (or even execution), or which may change as software executes. Within this text, procedural abstraction, data abstraction, and iteration abstraction are primarily discussed.

Procedural abstraction is found in applications, functions, procedures, subroutines, SAS macros, and other software modules, and exposes to the end user only the relevant details of functionality.

Procedural abstraction is the focus of Chapter 3

For example, the FREQ procedure employs procedural abstraction by shielding all but the necessary parameters (e.g., DATA, TABLES) from the view of SAS practitioners:

```
data somedata;
   length bday 8;
   format bday mmddyy8.;
   bday='06jan1946'd; output;
   bday='21oct1975'd; output;
   bday='15mar1994'd; output;
```

```
run;

proc freq data=somedata;
    tables bday;
run;
```

Thus, the end user calling FREQ must understand what inputs FREQ requires (e.g., the DATA and TABLES statements) and what output FREQ produces (i.e., frequency counts, optional output data set), but does not need to understand the FREQ *implementation*—the methods or complex algorithms through which FREQ generates results. Because FREQ methods are encapsulated (essentially within a *black box*), SAS Institute can redesign and refactor the procedure without changing the FREQ *specification*—the definition of how end users (i.e., SAS practitioners) call the FREQ procedure.

For example, in SAS 9.4, FREQ is *still* not multithreaded (unlike MEANS, SORT, SQL, and other higher-performing procedures), but SAS Institute could redesign FREQ to be multithreaded, release the updated software, and bless billions of SAS users with this tremendous advancement. So long as the FREQ *specification* remained consistent, SAS practitioners could continue to call FREQ as before, albeit with significantly improved performance. Thus, procedural abstraction enables developers to refactor and upgrade software more readily without interruption to end users.

Data abstraction is employed whenever variables (including macro variables) are used in lieu of literal values. Additionally, the FREQ procedure employs data abstraction when statements such as DATA and TABLES effectively operate as parameters that provide flexibility. A user-defined macro could operate similarly and utilize a DATA parameter to specify a data set to be transformed:

```
%macro transform(data= /* data set name */);
data transformed;
    set &data;
    * perform some transformation;
run;
%mend;

%transform(data=somedata);
```

Procedural *implementation* is introduced in Section 3.3, and procedural *specification* in Section 3.2

Data abstraction is the focus of Chapter 4

More complex data abstraction can be achieved through user-defined data structures, such as the cfg.txt control table created in Section 1.2. In this example, the data structure includes not only control data but also the implied rules that define how those data should be interpreted and transformed into explicit software instructions.

Iteration abstraction (or *iteration*) describes traversing a range of data or some other data structure, typically to perform element-level operations. Oftentimes, the same operation is performed on all elements, but in some cases, the tasks performed may differ.

Iteration abstraction is the focus of Chapter 5

The SOMANYHELLOS macro demonstrates iteration and prints "Hello World!" a variable number of times, specified at macro invocation:

```
%macro somanyhellos(n= /* number of iterations */);
%local i;
%do i=1 %to &n;
   %put Hello World!;
   %end;
%mend;


%somanyhellos(n=5);
```

Despite typing "Hello World!" only once in the code, the developer is greeted with five salutations in the SAS log:

```
Hello World!
Hello World!
Hello World!
Hello World!
Hello World!
```

From a business perspective, iteration abstraction provides two key advantages: increased developer productivity, because code length is reduced, and increased software productivity, in that software can generate more output through less (and minimal) code. From a more technical perspective, iteration facilitates software flexibility, configurability, and scalability because the number of loops can be varied at invocation (via the N argument) without modifying the macro implementation (i.e., the SOMANYHELLOS macro).

Arguments and *parameters* are defined and distinguished in Section 6.3

1.3.2 Modularity

Modularity is discussed within the context of OOP in Section 8.4.2, and the DYNO_LENGTH and DYNO_LABEL user-defined macro functions showcase modularity in Section 10.4.3

Software modularity, the second pillar of data-driven design, enables precision movements to be made, unadulterated by unrelated functionality. ISO defines *modularity* as the "degree to which a system or computer program is composed of discrete components such that a change to one component has minimal impact on other components."[6] If you are designing a marionette, modularity is critical because you do not want the same string controlling both mouth shape and leg movements—or you will end up with unwanted, unnatural dependencies, like a puppet that smiles when she runs but frowns when her legs stop moving.

Encapsulation and *information hiding* are discussed in Section 8.4.1

In a procedural language like SAS, modularity is often achieved by decomposing software into discrete functionality—macros, procedures, functions, and other modules that can be called as child processes. Controlling the inputs and outputs and ensuring that software interacts with a module only through predefined channels and with predefined control data enhances the separation among modules, allowing them to be used and reused more flexibly without unnecessary or unintended dependencies. The modules are *encapsulated*.

The Social Security Administration (SSA) maintains a sliding scale that determines—based on birth year—the age at which a recipient is eligible to receive full benefits.[7] If you were born in or before 1937, you are 100 percent eligible at the age of 65, whereas if you were born between the years of 1943 and 1954, you are not 100 percent eligible until the age of 66. These abridged business rules are hardcoded in the following DATA step, in which Elig is calculated to be either 100 or a missing value:

```
data trans (drop=age);
   set somedata;
   length age elig 8;
   age=intck('year',bday,date());
   if year(bday)<=1937 and age>=65 then elig=100;
   else if 1943<=year(bday)<=1954 and age>=66
      then elig=100;
run;
```

The data transformation could be made more modular, however, by extracting the business rules from the DATA step and placing them inside an FCMP function or macro function. For example, in the following SAS program, the SSA_ELIG macro now includes all business rules, which are executed when the SSA_ELIG macro is invoked in the DATA step:

```
%macro ssa_elig;
if year(bday)<=1937 and age>=65 then elig=100;
else if 1943<=year(bday)<=1954 and age>=66 then
elig=100;
%mend;


data trans (drop=age);
   set somedata;
   length elig age 8;
   age=intck('year',bday,date());
   %ssa_elig;
run;
```

This functionally equivalent solution is somewhat more modular because SSA_ELIG can be modified (to alter business rules) without modifying the DATA step. However, the program design is still monolithic because the macro is both defined and called within the same program file.

A more modular solution would instead store the SSA_ELIG macro inside a separate program (saved as ssa_rules.sas) so it could be called as a child process:

```
* saved as ssa_rules.sas;
%macro ssa_elig;
if year(bday)<=1937 and age>=65 then elig=100;
else if 1943<=year(bday)<=1954 and age>=66 then
   elig=100;
%mend;
```

The DATA step can be saved as ssa_main.sas, which calls the SSA_ELIG macro, its child process:

```
* saved as ssa_main.sas;
%let loc=d:\sas\;       * USER MUST CHANGE LOCATION *;
%include "&loc.ssa_rules.sas";
data trans (drop=age);
   set somedata;
   length elig age 8;
```

```
age=intck('year',bday,date());
%ssa_elig;
run;
```

Note that the %INCLUDE statement is required, and references (and executes) the SAS program file in which the SSA_ELIG macro is stored. Thus, %INCLUDE compiles the SSA_ELIG macro, which must occur before the SSA_ELIG macro can be called from within the DATA step.

With this revision, were Congress to legislate a new sliding scale for eligibility requirements, an analyst would be able to modify only the SSA_ELIG macro without having to touch the program file containing the primary DATA step. This improves the reusability of the macro because it can be independently maintained and modified, and improves the integrity of the DATA step because its code remains stable and untouched despite potential updates to the macro.

Section 11.1 details the unnecessary use of the SAS macro language, and how to overcome this common design flaw

The solution is now modular; however, it can be improved further by replacing the SSA_ELIG macro with a user-defined function. Because the macro only transforms data to produce a single return value (Elig), this functionality is more appropriately maintained within a user-defined FCMP function than a macro.

The SAS Function Compiler (aka the FCMP procedure) can be used to define the ELIG_FUNC function:

```
proc fcmp outlib=sasuser.myfuncs.ssa;
    function elig_func(dob);
        length age elig 8;
        age=intck('year', dob,date());
        if year(dob)<=1937 and age>=65 then elig=100;
        else if 1943<=year(dob)<=1954 and age>=66
            then elig=100;
        return(elig);
        endfunc;

quit;
```

Sections 6.5.1 and 6.5.2 demonstrate additional FCMP functions and subroutines

The Elig variable is now declared and calculated within the function, and passed back to the calling (i.e., parent) process using the RETURN function:

```
options cmplib=sasuser.myfuncs;
```

```
data trans;
   set somedata;
   length elig 8;
   elig=elig_func(bday);
run;
```

The solution employs abstraction—both procedural abstraction and data abstraction—as well as modularity, in defining and calling the ELIG_FUNC function. This abstraction facilitates reuse of the function by other programs that require the same data transformation business rules. Notwithstanding these improvements, data-driven design further requires data independence that has not yet been achieved but which is demonstrated in the next subsection.

1.3.3   Data Independence

Control data independence, the third pillar of data-driven design, requires that control data be maintained separately from the code interpreting them, and that control data be accessible to the processes or personnel intended to modify them. Data independence supports software configurability, one of the primary objectives of data-driven design, by allowing personnel who lack development experience (or even access to development software like Base SAS) to modify software functionality through control data alone.

With this understanding, although ELIG_FUNC is a beautifully crafted and devilishly handsome function, the control data it contains are literal values, defined in situ rather than interpreted from external control data. This is arguably not poor design; however, it does not embody *data-driven* design, which requires data independence—the separation of control data from code.

In the marionette scenario, a marionette operator might awkwardly— if not catastrophically—attempt to manipulate puppets directly, by holding them rather than using wires or wooden blocks to guide their movement. Control boards (or blocks) ensure smooth functioning of marionettes and prevent wires from getting crossed. Similarly, data-driven design requires external data structures that can be controlled remotely to guide functionality. Thus, neither your fingers nor your control data should be part of the show!

External data structures isolate control data but must be constructed such that their data can be unambiguously and consistently interpreted.

Continuing the example from Section 1.3.2, the control data that underpin the SSA business rules can be saved in a control file (ssa_scale.txt):

```
1900 - 1937, 65
1938, 65 and 2 months
1939, 65 and 4 months
1940, 65 and 6 months
1941, 65 and 8 months
1942, 65 and 10 months
1943 - 1954, 66
1955, 66 and 2 months
1956, 66 and 4 months
1957, 66 and 6 months
1958, 66 and 8 months
1959, 66 and 10 months
1960 - 3000, 67
```

The data structure requires an operation to interpret these raw control data and transform them into actionable business rules. The CREATE_RULES macro reads the control file, dynamically creates business rules, and aggregates all rules into the &BUSINESSRULES global macro variable:

```
%macro create_rules(ctrlfile= /* control file */);
%global businessrules;
%let businessrules=;
filename ctrl "&ctrlfile";
data _null_;
   infile ctrl dsd dlm=',' end=eof truncover;
     input dates :$12. ages :$20.;
   length agecutoff 8 date1 8 date2 8 rule $100
     ruletot $1000;
   retain ruletot '';
   date1=input(scan(dates,1,'-'),8.);
   date2=input(scan(dates,2,'-'),8.);
   agecutoff=input(scan(ages,1,'and'),8.);
   agecutoff=agecutoff+max(0,(input
     (scan(scan(ages,2,'and'),1,,'S'),8.)/12));
```

```
    rule=ifc(_n_=1,'if ','else if ')
        || strip(put(date1,8.)) || '<= year(dob)'
        || ifc(missing(date2),'','<='
        || strip(put(date2,8.)))
        || ' and age>=' || strip(put(agecutoff,8.3))
        || ' then elig=100;';
    ruletot=catx('',ruletot,rule);
    if eof then call symputx('businessrules',ruletot);
run;
%mend;
```

Through *metaprogramming*, the macro dynamically creates the &BUSINESSRULES global macro variable that contains the conditional logic that will be executed within the ELIG_FUNC function:

Metaprogramming techniques are contrasted with SAS arrays in Section 10.1.2, and Section 14.1.2 demonstrates a macro that writes code that interprets user-defined decision tables

```
if 1900<= year(dob) <=1937
    and age>=65.000 then elig=100;
else if 1938<=year(dob)
    and age>=65.167 then elig=100;
else if 1939<= year(dob)
    and age>=65.333 then elig=100;
else if 1940<= year(dob)
    and age>=65.500 then elig=100;
else if 1941<= year(dob)
    and age>=65.667 then elig=100;
else if 1942<= year(dob)
    and age>=65.833 then elig=100;
else if 1943<= year(dob)<=1954
    and age>=66.000 then elig=100;
else if 1955<= year(dob)
    and age>=66.167 then elig=100;
else if 1956<= year(dob)
    and age>=66.333 then elig=100;
else if 1957<= year(dob)
    and age>=66.500 then elig=100;
else if 1958<= year(dob)
    and age>=66.667 then elig=100;
else if 1959<= year(dob)
```

```
      and age>=66.833 then elig=100;
  else if 1960<= year(dob)<=3000
      and age>=67.000 then elig=100;
```

The CREATE_RULES macro must be invoked before the function is compiled, as ELIG_FUNC now relies on the &BUSINESSRULES macro variable, which contains the conditional logic that initializes the Elig variable:

```
%create_rules(ctrlfile=D:\sas\ssa_scale.txt);
proc fcmp outlib=sasuser.myfuncs.ssa;
    function elig_func(dob);
        length age elig 8;
        age=intck('year',dob,date());
        &businessrules;
        return(elig);
        endfunc;
quit;
```

Finally, a SAS developer wishing to apply the Social Security Administration business rules to the Somedata data set can do so by calling the ELIG_FUNC function:

```
options cmplib=sasuser.myfuncs;
data trans;
    set somedata;
    length elig 8;
    elig=elig_func(bday);
run;
```

Separately, a business analyst—having no knowledge of the SAS language—can modify the business rules by altering only the control file. Thus, within this new data-driven design paradigm, the software can flexibly incorporate evolving Social Security business rules while its code remains stable.

To recap, *procedural abstraction* is used to define and call the ELIG_FUNC function, enabling developers to maintain this module apart from the DATA step. *Data abstraction* ensures that ELIG_FUNC does not contain literal values but rather interprets control data that are supplied to the function. *Modularity* separates the ELIG_FUNC function from the DATA step that invokes it. Finally, *data independence* ensures that control data are maintained in a data structure apart from the code that interprets them, and that those data can be accessed and modified.

1.4   DATA-DRIVEN DESIGN PRINCIPLES

Whereas data-driven design *pillars* represent the high-level design concepts central to data-driven programming, data-driven design *principles* represent best practices that support data-driven design and development.

Data-Driven Design Principles

Data-driven design should be driven by requirements. Where functionally equivalent code-driven and data-driven design alternatives exist, stakeholders should examine requirements—including functional and performance requirements—to assess whether the more complex data-driven design is appropriate. This mitigates the tendency for every developer with a hammer to view every problem as a nail. Data-driven design is a solution for many, but not all, programming challenges.

Match the level and scope of abstraction with requirements. Select the appropriate abstraction level that delivers the required software flexibility, configurability, reusability, and overall dynamic functionality.

Favor built-in over user-defined data structures. User-defined data structures are essential but should be used only when built-in data structures are insufficient. If a built-in data structure is sufficient, but its associated operations are not, consider using the built-in data structure and developing new user-defined operations (that operate on it), rather than designing a custom data structure.

Favor data structures with intrinsic element decomposition. Data structures in which constituent elements are unambiguously differentiated are preferred over those for which data structure decomposition methods must be developed to identify and extract individual elements.

Identify inherited data structure characteristics. Data structures inherit characteristics from the superordinate data structure classes and file types in which they are maintained. Whether advantageous or not, characteristics (e.g., intrinsic element decomposition) and components (e.g., end-of-line markers, end-of-file markers) must be understood.

Never commingle control data with functionality. Control data should include just enough detail to be universally and unambiguously identified and extracted. Data operations can be implied, but should not be explicitly stated, within control data.

Maintain and pass control data simply and natively. Where possible, pass control data in their native formats or, if this impairs readability, through an interoperable format that facilitates their comprehension.

Identify master control data and maintain a single version. Where control data represent master data that are unique, far-reaching, and critical to an organization, master data management (MDM) principles should be implemented to maintain a single "golden" record, table, or other control file that is used for all dependent operations.

Hide complexity in the software implementation, not the invocation. The invocation (of some reusable software module) should not be encumbered with validity checks, control data transformation, or other functionality best concealed and maintained inside its implementation.

Future-proof to support backward compatibility. Faith in software reusability requires faith that current invocations of procedures, functions, and other software modules will not be invalidated by the subsequent release of software updates to those modules. The evolution of software is inevitable, so developers should strive to prioritize the backward compatibility of extant software functionality.

1.5   CONTROL DATA ARE SOFTWARE, TOO!

Definitively, control data are *data*—that subset of data that drive software operations and functionality; less apparent to some, however, control data are also *software*. Similar to the United States federal government, in which the Executive, Legislative, and Judiciary branches are coequal, control data are as important as their underlying code. Stated another way, code is as important as its underlying control data. Thus, and in contrast to some literature, data-driven programming does not aim to place control data *above* code but rather *on par with* code.

In a code-driven design paradigm, all functionality is delivered through code, which can comprise a single, monolithic program or a modular software product having multiple programs. Data-driven design, conversely, requires the cooperation of code and control data to deliver functionality. Despite these contrasting philosophies, for many software requirements, functionally equivalent code-driven and data-driven solutions can be conceptualized; that is, developers have a choice, and each alternative will deliver equivalent functionality.

But software quality comprises not only *functionality* but also *performance*—and a common performance requirement described in technical specifications is software configurability, which empowers especially end users to effect dynamic functionality through control data. In these cases, only data-driven design can deliver the flexibility and configurability that performance requirements demand.

Software configuration effectively offers a window into the software soul because stakeholders are able to make sometimes drastic changes to software functionality without altering its code. For example, the final solution in Section 1.3.3 demonstrates how fundamental Social Security Administration eligibility requirements can be modified by altering only the business rules contained within a configuration file.

Thus, it must be stated, that with great software design comes great responsibility. Where control data are intended to be modified by end users, system administrators, SAS practitioners, or other stakeholders, data entry controls and/or quality controls should be emplaced to ensure the security and integrity of those data. A misplaced parameter or malformed business rule could cause a software system to grind to a halt or, arguably worse, produce invalid or inaccurate data products. Reputations of developers and entire organizations have been sullied because control data were not controlled, and their integrity was compromised.

As a coequal of code, control data should be afforded the same security and scrutiny as the programs they support. For example, if a team tests and validates its code (and why would they not?!), control data should also be tested. This approach is commonly employed in functional testing in which specific test cases are used to validate input parameters for procedures and functions. *Positive tests* verify that functions perform correctly when supplied valid inputs, and *negative tests* demonstrate what functions do when invalid inputs are provided.

As another example, a common development best practice is to create incremental versions of code so that software can be "rolled back" to previous states if necessary—presumably, to a point prior to some failure, when software still functioned correctly. When *versioning* is employed, data-driven programming requires that not only code but also associated

Configuration and *customization* are differentiated in Section 16.1

Dynamic and static performance requirements are contrasted in Section 7.2.1

Control data integrity can be facilitated through policies such as *least privilege*, introduced in Section 2.2.3, as well as data quality controls, discussed in Section 8.3

Section 7.2 walks readers through the SDLC, discussing how planning, design, development, testing, and O&M phases can incorporate data-driven programming discussion

Versioning is discussed in Section 9.3

control data be versioned. Thus, capturing a software's state—at present or in the past—requires versioning both its code and control data.

In many software development environments, another best practice is to isolate production software in a production region so that it can run unfettered without risk of alteration. A change management policy may describe who can modify software, when they can modify software, and what paper trail of requests and approvals is first required. Security controls may further enforce this change management policy, disallowing access to a production codebase for those not approved to make a specific change. In these more restrictive environments, a data-driven design paradigm requires that not only code but also control data be brought under change management and release management policies.

As a final example, software documentation is a best practice that varies widely in its implementation—among developers, teams, organizations, and even software languages. Where a team has instituted guidelines for how to document its software, however, these guidelines should extend to both code and control data. Especially where user-defined data structures have been developed, documentation is required to ensure that subsequent developers understand how to create, interpret, and modify control data within user-defined data structures. This documentation helps ensure the consistent future use of user-defined data structures as well as their associated operations.

Understanding that control data are software, too, helps elucidate why data-driven programming first and foremost represents a design (rather than a development) consideration. Control data and their respective data structures should be incorporated throughout the software development life cycle (SDLC), including in software planning, design, development, and testing. By assessing how software requirements can be met through data-driven design, developers can conceptualize what data-driven methods should be implemented to achieve those objectives, and can build software that incorporates control data that drive its functionality.

1.6   SUMMARY

This chapter introduced abstract, data-driven design and contrasted it with concrete, code-driven design. No software is ever fully concrete or fully abstract; thus, data-driven programming describes the application of concepts, constructs, patterns, principles, and techniques—knowledge and

---

The SDLC O&M phase, introduced in Section 7.2.4, depicts a separate *production* region in which software runs after it is released

---

Section 14.1 demonstrates a user-defined data structure, the decision table, and documents the business rules that prescribe how the data structure must be maintained

tools that can improve software quality through increased flexibility, reusability, configurability, and maintainability.

This chapter also described how abstraction, software modularity, and control data independence are central pillars to data-driven design. Software modularity separates monolithic programs into discrete modules of code, making each easier to maintain and reuse. Data independence furthers the goal of modularity by additionally requiring that control data be separated from functionality—maintained outside of the code that interprets and operationalizes them. Finally, abstraction—including procedural, data, and iteration abstraction—simplifies and focuses by removing irrelevant or unnecessary aspects of software or data. Abstraction is the focus of the next four chapters.

Chapter 2.

THE ABSTRACTION ATTRACTION

This chapter has the following objectives:

- ❖ Define *abstraction* and demonstrate its importance throughout software design and development.

- ❖ Introduce the abstraction flavors—*procedural abstraction, data abstraction,* and *iteration abstraction.*

- ❖ Show how the SAS SORT procedure deftly models these three types of abstraction.

- ❖ Demonstrate abstraction levels within software design.

- ❖ Demonstrate how too much abstraction can be a bad thing.

The delicious Animal® Style Double-Double® 'n Cheese I buy at In-N-Out Burger is concrete; I taste it, savor it, devour it. The Double-Double image emblazoned on the drive-through marquee, however, is a mere abstraction, as is the icon on the touchscreen monitor on which the attendant enters my order. Still in line, I'm already salivating over the burger that will satiate my cravings, whereas the abstraction is only a representation (and simplification) of the former—a one-dimensional, low-resolution, tasteless, scentless, similitude.

But without this abstraction, the marquee would need to be draped with *actual* foodstuffs—and beef basking in the California sun just would not be appetizing hours into the day! The marquee and menu provide simplification, specifying the basic food products and the ways in which each can be customized. Despite its vastness, the menu is not limitless. In-N-Out will not let customers order undercooked beef because it could pose a health risk, nor do they serve ostrich patties. Thus, the menu is flexible to customer preference, but only in prescribed, predetermined ways.

The process between screaming my order into the microphone and receiving my food is an enigma to me—and represents another abstraction. As a customer, I need only understand that yelps into the microphone get me Double-Doubles, fries, and shakes. But the skilled Double-Double artisans inside the kitchen must competently interpret my order, and transform it into food magic. The processes are flexible, yet stable, ensuring that sufficient choices are possible, yet also ensuring that selecting the *same* options over time will yield predictable products, even at different In-N-Out establishments.

Some abstractions are so abstract that they bear little to no resemblance to what they aim to represent. Highly abstract works of art may evoke awe, confusion, contemplation, and visceral emotion from patrons while objectively evincing very little about the actual subject matter. Some of these works are destined to travel through time effectively as mirrors—a certainty to no one, and representing only what each individual intuits.

But other abstractions, such as the icons on the In-N-Out mobile app, or abstractions used within software, must be functional. When I click on the Double-Double, milkshake, and fries icons on my smartphone, there's no confusion about the food they represent, and when I arrive at the restaurant, my 1,600+ calorie snack is piping hot and ready to be devoured.[8] But for abstractions to be functional, they must be able to be unambiguously and universally decoded. If I had to click on an artichoke icon to order a milkshake and an avocado icon to order fries, it's not to say that these abstractions would be *wrong*—just functionally useless, because their relevance to the real-world constructs they aimed to represent would have been minimized, if not eliminated.

Abstraction

The International Organization for Standardization (ISO) defines *abstraction* as a "view of an object that focuses on the information relevant to a particular purpose and ignores the remainder of the information."[9] More than 100 years ago, Funk and Wagnalls provided a similar definition: "The act, process, or product of abstracting, or withdrawing the attention from other qualities or aspects of an object, in order to concentrate it upon some one quality or aspect."[10]

Specific to program design, Rod Ellis describes two aspects of abstraction: "the splitting up, or *partitioning*, of the design into discrete parts or components; the ability to treat these components individually in terms of their effects on the rest of the system, whilst ignoring their internal structure."[11]

Barbara Liskov and John Guttag clarify that "Abstraction is a way to do decomposition productively by changing the level of detail to be considered. When we abstract from a problem we agree to ignore certain details in an effort to convert the original problem to a simpler one."[12] They go on to extol that "Data abstraction is the most important method in program design."

The legendary Robert C. Martin remarks that "The most flexible systems are those in which source code dependencies refer only to abstractions not to concretions."[13] He warns that "Every time you see a duplication in the code, it represents a missed opportunity for abstraction."

And David Garbutt playfully captures the pith of abstraction, stating that "Abstraction allows you to avoid hard-coded hell, and encapsulation protects you from sharp tridents in the neighboring fire-pit."[14]

Software, too, employs abstraction to filter and focus—filtering irrelevant details that are not necessary to understand or implement software, and focusing end users (or processes) to interact through prescribed channels and methods. To this end, software abstraction must be unambiguous and actionable—sufficiently defined so that it can be interpreted and operationalized. After all, abstraction aims to improve the software experience of not only end users, by making software more flexible and configurable, but also developers, who can more easily reuse, repurpose, and maintain modules that are abstract.

This chapter introduces abstraction in software design. It shows the importance of determining the appropriate level of abstraction—that is, striking a balance between focusing on relevant aspects and filtering irrelevant details. Finally, it demonstrates that you can have too much of a good thing; both procedures and data can become overly abstract to the point that their usefulness is diminished.

2.1   PROC SORT – ABSTRACTION AT ITS FINEST

Somewhat ironically, it is often easiest to introduce software abstraction through concrete examples. The SAS SORT procedure orders a SAS data set, and provides a stellar archetype for illustrating abstraction, as it is one of the most recognizable and fundamental tools in Base SAS.

All functions and procedures inherently require abstraction to facilitate their flexibility and reuse, so this SORT sortie elucidates how procedural and iteration abstraction are in play, as well as how data abstraction is used to model real-world constructs and to create reusable data structures.

2.1.1   Data Abstraction

The following DATA step uses the DATALINES statement to read comma-delimited data to create the Personnel data set:

```
data personnel;
    infile datalines delimiter=',';
    length Emp_ID 8 First_Name $50 Last_Name $50;
    input Emp_ID First_Name $ Last_Name $;
    datalines;
1, Ron, Burgundy
2, Chazz, Michaels
3, Sky, Corrigan
4, Franz, Liebkind
5, Ricky, Bobby
6, Jacobim, Mugatu
```

;

The data themselves (irrespective of where they are maintained and how they are formatted) are an abstraction of the living, breathing persons who are listed (were they not all fictional, cinematic incarnations of Will Ferrell). Thus, despite the myriad nuanced aspects of Ron Burgundy's persona within *Anchorman*, he has been reduced (within these data) to a name and an employee ID only. This might be an adequate representation of Mr. Burgundy, or it might not; the appropriateness of the abstraction always depends on its intended use.

The SAS data set—that is, the abstract notion of *any* data set rather than *this* or a *specific* data set—is a data structure, as well as a data abstraction. Data structures define not only their format, content, and characteristics, but also operations that can be performed on data contained within the structure. For example, if you are asked to describe a SAS data set, you might conjure up words like "tabular," "variable," and "observation" to convey the "data set" concept to a SAS neophyte. However, the definition of a data structure should also reference how you can interact with the data structure, so descriptors of data set operations—like "sortable," "hashable," or "indexable"—would also be appropriate.

For example, as soon as data are ingested into the Personnel data set, they can be sorted, concatenated, joined, or interacted with through a host of other operations. Metadata contained within the Personnel data set (e.g., variable name, number, order, data type) are additionally made available through the built-in SAS Dictionary tables and views.

> SAS Dictionary tables are introduced in Section 12.4

Data structures that are robust, reliable, and have an abundance of associated operations will be more widely implemented than those that do not. Documentation of data structure rules, uses, misuses, and caveats is also paramount as this information enables subsequent developers to rely on data structures without having to infer functionality or guess how the data structures should be implemented. Without this standardization and documentation, user-defined data structures often exist ephemerally—destined to be discarded, forgotten, or worse, unnecessarily recreated.

> Section 1.2 demonstrates rules that can be defined to inform correct usage of a user-defined data structure

2.1.2   Procedural Abstraction

The SORT procedure itself is another type of abstraction, embodying *procedural abstraction*. Procedural abstraction effectively extends a software language by defining new operations that developers can utilize.[15] For example, in lower-level languages like C++, Java, or Python, developers can write their own sorting algorithms (e.g., bubble sort, merge sort, bucket sort), taking advantage of various sorting methodologies. As a fourth-generation language (4GL), however, SAS does this work for us, so we can focus on the more interesting challenges of data analysis and producing data products.

Procedural abstraction typically relies on parameterization in which parameters are defined within a software module and referenced when the module is called (i.e., invoked). For example, the SORT procedure orders the Personnel data set by last name, after which Ricky Bobby will appear first in the data set, *because if you ain't first, you're last!*

> In some cases, procedural abstraction relies on only environmental variables (including SAS automatic macro variables) to deliver dynamic functionality, as demonstrated in Section 6.7

```
proc sort data=personnel;
   by last_name;
run;
```

Procedural abstraction is a cornerstone of software design because it simplifies and standardizes common tasks like sorting data while making these operations as reusable and flexible as possible. Thus, the built-in SORT procedure ensures that SAS practitioners do not waste time writing user-defined sorting algorithms. Moreover, sorting flexibility is conferred through various SORT options. SORT uses the DATA option to specify the data set being sorted, but if omitted, sorts (by default) the last data set created. The BY statement effectively represents another parameter because it enables one or more SORT variables to be specified in series.

> Procedural *specification* is defined in Section 3.2

In addition to flexibility, procedural abstraction affords developers simplicity; that is, end users do not have to get in the weeds when we do not need to be there. For example, when interacting with the SORT procedure, developers must understand only the SORT *specification*, which describes how to invoke SORT, what parameters can be passed to the procedure, and what functionality it will deliver. Like other built-in procedures, SAS Institute provides the SORT specification within Base SAS product documentation.[16]

> *Encapsulation* and *information hiding* are defined and contrasted in Section 8.4.1

A third advantage of procedural abstraction is the *information hiding* that is gained through *encapsulation*. Because developers calling SORT are focused on its *specification*, we do not need to understand its *implementation*—the very technical methods that SORT uses behind the scenes to order data. For example, to use SORT effectively, I need to understand only its basic syntax, a few options, and the desired input and output. I do not need to understand, however, the internal algorithms that

SORT uses; these details are proprietary to SAS Institute, are unnecessary to me as a user, and remain hidden.

Procedural abstraction provides substantial benefits to end users, the SAS practitioners who rely on procedures like SORT. It also benefits SAS Institute developers, the fine ladies and gentlemen who write Base SAS software. From their development perspective, procedural abstraction increases the maintainability of the SAS application because built-in SAS procedures can be honed, refactored, and released more readily through software updates. So long as the *specification* remains consistent while only the *implementation* is modified, backward compatibility to previous versions of a procedure is achieved, and end users may not even perceive that a software upgrade has occurred.

Procedural implementation is defined and discussed in Section 3.3

For example, because information hiding shields end users from the nitty-gritty details of *how* the SAS language implements the SORT procedure, SAS Institute is able to modify and improve SORT behind the scenes, unbeknownst to SAS practitioners. So long as the SORT *invocation*—the interface through which SAS practitioners interact— remains consistent (or at least backward compatible to older software releases), legacy code that relies on SORT will not need to be changed, even as SAS Institute modifies SORT functionality through the years.

Backward compatibility for user-defined functions is demonstrated in Sections 3.3 and 10.2.4, in which software is refactored while extant functionality is preserved

Far from the realm of science fiction, this refactoring occurred when SAS Institute implemented multithreaded sorting in SAS 9. Although the SORT *specification* remained predominantly consistent with SAS 8, under the covers, the SORT *implementation* in SAS 9 began using a multithreaded, divide-and-conquer approach to achieve far greater performance. Thus, procedural abstraction is as much a benefit to those using software applications as those designing and developing them, because it facilitates incremental software upgrades with minimal disruption to end users.

For example, given this overhaul of SORT, one of the only outward signs (to SAS practitioners) of this rags-to-riches transformation was the addition of the THREADS/NOTHREADS options. SORT procedures written in SAS 8 continued to run when ported to SAS 9 (evincing backward compatibility), and where neither the THREADS nor the NOTHREADS option was specified, the default (THREADS) was automatically selected (beginning in SAS 9).

Given this increased performance, and coupled with backward compatibility, SAS Institute basically branded its newfangled SAS 9 SORT as "the same old SORT you're used to, just darn tootin' faster!" And this worked because SAS practitioners did not need to understand any multithreading intricacies; we only needed to know that our legacy SAS 8 code was future-proofed enough to run on the new SAS 9 platform—and that it would forever run faster.

Data abstraction is also essential to SAS Institute developers because the SAS data set sits inarguably at the center of the SAS universe. The versatility of the SAS data set (including its associated operations) facilitates the extension of Base SAS functionality. For example, the SORT procedure must first read a data set before its contents can be ordered. This data ingestion functionality, if decoupled from other SORT functionality, could be reused within other built-in SAS procedures that also read data sets. Thus, as core components are reused, the work necessary to develop and test new, unrelated software modules is decreased, and developer productivity increases.

Reuse is demonstrated in Section 10.2.3 in which a user-defined macro reuses a previous user-defined subroutine

Procedural and data abstraction play a pivotal role in software design, supporting both end users and developers. Although SAS practitioners lack permissions to modify the SORT procedure (why mess with perfection anyway?), we can learn from and emulate its functionality and performance in developing user-defined procedures, functions, and other software modules. Similarly, we can emulate the data abstraction of the SAS data set to develop reusable, user-defined data structures, as well as user-defined operations that interact with them.

Section 14.1 demonstrates a scalable, reusable, user-defined decision table

2.1.3 Iteration Abstraction

Iteration abstraction (or, simply, *iteration*) is the third type of abstraction discussed in this text. Iteration enables an operation to be performed repetitively despite being referenced (i.e., coded) only once. Iteration can be *external*, where iteration mechanics are exposed (such as a DO loop or %DO loop), or *internal*, where iteration mechanics are concealed (such as a DATA step that tacitly iterates a data set to read all observations). Both flavors of iteration abstraction increase developer productivity and software readability by reducing the amount of code required per operation.

Internal iteration and *external iteration* are introduced in Sections 5.2.1 and 5.2.2, respectively

SAS procedures utilize internal iteration to process observations within a data set. For example, the SORT procedure orders all observations in the Personnel data set without the need to reference observations individually:

```
proc sort data=personnel;
```

```
    by last_name;
run;
```

This flexibility enables SAS procedures like SORT to operate on *any* data set, irrespective of the number or type of observations it contains.

The DATA step similarly employs internal iteration to read, write, and transform observations; for example, each INPUT, SET, OUTPUT, PUT, and other statement is written once but is applied to all observations within the data set, yet the methods and mechanics used to control this repetition are concealed.

External iteration, on the other hand, is demonstrated when a DO loop iterates over a series of variables, observations, or other elements or objects. For example, the following DO OVER loop iterates over the Upper array to convert all character variables to uppercase:

```
data uppercase;
    set personnel;
    array upper _character_;
    do over upper;
        upper=upcase(upper);
        end;
run;
```

This example demonstrates both internal and external iteration. The _CHARACTER_ operand is known as a *special SAS name list* and represents a list of all character variables in the current data set. The ARRAY statement relies on internal iteration to parse _CHARACTER_ and dynamically create the Upper array; the looping mechanics are concealed, but we know they are at work. The DO OVER loop, conversely, represents external iteration because its looping mechanics are displayed.

> _CHARACTER_, _NUM_, and _ALL_ are the three *special SAS name lists*, which are discussed in Section 5.2.3

Without iteration, the preceding dynamic DATA step could be represented by a functionally equivalent concrete DATA step that explicitly references the two character variables:

```
data uppercase;
    set personnel;
    first_name=upcase(first_name);
    last_name=upcase(last_name);
run;
```

The benefits of the abstract method are apparent. First, the _CHARACTER_ operand represents all character variables, so the DATA step will flex as the name and/or number of variables changes. Second, as the number of variables increases, the abstract method will not require additional code whereas the concrete method will require one additional line per added variable.

2.2   ABSTRACTION LEVELS

Software abstraction removes irrelevant detail to allow developers to interact with software more effectively. Abstraction always involves balancing flexibility and simplicity, in that maximizing either will inherently reduce—and can compromise—the other. Make a procedure too *rigid* and it will lack the necessary abstraction that allows it to be reused in diverse circumstances, yet make the same procedure too *flexible* and it will have lost the benefits of simplicity and focus. The appropriate abstraction level requires an understanding of the technical need and often a bit of artistry.

The cover artwork illustrates levels of procedural abstraction. The larger marionette directly controls the smaller one while an unseen master directly controls the larger marionette and indirectly controls the smaller one. In general, the more indirect the pathway from a controller (i.e., end user or process) to its respective actions, the higher the level of procedural abstraction. Similarly, the more distant control data are from the real-world constructs they represent, the higher the level of data abstraction.

ISO defines *level of abstraction* as "a view of an object at a specific level of detail."[17] One of the best ways to conceptualize abstraction levels is to understand how they can be used to differentiate classes of programming languages.

Languages with a lower level of abstraction are closer to direct machine functionality, such as memory, storage, and power management functions. Thus, first-generation languages (1GLs, or machine languages) and second-generation languages (2GLs, or assembly languages) are less abstract because they control these basic hardware systems. These languages must be more concrete because they interact directly with specific hardware makes and models.

Higher-level languages are more abstract and allow developers to build, to the extent possible, software that functions equivalently irrespective of the hardware or operating system (OS) on which it runs. Third-generation languages (3GLs) operate at a higher level of abstraction and include C, C++, Java, Python, and other application development languages. Built-in functions and procedures enable developers to build software more efficiently in 3GLs than in lower-level languages. For example, 3GLs typically have hundreds of built-in functions and procedures that developers can utilize—without having to build the processes themselves.

The SAS language, a fourth-generation language (4GL), operates at an even higher level of abstraction. That is, SAS is even further removed from core machine functionality. This abstraction benefits SAS practitioners because we can rely on built-in SAS procedures, functions, statements, and other operations. It also means that SAS software (i.e., programs written in the SAS language) built on a Linux platform will run with few to no modifications on a Windows server or desktop. Behind the scenes, the SAS application is interacting uniquely with each platform, but these technical details are largely irrelevant to SAS practitioners and are obscured from our view.

> Abstraction must be balanced and appropriate, and the woes of over-abstraction are discussed in Section 2.3

2.2.1   Abstraction Levels vs. Articulation Points

Abstraction level typically speaks to the depth of an abstraction and its distance from some real-world construct that it models. The real-world construct could be an entity that data abstraction represents, or an action that procedural abstraction represents. Software components are said to be "more abstract" when they operate at higher abstraction levels.

Ambiguity can erupt, however, because software is sometimes described as being "more abstract" when it is more flexible—that is, when it has relatively more articulable joints at which the software can flex to deliver dynamic functionality. For example, the SORT procedure is *flexible* because it provides a number of ways in which developers can interact with it—altering the DATA option, BY statement, THREADS system option, or TAGSORT option, to name a few configurable items. Each option makes SORT more flexible, yet does not increase the procedure's abstraction level.

Rather, to achieve a higher level of procedural abstraction, a developer might write a macro that calls the SORT procedure. The RIGIDSORT macro calls SORT yet concretely defines the DATA option argument, OUT option argument, and BY statement argument:

```
%macro rigidsort();
proc sort data=onlythisinput out=onlythisoutput;
   by onlythisvar;
```

```
run;
%mend;
```

In very specific instances, RIGIDSORT might be preferred because its invocation is faster to type (when developing software) than the equivalent SORT procedure that it calls. For example, the following two methods are now functionally equivalent:

```
* method 1;
%rigidsort;

* method 2;
proc sort data=onlythisinput out=onlythisoutput;
   by onlythisvar;
run;
```

RIGIDSORT also might be useful were it necessary to shield developers from the full array of SORT options. However, this extreme *focus* comes at the tremendous cost of lost *flexibility* because RIGIDSORT is useless for any other sorting requirements; it *always* sorts the same data set and *always* by the same variable. Configurability is altogether vacated, which diminishes opportunity for reuse.

A more realistic example that creates an additional abstraction level for the SORT procedure might incorporate some but not all SORT options. For example, the SORTSORT macro calls the SORT procedure and enables the end user to specify the input data set name, output data set name, sort variables, FIRSTOBS, and OBS options:

```
%macro sortsort(dsn= /* data set being sorted */,
      dsnout= /* final data set name */,
      obs1= /* FIRSTOBS value */,
      obs2= /* OBS value */,
      sortvars= /* space-delimited BY variables */);
%local obsline;
%let obsline=;
%if %length(&obs1)>0 and %length(&obs2)>0
   %then %let obsline=(firstobs=&obs1 obs=&obs2);
proc sort data=&dsn &obsline out=&dsnout;
   by &sortvars;
```

```
run;
%mend;
```

The SORTCHOICE macro adds a second level of abstraction, and calls the SORTSORT macro:

```
%macro sortchoice(method= /* SORT or SQL */,
    dsn= /* data set being sorted */,
        dsnout= /* final data set name */,
        obs1= /* FIRSTOBS value */,
        obs2= /* OBS value */,
        sortvars= /* space-delimited BY variables */);
%if %upcase(&method)=SQL %then %let method=sqlsort;
%else %let method=sortsort;
%&method(dsn=&dsn, dsnout=&dsnout, obs1=&obs1,
    obs2=&obs2, sortvars=&sortvars);
%mend;


%sortchoice(method=sort, dsn=personnel,
    dsnout=sortout, sortvars=first_name);
```

A developer can interact with SORTCHOICE and need only specify a few SORT options—principally, the METHOD parameter, having the value of either SORT or SQL. Based on this parameterized input, SORTCHOICE orders the data set, either by calling the SORTSORT macro or by calling the SQLSORT macro.

In this example, the biggest clue to the additional abstraction level is the macro call that abstractly—rather than concretely—references the macro name (i.e., %&METHOD):

```
%&method(dsn=&dsn, dsnout=&dsnout, obs1=&obs1,
    obs2=&obs2, sortvars=&sortvars);
```

Before SORTCHOICE can be called with the SQL option (i.e., passing SQL to the METHOD parameter), the SQLSORT macro must be defined:

```
%macro sqlsort(dsn= /* data set being sorted */,
        dsnout= /* final data set name */,
        obs1= /* FIRSTOBS value */,
    obs2= /* OBS value */,
```

```
          sortvars= /* space-delimited BY variables */);
%local obsline;
%let obsline=;
%if %length(&obs1)>0 and %length(&obs2)>0
    %then %let obsline=(firstobs=&obs1 obs=&obs2);
%let sortvars=%sysfunc(tranwrd(&sortvars,
    %str( ),%str(,)));
proc sql noprint;
    create table &dsnout as
        select * from &dsn &obsline
        order by &sortvars;
quit;
%mend;
```

SORTCHOICE can now be invoked with the SQL option, which indirectly calls the SQLSORT macro to sort the Personnel data set utilizing the SQL procedure:

```
%sortchoice(method=sql, dsn=personnel, dsnout=sqlout,
    sortvars=first_name);
```

Thus, by modifying only the METHOD argument, SORTCHOICE uses an entirely different sorting algorithm—that otherwise would have required several lines of code to implement. Moreover, a SAS practitioner with no knowledge of the SQL procedure is now able to sort a data set using SQL. Finally, the implementation of how SORTCHOICE selects and operationalizes these diverse sorting methods is hidden from the invocation, which enables developers to modify SORTCHOICE (as well as SORTSORT and SQLSORT) behind the scenes. For example, a third sorting methodology that uses the hash object could be designed and incorporated into SORTCHOICE without compromising backward compatibility.

To be clear, the SORTCHOICE macro is *less flexible* (i.e., has fewer articulation points) than the built-in SORT procedure because SORTCHOICE contains only six parameters, and thus omits many built-in SORT options. However, SORTCHOICE is *more abstract* than SORT because it greatly simplifies the invocation of various sorting methods while removing unnecessary detail—that is, detail deemed unnecessary to meet this specific software requirement.

2.2.2   Traversing Abstraction Levels

Abstraction levels are best observed by isolating a single articulation point within software, and by subsequently displaying functionally equivalent solutions that provide successively greater abstraction. For example, the following REPORT procedure displays the Personnel data set created in Section 2.1.1:

```
title;
proc report data=personnel nocenter nowindows
      nocompletecols;
   column first_name last_name;
   define first_name / display
      style=[foreground=black];
   define last_name / display
      style=[foreground=blue];
run;
```

Only the text color is varied, which is initially defined as black for First_name and blue for Last_name. In this concrete example, the end user can modify the text color only by altering the program itself.

A higher level of abstraction can be achieved by empowering the end user to specify the text colors at report invocation. This could be accomplished by referencing a configuration file, or as demonstrated in the RPT1 macro, by parameterizing these values:

```
%macro rpt1(textcolor1= /* first_name color */,
   textcolor2= /* last_name color */);
title;
proc report data=personnel nocenter nowindows
      nocompletecols;
   column first_name last_name;
   define first_name / display
      style=[foreground=&textcolor1];
   define last_name / display
      style=[foreground=&textcolor2];
run;
%mend;
```

In this example, the method through which the text colors are passed to the macro (e.g., configuration file, parameterization) does not affect the level of abstraction. What matters is that substitution (via the &TEXTCOLOR1 and &TEXTCOLOR2 macro variables) is used to represent the text colors within the code. Thus, the RPT1 invocation is functionally equivalent to the preceding concrete REPORT procedure:

```
%rpt1(textcolor1=black, textcolor2=blue);
```

The color names themselves, however, are also abstractions of hexadecimal red-green-blue (RGB) values that are encoded by the SAS application or the OS. For example, the REGISTRY procedure prints a list of color names and values to the log:

```
proc registry list startat='colornames';
run;
```

Partial output of the REGISTRY procedure demonstrates the hexadecimal values—a lower level of abstraction than the associated color names (because the hexadecimal values are the actual values that the SAS application utilizes internally):

```
NOTE: Contents of SASHELP REGISTRY starting at subkey
[colornames]
[  colornames]
  Active="HTML"
[    HTML]
    AliceBlue=hex: F0,F8,FF
    AntiqueWhite=hex: FA,EB,D7
    Aqua=hex: 00,FF,FF
    Aquamarine=hex: 7F,FD,D4
    Azure=hex: F0,FF,FF
    Beige=hex: F5,F5,DC
    Bisque=hex: FF,E4,C4
    Black=hex: 00,00,00
    BlanchedAlmond=hex: FF,EB,CD
```

And with uncommon color names like "PapayaWhip" and "Thistle," aren't you glad that the REGISTRY procedure can help interpret this nonsense by providing hex codes?!

The SAS registry also enables existing named colors to be associated with new hexadecimal values, and new named colors to be added (with the REGISTRY IMPORT statement). This procedure is ideal when a SAS practitioner wants to modify color mappings *permanently*. However, in other cases, color mappings may only need to be modified *temporarily*—and data abstraction levels can save the day.

From the REGISTRY procedure output, the default hexadecimal values of black and blue are shown:

```
Black=hex: 00,00,00
Blue=hex: 00,00,FF
```

But what if a developer instead wanted to represent black as 0D1F4F and blue as 38508F whenever these color names were referenced within a program? A concrete method could replace the named colors with these hexadecimal values in the RPT1 macro invocation:

```
%rpt1(textcolor1=#0D1F4F, textcolor2=#38508F);
```

The colors are modified; however, this requires the developer to interact directly with the non-intuitive hexadecimal codes. More likely, a key stakeholder or decision maker may have requested the color shift, so these color selections should be saved somewhere for future use, like a configuration file that can be summoned when needed.

To begin this endeavor, the REGISTRY procedure output is piped to a text file (reg.txt) that is ingested as the Colors data set:

One principle of data-driven design recommends that control data should be passed intuitively, which SAS formats can facilitate, as demonstrated in Section 4.3.1

```
%let loc=d:\sas\;      * USER MUST CHANGE LOCATION *;
proc printto log="&loc.reg.txt" new;
run;
proc registry list startat='colornames';
run;
proc printto;
run;

data colors;
    infile "&loc.reg.txt" truncover delimiter=':';
    length color $32 hex $10;
    input color $ hex $;
    if missing(color) or length(hex)^=8 then delete;
```

```
    color=upcase(scan(color,1,'='));
    hex=upcase(compress(hex,','));
run;


proc sort data=colors;
    by color;
run;
```

The Colorconfig
configuration file is
revisited in Section
4.5.2, which
demonstrates file
type inheritance,
and in Section
16.3.3, in which
comments are
added to the file

Note that the &LOC macro variable must be initialized to a user-specified folder, after which the PRINTTO procedure saves the log file.

Next, a configuration file (colorconfig.txt) should be created that includes the new hexadecimal values for black and blue, as well as any new colors mappings, like your favorite beverages:

```
black=0D1F4F
blue=38508F
absinthe=25F95B
zaya=DE9421
fireball=DE8721
```

The following DATA steps and procedures subsequently read the configuration file, sort it by color name, join it with the Colors data set that was created by the REGISTRY procedure, and create the RGBHEX format:

```
data localcolors;
    infile "&loc.colorconfig.txt" truncover
        delimiter='=';
    length color $32 hex $10;
    input color $ hex $;
    color=upcase(color);
    hex=upcase(hex);
run;


proc sort data=localcolors;
    by color;
run;


data allcolors (rename=(color=start hex=label));
    merge colors (in=a) localcolors (in=b);
```

```
    by color;
    length fmtname $32 type $2;
    fmtname='rgbhex';
    type='c';          * denotes a character format;
run;


proc format library=work cntlin=allcolors;
run;
```

The RGBHEX format is created through data-driven methods that rely on the CNTLIN option to ingest external data into a SAS format. This best practice enables formats to be saved outside of SAS code so they can be maintained and modified more readily, including by stakeholders who have no access to the SAS application.

An updated RPT2 macro still parameterizes the values for the two text colors; however, &FONTCOLOR1 and &FONTCOLOR2 are transformed (via the RGBHEX user-defined format) into their respective hexadecimal codes:

The CNTLIN option of the FORMAT procedure is demonstrated in Sections 13.3.1, 13.4.3, and 13.5.2, and CNTLIN limitations are overcome in Section 15.3

```
%macro rpt2(fontcolor1= /* text color 1 */,
    fontcolor2= /* text color 2 */);
%let fontcolor1=#%sysfunc(putc(%upcase(&fontcolor1),
    rgbhex.));
%let fontcolor2=#%sysfunc(putc(%upcase(&fontcolor2),
    rgbhex.));
title;
proc report data=personnel nowindows nocenter;
    column first_name last_name;
    define first_name / display
        style=[foreground=&fontcolor1];
    define last_name / display
        style=[foreground=&fontcolor2];
run;
%mend;


%rpt2(fontcolor1=black, fontcolor2=blue);
```

The report is identical to the one produced by the RPT1 macro; however, the developer invoking RPT2 no longer must specify hexadecimal codes. Thus, in adhering to data-driven design principles, complexity has

Data-driven design principles, including complexity hiding, are enumerated in Section 1.4

been removed from the macro *invocation*, and has been concealed in the macro *implementation*. This practice encourages reuse because it facilitates user-defined modules that can be intuitively and readily implemented within new software products.

The RPT2 macro, in relying on the RGBHEX format, also has greater configurability because user-defined colors like Zaya and Absinthe can be used in the macro invocation, despite their not residing in the permanent SAS registry:

```
%rpt2(fontcolor1=zaya, fontcolor2=absinthe);
```

This subsection demonstrates two levels of data abstraction, in that end users are able to specify color names while developers maintain the configuration file that includes less abstract hexadecimal values. In this scenario, the higher abstraction level facilitates greater configurability, in that SAS practitioners are able to define, modify, and save color mappings without the need to modify code—or the permanent SAS registry, which can be a risky undertaking.

2.2.3   Stakeholder Interaction with Abstraction Levels

Selecting the correct abstraction level is a question of balance, as well as a question of the intended stakeholder. A SAS end user, a SAS practitioner, and a SAS system administrator might each operate at different levels of procedural or data abstraction within a single program.

Within the report-generating example in Section 2.2.2, the end user (invoking the RPT2 macro) might have little to no programming experience; however, he still has the ability to modify the text colors utilizing straightforward color names. This gives Peter the power to make a pretty report; he specifies the RPT2 macro parameters, but may be blind to how they are implemented. Peter is invoking RPT2 at a high level of abstraction, so he is very focused on prettiness, and is shielded from the many technical details that are irrelevant to his role.

At a lower level of abstraction, SAS developers are maintaining the program and RPT2 macro on which Peter relies. For example, the developer, Garrett, might maintain a configuration file (like colorconfig.txt) that includes the acceptable list of colors that can be parameterized by end users. Thus, if Peter attempts to pass "pretty pretty pink" as his desired background color, a parameter validation routine (not shown) might evaluate the color to be invalid, and either halt the program or substitute a default color.

Peter does not need to understand this lower level of abstraction and *how* the color inputs are validated; he only needs to be provided with the list of valid color names so he can invoke the RPT2 macro. Garrett, however, does need to understand how the color list will be validated because he must write the validation code.

Another benefit of hiding these details—the procedural implementation—from end users is that developers are free to maintain, improve, and expand software modules behind the scenes. In espousing data-driven design principles, the list of valid colors might be maintained in a configuration file (like colorconfig.txt) to which only developers have access. In this paradigm, developers could modify software functionality— the color list—by altering only this configuration file while leaving the underlying code untouched. In an alternative (less desirable) code-driven paradigm, the developers would instead need to modify the code directly to alter the color list each time a change was required.

Finally, at an even lower level of abstraction, SAS administrators or system administrators often control far-reaching aspects of software or the software environment. For example, you might not want Garrett (the developer) mucking around in the permanent SAS registry, so you only give him access to the user-defined color configuration file. However, Tracy, the savvy SAS administrator, would likely require registry access so she could permanently modify color mappings, if necessary. Moreover, she would likely have edit permissions to change the folder location of input and output files, perhaps by modifying autoexec.sas.

This scenario demonstrates not only the varying levels of abstraction, but also the practice of utilizing abstraction levels to prescribe or limit stakeholder interaction with various control data. This separation of duties facilitates software security because stakeholders can be granted access to specific control data based on their roles and responsibilities while denied access to more sensitive control data.

The International Information System Security Certification Consortium (ISC)[2] defines *least privilege* as "the practice of only granting a user the minimal permissions necessary to perform their explicit job function."[18] Least privilege aims to minimize the exposure of critical data, systems, and infrastructure to the risk of accidental or malicious modification or corruption. When considering the implementation of data

From the MDM perspective, Section 8.2 discusses the importance of protecting master data structures that will store critical control data, least privilege should always be an objective.

For example, you would not want end users modifying the list of valid report colors—because every shade of Crayola would eventually make its way into the color configuration file. Similarly, you might not want developers modifying the SAS registry because it might be maintained under a strict change control policy to facilitate data integrity, versioning, and rollback (if necessary). Thus, access to control data is often limited by stakeholder role, both to simplify stakeholder interaction with control data and to protect the data. Data-driven design can facilitate data integrity by restricting control data access (or edit permissions) to only necessary stakeholders.

2.3   ABSTRACTION AD ABSURDUM

Abstraction is fundamental to data-driven design because it facilitates the necessary flexibility and configurability that are hallmarks of data-driven programming. But take abstraction to an unhealthy extreme, and its benefits will be diminished if not extinguished. Thus, as abstraction comprises a balance between focus and flexibility, software requirements should dictate where this balance rests on the abstraction continuum.

Abstraction ad absurdum describes overly abstract software in which an unnecessary number (or degree) of abstraction levels are implemented. In extreme doses of procedural abstraction, software can become a poor facsimile of lower-level functionality that it models. Thus, each higher level of abstraction should provide some simplification and focus—and, correspondingly, less flexibility—than the next lower level of abstraction.

For example, in Section 2.2, the SORTSORT macro defines five parameters that can be specified to configure the SORT procedure: DSN, DSNOUT, OBS1, OBS2, and SORTVARS. However, if the TAGSORT, THREADS, and other SORT options were *all* incorporated into the SORTSORT macro, what would be the point of the macro? It would continue to be an abstraction—but an unnecessary one that would be a poor duplication of the out-of-the-box SORT functionality. Thus, note that abstraction *always* simplifies, so it should be less complex than the construct it models.

An absurd SORTSORTSORT macro could be defined that poorly mimics out-of-the-box SORT options in an unnecessarily complex format:

```
%macro sortsortsort(dsn= /* input data set */,
   dsnout= /* output data set */,
   sortvars= /* space-delimited variables */,
   tagsort= /* specifies TAGSORT option */,
   nodup= /* specifies NODUP option */,
   nodupkey= /* specifies NODUPKEY option */);
proc sort data=&dsn out=&dsnout &tagsort
      &nodup &nodupkey;
   by &sortvars;
run;
%mend;
```

Nothing is simplified; nothing is focused; nothing is gained from this abstraction because balance is shifted too far toward flexibility. In other words, there is no benefit to running SORTSORTSORT, and the user is better off running the out-of-the-box SORT procedure.

Conversely, a second abstraction failure pattern occurs when abstraction instead shifts too far toward focus and simplification, and thus away from flexibility. This can lead to rigidity that eliminates dynamic functionality. For example, in Section 2.2.2, the RPT2 macro is invoked with user-defined modifications to black and blue:

```
%rpt2(fontcolor1=black, fontcolor2=blue);
```

RPT2 provides simplification and value to end users; however, a developer might want to simplify the RPT2 invocation further and lump the black and blue arguments into a single, repeatable macro (BLACKANDBLUE):

```
%macro blackandblue();
%rpt2(fontcolor1=black, fontcolor2=blue);
%mend;


%blackandblue;
```

Yes, BLACKANDBLUE takes marginally less effort to invoke than the corresponding RPT2 macro that it calls; however, only a few keystrokes are eliminated, and no other benefits are apparent. In certain circumstances in which numerous parameters or other control data must be passed to a procedure, this degree of simplification may be warranted; however, in this example, the rigidity imposed by this additional level of abstraction is more senseless than not.

From this perspective, even the RPT2 macro might be considered too narrowly defined, with its pendulum swinging much closer to *focus* than *flexibility*. RPT2 only executes the REPORT procedure and always uses the Personnel data set, so parameterization probably should be added so that at least the data set name can be specified by the user at invocation. Moreover, RPT2 lacks some modularity because it commingles style (i.e., defining text colors) with substance (i.e., the report structure and contents).

Thus, a more useful and reusable macro might instead parse *any* SAS code, replace the named color values with user-defined hexadecimal color values, and then execute that revised code. This abstraction would remove the onus of specifying parameters and would allow color names to be replaced not only within the REPORT procedure but within *all* SAS procedures.

The INCLUDECC (include custom color) macro follows, which provides the updated functionality and flexibility:

> Section 16.5.2 demonstrates the benefits of using CSS to detangle style and substance

```
%macro includecc(folder= /* for temp SAS program */,
    file= /* SAS program file to load */,
    configfile= /* user-defined color config file */);
%local i;
data _null_;
    infile "&configfile" truncover dlm='=';
    length color $32 hex $10;
    input color $ hex $;
    call symputx('color' ||
        strip(put(_n_,8.)),lowcase(color),'l');
    call symputx('hex' ||
        strip(put(_n_,8.)),lowcase(hex),'l');
run;
data _null_;
    infile "&file" truncover;
    length line $200;
    input line $200.;
    %let i=1;
    %do %while(%symexist(color&i));
        if find(line,"=&&&color&i")>0 then do;
```

```
        line=tranwrd(line,"=&&&color&i",
        "=#&&&hex&i");
        end;
    %let i=%eval(&i+1);
    %end;
  file "&folder.temp.sas";
  put line;
run;
%include "&folder.temp.sas";
%mend;
```

The INCLUDECC macro is intended to replace the %INCLUDE macro statement, in that it reads a SAS program (specified in the FILE parameter), searches that program for named color assignment statements, and replaces named colors with their hexadecimal values (when those named colors appear in the user-defined configuration file specified within the CONFIGFILE parameter).

To replicate the functionality of the RPT2 macro, the RPT3 macro is defined and saved to a SAS program file (rpt3.sas):

```
* saved as rpt3.sas;
%macro rpt3(dsn= /* data set name */);
proc report data=&dsn nowindows nocenter;
  column first_name last_name;
  define first_name / display
    style=[foreground=black];
  define last_name / display
    style=[foreground=blue];
run;
%mend;
```

Note that RPT3 now again concretely defines the text colors as black and blue, rather than representing them abstractly. This shift enables a developer to build the report without significant use of abstraction and parameterization. The abstraction has been shifted from the RPT3 macro to the INCLUDECC macro that parses and interprets the code.

INCLUDECC can be invoked with the following code, which relies on the configuration file created in Section 2.2.2:

```
%let loc=d:\sas\;        * USER MUST CHANGE LOCATION *;
%includecc(folder=&loc, file=&loc.rpt3.sas,
    configfile=&loc.colorconfig.txt);
```

This invocation of INCLUDECC creates a temporary program file (temp.sas) that is loaded (with the %INCLUDE statement) and which can be subsequently called:

```
%macro rpt3(dsn= /* data set name */);
proc report data=&dsn nowindows nocenter;
column first_name last_name;
define first_name / display style=[foreground=#0d1f4f];
define last_name / display
style=[foreground=#38508f];
run;
%mend;
```

Note that black and blue have been replaced by the corresponding user-defined hex codes provided in the configuration file (colorconfig.txt). All tabs have been stripped, but readability is not crucial, because this temporary SAS program is run programmatically through RPT3:

```
%rpt3(dsn=personnel);
```

No more need to specify endless parameters that may or may not be used; a SAS practitioner need only save a macro as a SAS program file, include that program file in the INCLUDECC macro invocation, and subsequently call the macro (named in the program file).

This simplified example demonstrates much more flexible and useful abstraction; however, it does have several limitations, such as requiring that named colors in the configuration file be lowercase, and not being able to distinguish some user-defined colors (e.g., *reddishbrown* and *reddishbrownish* will be incorrectly interpreted as the same color). Notwithstanding these deficiencies, INCLUDECC provides a prototype for how abstraction and data-driven design could be utilized to build a code interpreter that dynamically rewrites software.

So, is building your own SAS code interpreter abstraction *ad absurdum*? Well, that depends on your software requirements and the design and development methods that are selected to fulfill them.

For most purposes, INCLUDECC constitutes overkill—unnecessary effort that could have been invested elsewhere. In some cases, it may not be abstract enough, or may not provide sufficient flexibility. Thus, understanding data-driven design patterns and principles, as well as the development methods that can operationalize them, is the first step in making this important assessment about the appropriateness of abstraction.

In the end, abstraction is like toilet paper—use too much, and it's going to be a rough ride; use too little, and you'll have a mess on your hands— quite literally. Finding abstraction that is *just right* sometimes requires a bit of trial and error, patience, and artistry.

2.4 SUMMARY

This chapter introduced abstraction, the most fundamental concept in data-driven design. Data abstraction, procedural abstraction, and iteration abstraction were defined, and examples demonstrated how each can facilitate increased software flexibility, configurability, and reusability. These three flavors of abstraction are the focus of the next three chapters, as the exploration of software abstraction continues.

The influence of abstraction within the SORT procedure was demonstrated as an archetype to be mimicked when designing and developing user-defined operations and data structures. The multithreading of SORT in SAS 9 (and its successful backward compatibility with SAS 8) demonstrated the benefits of encapsulation, in which the end user invoking a procedure has no awareness of the procedure's implementation, which comprises the procedure's guts and defines how it delivers functionality.

Abstraction levels and articulation points were contrasted, both of which must be balanced against a business need for flexibility and configurability. Finally, unhelpful abstraction was demonstrated in which the scale is tipped either too far toward *focus* or toward *flexibility*, either of which can compromise the objectives and success of abstraction.

Chapter 3.

PROCEDURAL ABSTRACTION

This chapter has the following objectives:

❖ Introduce procedural abstraction used to construct callable modules like procedures, functions, and subroutines.

❖ Define a module's *specification*, which describes inputs, outputs, functionality, vulnerabilities, and usage caveats.

❖ Define a module's *implementation*, the black box in which its functionality is contained.

❖ Define a module's *invocation*, the statement that calls a module.

❖ Differentiate procedural abstraction found in *built-in software* and in *user-defined software*.

❖ Introduce and differentiate SAS *procedures*, *functions*, and *subroutines*, each of which rely on procedural abstraction.

P rocedural abstraction is more generalizable than the name implies, and describes the abstraction in play whenever procedures, functions, subroutines, and other *callable software modules* are invoked (i.e., called) by referencing their name. Procedural abstraction supports software reuse and flexibility, both of which are facilitated through dynamic inputs (arguments) that deliver dynamic functionality through parameterization. That is, we love callable modules because we can run them again and again, and because we can alter their functionality by modifying only their arguments!

Procedural abstraction, like all aspects of software, begins with a business need—the reason that software is being developed. That need is ultimately translated into technical requirements that establish software functional and performance objectives. At a high level, software requirements for a function or procedure should convey general functionality, what inputs are required, what outputs are produced, what return values or return codes are generated, and any dependencies that exist. This information forms the basis of the procedural specification, and enables developers to build a module more accurately.

Thus, procedural abstraction makes big things happen from tiny statements; a couple of lines of SAS code can launch a complex statistical analysis—the complexity having been distilled (i.e., abstracted) into the few, standardized SAS keywords that are typed, parsed, and executed. That procedural abstraction facilitates software functionality is clear, but this abstraction occurs even outside of data-driven design. Rather, it is the dynamic communication between *calling* and *called* software modules—including the inputs, return codes, and return values—through which procedural abstraction embraces data-driven design.

As stakeholders plan and design a software module, they should anticipate the degree of flexibility it will require. For example, if a data transformation module is being constructed that will ingest a transactional data set that *always* has the same name, it is not necessary to use abstraction to represent the data set name; it can be hardcoded rather than parameterized. However, if the data set name could change over time, then it should be abstracted through *substitution*—passed as an argument that must be specified by developers, processes, or programs calling the module. This parameterization—through procedural abstraction—delivers the flexibility and configurability for which data-driven design is sought.

Procedural abstraction is introduced in Section 2.1.2, in which the SORT procedure is modeled

Parameters and *arguments* are defined and contrasted in Section 6.3

Section 6.1 demonstrates procedural abstraction that does *not* embody data-driven design

Call-by-reference and *call-by-value* methods of passing arguments are discussed in Section 6.5

3.1   PROCEDURAL DEFINITIONS

Procedural abstraction comprises the following software components:

- **Specification** – the documentation that describes a procedure (or other callable module), including its functionality, inputs, outputs, return codes, and return values, as well as risks, vulnerabilities, dependencies, and other usage caveats.
- **Implementation** – the code that performs the functionality described in the procedure's specification, including the *signature*, which declares parameter names, data types, identification methods, passing methods, and order.
- **Invocation** – the "call" that temporarily transfers program control from a *calling* program or process (aka, the *parent*) to the procedure or other *called* software module (aka, the *child*).

Signature components are explored in Section 6.2

These definitions—for *specification, implementation,* and *invocation*—hold fast whether describing built-in procedures or user-defined procedures, and whether describing procedures, functions, subroutines, or entire software applications, all of which rely on procedural abstraction. Before delving into procedural abstraction, several subsections clarify its components, nomenclature, and nuances.

3.1.1   Built-in vs. User-Defined Procedural Abstraction

Built-in software modules, such as functions, procedures, and subroutines, are those that ship (or download) with a software application; that is, the procedural specification and implementation are written by a software company (or open-source cooperative), and developers are only responsible for writing invocations that call these modules. For example, the SAS Institute wrote the SORT procedure, including its specification, which defines and documents its functionality, and its implementation, the underlying C code that does the work of ordering data sets. When an end user (i.e., SAS practitioner) relies on the SORT procedure to order data, the code that is written in Base SAS is the *invocation*.

Built-in and user-defined data structures are contrasted in Section 9.3

User-defined software components, conversely, are those in which the implementation and the specification are written by end users—not a software company or open-source cooperative. For example, a user-defined SAS macro might be written by a SAS developer but rely on built-in SAS functions, SAS procedures, or DATA step functionality. Thus, through user-defined modules, procedural abstraction effectively extends a language, providing or improving capabilities not delivered by native, built-in functionality.

User-defined procedures are instrumental because they enable developers to surpass barriers that are endemic within any programming language. Unfortunately, user-defined software modules are often riskier, less robust, less tested, and less documented than their built-in counterparts. However, by mimicking the design, functionality, performance, and documentation of built-in software components, SAS practitioners are well placed to design and develop repeatable processes that will stand the test of time while avoiding common failure patterns that too often plague user-defined software.

3.1.2   Clarifying Components of Built-in Modules

Within built-in procedures (available through commercially developed software), the specification and implementation are separate and distinct components. The *specification* represents documentation and is birthed early in the software development life cycle (SDLC). SAS Institute developers asking for "the specs" are typically asking for the design specifications—the blueprints that describe (at a high level) the software they have been instructed (and paid) to build. And throughout the SDLC, design specs may be incrementally defined and refined.

However, to an end user, such as a SAS practitioner who is relying on built-in SAS procedures, "the specs" represent the SAS 9.4 documentation that instructs users how to call Base SAS procedures, functions, and subroutines. In both instances, the *specification* represents documentation that is maintained apart from code, and which describes what a software module does and how to interact with it.

The *implementation,* conversely, represents the code itself—the C code in which Base SAS procedures are written. Thus, the implementation performs the work whereas the specification describes the high-level functionality of the work, as well as inputs, outputs, return values, and other intersections through which users or external software interact with callable software modules.

The importance of procedural signatures to parameterization is discussed in Section 6.2

Each implementation has a *signature*—a procedural definition that describes a module's parameters and their attributes. The International Organization for Standardization (ISO) defines a *signature* (also *signature type*) as the "definition of the parameters of a given operation, including their order, data types, and passing mode; the results if any; and the possible outcomes (normal vs. exceptional) that might occur."[19]

A representation (i.e., abstraction) of the signature also appears within the specification (i.e., product documentation), and describes the name, type, and order of all parameters. Note that the implementation *prescribes* the signature (and thus enforces it), whereas the specification only *describes* the signature (so SAS practitioners can sufficiently understand the procedure to use it). SAS practitioners must rely on the specification because the underlying code (in which Base SAS is written, and which contains the *real* signature) is inaccessible—as is typical for proprietary software applications.

When a SAS practitioner calls a built-in procedure like SORT, the arguments that are passed (e.g., SORT options like DATA and statements like BY) are evaluated against the signature within the SORT implementation. If the invocation is missing required arguments or has extraneous (i.e., undefined) arguments, these exceptions will be detected and handled, and notes, warnings, and runtime errors will be printed to the log. Thus, a signature not only defines procedural parameters but also acts as a quality control check to ensure that each invocation of a callable module has a valid signature that matches the implementation's signature.

In all instances in which a specification exists as external documentation (in that it does not reside within the code itself), developers must ensure that the specification remains synchronized with the implementation that it represents. As new functionality is added to a procedure's implementation, or as new parameters are added to the implementation's signature, these modifications must be updated within the respective specification to ensure that documentation remains accurate and represents current functionality.

3.1.3   Clarifying Components of User-Defined Modules

Although identical procedural components (i.e., specification, implementation, invocation) inhabit both built-in and user-defined procedures, user-defined procedures are often operationalized differently, especially within end-user development environments in which software modules are sparsely documented or are documented within the code itself.

Consider the MYFUNC user-defined macro function, which converts a parameterized value into an uppercase value, simulating %UPCASE functionality:

```
* returns uppercase value of text;
* RC=MYFUNC_RC;
* - 0 fail, 1 success;
%macro myfunc(p /* value to be upped */);
%let syscc=0;
%global myfunc_RC;
%let myfunc_RC=0;
%sysfunc(upcase(&p))
%if &syscc=0 %then %let myfunc_RC=1;
%mend;


%put %myfunc(yellow);
%put MYFUNC_RC: &myfunc_rc;
```

The log demonstrates conversion of the input to uppercase, with a return code of 1 indicating success:

```
YELLOW
MYFUNC_RC: 1
```

And that's all she wrote! The code succinctly describes the macro's functionality (uppercase conversion) and lists the two possible return codes (0 or 1) for the &MYFUNC_RC global macro variable. The first four lines of the code (including the three comments and %MACRO statement) effectively constitute the module's specification, and a SAS practitioner viewing only these four lines should be able to understand the macro's functionality, and to call the macro function without further access to its implementation.

The implementation (often referred to as the *macro definition*, or simply the *macro*) comprises all code between the %MACRO and %MEND statements in which the functionality occurs. The %MACRO statement itself represents the function's single-line signature because it prescribes the name, type (i.e., keyword vs. positional), and order of parameters. Within MYFUNC, only one parameter (i.e., the keyword parameter P) is defined, so parameter order is irrelevant. SAS macro parameters always have a character data type, so data type is also irrelevant. Even macros that declare no parameters will have a Null signature, in which empty parentheses denote that no arguments can be passed.

Confusion can arise when discussing user-defined macros, however, because the %MACRO statement—the *signature*—is simultaneously part of the specification and the implementation. Within the implementation, the signature *prescribes* (to the code) what parameters can be referenced when the macro is invoked, and within the specification, it *describes* (to SAS practitioners reading the code) what arguments can be passed. This overlap commonly occurs in user-defined SAS macro definitions, and Figure 3.1 demonstrates the intersection of the implementation and specification at the signature of a user-defined macro. This overlap pattern is also common in user-defined SAS functions (built with the FCMP procedure), in which function and subroutine functionality is often documented in the code itself.

Despite causing some confusion when formal procedural abstraction nomenclature is discussed, this macro construction nevertheless remains a best practice within the SAS language, as it supports software readability and eliminates the need for developers to duplicate the signature within an external specification (i.e., documentation).

Within a SAS end-user development paradigm, where *specification* is referenced in literature (or within this text), it should be interpreted to include comment headers and the %MACRO statement—the single statement defining the signature. The *implementation* also includes the

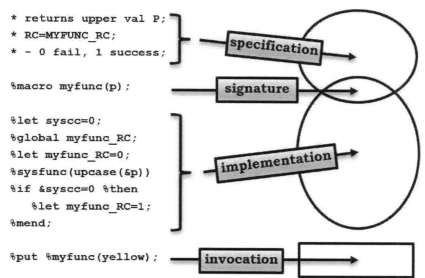

Figure 3.1 Signature Overlap in SAS Macro Procedural Abstraction

%MACRO statement, but adds the entire macro—from %MACRO to glorious %MEND. Thus, just as SAS practitioners are often simultaneously developers and end users, a user-defined SAS macro signature often will similarly straddle this developer-user divide, existing both within the procedural implementation and its specification.

3.2 SPECIFICATION

The specification defines and characterizes a software module; it is the blueprint that emerges from software planning and design, and should predate actual software development. ISO defines a *specification* as a "document that fully describes a design element or its interfaces in terms of requirements (functional, performance, constraints, and design characteristics) and the qualification conditions and procedures for each requirement."[20]

Software modules are born out of requirements that should describe some business need. The specification reflects that need by stating the functionality (and output, if any) of the module—what it *does*. Moreover, the specification states the inputs (and environmental constraints, if any) required by the module—what it *needs*. In many cases, the specification additionally describes vulnerabilities, risks, and other usage criteria or caveats. Noticeably absent from the specification is any information about *how* the module will (or does) deliver its functionality, as these details are contained only within the implementation and are hidden from end users.

For this reason, the specification itself is an abstraction; it describes functional output (like a fresh Double-Double) but says nothing of the process through which In-N-Out creates its mouth-watering hamburgers. The specification provides the link between the procedural invocation, through which end users or processes call a procedure, and the implementation, which executes the procedural instructions.

The specifications for built-in software components will generally be described within separate software product documentation. For example, SAS Institute publishes SAS language specifications online—throughout its extensive technical resources archive, as well as through stand-alone PDFs. Figure 3.2 demonstrates the SAS specification for the ANYDIGIT built-in function, which returns the first position in which a number is found in a character variable.[21]

User-defined software, too, can be elegantly and comprehensively described in stand-alone documentation—and this is most common where industry standards (e.g., FDA guidelines for pharmaceutical research)

ANYDIGIT Function

Searches a character string for a digit, and returns the first position at which the digit is found.

Categories:	Character
	CAS
Restriction:	This function is assigned an I18N Level 1 status unless a VARCHAR variable is used, or if the function is threaded or runs in DS2. If these exceptions occur, then this function is assigned an I18N Level 2 status. For more information, see Internationalization Compatibility.
Note:	This function supports the VARCHAR type.

Table of Contents

Syntax

ANYDIGIT(*string* <,*start*>)

Required Argument

string
is the character constant, variable, or expression to search.

Optional Argument

start
is an optional integer that specifies the position at which the search should start and the direction in which to search.

Figure 3.2 ANYDIGIT Built-in Function Specification

prescribe documentation requirements, where software modules are maintained in a centralized code repository (i.e., reuse library), or where users, teams, or organizations have adopted and enforced rigorous standards. This is to say that some user-defined specifications do mirror the professionalism and thoroughness evinced by SAS technical documentation, which only serves to maximize reuse of those user-defined modules.

This comprehensiveness contrasts sharply with less complex user-defined SAS modules that may lack any external documentation. In these cases, a module's entire specification—and, in fact, all documentation—may reside solely as comments within a SAS program file. Notwithstanding the pros and cons of this approach, it is important, nevertheless, to be able to both identify and understand the role of the software specification—even in barely documented software.

For example, the specification for the FINDVARS macro (defined in Section 3.3) includes the macro header comments, as well as the %MACRO statement, which declares its parameters:

```
* Creates a space-delimited var list as return value;
* Can be called from within a DATA step or PROC;
* Variables are ordered as they occur in the PDV;
* TYPE is NUM or CHAR, for numeric or character;
* No exception handling for missing/locked data set;
%macro findvars(dsn= /* data set in LIB.DSN format */,
    type= /* CHAR or NUM */);
```

Every SAS macro begins with the %MACRO statement, which includes the macro name followed by an enumeration of required or optional parameters, as well as their default values, if defined.

The specification describes the overall functionality of the module—why it exists. In straightforward modules, functionality might be conveyed through one or two statements, whereas more complex modules will require additional information.

When developers are making the critical decision about whether to reuse software modules (including those they have built, their team has built, or ones pillaged from white papers and other external resources), the specification is key to understanding whether existing code can be reused or refactored, or whether a new module must be built from scratch. Obviously, the former is preferred, and facilitates increased productivity gained through software reuse. Yet, without a specification that aptly describes and documents a software module, developers are likely to re-invent the wheel unnecessarily, and develop from scratch.

For example, without reading the FINDVARS macro itself (i.e., its implementation), a developer should be able to read only its specification and understand how to invoke the macro and what results will be produced. This abstract view of the FINDVARS macro benefits SAS practitioners, who are not required to understand every intricacy and idiosyncrasy of how FINDVARS delivers its functionality.

Instructions for invoking a module are also commonly included within a specification. The second comment in the preceding example states that FINDVARS "can be called from within a DATA step or PROC," which clarifies its utility and scope. Thus, as demonstrated in Section 3.4, the FINDVARS macro function can be embedded within the PRINT procedure to print all numeric variables (Emp_ID) in a data set:

```
data personnel;
    infile datalines delimiter=',';
    length Emp_ID 8 First_Name $50 Last_Name $50;
    input Emp_ID First_Name $ Last_Name $;
    datalines;
1, Ron, Burgundy
2, Chazz, Michaels
;

proc print data=personnel;
    var %findvars(dsn=personnel, type=num);
run;
```

Note that within the function's signature, *slashterisk* comments (i.e., /* */) further clarify the TYPE parameter by enumerating its valid values—CHAR and NUM. Within some SAS interfaces, such as SAS Enterprise Guide, when a user begins typing a user-defined macro invocation, slashterisk comments will appear in a popup box to facilitate entering each argument.

The FINDVARS specification defines what FINDVARS does (its functionality and return value) and what it needs (its parameter inputs). Some specifications end here, although information about a function's risks, limitations, or other caveats can lend invaluable insight to would-be developers as they assess a function's feasibility for reuse.

For example, the specification states that no exception handling exists for missing or locked data sets; thus, the following FINDVARS invocation (now referencing the nonexistent Peeps data set) results in failure:

```
%put %findvars(dsn=peeps, type=char);
```

```
WARNING: Argument 1 to function ATTRN referenced by the
%SYSFUNC or %QSYSFUNC macro function is out of range.
NOTE: Mathematical operations could not be performed
during %SYSFUNC function execution. The result of the
operations have been set to a missing value.
ERROR: A character operand was found in the %EVAL
function or %IF condition where a numeric operand is
required. The condition was: &vars
ERROR: The %TO value of the %DO I loop is invalid.
ERROR: The macro FINDVARS will stop executing.
```

The FINDVARS macro will similarly fail if another user or process maintains read-write access (i.e., an exclusive lock) on the data set that FINDVARS is attempting to interrogate. Exception handling could be implemented within the macro to detect these exceptions (e.g., a missing or locked data set) programmatically and, if implemented, should be documented inside the updated specification.

The importance of updating procedural specifications as functionality changes (over a software module's lifespan) is discussed in Section 10.2.4

Developers will often judge a book by its cover, and where software is concerned, that cover is the specification. A user-defined module whose functionality, strengths, and weaknesses are accurately documented will maximize the potential for developers to reach for and reuse an existing book—rather than unnecessarily writing their own.

3.3 IMPLEMENTATION

The implementation delivers functionality described in the specification of a procedure or other callable software module. Whereas the specification defines *what* a software module accomplishes, the implementation details *how* that functionality is delivered. ISO defines the *implementation* as a "process of translating a design into hardware components, software components, or both."[22]

For example, a SAS macro implementation is commonly referred to as the *macro definition*, and includes all that sumptuous code between %MACRO and %MEND. An initial implementation of the FINDVARS macro, referenced in the previous section, follows:

FINDVARS is refactored in Section 10.3.1 into a macro subroutine that initializes an indexed macro list, rather than returning a space-delimited list

```
%macro findvars(dsn= /* data set in LIB.DSN format */,
    type= /* CHAR or NUM */);
%local varlist dsid vars vartype i close;
%let varlist=;
%let dsid=%sysfunc(open(&dsn,i));
%let vars=%sysfunc(attrn(&dsid,nvars));
%do i=1 %to &vars;
    %let vartype=%sysfunc(vartype(&dsid,&i));
    %if (&vartype=N and %upcase(&type)=NUM)
        or (&vartype=C and %upcase(&type)=CHAR)
        %then %let varlist=
        &varlist %sysfunc(varname(&dsid,&i));
    %end;
%let close=%sysfunc(close(&dsid));
&varlist
%mend;
```

Thus, an implementation represents a lower level of abstraction (i.e., more concrete and granular) than its specification. A developer interested in reusing a module like the FINDVARS macro needs to understand the functionality described in its specification, but should not require access to the implementation (i.e., the macro itself) to comprehend and successfully call the macro. Of course, user-defined modules built in the SAS language are typically accessible to the SAS practitioners invoking them; however, a well-documented macro (or FCMP function or subroutine) should facilitate usage of the module without the user having to scrutinize the code to decipher its functionality.

In some cases, however, an understanding of the functionality contained within the implementation can assist developers in optimizing how they utilize a software module. For example, SAS documentation does not go to great lengths to describe the specific algorithms that the built-in FREQ procedure uses to calculate frequency distribution—nor does it need to. Rather, these very technical details are abstracted (within SAS documentation—that is, the FREQ *specification*) and hidden from SAS practitioners. But in some cases, some knowledge of *how* to FREQ—that is, its *implementation*—is beneficial; for example, when users are attempting to optimize FREQ performance or efficiency. And in these cases, SAS technical support can and does provide excellent technical guidance on the implementation of SAS built-in procedures and functions.

"Hiding" details may smack of scandal or intrigue, yet *information hiding* is a critical component of procedural abstraction that benefits both software developers and end users, as discussed in Chapter 2. Thus, when the core functionality of a procedure or function is *hidden*, end users are able to focus their attention only on the module's invocation, and developers are enabled to refactor or update the module's implementation to deliver even greater functionality or performance.

These benefits of procedural abstraction are as true for user-defined modules as they are for built-in modules. Consider the FINDVARS macro, which can be called once to specify *either* numeric or character variables, but which must be called twice to specify *both* numeric and character variables:

```
proc print data=personnel;
   var %findvars(dsn=personnel, type=num);
run;
```

```
proc print data=personnel;
   var %findvars(dsn=personnel, type=num)
      %findvars(dsn=personnel, type=char);
run;
```

Tired of having to invoke FINDVARS twice to enumerate both character and numeric variable names, a savvy SAS practitioner could subtly refactor FINDVARS so that omitting the TYPE parameter would list *all* variables in the user-specified data set, including both character and numeric variables:

```
* Creates a space-delimited var list as return value;
* Can be called from within a DATA step or PROC;
* Variables are ordered as they occur in the PDV;
* TYPE is NUM or CHAR, for numeric or character;
* if TYPE is omitted, all variables are selected;
```

```
* No exception handling for missing/locked data set;
%macro findvars(dsn= /* data set in LIB.DSN format */,
    type=ALL /* CHAR or NUM [ALL for CHAR and NUM] */);
%local varlist dsid vars vartype i close;
%let varlist=;
%let dsid=%sysfunc(open(&dsn,i));
%let vars=%sysfunc(attrn(&dsid,nvars));
%do i=1 %to &vars;
    %let vartype=%sysfunc(vartype(&dsid,&i));
    %if %upcase(&type=ALL) or (&vartype=N and
        %upcase(&type)=NUM) or (&vartype=C and
        %upcase(&type)=CHAR) %then %let
        varlist=&varlist %sysfunc(varname(&dsid,&i));
    %end;
%let close=%sysfunc(close(&dsid));
&varlist
%mend;
```

This version of the FINDVARS macro is refactored in Section 10.2.2 using *positional* parameters, as are more commonly observed within built-in functions

Now, when the TYPE argument is omitted from the function call, &TYPE will be initialized to ALL (the default value defined in the %MACRO statement), which returns all variable names, regardless of data type. For example, the following FINDVARS invocation prints all three variables (representing both character and numeric data types) from Personnel in the order in which they occur within the program data vector (PDV):

```
%put %findvars(dsn=personnel);
```

Emp_ID First_Name Last_Name

Macro functionality has been extended (i.e., expanded) while backward compatibility has been preserved; legacy code that relies on either the CHAR or NUM arguments for the TYPE parameter does not need to be changed. Neither do SAS practitioners need to understand *how* an omitted TYPE argument is able to generate all variables in a data set; they only need to understand that it does, which has been documented in the updated specification—both in comments preceding the macro definition and in the slashterisk comment following the TYPE parameter declaration.

Data-driven programming promotes software flexibility and configurability, but it also promotes software reuse. When software

Backward compatibility, which promotes software reuse, is introduced as a data-driven design principle in Section 1.4, and its role in supporting user-defined functions is demonstrated in Section 10.2.4

modules are updated and backward compatibility is *not* prioritized and is lost, end users often face the difficult dilemma of either having to run less functional software (that at least does not break legacy code), or having to upgrade to a higher-functioning module (albeit one that requires manual updates to all legacy calls to the former module). Rather than forcing this Sophie's choice on SAS practitioners, a far more prudent approach prioritizes backward compatibility, where possible, to deliver both superior functionality and future-proofed software.

3.4 INVOCATION

An invocation (or call) temporarily passes program control from a calling program (i.e., parent process) to a called module (i.e., child process). Data-driven design typically requires that one or more parameters be defined in the callable module and passed as arguments from the calling program. When the called module terminates, it may pass a return value or one or more return codes to the calling program, and it may produce additional output, interact with data objects, or deliver additional functionality. Similarly, when SAS programs run in batch mode, they are invoked from the operating system (OS) and control returns to the OS when the called process exits.

An invocation *should* mirror its respective specification, in that the signature provided in the invocation should match the signature described in documentation; however, invocations *must* mirror the actual signature that is defined within the implementation, where parameters are declared. Thus, as mentioned previously, whereas a specification only *describes* the signature, the implementation *prescribes* (and governs) the signature.

The FINDVARS macro is defined in Section 3.3, and can be used to demonstrate two separate invocation failure patterns that occur when signatures within the invocation and implementation do not match.

The following invocation contains an undefined parameter (COLOR), not included in the implementation's signature:

```
%put %findvars(dsn=personnel, type=, color=blue);
```

SAS does not know how to interpret the COLOR argument (that lacks a corresponding COLOR parameter), so it prints an error message:

```
ERROR: The keyword parameter COLOR was not defined with
the macro.
```

Similarly, an invocation can fail if it omits arguments that are required by the procedural specification. However, whereas the failure of supernumerary parameters is quick and obvious (because SAS halts immediately when the incorrect FINDVARS call executes), the failure of omitted parameters can be silent but deadly, producing functional failure but not evincing runtime errors or warnings in the log or within automatic macro variables (e.g., &SYSCC, &SYSERR).

For example, the following invocation of FINDVARS omits the TYPE argument, which is OK because this parameter is optional; however, the invocation also omits the DSN argument, which is NOT OK because the macro needs to know in which data set to look to find variables:

```
%put %findvars();
```

Given these omissions, the output may be surprising, with the log indicating neither warning nor runtime error, yet still enumerating the now-familiar variable names within the Personnel data set:

```
Emp_ID First_Name Last_Name
```

It turns out that when the required DSN argument is omitted, the &DSN local macro variable is initialized to missing, and the following OPEN function is dynamically generated inside FINDVARS:

```
OPEN(,1);
```

And it also turns out that the first OPEN parameter (denoting data set name) is optional and, if omitted, is initialized to the value of the _LAST_ SAS system option, which represents the last data set that was created.

Thus, if you intended to interrogate the Personnel data set and accidentally omitted the DSN argument, you would still arrive at the correct results; however, if any subsequent data set had been created prior to invoking FINDVARS, your output would differ. This is undesirable functionality because the macro risks producing an undetected failure that yields neither warning nor runtime error.

Exception handling could be implemented to validate programmatically that the DSN argument has been supplied, and if the required argument has been omitted, the macro could terminate and communicate this error. Additional exception handling could validate that the referenced data set (and its library, if referenced) does, in fact, exist. The

Exception handling within the SAS macro language is demonstrated in Sections 4.6 and 6.4.1

following final refactoring of FINDVARS implements these two exception handling routines:

```
/*
Creates a space-delimited var list as return value
Can be called from within a DATA step or PROC
Variables are ordered as they occur in the PDV
TYPE is NUM or CHAR, for numeric or character
If TYPE is omitted, all variables are selected

Return codes (and SYSCC set to 4) for the following:
 - _ERROR_ARG_MISSING_ - required DSN arg is missing
 - _ERROR_DATASET_MISSING_ - DSN argument provided, but
      the referenced data set and/or library is missing
No exception handling for exclusively locked data set
*/
%macro findvars(dsn= /* data set in LIB.DSN format */,
    type=ALL /* CHAR or NUM [ALL for CHAR and NUM] */);
%let syscc=0;
%if %length(&dsn)=0 %then %do;
    %let syscc=4;
    _ERROR_ARG_MISSING_
    %return;
    %end;
%else %if %sysfunc(exist(&dsn))^=1 %then %do;
    %let syscc=4;
    _ERROR_DATASET_MISSING_
    %return;
    %end;
%local varlist dsid vars vartype i close;
%let varlist=;
%let dsid=%sysfunc(open(&dsn,i));
%let vars=%sysfunc(attrn(&dsid,nvars));
%do i=1 %to &vars;
    %let vartype=%sysfunc(vartype(&dsid,&i));
    %if %upcase(&type=ALL) or (&vartype=N and
        %upcase(&type)=NUM) or (&vartype=C and
```

```
    %upcase(&type)=CHAR) %then %let
    varlist=&varlist %sysfunc(varname(&dsid,&i));
  %end;
%let close=%sysfunc(close(&dsid));
&varlist
%mend;
```

Omitting the DSN argument (or passing a Null value) now produces an error message:

```
%put %findvars();
```

```
_ERROR_ARG_MISSING_
```

And specifying a non-existent data set (or library) also produces an error message:

```
%put %findvars(dsn=peeps);
```

```
_ERROR_DATASET_MISSING_
```

Rather than modifying the *functionality* of FINDVARS, this refactoring has improved the macro's *performance* (i.e., robustness). Argument validation—and the documentation thereof within the specification—is critical, especially where end users manually call modules. Yet, in all cases, the implementation—not its associated invocations—bears the responsibility of ensuring that only valid arguments have been passed.

3.5 PROCEDURES

Procedural abstraction is central to not only procedures but also applications, functions, subroutines, macros, and other callable software modules. Built-in procedures provide out-of-the-box functionality to would-be developers, and are a primary draw in attracting users to one application or language over another. Apropos data-driven design, SAS built-in procedures, functions, and subroutines provide archetypes that SAS practitioners can use to model the design of our own user-defined modules.

ISO defines a *procedure* as a "2. portion of a computer program that is named and that performs a specific action" and, more restrictively, as a "3. routine that does not return a value."[23] Procedures can have one or more parameters, and often modify some object or produce some output.

Procedures provide repeatable yet configurable functionality when the arguments passed to them are varied.

Historically, *procedure* has enjoyed an expansive definition. For example, in a 1991 comparative analysis of programming languages, Linda Weiser Friedman contends that "The word *procedure* is often used generically to denote any subprogram (even a function, which would then be called a *value-returning procedure* or *typed procedure*)."[24] Through the ages and across languages, never disputed is a procedure's status as a *callable software module that provides functionality.*

Within the SAS language, built-in procedures are invoked using "PROC" and the procedure's name, in addition to required or optional procedural statements and arguments. It is the SAS language's integral reliance on procedures for which it is labeled a "procedural language."

Procedures often act upon a data object (like a SAS data set) that is *passed by reference*, in which a pointer to the data object (i.e., the data set name) is passed to the procedure. For example, the following SORT invocation passes the name of the data set (Personnel) and the variable name (First_name) by which the data set will be ordered:

Call by reference is introduced in Section 6.5.2

```
data personnel;
    infile datalines delimiter=',';
    length Emp_ID 8 First_Name $50 Last_Name $50;
    input Emp_ID First_Name $ Last_Name $;
    datalines;
1, Ron, Burgundy
2, Chazz, Michaels
3, Sky, Corrigan
4, Franz, Liebkind
5, Ricky, Bobby
6, Jacobim, Mugatu
;

proc sort data=personnel;
    by first_name;
run;
```

The data within Personnel are not passed directly (i.e., by value) through the SORT invocation, but rather indirectly because only the name of the object (Personnel) is passed (by reference). SORT modifies the Personnel data set but produces no other output or return value; however, SAS automatic macro variables such as the &SYSCC (system current condition) and &SYSERR (system error) are updated if a warning or runtime error occurs while SORT is running.

For example, when the SORT invocation is updated, and now specifies a variable that does not exist in the Personnel data set, a runtime error is produced in the log, and &SYSCC and &SYSERR are automatically initialized to 3000:

```
%let syscc=0;
proc sort data=personnel;
   by missing_variable; * variable does not exist;
run;
%put SYSCC: &syscc;
%put SYSERR: &syserr;
```

The log demonstrates both the failure and the automatic macro variables, the latter of which can be used in exception handling routines to detect and respond to failures programmatically:

Exception handling (to detect invalid arguments) is demonstrated in Section 6.4.1

```
%let syscc=0;
proc sort data=personnel;
   by missing_variable;
ERROR: Variable MISSING_VARIABLE not found.
run;

NOTE: The SAS System stopped processing this step
because of errors.
NOTE: PROCEDURE SORT used (Total process time):
      real time               0.00 seconds
      cpu time                0.00 seconds

%put SYSCC: &syscc;
SYSCC: 3000
%put SYSERR: &syserr;
SYSERR: 3000
```

For example, conditional logic after the failed SORT procedure could evaluate the value of &SYSCC (3000), determine a failure had occurred, terminate the program, and notify stakeholders via email.

When assessing the scope of procedural parameters, it is critical to inspect the procedure's *specification*, not its *invocation*. For example, the MEANS procedure can be called with no arguments or options, in which case it analyzes all variables in the last data set that was created:

```
proc means;
run;
```

This bare-bones usage does not imply that MEANS has no defined parameters. Rather, in this example, MEANS parameters are initialized to default values because arguments are not provided in the invocation. For example, the DATA parameter, through which SAS practitioners typically specify the data set to be analyzed, is initialized to the _LAST_ SAS system option, which represents the last data set that had been created. Only through inspection of SAS documentation of the MEANS procedure can SAS practitioners understand the functionality of MEANS, including the full extent of its parameters, options, and default settings.

3.5.1   User-Defined Macro Procedures

SAS practitioners are able to develop callable, reusable software modules—including procedures, functions, and subroutines—using the SAS macro language. *Macro procedures*, although seldom referenced as such, are simply those user-defined macros that fail to meet the criteria for either a *macro function* or a *macro subroutine*, both of which are defined and discussed later in this chapter. In general, SAS user-defined macro procedures are denoted only as *macros*, whereas it is more important that *macro functions* and *macro subroutines* be distinguished as such, given their narrower definitions.

One of the hallmarks of macro procedures is their ability to contain step boundaries—including DATA steps, RUN statements, and SAS built-in procedures—none of which can be executed within a user-defined macro function or a user-defined macro subroutine. It is for this reason that user-defined macro functions and subroutines can typically operate within a DATA step or a SAS built-in procedure, whereas macro procedures cannot.

The FINDVARSPROC macro relies on the DICTIONARY.Columns table to select either all character or all numeric variable names from a user-specified data set:

SAS Dictionary tables are introduced in Section 12.4, and are integral to interrogating the structure of SAS data sets

```
* Creates a space-delim global macro variable VARLIST;
* CANNOT be called from within a DATA step or PROC;
* Variables are ordered as they occur in the PDV;
* TYPE is NUM or CHAR, for numeric or character;
* No exception handling for missing/locked data set;
%macro findvarsproc(dsn= /* data set LIB.DSN */,
    type= /* CHAR or NUM */);
%global varlist;
%let varlist=;
%local lib;
%if %length(%scan(&dsn,2,.))=0 %then %let lib=WORK;
%else %do;
    %let lib=%scan(&dsn,1,.);
    %let dsn=%scan(&dsn,2,.);
    %end;
proc sql noprint;
    select name into : varlist separated by " "
    from dictionary.columns
    where upcase(libname)="%upcase(&lib)"
        and upcase(memname)="%upcase(&dsn)"
        and upcase(type)="%upcase(&type)";
quit;
%mend;
```

If the specified data set exists, is not exclusively locked (which occurs when a data set is being created or modified), and contains one or more variables of the user-specified data type (CHAR or NUM), the &VARLIST global macro variable is initialized to a space-delimited list of all relevant variable names. In all other cases, &VARLIST is initialized to an empty string.

The following invocation prints all character variables (First_Name and Last_Name) from Personnel (created in Section 2.1.1):

```
%findvarsproc(dsn=personnel, type=CHAR);
```

```
%put VARLIST: &varlist;
```

The output lists the variable names for all character variables in the Personnel data set:

```
VARLIST: First_Name Last_Name
```

Note that because FINDVARSPROC runs the SQL procedure, it cannot be called from inside a DATA step or SAS procedure. Thus, FINDVARSPROC must be invoked before any process that requires &VARLIST. In the next section, this limitation is overcome by converting the macro from a user-defined *procedure* to a user-defined *function*.

Finally, note that throughout SAS literature and documentation (and including within this text), SAS macros that contain step boundaries are most commonly referenced simply as *macros* rather than more formally as *macro procedures*. Thus, only the user-defined *macro function* and *macro subroutine* exhibit functionality distinct enough to warrant referencing their full names.

3.6 FUNCTIONS

Functions are often distinguished from procedures in that they produce a return value whereas procedures do not. ISO defines a *function* as a "software module that performs a specific action, is invoked by the appearance of its name in an expression, receives input values, and returns a single value."[25] That is, functions represent another—yet more specific—breed of callable software modules.

Like procedures, functions typically define one or more parameters; however, this cardinal rule can be broken in some cases. The following DATA step relies on the DATE function (which defines no parameters) to generate the current date:

User-defined parameter-less functions and procedures are discussed and demonstrated in Section 6.7

```
data _null_;
    dt=date();
    put dt=mmddyy10.;
run;
```

This parameter-less pattern is uncommon, albeit typical when functions rely on environmental or system variables as their only input.

Within the SAS language, functions are divided into several categories, such as arithmetic, statistical, character, date, and input/output (I/O). For example, the following DATA step utilizes the CATX function to concatenate the First_name and Last_name variables to create the Name variable:

```
data cat;
   set personnel;
   length name $50;
   name=catx(' ',first_name, last_name);
run;
```

Name is initialized to the CATX return value. The same CATX function can utilize any character or string as a user-specified delimiter, can concatenate two or two hundred variables, and can utilize variable names or literal values as arguments.

For example, the following CATX function uses an asterisk as a separator and concatenates the variables One and Three, and the literal value 2, to initialize the Concat variable:

```
data cat2;
   length one three $1 concat $20;
   one='1';
   three='3';
   concat=catx('*',one,'2',three);
   put concat;
run;
```

Concat is initialized to the following value, which is printed to the log:

```
1*2*3
```

Thus, procedural abstraction facilitates functional flexibility that promotes the reuse of functions. CATX executes with great aplomb, relying on *internal iteration* to parse its list of arguments. In other words, CATX iterates across the delimited list of input values, yet conceals the methods through which it iterates. This iteration abstraction maximizes the flexibility and scalability of CATX because CATX can concatenate a scalable number of values.

Internal iteration is introduced in Section 5.2.1

3.6.1   User-Defined Macro Functions

Functions typically contain one or more input parameters, and always produce a return value. So-called *user-defined macro functions* approximate the functionality of a function within the SAS macro language, but because they are not true functions, it is essential to define this anecdotal usage, however prevalent it may be within SAS circles and literature.

Within this text, *user-defined macro functions* describe SAS macros that:

1. declare zero or more keyword or positional parameters
2. contain no step boundaries (e.g., DATA steps, SAS procedures, RUN statements)
3. *resolve to* (rather than *return*) a value

The prohibition of step boundaries is essential, as it enables user-defined macro functions to be placed inside the DATA step and SAS procedures, just as built-in functions can be utilized within Base SAS.

Note the key distinction that true functions *return* a value, whereas user-defined SAS macro functions *resolve to* a value. That is, the macro facility interprets macro language within a program, and *resolves* (i.e., converts) the whole of the macro code into a single value that is available for use when the non-macro code subsequently executes.

For example, the following user-defined macro function *resolves* to the character value "dinosaur":

```
%macro func();
%local rc;
%let rc=dinosaur;
&rc
%mend;
```

The statement that lacks a semicolon (&RC) is a tell-tale sign of a user-defined macro function, as the macro processor resolves this line to the value of &RC, but does not append a trailing semicolon. For this reason, calls to user-defined macro functions can occur within the DATA step and SAS procedures, and even inline with additional code.

Consider the following three invocations of FUNC that take advantage of this nimbleness:

```
%put %substr(%func,1,4);

data _null_;
    length word abbr $10;
    word="%func";
```

```
   abbr=substr("%func",1,4);
   put word= abbr=;
run;
```

FUNC performs admirably when embedded within the built-in macro function %SUBSTR, as well as when nestled inside the built-in SUBSTR function (in a DATA step), as shown in the log:

```
dino
```

```
word=dinosaur abbr=dino
```

It is this versatility of SAS user-defined macro functions with which SAS practitioners are so enamored, and why user-defined macro functions are often favored over their non-function macro counterparts.

In this section, the FINDVARSPROC *macro procedure* in Section 3.5.1 is refactored into the FINDVARS *macro function*. FINDVARS is considered to be a macro function because it resolves to a single value (the local macro variable &VARLIST) and contains no step boundaries:

```
* Creates a space-delimited var list as return value;
* Can be called from within a DATA step or PROC;
* Variables are ordered as they occur in the PDV;
* TYPE is NUM or CHAR, for numeric or character;
* No exception handling for missing/locked data set;
%macro findvars(dsn= /* data set in LIB.DSN format */,
    type= /* CHAR or NUM */);
%local varlist dsid vars vartype i close;
%let varlist=;
%let dsid=%sysfunc(open(&dsn,i));
%let vars=%sysfunc(attrn(&dsid,nvars));
%do i=1 %to &vars;
    %let vartype=%sysfunc(vartype(&dsid,&i));
    %if (&vartype=N and %upcase(&type)=NUM)
        or (&vartype=C and %upcase(&type)=CHAR)
        %then %let varlist=
        &varlist %sysfunc(varname(&dsid,&i));
      %end;
%let close=%sysfunc(close(&dsid));
```

```
&varlist
%mend;
```

Note that the signature (that declares parameters) is identical in both macros; however, the functionality and invocations of the macros differ. Both macros store results (i.e., the space-delimited list of data set variable names) in the &VARLIST macro variable; however, they utilize different methods to communicate these results to the calling process.

The macro procedure (FINDVARSPROC) communicates with its calling process by declaring a *global macro variable* (&VARLIST), and initializing it to the space-delimited list of variable names. Thereafter, the calling process can substitute &VARLIST wherever this list should be placed within code— so long as FINDVARSPROC has already been run prior to usage of &VARLIST.

The macro function (FINDVARS), on the other hand, declares &VARLIST as a *local macro variable*; thus, the calling process cannot access &VARLIST. FINDVARS instead stows &VARLIST in a semicolon-free line of code that, upon macro interpretation, resolves to the identical space-delimited list of variable names.

The following invocation of FINDVARS prints all character variable names (First_Name and Last_Name) in the Personnel data set, which is created in Section 3.5:

```
%put %findvars(dsn=personnel, type=char);
```

```
First_Name Last_Name
```

User-defined macro functions can be called from within the DATA step, as the following invocation of FINDVARS demonstrates:

```
data testdata;
    length varsindsn $50;
    varsindsn="%findvars(dsn=personnel, type=char)";
run;
```

The DATA step declares the VarsinDSN variable, and initializes it to a space-delimited list of all character variables in the Personnel data set.

Similarly, user-defined macro functions can be called from within SAS procedures; thus, FINDVARS can be called within PRINT to display only numeric variables within the Personnel data set:

```
proc print data=personnel;
   var %findvars(dsn=personnel, type=num);
run;
```

FINDVARS and FINDVARSPROC produce identical results, but cannot be said to be *functionally equivalent* because their invocations occur through different methods and because their results are communicated (to calling processes) through different methods.

Anecdotally, &VARLIST is referred to as a *return value*. In truth, however, SAS user-defined macro functions *resolve* rather than *return* values. Although SAS practitioners should understand the return-vs-resolve distinction, speaking of "macro return codes" and "macro return values" is commonplace throughout SAS literature, and is embraced in this text to facilitate consistency.

3.6.2 User-Defined FCMP Functions

The FCMP procedure empowers SAS practitioners to create user-defined functions and subroutines. Similar to user-defined macro functions, FCMP functions can declare zero or more parameters, and always return a single value.

Several aspects of FCMP functions are more restrictive than those of user-defined macro functions. For example, user-defined macro functions can declare positional and keyword parameters, whereas FCMP functions can declare only positional parameters. Similarly, user-defined macro functions can declare optional parameters, whereas FCMP functions must be invoked with all declared parameters passed. Finally, user-defined macro functions can specify a default value for arguments that are omitted, whereas FCMP functions cannot.

Despite these limitations, FCMP functions are *real* functions, in that they *return* rather than *resolve* a value (as user-defined macro functions do). Moreover, FCMP functions can declare character and numeric parameters, whereas user-defined macro functions can declare only character parameters. Finally, FCMP functions can declare array parameters—a tremendously useful skill that macros have yet to master.

Although the full functionality and syntax of FCMP far exceed the scope of this text, the FUNCTION statement (within the FCMP procedure) declares a user-defined function, and the ENDFUNC statement terminates the function.

For example, consider the Personnel data set (created in Section 3.5) and the need to create a variable that concatenates (and delimits) the last and first names—Last_name and First_name, respectively. The following FCMP procedure declares the SWAP_ADD_C function, which performs this concatenation:

```
proc fcmp outlib=sasuser.myfuncs.char;
   function swap_add_c(first $, last $) $;
      length last_comma_first $50;
      last_comma_first=strip(last) || ', '
         || strip(first);
      return(last_comma_first);
      endfunc;
quit;
```

The SWAP_ADD_C function is saved to the SASUSER.Myfuncs data set, and can be called subsequently by separate SAS programs. For example, the following OPTIONS statement instructs SAS to inspect the SASUSER.Myfuncs data set for user-defined functions, and the DATA step calls SWAP_ADD_C to initialize the New_name variable:

```
options cmplib=sasuser.myfuncs;

data _null_;
   set personnel;
   length new_name $60;
   new_name=swap_add_c(first_name, last_name);
   put new_name=;
run;
```

The log demonstrates that SWAP_ADD_C has transformed the Last_name and First_name variables into a new concatenated variable:

```
new_name=Michaels, Chazz
new_name=Liebkind, Franz
new_name=Mugatu, Jacobim
new_name=Bobby, Ricky
new_name=Burgundy, Ron
new_name=Corrigan, Sky
```

In general, SAS user-defined FCMP functions are used to transform data within a data set or hash object, whereas SAS user-defined macro functions facilitate metaprogramming and are used to write code dynamically. Both types of user-defined functions are powerful tools, although they solve different sets of programming challenges.

3.7 SUBROUTINES (AKA SAS CALL ROUTINES)

Subroutines are relics of procedural languages like COBOL and PL/I that stubbornly persist in Base SAS and the SAS macro language. IEEE defines a *subroutine* as a "routine that returns control to the program or subprogram that called it" but further notes the ambiguity that "The terms 'routine,' 'subprogram,' and 'subroutine' are defined and used differently in different programming languages."[26] To their credit, SAS subroutines persist because they deliver niche functionality not provided by functions or other SAS callable modules.

IEEE denotes the confusion evinced by *subroutine*; yet one would hope that at least *within* a specific language (like SAS), *subroutine* would be defined and used consistently in formal documentation like technical specifications. However, SAS Institute has regularly commingled *subroutine, routine, CALL subroutine, call routine,* and *CALL routine* for several decades in describing SAS subroutines. The next subsection explores the semantic history of the SAS subroutine, illustrates the failure of SAS Institute to standardize its own terminology, and lobbies for the consistent use of "subroutine" in documentation and literature.

Semantic pettifoggery aside, SAS subroutines are distinguished in that they do not return a value (as functions do), and can modify the value of one or more arguments (within the calling program). Built-in SAS subroutines and user-defined SAS subroutines (the latter of which are constructed using the FCMP procedure) must be invoked using the CALL statement or %SYSCALL macro statement. User-defined SAS macro subroutines can also be designed, and represent macros that return no value, do not contain step boundaries, and can modify one or more arguments; they require neither CALL nor %SYSCALL to be invoked.

SAS subroutines do not represent a subset or subordinate class of functions, as sometimes described—even in SAS documentation—they are their own thing. Thus, within the SAS language, subroutines—as well as procedures and functions—represent callable software modules that facilitate procedural abstraction. Imagine the SAS subroutine as the less

> Section 6.8.1 discusses the dichotomy between values *returned* by functions yet *modified* by subroutines

> In truth, FCMP functions can also modify multiple arguments by listing them in the OUTARGS statement, as discussed in Section 6.5.2

popular, slightly emo, half-twin brother of the SAS function. Although you won't often want to play with the SAS subroutine, neither should you lock him away under the stairs to be forgotten.

3.7.1   A Convoluted History of the SAS Subroutine

Base SAS stands on the shoulders of giants, and borrows especially from the PL/I procedural language that still powers some mainframe machines today. PL/I defines three types of "procedures"—MAIN, function, and subroutine.[27] Sound familiar? These terms correspond to today's SAS procedures (i.e., MAIN), SAS functions, and SAS subroutines.

In fact, Joan K. Hughes (aka Auntie Joan) contrasts PL/I functions and subroutines way back in 1973—yes, years before the genesis of the SAS language—so splendidly that her words bear repeating in 2023:

> "Functions versus Subroutines: A function is a procedure that returns a single value to the invoking procedure. By contrast, a subroutine cannot return a value to the point of invocation. The value of arguments, in certain cases, may be modified by the subroutine, and in this way results are effectively returned to the invoking program. A subroutine may return none, one, or many results to the invoking procedure through the modification of arguments in the subroutine call."[28]

And although Joan was speaking specifically of the PL/I language, her definition (half a century later) remains an accurate depiction of the Base SAS and SAS macro languages, and their use of functions and subroutines.

A 1980 PL/I primer similarly defines a *subroutine* as "a procedure whose construction allows the return of an arbitrary number of results for each invocation"; it states that "A subroutine is invoked by means of a CALL statement."[29] Thus, from the PL/I language, Base SAS "borrows" not only the subroutine definition but also the CALL statement that invokes both SAS built-in and user-defined subroutines! Moreover, user-defined subroutines created using the FCMP procedure are declared using the SUBROUTINE statement!! #nostalgia.

Despite the clear similarities between the PL/I subroutine and the SAS subroutine, SAS documentation unfortunately has used *subroutine*, *routine*, *CALL subroutine*, *call routine*, and *CALL routine* seemingly interchangeably for three decades—despite describing a single construct. This has contributed to the false representation (even by current SAS documentation) and false interpretation (by many SAS practitioners) that these separate terms describe separate software constructs; to be clear, they do not. Moreover, certain terms seem to have been favored—at specific points in time, or by specific SAS Institute publications—over others, further confounding users.

Early confusion in *subroutine* terminology is apparent in the *SAS User's Guide: Basics, 1982 Edition*.[30] Of the five terms—*subroutine, routine, CALL subroutine, call routine,* and *CALL routine*—only *call routine* and *CALL subroutine* appear in the book's index, with the "CALL Subroutines" section describing:

> "SAS provides a series of subroutines that give you more control over the seed stream and the random number stream than is possible with random number generating functions. These random number generating subroutines are invoked with CALL statements."

Thus, once upon a time, SAS subroutines supported primarily random number functionality, with the publication further stating that "For cases where you want more control of the number streams, use the CALL subroutine (described in RANUNI) corresponding to the random number function." These original SAS subroutines include: RANBIN, RANCAU, RANEXP, RANGAM, RANNOR, RANPOI, RANTBL, RANTRI, and RANUNI. Despite the simplicity and focus of subroutine functionality at this early stage in SAS history, SAS documentation was already conflating "CALL statement" with "CALL subroutine," and was using "CALL subroutine" and "subroutine" interchangeably.

Adding confusion, the book's index for "call routine" directs to the "CALL Statement" entry, which describes:

> "The purpose of the CALL statement in the DATA step is to invoke or call a routine. The routine is called each time the CALL statement is executed. You can write your own call routine in assembler or FORTRAN to process observations in a SAS data set and then invoke this routine with a CALL statement."

Yet, after this explanation that the CALL statement is used to invoke a "routine" (which contrasts with the earlier explanation that the CALL statement invokes *subroutines*), the very next sentence conflates subroutines and functions by stating "For example, the SYMPUT function [sic] is used to give the value of an ordinary SAS variable to a macro variable." Adding more fuel to the conflagration, the book's index lists the "SYMPUT call routine," which directs to a section that repeatedly references "the SYMPUT function [sic]." To be clear, SYMPUT is a SAS subroutine and has never been a function! It is no wonder, given this 1982 trainwreck of technical jargon, that SAS subroutines have been inconsistently referenced throughout their existence.

By 1988, the *SAS Language Guide for Personal Computers, Release 6.03 Edition* has only one *subroutine* term—*CALL subroutines*—listed in its index.[31] Notwithstanding, the "Call Statement" entry denotes that "The purpose of the CALL statement in the DATA step is to invoke or call a routine. The routine is called each time the CALL statement is executed." The text continues and enumerates all SAS "routines," which include nine random number subroutines (RANBIN, RANCAU, RANEXP, RANGAM, RANNOR, RANPOI, RANTBL, RANTRI, and RANUNI), SOUND, SYMPUT, and SYSTEM. From this account, SAS seemed poised to clarify that *subroutines* and *routines* could be used interchangeably, which would not have been a terrible world to inhabit.

However, a contemporaneous SAS publication for the same SAS software release upends this sense of consensus. The *SAS Language: Reference, Version 6, First Edition* instead denotes that "The CALL statement invokes a SAS CALL routine. SAS CALL routines can assign variable values and perform other system functions."[32] Moreover, the index correspondingly lists "CALL routine" rather than "CALL subroutine." Thus, in the late 1980s and early 1990s (at least within some SAS documentation), there is an effort underway to replace *subroutine* nomenclature with *CALL routine*. Notwithstanding, this also would not have been a terrible world to inhabit—had the terminology shift toward *routine* been universally applied, but of course it was not.

Documentation surrounding the introduction of the %SYSCALL macro statement (which invokes subroutines) similarly favored *routine* over *subroutine*. For example, the *SAS Macro Language: Reference, First Edition*, published in 1997, describes that "%SYSCALL invokes a SAS call routine"; elsewhere, however, "CALL routine" is capitalized.[33] At that time, %SYSCALL was used to call either built-in subroutines or user-defined subroutines, the latter of which were created using the SAS/TOOLKIT software (because the FCMP procedure did not exist).

Thus, in 1991, the *SAS/TOOLKIT Software: Usage and Reference, Version 6, First Edition* does consistently reference "CALL routines." It states: "A SAS CALL routine is a builtin [sic] expression that can change the value of any of the arguments passed to it, but does not return a value."[34] SAS/TOOLKIT empowered SAS practitioners to write functions and subroutines in C, FORTRAN, PL/I, or IBM assembler.

But increasingly, SAS practitioners wanted to write user-defined functions and subroutines in a familiar tongue—Base SAS. Out of this necessity was born the FCMP procedure, which empowered SAS practitioners to write user-defined functions and subroutines, but which also revived the *subroutine* nomenclature in both FCMP syntax and documentation.

For example, the 2003 SAS Institute publication *The FCMP Procedure* commences by declaring that "The SAS Function Compiler (FCMP) Procedure allows users to create, test, and store SAS functions and subroutines for use by other SAS procedures."[35] Thereafter, SAS practitioners are introduced to the SUBROUTINE and ENDSUB statements: "The subroutine begins with the SUBROUTINE statement...and each is completed with an ENDSUB statement." Curiously, the publication defines subroutines as being subordinate to functions, and both subroutines and functions as being "routines":

"Functions are equivalent to "routines" as used in any other programming language. They are independent computations blocks that require zero or more arguments. The subroutine is a special type of function that has no return value."

This alleged hierarchy—the notion that SAS subroutines are subordinate to (or a subset of) SAS functions—is no longer promulgated by SAS documentation, which now embraces the separate-but-different model. Notwithstanding, the 2003 return to *subroutine* in FCMP syntax and documentation represented a welcome undoing of the routine/call routine/CALL routine chaos that had plagued previous documentation. But alas, the calm was not to last.

Current SAS documentation again favors *CALL routine* over *subroutine*; however, this is applied inconsistently, with built-in subroutines more commonly called *CALL routines* and user-defined subroutines referenced erratically as either *CALL routines* or *subroutines*.

Consider the current *Base SAS 9.4 Procedures Guide, Seventh Edition*, which first describes that the FCMP procedure "Enables creation, testing, and storage of SAS functions and subroutines before they are used in other SAS procedures." The documentation subsequently describes that the FCMP procedure "Enables you to create, test, and store SAS functions, CALL routines, and subroutines before you use them in other SAS procedures or in DATA steps." This subtle shift in phrasing denotes a huge distinction because the second description implies that CALL routines and subroutines are separate constructs; once again, they are not!

The publication continues to spew chaos under the header "What Does the FCMP Procedure Do?":

> "The SAS Function Compiler (FCMP) procedure enables you to create, test, and store SAS functions, CALL routines, and subroutines before you use them in other SAS procedures or DATA steps. PROC FCMP provides the ability to build functions, CALL routines, and subroutines using DATA step syntax that is stored in a data set. The procedure accepts slight variations of DATA step statements, and you can use most features of the SAS programming language in functions and CALL routines that are created by PROC FCMP. You can call PROC FCMP functions and CALL routines from the DATA step just as you would any other SAS function, CALL routine, or subroutine."

This unnecessary imprecision at the hands of SAS Institute only stymies the adoption of FCMP by SAS practitioners, who must painfully parse SAS documentation in an attempt to discover what differences exist between *CALL routines* and *subroutines*. No differences exist—only inconsistent nomenclature surrounding subroutines! Seriously, this is why we can't have nice things!!

The 2021 edition of the SAS publication *SAS 9.4 Functions and CALL Routines: Reference, Fifth Edition* might understandably reference only *CALL routines*—you know, because *CALL routine* is in the name. However, 59 instances of *subroutine* persist in this publication—all of which are used to reference various SAS subroutines that relate to random number generation.[36] Elsewhere in the publication, however, 1,257 references to *CALL routine* are made. Thus, even extant SAS publications cannot uniformly discuss the SAS subroutine.

The SAS subroutine has clearly endured an identity crisis—apparent even at its introduction within SAS documentation, and indurated through decades of confusing and even conflicting SAS technical specifications. Despite this rough childhood, subroutines nevertheless fulfill a functional niche within Base SAS and the SAS macro language. It is for this reason that subroutines—by any name—should juxtapose functions in every SAS practitioner's toolkit, and why user-defined subroutines are invaluable to data-driven design.

3.7.2   User-Defined Macro Subroutines

The SAS macro language defines neither user-defined functions nor user-defined subroutines. Nevertheless, just as user-defined macro functions are anecdotally defined within Section 3.6.1, user-defined macro subroutines are anecdotally defined herein. This text adopts the definition that a user-defined macro subroutine declares zero or more parameters, does not contain step boundaries, and does not resolve to a value.

SAS macro subroutines can optionally modify the values of the arguments passed to them. Note that all modifiable arguments must be passed *by reference*—not *by value*—so the subroutine can reinitialize the macro variables within the subroutine. Moreover, this reinitialization requires access to macro variables both inside and outside of the subroutine, so macro variables must either have global scope or be locally declared in a calling macro, in which case that local scope will be inherited by called child processes.

The FINDVARS_IDX macro subroutine, shown in Section 10.3.1, initializes the values within an indexed macro list (a user-defined data structure)

For example, consider the requirement to build a callable software module that swaps values between two macro variables. A user-defined macro subroutine can deliver this functionality because subroutines are able to modify the arguments passed to them. The SWAP subroutine declares and initializes a local macro variable &TEMP to the value passed to its first parameter (A), then reinitializes the first argument to the value passed to the second parameter (B), and finally reinitializes the second argument to the value held in &TEMP:

```
%macro swap(a /* [REF] */,
    b /* [REF] */);
%local temp;
%let temp=&&&a;
%let &a=&&&b;
```

```
%let &b=&temp;
%mend;
```

If two global macro variables (&VAR1 and &VAR2) are declared, initialized, and passed as arguments to SWAP, the value in &VAR1 (first) and the value in &VAR2 (last) will be swapped:

```
%global var1 var2;
%let var1=first;
%let var2=last;
%swap(var1, var2);
%put &=var1 &=var2;
```

Note that the macro variable names (&VAR1 and &VAR2) are required to be passed by reference; thus, their ampersands are omitted from the SWAP call.

The log demonstrates that SWAP reinitialized &VAR1 to "last" and &VAR2 to "first":

```
VAR1=last VAR2=first
```

But what happens if the SWAP subroutine is called, and the arguments have not been declared as global macro variables (or as local macro variables having accessible, inherited scope)? This exception is generated by the following invocation:

```
%swap(miss1, miss2);
```

The log demonstrates that this exception results in a very unhappy SAS session and a failed process:

```
WARNING: Apparent symbolic reference MISS1 not resolved.
WARNING: Apparent symbolic reference MISS2 not resolved.
WARNING: Apparent symbolic reference MISS2 not resolved.
ERROR: The text expression &MISS2 contains a recursive
reference to the macro variable MISS2.
The macro variable will be assigned the null value.
```

To detect and handle this exception, a user-defined macro function can be designed in lieu of a subroutine. The SWAP_FUNC function performs the same swapping functionality as the SWAP subroutine, but now returns 0 to indicate success and 42 to indicate failure:

```
* returns 0 for success, 42 for failure;
%macro swap_func(a /* [REF] */,
    b /* [REF] */);
%let syscc=0;
%if %symglobl(&a) and %symglobl(&b) %then %do;
    %local temp;
    %let temp=&&&a;
    %let &a=&&&b;
    %let &b=&temp;
    %end;
%else %let syscc=42;
&syscc
%mend;
```

SWAP and SWAP_FUNC are functionally equivalent, in that each swaps the values of two global macro variables; however, SWAP can be called directly, whereas the return value of SWAP_FUNC must be utilized or saved to a macro variable (such as &RC in the following example):

```
%let rc=%swap_func(miss1, miss2);
%put &=rc;
```

The log indicates that SWAP_FUNC detected the missing macro variables (&MISS1 and &MISS2), and thus did not attempt to perform the swap:

RC=42

The use of exception handling is preferred, as it produces more robust, reliable software. For example, the return value &RC can now be evaluated, and can drive subsequent dynamic processing based on whether SWAP_FUNC succeeded or failed. In part, this exception handling demonstrates why functions are typically preferred to subroutines, even when performing functionally equivalent work.

It bears repeating, as stated in Section 3.6.1, that neither user-defined macro functions nor user-defined macro subroutines are true constructs in the SAS macro language; both are the nearest representations that the SAS macro language supports, and this differentiation is intended only to drive design best practices through mimicry of built-in components and nomenclature. However, true user-defined functions (introduced in Section

3.6.2) and true user-defined subroutines (introduced in the next subsection) can be designed using the FCMP procedure.

3.7.3   User-Defined FCMP Subroutines

The FCMP procedure empowers SAS practitioners to create user-defined functions and subroutines. User-defined subroutines can declare zero or more parameters (within the SUBROUTINE statement), and can modify zero of more arguments (within the OUTARGS statement). Subroutines never return a value, and thus omit the RETURN function that user-defined functions require.

Consider the requirement proposed in Section 3.7.2, in which a callable module needed to be developed to swap the values of two global macro variables. A similar requirement might describe the functionality of a callable module that swaps the values of two variables within a data set— and this functionality is delivered through a user-defined subroutine.

The SWAP_CHAR subroutine swaps the values of two character variables, which are parameterized as A and B:

```
proc fcmp outlib=sasuser.myfuncs.char;
   subroutine swap_char(a $, b $);
      outargs a, b;
      length temp $1000;
      temp=a;
      a=b;
      b=temp;
      endsub;
quit;
```

Note that the data types of all parameters must be declared in the SUBROUTINE statement, so this character-specific subroutine swaps only the values of two character variables—not numeric. Also note that because both A and B are being modified (within the calling program), the OUTARGS statement must list both A and B to denote call by reference.

The Personnel data set (created in Section 3.5) is read, and the values within the First_name and Last_name variables are swapped:

```
options cmplib=sasuser.myfuncs;


data _null_;
```

```
   set personnel;
   call swap_char(first_name, last_name);
   put first_name= last_name=;
run;
```

Note that user-defined subroutines—unlike user-defined functions like SWAP_ADD_C, which was defined in Section 3.6.2—must be prefaced by the CALL statement when invoked.

The log demonstrates that all first and last names in the Personnel data set have been swapped:

```
First_Name=Michaels Last_Name=Chazz
First_Name=Liebkind Last_Name=Franz
First_Name=Mugatu Last_Name=Jacobim
First_Name=Bobby Last_Name=Ricky
First_Name=Burgundy Last_Name=Ron
First_Name=Corrigan Last_Name=Sky
```

User-defined subroutines are useful in delivering certain, specific functionality in which a return value does not need to be generated. However, one of their most cited characteristics—the ability to modify arguments in the calling program—lies not with the SUBROUTINE statement, but rather with the OUTARGS statement. And for this reason, a user-defined function could be designed to deliver equivalent functionality as the SWAP_CHAR subroutine; the only difference would be the return of a return value. It is, in part, for this reason that subroutines remain far less common than their function counterparts.

3.8 SUMMARY

This chapter introduced procedural abstraction, one of the three abstraction flavors that underpins data-driven design. Procedural abstraction enables developers to build modular, reusable software components that can benefit not only themselves but also their teams, organizations, and even outside stakeholders who can use and reuse the modules they create.

This chapter introduced and differentiated three varieties of callable software modules—procedures, functions, and subroutines. Built-in procedures primarily operate on the SAS data set. Functions and subroutines were contrasted, and user-defined functions and subroutines were introduced that leverage the FCMP procedure. User-defined macro functions and macro subroutines were also anecdotally defined.

Through parameterization, user- and process-specified arguments can be passed into procedures, functions, and applications to deliver flexibility—the dynamic functionality central to data-driven programming. This flexibility also promotes configurability, in that SAS practitioners and other end users are able to modify only a procedure's arguments (within its invocation) to produce varied results that meet changing user needs. In the next two chapters, data abstraction and iteration abstraction, as well as their respective roles in data-driven design, are explored.

Chapter 4.

DATA ABSTRACTION

This chapter has the following objectives:

- ❖ Define data abstraction and its benefits.

- ❖ Introduce abstract data types (ADTs) and demonstrate how they inspire less abstract data types and data structures.

- ❖ Demonstrate built-in SAS data types, including character and numeric variables.

- ❖ Discuss built-in SAS data structures, including the SAS data set and the hash object.

- ❖ Introduce the built-in quasi-data structure, the SAS array, which facilitates containerizing and referencing SAS variables in aggregate.

- ❖ Demonstrate how *user-defined* data structures (like macro lists) and their associated operations can be designed and developed from superordinate *built-in* data structures.

- ❖ Introduce the concepts of inheritance, tokenization, functional extension, and backward compatibility that should inform the planning and design of all user-defined data structures.

hereas *procedural abstraction* describes functionality that is abstractly represented within a procedure's specification, *data abstraction* describes the organization and characteristics of data, as well as operations that can be performed on those data. The International Organization for Standardization (ISO) defines *data abstraction* as the "process of extracting the essential characteristics of data by defining data types and their associated functional characteristics and disregarding representation details."[37] Data abstraction simplifies our world, allowing us to focus on only relevant attributes while filtering out unnecessary detail.

A symbiosis exists between data structures and their respective operations—the functions, procedures, and other processes that act upon those data structures. For example, the strength and ubiquity of the SAS data set—the primary built-in data structure of the SAS language and application—are derived in part from the data set's "essential characteristics of data," to borrow from the ISO definition. Thus, we know and love the SAS data set because it provides a standardized, tabular structure in which we can store, access, and transform data. In fact, whenever another file type (e.g., CSV, XML, spreadsheet) is encountered, our instinctual first action is typically to convert the "foreign" data object into a SAS data set—and this instinct serves us well.

For example, a comma-separated values (CSV) file has little analytic utility in its native format because the strength of CSV files (and other canonical files) lies in their interoperability. That is, CSV files can be read by most applications that ingest data, but the files are rarely used outside of input/output (I/O) and data transfer operations. Once a CSV file is converted to a SAS data set, however, the breadth of Base SAS procedures, functions, and other operations can interact with those data. For example, within a text editor, you could manually and painstakingly "sort" a CSV file by a variable (i.e., a comma-delimited position within the file); however, the same data (stored as a SAS data set) could be sorted effortlessly using built-in SAS operations, such as the SORT or SQL procedures or the hash object.

In addition to built-in data structures, user-defined data structures can further extend the functionality of software by facilitating non-native operations. As user-defined data structures are designed, standardized, and reused over time, they become more reliable and part of the software substrate. Thus, just as developers often have a toolkit of their favorite user-defined macros, functions, and subroutines they have built and refined over the years, so too might they have a toolkit of user-defined *data structures* on which they also rely. And when those user-defined data structures have accumulated a bevy of associated user-defined operations, the stability and sustainability of each—the data structures and their respective operations—are maximized.

Barbara Liskov and John Guttag decry "Data abstraction is the most important method in program design."[38] This sentiment is especially true in data-driven design, in which data structures containerize the control data that provide software instruction. In so doing, data structures promote data independence because control data can be maintained apart from code, as well as within interoperable formats that facilitate the widest range of use by the broadest array of applications and languages.

J.A. Zimmer, in speaking of data abstraction, states that "The value of data increases with its ease of use, and the ease of use increases with the appropriateness of the basic manipulations that are available."[39] This chapter introduces built-in data structures and their respective operations—archetypes from which SAS practitioners can learn to model our own user-defined data structures and user-defined operations. Pitfalls of user-defined data structures are also introduced in the hopes of supplanting common failure patterns with flexible, reusable data structures and operations.

4.1 ABSTRACT DATA TYPES (ADTS)

Many discussions about data abstraction begin with the notion of abstract data types (ADTs), which comprise the abstract representations of how data are defined, structured, related, and utilized. ISO defines an *abstract data type* as a "data type for which only the properties of the data and the operations to be performed on the data are specified, without concern for how the data will be represented or how the operations will be implemented."[40] ADTs are so abstract that they exist only conceptually. That is, ADTs are not found in code but rather are used to define, differentiate, communicate, and understand high-level attributes and aspects of data types and data structures.

At a lower level of abstraction, ADTs are operationalized within specific software languages through data types and data structures. For example, the string ADT represents the abstract notion of a data type (in an unspecified language) that contains a collection of alphanumeric characters. As part of this ADT definition, and irrespective of any specific programming language, strings can be printed, concatenated, capitalized, and have a host of other operations performed on them.

Within the SAS language, the string ADT is operationalized through the SAS character data type. Thus, SAS character variables will exhibit most of the characteristics of the string ADT, and many of the theoretical operations attributed to string ADTs will be available within Base SAS through built-in character functions and other operations.

However, because the string ADT is only an abstraction, differences will exist in how it is operationalized across individual programming languages. For example, within the SAS language, the following code prints "Hello World!" and then prints only the first letter of this message (H):

```
data _null_;
   note='Hello World!';
   shortnote=substr(note,1,1);
   put note;
   put shortnote;
run;
```

Conversely, Python strings, unlike SAS character variables, are explicitly indexed, so any character within a string can be accessed by referencing its position. Indexing in Python begins at 0, so note[0] retrieves the first character of the Note variable without the need to call a substring function—as is required in SAS, with SUBSTR delivering this functionality. The functionally equivalent Python code to the preceding DATA step follows:

```
note='Hello World!'
print(note)
print(note[0])
```

Thus, although both SAS and Python have representative data types that model the string ADT, these data types differ, including both how data are stored and how they are operationalized. Common ADTs include integers, real numbers, characters, strings, Boolean, lists, arrays, records, and tables, not all of which may be represented as built-in data types or data structures within a specific language. Moreover, and as demonstrated in the preceding examples, language-specific data types or data structures that represent the same ADT can be implemented in vastly different ways, and have different operations that can be performed on them.

Even where built-in data types and structures for specific ADTs are not available within a software language, savvy developers can sometimes mimic their functionality by building user-defined data-structures and their associated operations. Thus, the exploration of ADTs and their associated data types and data structures (and how these are operationalized in languages other than Base SAS) can benefit the SAS practitioner desiring to design and hone user-defined data structures (and their operations) within the SAS language.

4.2   FROM ADTS TO DATA TYPES AND STRUCTURES

ADTs provide the conceptual models that define data and their respective operations, whereas data types and data structures operationalize ADTs within a specific language. Base SAS defines only two data types, numeric and character, that are relied upon by its two principal built-in data structures, the SAS data set and the hash object, as well as SAS arrays.

Data types generally represent simpler ADTs, such as integers, real numbers, characters, strings, and Boolean values. The Institute of Electrical and Electronics Engineers (IEEE) defines *data type* as a "class of data, characterized by the members of the class and the operations that can be applied to them."[41] Data types are often named after their respective ADTs, which is helpful, but which can also cause confusion. For example, within Python, the string ADT is represented by the string data type.

Data structures, on the other hand, more commonly represent more complex ADTs, such as tables, records, lists, dictionaries, and arrays. ISO defines a *data structure* as the "physical or logical relationship among data elements, designed to support specific data manipulation functions."[42] Thus, data structures are containers that can hold multiple data elements and, in some cases, subordinate data structures. For example, SAS arrays are defined and exist wholly inside the SAS data set data structure. In other languages, however, arrays are distinct data types or data structures, rather than subordinate to the table ADT. This is all to say that although ADTs often can be discussed in language-agnostic terms, data types and data structures seldom can, as their definitions and implementations can vary significantly from one language to another.

SAS arrays are introduced in Section 4.4.3, and are contrasted with SAS macro metaprogramming in Section 10.1.2

Within SAS, the numeric data type represents several ADTs, including integers, real numbers, doubles, dates, and times. SAS employs formatting to distinguish how these various breeds of numeric data are displayed and

Abstract Data Type	SAS Data Type or Data Structure
character	character
string	character
integer	numeric (with no decimal formatting)
real number	numeric (with decimal formatting)
date/datetime	numeric (with date or datetime formatting)
Boolean	not available, but partially mimicked through operations
list	not available, but partially mimicked through delimited character strings or macro variables
array	array (with limitations)
record	observation (within a data set)
table	data set and in-memory hash object
data map (or map)	SAS format (with one-to-one relationships)
multimap	SAS format (with many-to-one relationships)

Table 4.1 ADTs and Equivalent SAS Data Types and Data Structures

interpreted. Similarly, within SAS, the character data type represents both character and string ADTs, which are differentiated in some languages.

Table 4.1 lists some common ADTs and their corresponding SAS data types and structures. Note that some ADTs are not available, others are mimicked through built-in functionality, and still others can be mimicked through user-defined data structures.

For example, the SAS data set is a built-in data structure that corresponds to the table ADT, and the SAS observation is a built-in data structure (subordinate to the data set data structure) that corresponds to the record ADT. That is, a data set represents the SAS implementation of the abstract *table* concept; it contains many table-esque features (e.g., organized into columns and rows, one or more variables comprising various data types, one or more records), and supports many table-esque operations (e.g., creation, deletion, indexing, sorting, record insertion). However, SAS data sets do differ substantially from how other languages or applications—especially relational database management systems (RDBMS)—interpret and operationalize the table ADT.

4.3   BUILT-IN DATA TYPES

SAS has two built-in data types, character and numeric, which are sometimes referred to as *primitive* data types (also *atomic* data types or *basic* data types). ISO defines an *atomic type* as a "data type, each of whose members consists of a single, nondecomposable data item."[43] Thus, within SAS, character and numeric data types form the building blocks with which built-in and user-defined data structures are constructed.

The SAS character data type represents both the character ADT (which is typically conceptualized as a single, alphanumeric character) and the string ADT (which is conceptualized as a series of characters). Similarly, SAS numeric data represent multiple ADTs, such as integers, real numbers, dates, and datetime values. Despite having only two data types, the SAS language supports the diverse nature of data through a smorgasbord of built-in SAS formats and informats, and through the ability of end users to construct user-defined formats and informats.

SAS formats, in addition to modeling the diversity of data, facilitate core operations like data validation, cleaning, and classification. For example, SAS formats can represent a numeric data type as a date value, a currency value, or a Boolean value, despite the underlying data type remaining numeric.

> Formats that facilitate data validation, cleaning, and classification are demonstrated in Sections 13.3.1, 13.4.3, and 13.5.2, respectively

The following DATA step creates the Pres data set that is relied upon throughout this chapter:

```
data pres;
   infile datalines dsd;
   length fname $20 lname $20 num 3 dt1 8 dt2 8
      vp $100;
   input fname $ lname $ num dt1 : mmddyy10.
      dt2 : mmddyy10. vp $;
   format dt1 dt2 mmddyy10.;
   label fname='First Name' lname='Last Name'
      num='Number' dt1='Term Start' dt2='Term End'
      vp="President's VPs";
   datalines;
George, Washington, 1, 04/30/1789, 03/04/1797, John
Adams
John, Adams, 2, 03/04/1797, 03/04/1801, Thomas Jefferson
Thomas, Jefferson, 3, 03/04/1801, 03/04/1809, "Aaron
Burr, George Clinton"
James, Madison, 4, 03/04/1809, 03/04/1817, "George
Clinton, Elbridge Gerry"
```

> Formats that facilitate dynamic stoplight reporting are demonstrated in Sections 16.5.1 and 16.5.2

```
James, Monroe, 5, 03/04/1817, 03/04/1825, Daniel
Tompkins
John, Adams, 6, 03/04/1825, 03/04/1829, John Calhoun
Andrew, Jackson, 7, 03/04/1829, 03/04/1837, "John
Calhoun, Martin Van Buren"
Martin, Van Buren, 8, 03/04/1837, 03/04/1841, Richard
Johnson
William, Harrison, 9, 03/04/1841, 04/04/1841, John Tyler
John, Tyler, 10, 04/04/1841, 03/04/1845, VACANT
James, Polk, 11, 03/04/1845, 03/04/1849, George Dallas
Zachary, Taylor, 12, 03/04/1849, 07/09/1850, Millard
Fillmore
Millard, Fillmore, 13, 07/09/1850, 03/04/1853, VACANT
Franklin, Pierce, 14, 03/04/1853, 03/04/1857, William
King
James, Buchanan, 15, 03/04/1857, 03/04/1861, John
Breckinridge
Abraham, Lincoln, 16, 03/04/1861, 04/15/1865, "Hannibal
Hamlin, Andrew Johnson"
;
```

The Pres data set represents the first sixteen U.S. presidents, and includes their order of election, inauguration date, term end date, and vice president(s). Note that when multiple vice presidents served under a single president, the vice president names are separated by commas within the VP variable, which—spoiler alert!—represents a user-defined list data structure constructed upon the built-in SAS character data type. The following subsections demonstrate how rudimentary control data, comprising built-in data types, can facilitate data-driven programming.

4.3.1 Numeric Data Type

The Pres data set contains three numeric variables—Num, Dt1, and Dt2. Num represents presidential order and is displayed as an integer; Dt1 and Dt2 represent the inauguration date and term end date, respectively, and are displayed using the SAS MMDDYY10 format.

The SELECTPRES macro selects a subset of presidents based on their term order (Num), which is parameterized as STARTNUM:

```
* default to all presidents if STARTNUM is missing;
%macro selectpres(newdsn= /* data set subset */,
    startnum= /* [OPT] first president to select */);
%local firstobs;
%if %length(&startnum)>0 %then
    %let firstobs=(firstobs=&startnum);
data &newdsn;
    set pres &firstobs;
run;
%mend;
```

The following SELECTPRES invocation selects only presidents ten through 16, and saves these observations in the Somepres data set:

```
%selectpres(newdsn=somepres, startnum=10);
```

The invocation and implementation are straightforward, in part because the parameter format matches the internal data with which it is interacting. Thus, the STARTNUM argument (10), which is initialized as the &STARTNUM macro variable, can be utilized by the FIRSTOBS statement, which requires numeric input (formatted as an integer).

By adding the INAUGDT parameter, SELECTPRES can be modified so that the inauguration date can also be utilized to select a subset of data:

```
* if multiple OPTional parameters are selected;
* then AND is the evaluation operator used;
%macro selectpres(newdsn= /* data set subset */,
    startnum= /* [OPT] first president to select */,
    inaugdt= /* [OPT] inaug date (SAS date format) */);
%local firstobs where;
%if %length(&startnum)>0 %then
    %let firstobs=(firstobs=&startnum);
%if %length(&inaugdt)>0 %then
    %let where=where dt1>=&inaugdt;
data &newdsn;
    set pres &firstobs;
    &where;
run;
%mend;
```

The Dt1 evaluation requires &INAUGDT to be a numeric variable because it is evaluated against Dt1, a numeric variable. For example, a user might attempt to select all presidents inaugurated after 1810 with the following invalid call:

```
%selectpres(newdsn=somepres, inaugdt=01/01/1810);
```

However, SELECTPRES fails to generate the desired results because the INAUGDT argument is not a number, but rather a text value formatted as a built-in SAS date format (MMDDYY10):

```
NOTE: There were 0 observations read from the data set
WORK.PRES.
      WHERE dt1>=0.0005524862;
NOTE: The data set WORK.SOMEPRES has 0 observations and
6 variables.
```

Rather, to select only presidents inaugurated after 1810, an end user would first need to write SAS code to translate January 1, 1810, to a SAS date:

```
data _null_;
   length dt 8;
   dt='01jan1810'd;
   put dt;
run;
```

The output indicates that 01/01/1810 corresponds to -54786, the SAS date that can be passed in the INAUGDT argument to generate valid results. The updated call now selects all presidents inaugurated after January 1, 1810:

```
%selectpres(newdsn=somepres, inaugdt=-54786);
```

With this modification, SELECTPRES now generates the desired data set having 12 observations, as shown in the log:

```
NOTE: There were 12 observations read from the data set
WORK.PRES.
      WHERE dt1>=-54786;
NOTE: The data set WORK.SOMEPRES has 12 observations and
6 variables.
```

But at what cost? The end user was forced to first transform the user-readable MMDDYY10 date into the machine-readable (aka human-inscrutable) -54786 date. This is never ideal.

One data-driven design principle requires that complexity be hidden, whenever possible, in the procedural implementation rather than exposed to the end user in the invocation. In lieu of forcing end users to compute numeric values for SAS dates (e.g., -54786) prior to macro execution, the SELECTPRES macro could be refactored so that the INAUGDT parameter would accept values in the MMDDYY10 (or other human-readable) format:

```
%macro selectpres(newdsn= /* data set subset */,
    startnum= /* [OPT] first president to select */,
    inaugdt= /* [OPT] inaug date (MM/DD/YYYY) */);
%local firstobs where;
%let inaugdt=%sysfunc(inputn(&inaugdt,mmddyy10.));
%if %length(&startnum)>0 %then
    %let firstobs=(firstobs=&startnum);
%if %length(&inaugdt)>0 %then
    %let where=where dt1>=&inaugdt;
data &newdsn;
    set pres &firstobs;
    &where;
run;
%mend;
```

The refactored SELECTPRES macro now can be invoked with an intuitive date that facilitates comprehension, not obfuscation:

```
%selectpres(newdsn=somepres, inaugdt=01/01/1810);
```

Within SELECTPRES, the INPUTN function translates the formatted date (&INAUGDT) into a SAS date—a numeric value that can be evaluated against Dt1 by the WHERE statement. This simple data abstraction ensures that end users can more readily call the macro, and thus encourages future reuse of the macro.

4.3.2   Character Data Type

The Pres data set contains three character variables—Fname, Lname, and VP. SELECTPRES can be further refactored so that end users can select observations based on the president's first name:

```
%macro selectpres(newdsn= /* data set subset */,
    startnum= /* [OPT] first president to select */,
    inaugdt= /* [OPT] inaug date (MM/DD/YYYY) */,
    fname= /* non-case sensitive first name */);
%local firstobs where;
%let inaugdt=%sysfunc(inputn(&inaugdt,mmddyy10.));
%if %length(&startnum)>0 %then
    %let firstobs=(firstobs=&startnum);
%if %length(&inaugdt)>0 %then
    %let where=where dt1>=&inaugdt;
%if %length(&fname)>0 %then
    %let where=%sysfunc(ifc(
    %length(&where)=0,,&where and,where))
    upcase(fname)="%upcase(&fname)";
%if %length(&where)>0 %then %let where=&where;
data &newdsn;
    set pres &firstobs;
    &where;
run;
%mend;
```

If both the INAUGDT and FNAME arguments are specified, the AND operator is dynamically applied (using the IFC function) to create an intersection of the two requirements. For example, the following invocation selects all observations (only one, John Tyler) for which the president was named John *and* was inaugurated after 1830:

```
%selectpres(newdsn=somepres, inaugdt=01/01/1830,
    fname=john);
```

The FNAME parameter is straightforward because it accepts a character argument, and is compared to a character variable (Fname) within the SELECTPRES DATA step. Thus, the FNAME parameter requires neither mapping nor transformation prior to evaluation.

The VP variable is more complex, however, because a built-in character data type is *prescribed*, upon which a user-defined list data structure is *described*. That is, the SAS language (i.e., the LENGTH statement in the DATA step in Section 4.3) declares VP as having character data type, which SAS enforces, and which SAS practitioners cannot override. Yet the usage of VP to store comma-delimited character values represents a user-defined list data structure built upon the superordinate character data type. Thus, the VP list, as a user-defined data structure, must be manually parsed, validated, and operationalized through user-defined operations.

For example, consider a final requirement to be able to select observations based on the vice president's full name. The VP parameter is now declared; however, the INAUGDT and FNAME parameters have been removed to improve readability:

```
%macro selectpresbyvp1(newdsn= /* data set subset */,
    vp= /* [OPT] VP name, non-case sensitive */);
%local where;
%if %length(&vp)>0 %then
    %let where=where upcase(vp)="%upcase(&vp)";
data &newdsn;
    set pres;
    &where;
run;
%mend;
```

Invoking the SELECTPRESBYVP1 macro can be used to find all occurrences of Vice President John Calhoun:

```
%selectpresbyvp1(newdsn=somepres, vp=John Calhoun);
```

But wait—the log demonstrates that only one observation was selected, John Calhoun's vice presidency under John Adams, with the macro failing to find his vice presidency under Andrew Jackson:

```
NOTE: There were 1 observations read from the data set
WORK.PRES.
      WHERE UPCASE(vp)='JOHN CALHOUN';
NOTE: The data set WORK.SOMEPRES has 1 observations and
6 variables.
```

This failure occurs because the WHERE statement compares the &VP macro variable to the entire VP variable, which is "John Calhoun" for President John Adams but is "John Calhoun, Martin Van Buren" for Andrew Jackson's presidency. Thus, because the VP variable has a *character* data type, but is masquerading as a comma-delimited *list*, the one-to-one evaluation cannot parse the more complex, comma-delimited values.

Element decomposition and evaluation of the VP variable is thus required so that its constituent elements can be extracted and compared to the &VP macro variable. An updated macro now uses the DO WHILE loop to iterate across the user-defined list:

```
%macro selectpresbyvp2(newdsn= /* data set subset */,
    vp= /* [OPT] VP name, non-case sensitive */);
data &newdsn (drop=i found);
    set pres;
    i=1;
    found=0;
    do while(length(scan(vp,i,','))>1);
        if upcase(scan(vp,i,','))="%upcase(&vp)"
            then found=1;
        i=i+1;
        end;
    if found;
run;
%mend;
```

The DO WHILE loop employs *external* iteration, introduced in Section 5.2.2

The identical invocation (calling the refactored macro) now creates the Somepres data set (having two observations), which includes both presidents for which John Calhoun served as vice president:

```
%selectpresbyvp2(newdsn=somepres, vp=John Calhoun);
```

The log demonstrates the selection of two observations:

```
NOTE: There were 16 observations read from the data set
WORK.PRES.
NOTE: The data set WORK.SOMEPRES has 2 observations and
6 variables.
```

Note that as the complexity of a character variable increases, mapping, iteration, or other transformation may be required to validate or utilize that variable or its constituent elements, if defined. This is especially true when the underlying data type or data structure that is prescribed differs from a user-defined data structure that may sit atop that substrate. And in all such cases, user-defined operations must be engineered to cross the chasm between the built-in substrate and the user-defined reality.

For example, anecdotally, the VP variable could be called a *list* or *comma-delimited list*, in reference to its user-defined usage; from a technical perspective, however, its true data type remains character—nothing more, nothing less. Thus, when the SELECTPRESBYVP1 macro fails to return two observations (i.e., both presidents), it fails not with a syntax error or runtime error, but rather with a logic error, resultant from the failure to decompose the comma-delimited VP variable into its constituent character values. Because the SAS language lacks a built-in list data structure and one must be engineered, so too must SAS practitioners design, develop, test, and implement associated user-defined operations that support the user-defined list data structure.

4.3.3 Data Formats (Mappings)

Data mappings (or *mappings*) transform data or how data are represented within a data structure or data product. Within SAS, data mappings are operationalized principally through the FORMAT procedure, which creates mappings, and the FORMAT and INFORMAT statements and the PUT and INPUT functions, which apply mappings. Formats can be applied to change how data are displayed temporarily (for the duration of a DATA step or SAS procedure), or permanently, to include even changing a variable's data type.

IEEE defines a *mapping* as an "assigned correspondence between two things that is represented as a set of ordered pairs."[44] A *multimap* sometimes further distinguishes a mapping in which the second half of each ordered pair can comprise a series of elements. Because SAS formats can represent both one-to-one and many-to-one relationships, they provide mapping and multimap functionality.

Data mappings provide critical data abstraction, enabling software to interpret and interact with data on a lower level of abstraction while end users interact with data on a higher, more readable level. For example, the DATA step in Section 4.3 relies on the INPUT statement to ingest data and specifies that the Dt1 and Dt2 variables should be read with the MMDDYY10 SAS informat. Thus, George Washington was inaugurated on April 30, 1789, and served through March 4, 1797, represented as 04/30/1789 and 03/04/1797, respectively. The use of the MMDDYY10 informat and format enables these dates to be both ingested and visualized

In addition to relying on formats, data mappings can utilize lookup tables, user-defined functions, and hash objects, as demonstrated in Sections 13.4 and 13.5

in a readable date format, despite their underlying data type remaining numeric.

Behind the scenes, however, SAS dates are stored as numeric data, which can be observed when the MMDDYY10 format is removed. The following DATA step removes the date format (by specifying the 8 format) to expose the native numeric nature of SAS dates:

```
data noformats;
   set pres (obs=1);
   format dt1 dt2 8.;
   put fname lname dt1 dt2;
run;
```

Note that SAS date values are calculated and stored as *the number of days since January 1, 1960,* with prior dates represented as negative integers. The log shows these raw dates with numeric formatting:

```
George Washington -62336 -59471
```

Thus, the MMDDYY10 format enables dates to be displayed in a more natural, readable format. Without this built-in data mapping, developers would be left with two equally unattractive solutions: either store dates as raw numbers (which lack readability), or process dates as character strings (which lack the ability to have date-specific calculations performed on them).

Thus, data mappings can bridge data abstraction levels while extending the scope and utility of data types. Data-driven design, which aims to maintain and pass control data in simple, readable, interoperable formats, relies heavily on SAS formats and informats (as well as other data mapping methods) to facilitate control data that are simultaneously optimized for end user readability and software operations. That is, control data must be useful to and readable by both the end users supplying them and the code interacting with them. Data mappings ensure that people *and* processes get their control data in the respective formats of their choosing— without the burden of maintaining multiple, differently formatted copies of the same control data.

4.4   BUILT-IN DATA STRUCTURES

Despite the widespread applicability of and love for SAS, the SAS language supports a paucity of built-in data structures. Part show pony, part workhorse, the SAS data set is both pretty and powerful, and understandably the first data structure to which SAS neophytes are introduced. In fact, many experienced SAS practitioners carry out successful careers without ever venturing beyond the confines of the SAS data set.

But SAS built-in data structures also include hash objects, dictionary objects, and arguably, SAS formats. Dictionary objects can be utilized within the FCMP procedure but are not discussed in this text. SAS formats operationalize data *mappings* and *multimaps* (one-to-one and many-to-one relationships, respectively), and are demonstrated throughout the text. SAS formats, however, are not typically described as "data structures" but rather in terms of the very specific mapping functionality they provide.

The hash object is a built-in data structure that all savvy SAS practitioners should embrace to facilitate higher-performing, in-memory operations. Hash objects also represent a true data structure, whereas SAS arrays, albeit powerful, are *truly built-in* yet are not *truly data structures*; thus, a SAS array represents only a quasi-data structure, and cannot facilitate faster or more efficient data processing. No shade should be thrown, however, because arrays can make your software more flexible, maintainable, and readable while rendering your development experience more productive and enjoyable!

The following subsections succinctly introduce the SAS data set, hash object, and SAS array. Thereafter, user-defined data structures are introduced, which inherit both their functionality and limitations from the superordinate built-in data types (or built-in data structures) from which they are molded. In other words, a healthy understanding of built-in data types (and data structures) is required before user-defined data structures (and user-defined operations) can be designed and developed to extend the functionality of a programming language.

4.4.1 SAS Data Set

The SAS data set represents a friendly, familiar, flexibly powerful data structure that has thrived for decades. Inarguably the cornerstone of the SAS language and the SAS application, the SAS data set derives its strength in part from this continuity, as well as from the DATA step and countless procedures, functions, and other operations that leverage the data set data structure. That is, data structures—both built-in and user-defined—

increase in value as they are reused over time, and commensurate with the number and diversity of operations that support them.

Creating a sample data set reveals just the tip of this awesomeness. The following DATA step creates the Grades data set, which simulates school grades of some U.S. presidents:

```
data grades;
    infile datalines dsd;
    length fname $20 lname $20 grades1 grades2
        grades3 8;
    input fname $ lname $ grades1 grades2 grades3;
    datalines;
George, Washington, 97, 92, 95
John, Adams, 89, 92, 95
Andrew, Johnson, 96, 95, 92
;
```

Although *this* data set has only five variables, the data set data structure—that is, the data set *class* or the abstract notion of *any* SAS data set—can support nearly limitless character and numeric variables, and nearly limitless observations.

This data structure flexibility and scalability is demonstrated in the following DATA step and SQL procedure, which add a new month of grades to the Grades data set to create Newgrades:

```
data mogrades;
    infile datalines dsd;
    length fname $20 lname $20 grades4 8;
    input fname $ lname $ grades4;
    datalines;
George, Washington, 94
John, Adams, 89
Andrew, Johnson, 92
;
run;

proc sql;
    create table newgrades as
        select * from grades a, mogrades b
```

```
    where a.fname = b.fname and a.lname = b.lname;
quit;
```

Newgrades and Grades differ, but each represents an instance of the same abstract data set data structure. Although not further discussed in this section, within an object-oriented programming (OOP) paradigm, the abstract notion of *any* SAS data set is referred to as a *class*, whereas an instantiation of that class (to create a specific data set, like Grades or Newgrades) is referred to as an *object*.

Classes and *objects* are introduced within an OOP paradigm in Section 8.4

Additional flexibility of the data set data structure can be demonstrated by adding an observation, which is accomplished with two additional DATA steps that update Newgrades by adding James Madison:

```
data newstudent;
    infile datalines dsd;
    length fname $20 lname $20 grades1 grades2
        grades3 grades4 8;
    input fname $ lname $ grades1 grades2
        grades3 grades4;
    datalines;
James, Madison, 77, 84, 79, 82
;


data newgrades;
    set newgrades newstudent;
run;
```

As before, the specific data set (Newgrades) is flexibly modified, yet still represents an instance of the same data set data structure—the data set *class*. This flexibility extends the ways in which data sets can be utilized to solve diverse problems, and underscores why SAS software has been so successful despite its primary reliance on one built-in data structure—the SAS data set.

In addition to modifying SAS data sets through the DATA step, the SAS language boasts hundreds of built-in procedures (aka PROCs) that can interpret and manipulate SAS data sets. Thus, with SAS procedures operating *on*—and SAS functions and subroutines (usually) operating *within*—SAS data sets, it is this cumulative built-in functionality that renders the SAS data set so powerful, and ergo, lovable.

4.4.2   Hash Object

The SAS hash object represents a tabular, in-memory, built-in data structure that can be operationalized within the DATA step, the FCMP procedure, and the DS2 language. In-memory processing facilitates high-performance data lookup that can be markedly faster than functionally equivalent disk-storage processing methods. Within data-driven design, tabular control data often can be maintained within a hash object to support data validation, standardization, or transformation objectives.

A hash object defined within a DATA step exists only for the duration of that DATA step; when execution completes, the hash object is destroyed. Notwithstanding their ephemeral nature, hash objects can still represent the fastest method of data retrieval. For example, the following DATA step declares the hash object H, an in-memory representation of the Pres data set (created in Section 4.3):

```
data hashed (drop = rc);
   set newgrades;
   length dt1 dt2 8;
   if _n_ = 1 then do;
      declare hash h(dataset: 'pres');
      rc = h.defineKey('fname', 'lname');
      rc = h.defineData('dt1', 'dt2');
      rc = h.defineDone();
      call missing(dt1, dt2);
      end;
   rc = h.find();
   format dt1 dt2 mmddyy10.;
   put fname lname dt1 dt2;
run;
```

The DECLARE statement births the hash object (H), with the DATASET option specifying that the object should be created from the Pres data set. Only those variables subsequently enumerated in the DEFINEKEY and DEFINEDATA methods will be created within the hash object; thus, the VP variable is never ingested into memory, and cannot be evaluated or returned during a subsequent hash lookup.

The DEFINEKEY method identifies the variable(s) that comprise the hash object index. As two or more variables are enumerated (Fname and

Lname), the hash object declares a *composite index*—two or more variables that uniquely identify each record of the hash object. Thus, if Newgrades contains an observation not found in Pres (such as Andrew Johnson), the lookup (of that observation) will return no value(s).

The DEFINEDATA method identifies the variable(s) that comprise attributes of the hash object—data that can be returned when a hash object lookup succeeds. Thus, when James Madison (the fourth observation in Newgrades) is found within the hash object, the associated variables Dt1 and Dt2 (corresponding to Madison's inauguration and last day in office, respectively) are retrieved from the hash object, and added to the Newgrades data set.

Finally, the FIND method performs the hash object lookup. It returns Dt1 and Dt2 for presidents George Washington, John Adams, and James Madison. Yet, as Andrew Johnson is omitted from the Pres data set (used to populate the H hash object), the FIND method fails to locate Andrew Johnson, so his Dt1 and Dt2 variables (within the Hashed data set) are initialized to missing values.

The log shows the four observations in the Newgrades data set—three of which were found in the hash object:

```
NOTE: There were 16 observations read from the data set
WORK.PRES.
George Washington 04/30/1789 03/04/1797
John Adams 03/04/1797 03/04/1801
Andrew Johnson  .  .
James Madison 03/04/1809 03/04/1817
```

When the DATA step terminates, the H hash object is deleted from memory. The full extent of hash object functionality lies outside the scope of this text; however, even this scant introduction demonstrates some of the complexity in hash object design and utilization—complexity that arguably has retarded the adoption of hash methods by many SAS practitioners.

However, hash objects can be made more palatable by removing this complexity from the DATA step. Procedural abstraction, facilitated through the FCMP procedure, provides this filtration and finesse. Thus, the logic contained within the H hash object declaration, initialization, and operationalization can be transported from the DATA step to an FCMP function or subroutine.

Hash objects created within FCMP functions and subroutines are demonstrated in Section 13.3.3

The following user-defined subroutine (Pres_lookup) now delivers reusable functionality through the FCMP procedure:

```
proc fcmp outlib=sasuser.myfuncs.char;
   subroutine pres_lookup(fname $, lname $, dt1, dt2);
      outargs dt1, dt2;
      declare hash h(dataset: 'pres');
      rc = h.defineKey('fname', 'lname');
      rc = h.defineData('dt1', 'dt2');
      rc = h.defineDone();
      rc = h.find();
      endsub;
quit;
```

All hash object functionality is now hidden within the subroutine implementation, and SAS practitioners calling the Pres_lookup user-defined subroutine may not even be aware that a hash object is utilized to perform the data lookup. For example, the following DATA step calls Pres_lookup to initialize the values of Dt1 and Dt2 to each president's inauguration day and last day in office, respectively—with no reference to hash syntax, methods, or other functionality:

```
options cmplib=sasuser.myfuncs;
data hashed;
   set newgrades;
   length dt1 dt2 8;
   format dt1 dt2 mmddyy10.;
   call missing(dt1, dt2);
   call pres_lookup(fname, lname, dt1, dt2);
   put fname lname dt1 dt2;
run;
```

For those SAS practitioners skeptically perched atop the fence who have yet to delve into either FCMP or hash object syntax, the FCMP-hash cloacal kiss can provide the impetus to explore and adopt these tangled lovers. Hash has been selectively bred to deliver altogether singular functionality—that of table lookups—and the procedural abstraction afforded by FCMP hides the complexity for which hash methods are sometimes avoided.

4.4.3   SAS Array

The SAS array is a *quasi*-data structure that can be initialized inside SAS data sets, and is used only to reference a series of same-type variables. The SAS built-in array differs substantially from array data types and array data structures defined in other languages. SAS documentation clarifies: "Arrays in SAS are different from those in many other programming languages. In SAS, an array is not a data structure. An array is just a convenient way of temporarily identifying a group of variables."[45] Notwithstanding its uniqueness, the SAS array is a mighty tool that facilitates data abstraction and iteration abstraction in data-driven design.

Methods of iterating SAS arrays are demonstrated and contrasted in Section 5.2.3

Arrays temporarily transform a series of variables into an object that can be referenced collectively through functions and other DATA step operations. DO loops iterate over array elements, and operators such as OF enable functions to reference array objects while operating on their individual, constituent elements. Data abstraction is in play whenever this type of one-to-many or object-to-elements relationship exists. This abstraction simplifies code, by removing unnecessary complexity, and can facilitate more flexible software modules, as dynamic array *elements* contort to support data variability while their parent array *object* remains stable.

Section 10.1.2 uses the OF operator to reference arrays within built-in functions

For example, consider the need to compute the average (i.e., mean) of a president's grades within the Grades data set (created in Section 4.4.1). The following DATA steps recreate this data set, and subsequently calculate mean scores for each president:

```
data grades;
    infile datalines dsd;
    length fname $20 lname $20 grades1 grades2
        grades3 8;
    input fname $ lname $ grades1 grades2 grades3;
    datalines;
George, Washington, 97, 92, 95
John, Adams, 89, 92, 95
Andrew, Johnson, 96, 95, 92
;
run;
```

```
data avggrades;
   set grades;
   avg=mean(grades1, grades2, grades3);
   format avg 8.1;
   put fname lname avg;
run;
```

The log demonstrates average grades—calculated with the built-in MEAN function—for each president:

```
George Washington 94.7
John Adams 92.0
Andrew Johnson 94.3
```

But what if dozens or hundreds of individual grades needed to be evaluated? SAS could still calculate these data with ease, but it could be a headache for SAS practitioners to code. Moreover, if additional calculations (e.g., median, mode) were required, the list of grade variables would need to be repeated for each calculation.

For example, to calculate the median and standard deviation, two additional lines of code are required—each of which must again enumerate all grade variables:

```
data avggrades;
   set grades;
   avg=mean(grades1, grades2, grades3);
   med=median(grades1, grades2, grades3);
   std=std(grades1, grades2, grades3);
   format avg med std 8.1;
   put fname lname avg= med= std=;
run;
```

A superior solution that is both more scalable and maintainable instead declares an array that containerizes all grade variables so they can be referenced as a collective object. The following DATA step incorporates the ARRAY statement, which declares the Grades array:

```
data avggrades;
   set grades;
   array grades[*] grades1 grades2 grades3;
   avg=mean(of grades[*]);
```

```
     med=median(of grades[*]);
     std=std(of grades[*]);
     format avg med std 8.1;
     put fname lname avg= med= std=;
run;
```

The MEAN, MEDIAN, and STD functions now use the OF operator to specify the Grades array; individual variables no longer must be repeatedly enumerated in this functionally equivalent solution:

```
George Washington avg=94.7 med=95.0 std=2.5
John Adams avg=92.0 med=92.0 std=3.0
Andrew Johnson avg=94.3 med=95.0 std=2.1
```

Scalability is improved because the variables are now enumerated only once in the code—within the ARRAY statement—with all subsequent references to these variables abstractly made to the array object (grades[*]), not its constituent elements.

Arrays are also favored where data evaluation (or calculation) must be performed across a series of variables. For example, given the Founding Fathers' less-than-exemplary academics, a formula could be applied to each grade to inflate it a configurable number of points (the &PLUS macro variable) while ensuring no grade exceeded 100.

The following DATA step implements a DO loop that iterates across each variable in the Grades array to increase all values by a parameterized amount (&PLUS), which is arbitrarily set to 2:

```
%let plus=2;
data avggrades;
   set grades;
   array grades[*] grades1 grades2 grades3;
   do i=1 to dim(grades);
      grades[i]=min(100,grades[i]+&plus);
      end;
   avg=mean(of grades[*]);
   med=median(of grades[*]);
   std=std(of grades[*]);
   format avg med std 8.1;
   put fname lname avg= med= std=;
```

```
run;
```

Note that the MIN function is utilized to ensure that no inflated grade exceeds 100. The code executes, and the log demonstrates the slight grade inflation:

```
George Washington avg=96.7 med=97.0 std=2.5
John Adams avg=94.0 med=94.0 std=3.0
Andrew Johnson avg=96.3 med=97.0 std=2.1
```

The array-based solution is neither faster nor more efficient than a functionally equivalent array-less version (not shown). However, the array solution is faster to develop, owing to a substantial reduction in code, and faster to modify, because grade variables can be added to or removed from the single ARRAY statement.

Preloading of control tables using temporary arrays is introduced in Section 11.1.5, and demonstrated in Section 11.2

Within data-driven design, arrays can be employed to preload control data into a data set, and to iteratively evaluate that data set against the data rules or business rules contained in the array. SAS temporary arrays are especially well-suited for control data preloading, as the array variables are automatically deleted at the termination of the DATA step.

A one-dimensional SAS array can represent a series of values or SAS variables, and often can replace unnecessary user-defined macro lists. Similarly, a two-dimensional SAS array (or two or more one-dimensional SAS arrays) can represent tabular control data, and greatly simplify their evaluation. The benefit of employing a built-in array (over a user-defined data structure) is the array's reliance on commensurate built-in functionality, including built-in operations that can iterate and evaluate arrays with ease and without risk. Thus, as in all cases, SAS practitioners should leverage the design and development of user-defined data structures only after identifying that all built-in data structures (including SAS data sets, hash objects, and arrays) are incompatible with (or cannot deliver) the functionality being sought.

4.5   USER-DEFINED DATA STRUCTURES

Data structures vary in complexity from series data, such as lists and one-dimensional arrays, to tables, configuration files, and beyond. Built-in data structures within SAS and other languages flexibly accommodate reuse for diverse purposes. Moreover, the host of built-in operations that can interact with built-in data structures further incites their appeal, and built-in data structures should be favored whenever they can deliver required functionality; alas and alack, sometimes they cannot.

Where user-defined data structures must be designed and developed, the scope and lifespan of their intended use should be considered. Are you building a configuration file data structure that will be used to drive a single program? Or are you building a configuration file *template* that can be reused to drive unrelated SAS programs in the future, and to flexibly accommodate their unrelated (and possibly unruly) control data? Even if intended to drive only a single program, is that user-defined configuration file expected to flex over the years to facilitate dynamic input, or will it remain relatively stable?

> Additional design considerations for user-defined configuration files are discussed in Sections 16.3 and 16.3.1

Thus, just as conversations about software quality characteristics (e.g., reliability, robustness, modularity, configurability, reusability) should occur in software planning and design, so too must stakeholders consider the quality of the data structures they are envisioning and ultimately engineering. Just as *procedural abstraction* effectively extends the functionality of a software language by enabling developers to write user-defined functions and subroutines, *data abstraction* similarly extends software functionality—through the creation of user-defined data structures and their associated operations.

> Axes that distinguish control data structures are discussed in Section 9.1

The next subsections demonstrate how the *list*, a common ADT not available natively in the SAS language, can be operationalized by designing a user-defined data structure. Throughout this demonstration, concepts such as inheritance, operational extensibility, and backward compatibility—which are germane to *all* user-defined data structures, not only the list—are discussed in relation to *this* specific data structure.

4.5.1   Mimicking the List ADT in SAS

The *list* is a common ADT that ISO defines as a "set of data items, each of which has the same data definition."[46] Lists can be counted, ordered, iterated, searched, concatenated, deduplicated, and so much more. Although list data types are available in many languages, the list ADT does not have a corresponding built-in data structure within the SAS language.

Throughout SAS literature, thousands of SAS practitioners have mimicked the list ADT structure and functionality using the SAS macro language, thus expanding the range of operations that can be performed within SAS. Whereas *macro lists* are discussed more fully in Chapter 10,

Favoring data
structures that
support intrinsic
element
decomposition is a
data-driven design
principle, introduced
in Section 1.4, and
described in
Section 9.6

the following subsections instead operationalize the list ADT within a comma-delimited character variable—anecdotally, the *SAS list*.

For example, the Pres data set (created in Section 4.3) contains the VP character variable anecdotally referred to as a *list*; that is, the built-in data type is *prescribed* to be character, whereas the user-defined data structure (that sits atop the built-in data type) is *described* as a comma-delimited list. And because *prescription* trumps *description* in the world of data types and data structures, although myriad built-in SAS operations support the character data type, SAS practitioners must engineer user-defined operations to interact with user-defined data structures like the list.

For example, within the Pres data set, the VP values for the first three observations follow:

```
John Adams
Thomas Jefferson
Aaron Burr, George Clinton
```

The VP variable in both the first and second observations contains a single element; however, the third observation contains two elements—two comma-delimited values containerized within a single character variable. This packaging is useful because more information can reside in a single variable. But as a wise fortune cookie once admonished me, "What has been packed...must be unpacked. Your lucky number is 42."

Thus, despite their undeniable utility, lists—as operationalized within the SAS language, including both user-defined SAS lists and user-defined macro lists—also represent a bastardization of the list ADT when compared to the multitude and flexibility of built-in list capabilities available in other languages. In this example, the inadequacy is demonstrated in that the "list" of U.S. presidents is in fact a single variable that must be iterated and unpacked using user-defined operations and, in extreme cases (such as when special characters are present), acrobatics.

Notwithstanding their limitations, user-defined lists are invaluable to SAS software when implemented consistently and reliably. In addition to lists, other ADTs that are not natively represented within SAS can be modeled to extend SAS functionality. Designing user-defined data structures can be a complex endeavor because elements often must be decomposed through user-defined parsing operations and because other user-defined operations must be built. Data structure design should also consider factors such as the intended data structure users, scope, file type, longevity, and data validation methods.

Before embarking on a quest to design and develop a user-defined data structure, the first objective should be to ensure that the desired functionality and performance cannot be achieved through built-in data structures and their respective operations. Despite their benefit and true necessity in many instances, user-defined data structures are riskier than their built-in counterparts because developers must build the software components that interpret and interact with them.

User-defined data structures also tend to be poorer performing—both slower and less efficient than their built-in counterparts. This is not surprising, considering that the operations that support user-defined data structures must be built in the programming language itself, whereas built-in data structures can rely on lower-level (i.e., less abstract) languages.

For example, the SAS application is not written in the SAS language—but rather in C—a lower-level, third-generation language (3GL) with more direct access to core computer functionality. SAS user-defined data structure operations, on the other hand, must be written in SAS, a fourth-generation language (4GL). User-defined data structures are still essential to extend software functionality and to meet many software requirements, but they will always have limitations. Notwithstanding, by understanding overarching ADTs and how they are operationalized (as data types and data structures) within other languages, SAS practitioners can best mitigate and overcome these limitations when designing user-defined data structures and their respective operations in the SAS language.

4.5.2   Data Structure Inheritance

User-defined data structures always must be derived from some superordinate data type, data structure, or file type, and thus demonstrate inheritance, an aspect of data abstraction. IEEE defines *inheritance* as the "semantic notion by which the responsibilities (properties and constraints) of a subclass are considered to include the responsibilities of a superclass, in addition to its own, specifically declared responsibilities."[47] That is, higher-level data structures inherit characteristics from lower-level data types, data structures, and file types on which they are based—and these characteristics include not only functionality but also limitations.

Section 4.5.1 introduces the SAS list, a user-defined data structure operationalized as a series of character values within a character variable.

Specifically, the VP variable is declared as a built-in character data type but is used and referenced as a user-defined list. Thus, VP functionality—the operations that can be performed on this user-defined list—are character-specific rather than list-specific because VP inherits its functionality from its declared character data type.

For example, the use of the built-in LOWCASE character function lowers the case of the VP variable:

```
data _null_;
   set pres (obs=3);
   length newvar $100;
   newvar=lowcase(vp);
   put newvar=;
run;
```

LOWCASE is a built-in *character* function and operates by interacting not with the user-defined list data structure but rather with its superordinate *character* data type. That is, LOWCASE fails to perceive the comma-delimited data structure that has been described. Notwithstanding, this functionality is useful because all list elements can be transformed in one fell swoop, as demonstrated in the log:

```
newvar=john adams
newvar=thomas jefferson
newvar=aaron burr, george clinton
```

As a second example, the built-in SUBSTR character function can also be applied to the VP list because it is, in fact, a character variable. The following DATA step attempts (but fails) to obtain the first letter of each vice president's first name:

```
data _null_;
   set pres (obs=3);
   length newvar $1;
   newvar=substr(vp,1,1);
   put newvar=;
run;
```

Although syntactically valid, the use of SUBSTR on VP is logically incorrect because it fails to capture the "G" in George Clinton—the second element in the two-element list:

```
newvar=J
newvar=T
newvar=A
```

Thus, although SUBSTR is a character function and syntactically *can* operate on the VP character variable, it typically *should not* be used because VP has been operationalized as a user-defined list. Tokenization and decomposition of VP into its constituent elements (i.e., individual vice presidents) would first be required before SUBSTR should be applied.

Thus, although the panoply of built-in SAS character functions (and other DATA step character operations) could be applied to the VP character variable, SAS practitioners must be cautious in application of this functionality—because the user-defined list nature of VP must be enforced through user-defined functionality. For this reason, some of the first user-defined operations typically engineered for user-defined data structures are tokenization and decomposition (of and into constituent elements), as demonstrated in the next subsection. Only after constituent elements have been extracted from a user-defined list should SAS built-in character functions (or other operations) be applied to those individual elements.

As a third example, the VP list—declared as a character data type but described as a SAS list of character elements—inherits not only functionality but also limitations from its superordinate character data type. The built-in LENGTH statement demonstrates one such limitation, as it declares the maximum number of characters that a character variable can contain.

Consider the following DATA step, which declares the VP variable to have a length of 20 (rather than 100) characters:

```
data _null_;
    length vp $20;
    set pres (obs=3);
    put vp=;
run;
```

The code executes but is functionally incorrect because it truncates the list of vice presidents in the third observation:

```
vp=John Adams
vp=Thomas Jefferson
vp=Aaron Burr, George C
```

However, this functional limitation stems not from the user-defined list data structure but rather from its superordinate built-in character data type—declared as a length of 20 characters. Thus, as all built-in data types, data structures, and file types inherently have limitations that prescribe their structure, format, and usage, all derivative user-defined data structures will inherit those same limitations.

User-defined data structures can also inherit functionality (and limitations) from their superordinate *file types* inasmuch as data structures. Two of the most ubiquitous characteristics inherited from file type include end-of-line (EOL) and end-of-file (EOF) markers. For example, when defining a user-defined configuration file within a superordinate text file, SAS practitioners do not need to engineer operations to detect either EOL or EOF because these markers are encoded into the file type definition. The SAS language is flexible enough to allow users to *choose* to interact with these built-in markers (for example, through the FLOWOVER, MISSOVER, STOPOVER, and TRUNCOVER options of the INFILE statement, or the END option of the SET statement), but the point is that EOL and EOF markers inhabit all text files—irrespective of whatever user-defined data structures may be maintained within these files.

Note that as a user-defined data structure increasingly differs from its superordinate data type or data structure, SAS practitioners will need to engineer increasingly more (or more complex) user-defined operations to enforce, interact with, and operate on the user-defined data structure. For example, the VP list represents a series of comma-delimited *character* values within a *character* variable. However, this gap widens when a "list" instead is defined as a series of *numeric* values within a *character* variable because user-defined operations must be added to restrict list content to only numbers. For this reason, the built-in substrate upon which user-defined data structures are designed always should be carefully selected to minimize the *prescription-description gap*—the inherent gap between superordinate prescription and subordinate user-defined description.

The *prescription-description gap* is defined and discussed in Section 9.6

4.5.3   Data Structure Tokenization

Section 4.5.1 introduces the concept of the *SAS list*, a user-defined series of delimited values maintained within a character variable. SAS lists operate as containers, enabling developers to reference or interact with them as a single object or as a collection of values; however, SAS lists are not true lists (per the list ADT) because they do not contain distinct elements. The delimited values within a list, although often anecdotally referenced as *elements* or *items* (even throughout this text), must be parsed and extracted programmatically, and thus more precisely represent *values*, not *elements*.

But because these elements must be able to be universally and unambiguously differentiated from each other, some user-defined delimiter always must separate elements within a user-defined list. In this text, SAS lists are operationalized as comma-delimited values within a character variable, in which the occurrence of any comma within the list variable denotes the termination of the prior (and the start of the subsequent) element. SAS lists, however, could also be defined as space-delimited numbers within a character variable; the possibilities for user-defined list construction are endless, so long as the data structure definition that is selected is supported by operations that can competently parse list elements.

Tokenization describes the process whereby data are parsed or decomposed into *tokens*—constituent elements that convey identifiable meaning—and *non-tokens*—actual data that convey information. For example, prior to program execution, the SAS macro processor reads SAS code and tokenizes it into elements that have distinct meaning. Thus, when the macro processor encounters the &PLUS macro variable in Section 4.4.3, it recognizes the ampersand (&) and immediately identifies &PLUS is a macro variable whose value should be used during execution. Similarly, when the macro processor reads the %LET statement, it recognizes the percent sign (%) as the start of a macro statement—specifically, the macro keyword %LET.

Tokenization can also describe the parsing of data structures into their constituent elements. Built-in data structures are automatically tokenized, and thus do not require user-defined operations to parse them; their elements are said to be *intrinsically decomposed*. For example, you can reference a SAS variable within code and trust that it will not be corrupted by data from neighboring variables (within its data set)—because the data set, a built-in data structure, automatically tokenizes both observations and variables.

However, tokens must be defined (and associated tokenization operations built) whenever developers design a user-defined data structure. For example, a user-defined list comprises a series of elements, so it requires only one delimiter; thus, a comma-delimited list uses the comma symbol to delimit all elements, but requires user-defined operations to parse and extract its comma-delimited values.

Defining the comma as a delimiter, however, also requires that the comma *not* appear within the list elements themselves. For example, the Pres data set (created in Section 4.3) contains the comma-delimited VP variable, whose first three values include:

```
John Adams
Thomas Jefferson
Aaron Burr, George Clinton
```

But what if each vice president's name instead had been stored in last-name-comma-first-name format while still containerized within a comma-delimited list? This transformation would engender chaos in which elements could no longer be reliably differentiated because the comma symbol would delimit both *within* an element and *between* elements:

```
Adams, John
Jefferson, Thomas
Burr, Aaron, Clinton, George
```

Thus, as delimiters—and, in fact, all tokens—are conscripted for use within user-defined data structures, care must be exercised to ensure that they are reliable—that is, universally and unambiguously interpreted.

Masking is one method to extend the functionality and flexibility of a data structure, by effectively enabling a delimiter to appear within a data element (e.g., in a non-delimiter role) through distinct symbology. For example, a CSV file employs masking when double quotes enclose all comma-delimited elements, enabling a comma to appear both *within* elements (to denote data) and *between* elements (to denote a delimiter).

In some cases, multiple delimiter tokens may be warranted within a single user-defined data structure. For example, a two-dimensional or tabular data structure could be defined in which one token delimits the first dimension and a second token delimits the second dimension. Thus, the VP character variable could be operationalized to represent a user-defined table, with commas delimiting vice presidents and asterisks delimiting the last and first names thereof:

```
Adams*John
Jefferson*Thomas
Burr*Aaron,Clinton*George
```

Given this multi-level paradigm, commensurate operations would need to be designed that first decompose VP into vice presidents (tokenizing by comma), and subsequently decompose these elements into last and first names (tokenizing by asterisk). In many instances, however, those pioneering practitioners wont to fashion multidimensional user-defined data structures are better served by embracing built-in data structures and the built-in functionality that SAS data sets, hash objects, and arrays provide.

4.5.4   Data Structure Functional Operations

User-defined data structures nearly always require the development of associated user-defined operations. As *data structure* conveys the containerization of multiple data elements into some composite, operations must facilitate the identification of constituent elements through tokenization and decomposition, as discussed previously.

For example, in Section 4.5.2, the following DATA step failed (i.e., executed without runtime error but produced invalid output) on the third observation because the VP variable contained two elements (i.e., vice presidents), although only one could be extracted:

```
data _null_;
   set pres (obs=3);
   length newvar $1;
   newvar=substr(vp,1,1);
   put newvar=;
run;
```

To remedy the parsing failure, a loop can be constructed in which SCAN identifies and iterates across all commas within the VP variable:

```
data _null_;
   set pres (obs=3);
   length newvar $1;
   do i=1 to countw(vp,',');
      newvar=substr(strip(scan(vp,i,',')),1,1);
      put newvar=;
      end;
run;
```

The results now demonstrate that both Aaron Burr's (A) and George Clinton's (G) first initials are extracted:

newvar=J

newvar=T

newvar=A

newvar=G

This same tokenization and decomposition will be required in subsequent operations that interact with this user-defined list, so placing iteration functionality within a reusable function (or other callable software module) can often eliminate redundant iteration.

For example, consider a new requirement to identify the first vice president (alphabetically by first name) within VP. Thus, in James Madison's first term (observation 4), VP resolves to "George Clinton, Elbridge Gerry" so the first value alphabetically should resolve to "Elbridge Gerry."

The LIST_FIRST user-defined function produces this functionality, relying on COUNTW to evaluate list size and on SCAN to parse and decompose the list:

```
proc fcmp outlib=sasuser.myfuncs.char;
    function list_first(list $) $;
        length first $20;
        do i=1 to countw(list,',');
            element=strip(scan(list,i,','));
            if i=1 then first=element;
            else if element < first then first=element;
            end;
        return(first);
        endfunc;
quit;
```

Unlike the previous DATA step, however, all tokenization and iteration mechanics have now been removed from the DATA step and abstracted to the user-defined function. Thus, when a subsequent DATA step calls LIST_FIRST, it can pass the VP user-defined list as an argument and trust that the function will correctly interpret the delimited data:

```
options cmplib=sasuser.myfuncs;
```

```
data _null_;
   set pres (obs=4);
   length vp_alpha $20;
   vp_alpha=list_first(vp);
   put vp= vp_alpha=;
run;
```

The log shows that for each of the first four observations, the correct (i.e., first alphabetically) vice president was selected for each president's term:

```
vp=John Adams vp_alpha=John Adams
vp=Thomas Jefferson vp_alpha=Thomas Jefferson
vp=Aaron Burr, George Clinton vp_alpha=Aaron Burr
vp=George Clinton, Elbridge Gerry vp_alpha=Elbridge
Gerry
```

Moreover, LIST_FIRST demonstrates scalability in processing both single-element lists (first and second observations) and multi-element lists (third and fourth observations). LIST_FIRST represents a reusable function that can be applied to not only the VP list but any similarly defined comma-delimited SAS list. Thus, this new operation can be said to *extend the functionality* of the user-defined SAS list data structure. That is, the next time a SAS practitioner has decided to maintain data in a list, he will not need to recreate this functionality.

For example, the following DATA step enumerates some favorite fruits in the Fruits variable—prescribed as a SAS character variable but described as a user-defined comma-delimited list:

```
data my_favorites;
   length fruits $100 first $20;
   fruits='orange, kiwi, mango, persimmon';
   first=list_first(fruits);
   put first=;
run;
```

Because the SAS practitioner has selected an existing user-defined data structure, the program can rely on that data structure's associated user-defined operations (like LIST_FIRST). The log demonstrates that kiwi has been selected as the first fruit (alphabetically) from the list:

```
first=kiwi
```

As the number and variety of user-defined operations that support a user-defined data structure increase, the versatility and likely longevity of that data structure will commensurately increase. Thus, as data abstraction defines not only data structures but also the operations that act upon them, the success of one depends on the other. SAS practitioners are more likely to reach for and consistently reuse a user-defined data structure they know and trust—one that has been aptly documented and which has a breadth of associated user-defined operations that can be leveraged with confidence.

4.5.5   Data Structure Backward Compatibility

Backward compatibility describes the retention of software functionality even after some change has been made—whether preventative maintenance, corrective maintenance, adaptive maintenance, or requirements maintenance. That is, whether software was modified to correct a defect, mitigate risk, improve performance, or add new functionality, a common requirement decries that *the stuff that worked before the modification should still work after the modification!*

Callable software modules commonly declare parameters that must be passed at invocation, or define data structures that similarly drive dynamic functionality. Where adaptive maintenance or requirements maintenance are performed on a callable module to extend its functionality, control data often must be modified to support new operations or configurable options. Thus, a common question and concern becomes whether an updated version of some procedure, function, or subroutine will break legacy invocations thereof that relied on the previous or past version. Where backward compatibility is prioritized, legacy calls to a historic module will continue to function consistently—even after the module's implementation has been updated to extend its functionality.

For example, when the SORT procedure was upgraded and multithreaded in SAS 9, previous calls to SORT (written in SAS 8) still functioned without issue. SAS Institute had prioritized backward compatibility because it had not wanted all SORTs around the world to stop functioning suddenly like some zero-day attack had occurred. And this is the narrow vein in which backward compatibility is typically discussed—ensuring that when your code changes, your historic functionality (and especially legacy invocations) will not.

The multithreaded refactoring of the SORT procedure is discussed in Sections 2.1.2 and 3.3

But as data abstraction defines not only data structures but also their respective operations, backward compatibility must extend beyond *securing code* to *securing data structures*. Thus, and especially within a data-driven design paradigm, user-defined data structures that house control data must be protected from modification that could invalidate legacy usage of these structures. Before populating any control data into a user-defined data structure, consider all the ways in which the data structure is intended to be used—and all the ways (or data) that will be expressly prohibited. This *future-proofing* results in a more reliable, sustainable, enduring user-defined data structure that can flex to the anticipated variability of the control data it has been designed to maintain.

For example, in Section 4.5.3, an alternative (yet troubling) format for the VP variable is expressed, in which commas are used both within and between elements, causing ambiguity where multiple vice presidents served one presidential term (as in the third observation):

```
Adams, John
Jefferson, Thomas
Burr, Aaron, Clinton, George
```

An ambitious SAS practitioner might redefine the SAS list definition from "comma-delimited values inside a character variable" to "comma-delimited *quoted* values inside a character variable." For example, the inclusion of double quotes around Aaron Burr and George Clinton does improve readability and eliminate ambiguity:

```
Adams, John
Jefferson, Thomas
"Burr, Aaron", "Clinton, George"
```

The following DATA step creates the Pres_new_format data set, which demonstrates this new quoted data structure format:

```
data pres_new_format;
   infile datalines dsd;
   length fname $20 lname $20 num 3 dt1 8 dt2 8
      vp $100;
   input fname $ lname $ num dt1 : mmddyy10.
      dt2 : mmddyy10. vp $;
   format dt1 dt2 mmddyy10.;
```

```
      label fname='First Name' lname='Last Name'
         num='Number' dt1='Term Start' dt2='Term End'
         vp="President's VPs";
      datalines;
George, Washington, 1, 04/30/1789, 03/04/1797, 'Adams,
John'
John, Adams, 2, 03/04/1797, 03/04/1801, 'Jefferson,
Thomas'
Thomas, Jefferson, 3, 03/04/1801, 03/04/1809, '"Burr,
Aaron", "Clinton, George"'
James, Madison, 4, 03/04/1809, 03/04/1817, '"Clinton,
George", "Gerry, Elbridge"'
;
```

The new data structure can be tested against legacy operations by calling the user-defined LIST_FIRST function (defined in Section 4.5.4) on the new VP variable:

```
data _null_;
   set pres_new_format;
   length vp_alpha $20;
   vp_alpha=list_first(vp);
   put vp= vp_alpha=;
run;
```

Not surprisingly, the log demonstrates that the VP_alpha variable is now incorrect because it includes a double quotation mark (when one appears in the respective VP variable):

```
vp=Adams, John vp_alpha=Adams
vp=Jefferson, Thomas vp_alpha=Jefferson
vp="Burr, Aaron", "Clinton, George" vp_alpha="Burr
vp="Clinton, George", "Gerry, Elbridge"
vp_alpha="Clinton
```

Thus, because the SAS practitioner effectively redefined the list data structure to include the option of quoted elements, legacy operations—such as the LIST_FIRST function—have been invalidated.

This juncture represents the age-old balancing act between backward compatibility and future functionality. You do not want to deprive yourself or your users of the benefits of improved, more flexible software—including both callable modules and the data structures that support them. On the other hand, you neither want to make so many modifications so often that your legacy invocations fail, or your legacy user-defined data structures can no longer be parsed—because backward compatibility has been vacated.

In this example, the decision boils down to either updating the definition of the comma-delimited SAS list (and the operations that utilize it), or creating a new user-defined data structure (and the operations that will utilize it). An examination of the proposed new data structure (a comma-delimited list with optional quotations masking interior commas) illustrates some of the complexity that will be encountered:

- Can quoted and unquoted elements appear in the same list?
- Can multiple quoted elements appear in the same list?
- Can both single and double quotes be utilized to mask interior commas?
- If both single and double quotes can be utilized, can they be utilized separately within a single list?
- If an unmatched quote is encountered, will this trigger a failure? Should it be deleted? Or should it be incorporated into the element's data?
- Can either quoted or unquoted elements be empty?

For example, the following LIST_FIRST_Q function redefines the prior LIST_FIRST function, and is now capable of evaluating commas that are masked within double quotes:

```
proc fcmp outlib=sasuser.myfuncs.char;
    function list_first_q(list $) $100;
        length new_list $100 element $100 first $100;
        new_list=strip(list);
        n=1; * counts elements in list;
        * this loop selects the next element to evaluate;
        do while (lengthn(new_list)>0 and n<100);
            c=findc(new_list,',',1);
            q1=findc(new_list,'"',1);
            if q1>0 then q2=findc(new_list,'"',q1+1);
            else q2=0;
            * quotes precede comma or EOL;
```

```
        if q1^=0 and q2^=0 and (q1<c or c=0) then do;
           element=strip(substr(new_list,q1+1,
              q2-1-q1));
           new_list=strip(substr(new_list,q2+1));
           * remove trailing comma;
           if substr(new_list,1,1)=',' then new_list=
              strip(substr(new_list,2));
           else new_list='';
           end;
        * no quotes, or comma precedes quotes;
        else if (q1=0 and q2=0) or c<q1 or c=0
              then do;
           if c>0 then do;
              element=strip(substr(new_list,1,c-1));
              new_list=strip(substr(new_list,c+1));
              end;
           else do;
              element=strip(substr(new_list,1));
              new_list='';
              end;
           end;
        else return('_ERROR_');
        * evaluate current element w/ past elements;
        if n=1 then first=element;
        else if element < first then first=element;
        n+=1;
        end;
     return(first);
     endfunc;
  quit;
```

The majority of the complexity and code results from the necessity to now differentiate masked commas (within double quotes) from unmasked commas (that delimit elements). In fact, the same two lines of code that appeared in LIST_FIRST still provide the entire logic that evaluates whether the current element is alphabetically first among all elements in the list:

```
if n=1 then first=element;
```

```
else if element < first then first=element;
```

Thus, the remainder of the code interprets the mildly more complex definition of the SAS list, which now can incorporate double quotes. This arguably unnecessary opus also underscores the best practice of utilizing built-in data structures (in lieu of user-defined data structures) whenever possible, so that text-parsing shenanigans like these can be avoided.

Section 11.1.5 demonstrates how the reliance on built-in data structures like the SAS data set can more aptly handle symbols and other special characters that appear in data

Apropos backward compatibility, however, this degree of complexity can be warranted when it allows legacy calls to the LIST_FIRST function to continue to function while also extending LIST_FIRST functionality. For example, the following DATA steps demonstrate that LIST_FIRST_Q is backward compatible to LIST_FIRST functionality:

```
data more_favorites;
    length fruits $100;
    fruits='orange'; output;
    fruits='orange, kiwi'; output;
    fruits='"cherry"'; output;
    fruits='"plum, pear"'; output;
    fruits='mango, banana, "kumquat, cherry"'; output;
    fruits='"mango, banana", kumquat, cherry'; output;
    fruits='"strawberry, raspberry, blueberry", "kumquat,
grape", tangerine'; output;
run;


options cmplib=sasuser.myfuncs;
data _null_;
    set more_favorites;
    length first_fruit $50;
    first_fruit=list_first_q(fruits);
    put first_fruit=;
run;
```

Thus, were LIST_FIRST_Q to be renamed LIST_FIRST (and inherently overwrite and replace the legacy function), historic calls to LIST_FIRST would continue to run. However, as neither LIST_FIRST nor LIST_FIRST_Q contain exception handling that could prevent failure were invalid data passed, their functionality under *exceptional* conditions could vary dramatically. For example, if passed copious or invalid data, one function might fail *saliently* with a runtime error while the other function might fail *silently* (and inarguably more *heinously*) by instead producing invalid results. Thus, within any production environment, *far more testing*—including regression testing of both legacy invocations and legacy data—would be required before LIST_FIRST_Q could replace its predecessor.

Notwithstanding these real-world caveats, the results from the prior DATA step demonstrate that LIST_FIRST_Q is able to parse both single- and multi-element lists, as well as quoted and unquoted elements:

```
first_fruit=orange
first_fruit=kiwi
first_fruit=cherry
first_fruit=plum, pear
first_fruit=banana
first_fruit=cherry
first_fruit=kumquat, grape
```

However, the newfangled SAS list data structure (comma-delimited and optionally quoted) now requires quite a bit of code to be tokenized into elements. Further, this logic must be replicated within all subsequent operations that are built to interact with this data structure. Thus, a more sustainable, long-term approach to designing future operations might instead extract this tokenization and iteration logic from LIST_FIRST_Q and place it in a new user-defined function (not demonstrated) that identifies only the "current" element within some list.

To be clear, backward compatibility will not always be possible, nor even prudent. Especially where functionality is being greatly expanded, it may be impossible to cling to the remnants of once-great user-defined data structures, no matter how near and dear they may be to our hearts. Moreover, complexity alone may mandate that SAS practitioners eschew a user-defined data structure in lieu of the reliability, functionality, security, and stability of a built-in data structure.

4.6   CONTROL DATA INDEPENDENCE

Control data should not be commingled with functionality, as this unwanted dependency limits the flexibility and extensibility of the data. When a user-defined data structure is being designed, developers should conceptualize the ways in which its data might be used. For example, having some awareness of the breadth of eventual operations that are planned for a theorized user-defined data structure enables SAS practitioners to build a sufficiently robust data structure that flexibly handles the expected control data variability.

The operations that are envisioned, however, should not be attached to the control data themselves, as this creates undesirable (and unnecessary) coupling. Consider the SELECTPRES macro, which selects a subset of observations using the OBS option:

```
%macro selectpres(newdsn= /* data set subset */,
    obs= /* [OPT] first president to select */);
data &newdsn;
    set pres &obs;
run;
%mend;


%selectpres(newdsn=somepres, obs=(obs=10));
```

SELECTPRES is functional but ugly; the OBS parameter requires its argument to include not only the observation number (control data) but also the OBS option name (functionality). This convoluted invocation succeeds in reducing some complexity inside the macro implementation, but at great expense to the clarity of the invocation itself; where possible, complexity always should be hidden *inside* the implementation.

SELECTPRES can be further obfuscated by commingling the NEWDSN argument with its intended functionality. In this functionally equivalent example, SELECTPRES now ludicrously requires the DATA statement to appear inside the NEWDSN argument:

```
%macro selectpres(newdsn= /* data set subset */,
    obs= /* [OPT] first president to select */);
&newdsn;
    set pres &obs;
run;
%mend;


* selects some presidents;
%selectpres(newdsn=data somepres,
    obs=(obs=10));
```

User-defined data structure rules are discussed in Section 9.6, and are demonstrated in Sections 1.2 and 14.1

Data independence, a pillar of data-driven design, is introduced in Sections 1.3 and 1.3.3, and is contrasted with modularity in Section 4.7

Yes, the macro implementation is made simpler, but at tremendous cost to the quality of the invocation; these control data are not only being parameterized but, undeniably, traumatized!

For example, the NEWDSN argument (i.e., the data set name) would also be useful in evaluating whether a data set exists. Consider an updated software requirement in which the macro must terminate (via the %RETURN statement) if the EXIST function evaluates that the data set (parameterized through NEWDSN) already exists. The NEWDSN argument, which unnecessarily includes "DATA" (i.e., functionality) would first need to be parsed so that the data set name could be extricated from this hot mess.

Central to data-driven design, *control data independence* requires that control data be separated from the code interpreting and acting upon them. Thus, to achieve data independence, the NEWDSN argument should contain only the data set name, and the OBS argument should contain only the number of observations.

A refactored SELECTPRES now espouses data independence, and implements exception handling, relying on the %RETURN statement to terminate the macro if the parameterized data set already exists:

```
%macro selectpres(newdsn= /* data set subset */,
    obs= /* [OPT] first president to select */);
%if %sysfunc(exist(&newdsn)) %then %return;
%if %length(&obs)>0 %then
    %let obs=(obs=&obs);
data &newdsn;
    set pres &obs;
run;
%mend;


%selectpres(newdsn=somepres, obs=10);
```

The newly unencumbered NEWDSN argument, represented as the &NEWDSN macro variable, now can be evaluated by the EXIST function—without the need to detangle these control data from extraneous functionality. More complex, user-defined control data, such as configuration files and control tables, also must ensure they evince this same control data simplicity and data independence.

Data independence is discussed as a configuration file design consideration in Section 16.3.1

4.7   DATA INDEPENDENCE AND MODULARITY

So, are data independence and software modularity the same thing? Not quite, but they are similar, and data independence does depend on a degree of software modularity.

The following single-line configuration file (rptconfig1.txt) contains control data that drive the font color in a SAS report:

```
style=[foreground=blue]
```

The software embodies modularity in that the data structure is separate from the program that utilizes it—the RPT1 macro:

```
%macro rpt1(config= /* configuration file */);
%local color;
data _null_;
   infile "&config" truncover;
   length color $32;
   input color $;
   call symputx('color',color,'l');
run;
proc report data=pres nocenter nowindows
      nocompletecols;
   column fname lname dt1 dt2;
   define fname / display
      &color;
   define lname / display
      &color;
   define dt1 / display;
   define dt2 / display;
run;
%mend;


%let loc=d:\sas\;     * USER MUST CHANGE LOCATION *;
%rpt1(config=&loc.rptconfig1.txt);
```

The RPT1 macro substitutes the &COLOR macro variable with the dynamic STYLE statement supplied by the configuration file. The control data are modular in that they are apart from the code. Thus, an analyst or

The concept of *least privilege*, including the role it can play in data-driven design, is discussed in Section 2.2.3

end user could be granted permission to modify only the configuration file—but not the code—which would protect the software through the *least privilege* best practice. Moreover, SAS practitioners could modify the RPT1 macro while not influencing its underlying control data.

Despite this modularity, however, control data independence has not yet been achieved because the control data (BLUE) are intertwined with the STYLE statement. Thus, if the same control data were needed for a separate purpose or process, the commingled functionality (i.e., STYLE statement) would need to be removed before BLUE could be used. This is not to say that RPT does not demonstrate *some* data-driven design—only that this macro's design could be improved through control data independence.

The following revised configuration file (rptconfig2.txt) demonstrates both modularity and data independence, in that no functionality is supplied or implied by the color—it's just plain blue:

```
blue
```

The revised macro now must supply the functionality that was removed from the configuration file; however, it is always better to maintain this complexity in the implementation rather than in the control data or the invocation:

```
%macro rpt2(config= /* configuration file */);
%local color;
data _null_;
   infile "&config" truncover;
   length color $32;
   input color $;
   call symputx('color',color,'l');
run;
proc report data=pres nocenter nowindows
      nocompletecols;
   column fname lname dt1 dt2;
   define fname / display
      style=[foreground=&color];
   define lname / display
      style=[foreground=&color];
   define dt1 / display;
   define dt2 / display;
```

```
run;
%mend;
```

```
%let loc=d:\sas\;       * USER MUST CHANGE LOCATION *;
%rpt2(config=&loc.rptconfig2.txt);
```

The two macros are functionally equivalent, but the flexibility of the control data has been expanded in the second example because the configuration file control data (BLUE) can now be referenced by other statements or processes beyond the FOREGROUND attribute, or even beyond the STYLE statement or REPORT procedure.

The use of positional and key-value pair attribute identification methods are discussed in relation to configuration file design in Sections 16.3.4 and 16.3.5

But has the flexibility been increased *too* far? For example, were the functionality of the report expanded to include not only FOREGROUND but also BACKGROUND and other user-specified attributes, the configuration file could become a meaningless jumble of unordered, unattributable colors. Thus, a balance must be struck between functionality and flexibility while ensuring that all arguments can be reliably and unambiguously identified and interpreted.

To address these concerns, a final configuration file (rptconfig3.txt) is created, in which the parameters (e.g., FOREGROUND, BACKGROUND) and their respective arguments (e.g., blue, gray) are defined in *key-value pairs* that clarify the intent of each color:

```
foreground=blue
background=gray
```

Blue and gray are now clearly identifiable (i.e., assigned to specific parameters) within the data structure, and the STYLE statement (i.e., functionality) remains apart from the data structure to facilitate data independence.

The refactored RPT macro reads rptconfig3.txt and dynamically initializes the local macro variables &FOREGROUND and &BACKGROUND to blue and gray, respectively:

```
%macro rpt3(config= /* configuration file */);
%local color;
data _null_;
    infile "&config" truncover dsd delimiter='=';
    length var $32 val $32;
    input var $ val $;
```

```
      call symputx(var,val,'1');
run;
proc report data=pres nocenter nowindows
      nocompletecols;
   column fname lname dt1 dt2;
   define fname / display
      style=[foreground=&foreground
background=&background];
   define lname / display
      style=[foreground=&foreground
background=&background];
   define dt1 / display;
   define dt2 / display;
run;
%mend;


%let loc=d:\sas\;      * USER MUST CHANGE LOCATION *;
%rpt3(config=&loc.rptconfig3.txt);
```

Each of the three macros (RPT1, RPT2, and RPT3) can be considered to be functionally equivalent in that they produce the same report—with RPT3 extending functionality through the additional declaration of the BACKGROUND parameter, as defined in its configuration file. However, RPT1 fails to achieve control data independence, and RPT2 inadequately identifies to which parameter its argument should be assigned. Thus, the more maintainable and scalable solution is RPT3, whose initial DATA step facilitates ingestion of limitless arguments for assignment to macro variables.

For example, consider the updated configuration file (rptconfig4.txt), in which the order and placement of the two parameters have been altered, and two unknown parameters have been added:

```
sideground=hazel
background=gray
foreground=blue
upsidedownground=purplish orange
```

The RPT3 macro can be pointed at the new configuration file to derive color assignments therefrom, and to generate the report of presidential term dates (shown in Table 4.2):

```
%let loc=d:\sas\;        * USER MUST CHANGE LOCATION *;
%rpt3(config=&loc.rptconfig4.txt);
```

Despite introducing two unknown parameters, the DATA step in RPT3 flexibly accommodates, and declares two additional macro variables—&SIDEGROUND and &UPSIDEDOWNGROUND. Their values are initialized and never referenced thereafter, but this causes no issues. This maintainability and scalability allows additional parameters to be designed

First Name	Last Name	Term Start	Term End
George	Washington	04/30/1789	03/04/1797
John	Adams	03/04/1797	03/04/1801
Thomas	Jefferson	03/04/1801	03/04/1809
James	Madison	03/04/1809	03/04/1817
James	Monroe	03/04/1817	03/04/1825
John	Adams	03/04/1825	03/04/1829
Andrew	Jackson	03/04/1829	03/04/1837
Martin	Van Buren	03/04/1837	03/04/1841
William	Harrison	03/04/1841	04/04/1841
John	Tyler	04/04/1841	03/04/1845
James	Polk	03/04/1845	03/04/1849
Zachary	Taylor	03/04/1849	07/09/1850
Millard	Fillmore	07/09/1850	03/04/1853
Franklin	Pierce	03/04/1853	03/04/1857
James	Buchanan	03/04/1857	03/04/1861
Abraham	Lincoln	03/04/1861	04/15/1865

Table 4.2 HTML Output from RPT3 Macro

and added to the configuration file prior to the development of the corresponding code that will interpret and implement them.

This is all to say that data abstraction takes many forms, and the "correct" solution will evade the SAS practitioner seemingly seeking perfection. Data-driven design best practices and principles (such as not commingling control data with code) should be embraced, but ultimately, the data structure that is selected to maintain control data—whether built-in or user-defined—must strike a balance between abstraction and flexibility that delivers the requisite functionality and performance.

4.8 SUMMARY

Data abstraction describes not only data types and data structures, but also the operations that interact with them. This chapter introduced the concept of abstract data types (ADTs)—conceptualized notions of data types and structures, irrespective of any specific programming language. A healthy foundation in ADTs allows SAS practitioners to envision and operationalize user-defined data structures within the SAS language.

This chapter introduced the character and numeric built-in data types, and the data set and hash object built-in data structures; the SAS array, a built-in quasi-data structure, was also demonstrated. In gaining an understanding of built-in data types and data structures and their associated operations, SAS practitioners can better model and implement our own user-defined data structures.

The SAS list, a user-defined data structure, was introduced, and two comma-delimited variations thereof—one quoted and one unquoted—were demonstrated and contrasted. High-level concepts of data structure inheritance, data structure tokenization and parsing, and data structure functional extension were demonstrated, all of which can be applied to non-list user-defined data structures.

The extent to which user-defined data structures can be made more reliable, robust, flexible, and functional will support their use and reuse. Well-crafted user-defined data structures that are accompanied by reliable user-defined operations support the subsequent reuse of these data structures, thus maximizing the ease with which control data can be maintained, accessed, and modified—both by personnel and processes.

Chapter 5.

ITERATION ABSTRACTION

This chapter has the following objectives:

❖   Introduce iteration abstraction.

❖   Define and contrast *internal iteration* and *external iteration*.

❖   Define and contrast *implicit iteration scope* and *explicit iteration scope*.

❖   Demonstrate how iteration reduces code length and complexity, and increases developer productivity.

❖   Demonstrate and contrast iteration within the DATA step and SAS macro language.

❖   Demonstrate how SAS arrays can replace macro lists for some iteration use cases.

I teration abstraction—that is, *iteration*—describes the traversal of data structures, and inherently decomposes data objects into their constituent elements. Thus, iteration facilitates element-level operations, including the ability to perform the same operation across all (or some subset of) elements within a data structure. The International Organization for Standardization (ISO) focuses on this repetition in defining *iteration* as the "process of performing a sequence of steps repeatedly."[48]

From a data-driven design perspective, control data drive iteration, so this chapter differentiates iteration methods, and demonstrates iteration of both built-in and user-defined data structures. For example, where a counter variable is being incremented to track the current position within a list, macro list, or SAS array, this counter variable represents control data—it *controls* the looping mechanics that facilitate iteration. And in some cases, the data structure *itself* being iterated will contain additional control data that further drive processing.

Sections 10.2 and 10.3 introduce macro lists and indexed macro lists, respectively

Thus, iteration is critical to data-driven design because control data are often grouped together within linear or tabular data structures. For example, it might be useful to list the months of the year within a single, comma-delimited macro variable—anecdotally, a *macro list*—that can drive subsequent analysis or reporting. This aggregation—or *containerization*—is commonplace but must include methods that allow individual elements (e.g., months) to be identified and extracted. Thus, if you bundle a bunch of control data together, your code needs to be able to parse and separate those data when element-level analysis is subsequently required.

Iteration is a form of abstraction because it allows processes to be developed without foresight (or with measured foresight) into the eventual size or scope of the data they will process. Thus, iteration promotes process scalability—it enables the same PRINT procedure to print ten or 10 million observations, with no change to the underlying code. Even where scalability is not being sought, iteration is often implemented to improve productivity; developers can get more done by typing less code because statements can be typed once yet executed repeatedly.

Where built-in data structures or their respective iteration methods are insufficient for software requirements, developers can construct user-defined data structures and iteration methods. User-defined data structures and methods, albeit required in certain circumstances, are nearly always less desirable (than their built-in counterparts) because they are typically riskier, slower, and less efficient. Notwithstanding these

154

limitations, by observing built-in data structures and their associated iteration operations, SAS practitioners are better equipped to construct user-defined data structures and to build processes that iterate across them.

5.1   WHY ITERATION?

Because I'm lazy. And because you are, too! Even the inimitable Art Carpenter is fond of telling his fawning, fangirling students that his capacity for "writing the same code" is exceeded when he hits the third iteration.

Like so many programming texts before it, *Data-Driven Development* commences in Section 1.2 with "Hello World!" basics, and this timeless message can be printed using two functionally equivalent methods that leverage the PUT and %PUT statements, respectively:

```
data _null_;
   put 'Hello World!';
run;


%macro hello;
%put Hello World!;
%mend;


%hello;
```

Similarly, when two Hellos are required, the following concrete methods double the salutations—albeit, with double the work:

```
data _null_;
   put 'Hello World!';
   put 'Hello World!';
run;


%macro hello;
%put Hello World!;
%put Hello World!;
%mend;


%hello;
```

However, when even more Hellos are required, this unscalable development pattern should be abandoned. Consider the pleasantries that must be exchanged when Art greets a roomful of enamored students—an arbitrary threshold for static coding is surpassed, and iteration should be embraced.

The following functionally equivalent methods now deliver 100 Hellos a piece:

```
data _null_;
   do i=1 to 100;
      put 'Hello World!';
      end;
run;

%macro hello;
%local i;
%do i=1 %to 100;
   %put Hello World!;
   %end;
%mend;


%hello;
```

It is this simplicity, scalability, and productivity that makes iteration inarguably one of the most fundamental tools in software design. The examples also demonstrate why iteration must be done right—because one mistake, whether resulting in functional failure or inefficiency, can be replicated 100 or one million times over.

Within data-driven programming, iteration is especially important because control data that are passed as complex parameters or extracted from data structures must be parsed and iterated.

5.2   DIFFERENTIATING ITERATION

This chapter introduces iteration patterns and methods that exist in the SAS language, including the SAS macro language. To make sense of this journey, two axes—think *differential criteria*, not *Patrick Bateman*—are introduced, along which iteration methods can be described and identified:

- **Internal vs. external iteration** – *External iteration* exposes looping mechanics, whereas *internal iteration* conceals them.
- **Implicit vs. explicit iteration scope** – *Explicit iteration scope* exposes the element-level contents of the data structure being iterated, whereas *implicit iteration scope* does not.

Programming languages include built-in operations that iterate across built-in data structures. For certain operations, the iteration methods are *internal*, in that they occur behind the scenes. For example, the PRINT procedure continues printing until all observations in a data set have been exhausted, just as the DATA step automatically reads all observations (using the SET statement) until it reaches the end of file (EOF).

In other cases, the iteration mechanics are *external*, such as when DO and %DO loops are used, or when a counter is incremented to advance to the next element in a data structure. SAS built-in input/output (I/O) functions, such as FETCH and FETCHOBS, can also be used to read observations from a data set, and can facilitate equivalent functionality (to the SET statement), albeit with more granular data ingestion options provided through external iteration.

Internal and *external iteration*, and *implicit* and *explicit iteration scope*, are contrasted and demonstrated with the ARRAY statement in Section 10.1.2*

The following DATA step creates a data set (South_Park) that contains an abridged list of voice actors from the family-friendly Comedy Central show *South Park*:

```
data south_park;
    infile datalines dsd;
    length id 3 actor $30 characters $500;
    input id actor $ characters $;
    label id='ID' actor='Actor' characters=
        'South Park Character(s)';
    datalines;
1,Trey Parker,"Eric Cartman,Stan Marsh,Randy Marsh,Jimmy
Valmer,Herbert Garrison"
2,Matt Stone,"Kenny McCormick,Kyle Broflovski,Gerald
Broflovski,Butters Stotch,Tweek Tweak"
3,Isaac Hayes,Chef
4,Mona Marshall,"Sheila Broflovski,Wendy Testaburger"
5,April Stewart,"Sharon Marsh,Liane Cartman"
;
```

All voice actors (Actor) are mapped to a user-defined list (Characters) of the one or more characters they voice, and an arbitrary actor ID uniquely identifies each actor. Note that several actors, especially the show's illustrious creators, Trey Parker and Matt Stone, voice multiple characters. Thus, whereas the Actor variable represents a single voice actor, the Characters variable is a comma-delimited list (i.e., a user-defined data structure) having one or more South Park characters.

5.2.1 Internal Iteration

Internal iteration traverses a data structure without revealing the iteration mechanics; the iteration is abstracted and hidden from the view of developers. This concealment is beneficial because it allows a statement, function, procedure, or other software module to scale to accommodate varying quantities of data while hiding this complexity.

Internal iteration is a driving force behind the DATA step and built-in SAS procedures. For example, the following DATA step copies all South_Park observations using a single SET statement—with no apparent looping in sight:

```
data copysouthpark;
   set south_park;
run;
```

Internally, SET iterates, and dutifully reads one observation after another from the South_Park data set. This internal iteration also detects the last observation, irrespective of the number of observations that are read, thus facilitating scalability—because both big and small data sets can be read with the single SET statement.

Internal iteration benefits not only the SAS practitioners who rely on the DATA step but also the SAS Institute software developers who build the SAS application. For example, because the iteration is abstracted inside the DATA step, this enables SAS Institute software developers to refine and refactor the DATA step implementation (i.e., the methods that deliver its functionality) as long as the DATA step invocation (i.e., how SAS practitioners utilize the DATA statement) does not change. Thus, if a faster method of iterating observations is magically discovered or engineered, SAS Institute can refactor the DATA step to include this wizardry— unbeknownst to SAS practitioners who continue using the DATA step and the SET statement without interruption.

Statements placed inside the DATA step also inherently iterate over the entire data set being ingested. For example, the following DATA step prints each actor's name to the log, albeit requiring only a single PUT statement to print an unlimited number of observations:

```
data _null_;
   set south_park;
   put actor;
run;
```

Internal iteration also drives the SAS procedures that we know and love. The following SORT procedure sorts the South_Park data set by the actor's first name but does not expose the underlying iteration:

```
proc sort data=south_park out=sorted;
   by actor;
run;
```

The internal iteration that occurs within the DATA step and SAS procedures effectively treats each observation as an element. Observations are read in sequence, with the exception of multithreaded processing (not discussed in this text), in which observations are read in parallel. Thus, despite representing a two-dimensional matrix (of rows and columns), the data set is iterated one observation at a time as though it were a linear data structure.

Internal iteration can also occur inside select SAS statements. For example, the KEEP option in the DATA statement lists the variables to be retained in a data set. KEEP demonstrates internal iteration because it can accept a series of space-delimited variables, yet hides the mechanics of how the series is processed:

```
data subset (keep=actor characters);
   set south_park;
run;
```

Because Actor and Characters are the only two character variables within the South_Park data set, equivalent functionality could be gained by using the automatic variable _CHARACTER_:

```
data subset (keep=_character_);
   set south_park;
run;
```

CHARACTER, _NUM_, and _ALL_ are the three *special SAS name lists*, which are discussed in Section 5.2.3

Similarly, despite _CHARACTER_ representing multiple variables, the mechanics that iterate this *special SAS name list* are not observed within the code. Developers can interact with both the DROP and KEEP options in a number of ways that showcase their use of internal iteration.

In one final example, a trailing colon instructs KEEP to retain all variables that begin with the letter A:

```
data subset (keep=a:);
   set south_park;
run;
```

The OF operator also facilitates internal iteration across a list of variables. For example, consider that you want to create a new variable (Concat) that concatenates the actors and their respective characters. Without OF, you might use the following code:

```
data concat;
   set south_park;
   length concat $500;
   concat=catx(':',actor,characters);
run;
```

A second, functionally equivalent alternative instead uses the OF operator to concatenate all character variables:

```
data concat;
   set south_park;
   length concat $500;
   concat=catx(':',of _character_);
run;
```

Arrays are introduced in Section 4.4.3

A third, functionally equivalent solution utilizes the ARRAY statement to define the Charvars array, which can also be referenced by the OF operator:

```
data concat;
   set south_park;
   array charvars[*] actor characters;
   length concat $500;
   concat=catx(':',of charvars[*]);
run;
```

Note that in this final example, the ARRAY statement effectively builds a variable list equivalent to the _CHARACTER_ value. However, in more complex scenarios in which Concat needs to concatenate *some* but not *all* character variables, an array (unlike _CHARACTER_) can facilitate this precision by containerizing only a subset of character variables.

Internal iteration always conceals iteration mechanics; however, individual elements of the linear data structure being traversed often can be identified or extracted. The following DATA step prints only the second observation of the South_Park data set, relying on the _N_ automatic variable:

```
data _null_;
   set south_park;
   if _n_=2 then put _all_;
run;
```

A functionally equivalent solution uses the FIRSTOBS and OBS options to subset the data as they are ingested by the SET statement:

```
data _null_;
   set south_park (firstobs=2 obs=2);
   put _all_;
run;
```

Thus, the hiding of iteration mechanics does not imply that developers or processes cannot access individual elements within the data structure being traversed. For example, the _N_ automatic variable tracks the number of iterations within a DATA step, and the _I_ automatic variable tracks the number of iterations within an array. However, in general, internal iteration is used to traverse an entire data structure—from the first element to the last.

5.2.2   External Iteration

External iteration is generally the "iteration" that comes to mind when the term is mentioned—because it's right there in your face. External iteration exposes the mechanics of iteration, and oftentimes the *iteration scope* as well. Within the SAS language, external iteration mechanics comprise the various DO and %DO loops that facilitate traversing data structures, including DO, DO WHILE, DO UNTIL, DO OVER, %DO, %DO %UNTIL, and %DO %WHILE.

Iteration scope is introduced in Section 5.2.3, in which *implicit* and *explicit* scope are contrasted

Note that the %DO %OVER statement is conspicuously absent (because it does not exist); as macros have no built-in data structure that corresponds to a SAS array (or list), there is no equivalent data structure over which a %DO %OVER statement could iterate.

In all cases for which built-in internal iteration methods do not exist, external iteration must be implemented to iterate across data structures. However, SAS literature is replete with examples in which internal iteration could have been used, but in which external iteration was (unnecessarily) used instead. To be clear, the use of external iteration is not always disadvantageous; however, like all techniques within the data-driven design toolbox, SAS practitioners should be cognizant of internal iteration methods so they can be considered when developing user-defined functionality.

For example, the following DATA step creates the Voices variable, which represents the number of characters voiced by each South Park actor:

```
data howmany;
   set south_park;
   voices=1;
   do while(length(scan(characters,voices,','))>1);
      voices+1;
      end;
   voices=voices-1;
run;
```

The DO WHILE loop represents external iteration because the mechanics of the loop are visible rather than concealed. However, this external iteration is unnecessary because the COUNTW function offers a simpler, functionally equivalent solution using internal iteration:

```
data howmany;
   set south_park;
   voices=countw(characters,',');
run;
```

Within SAS, external iteration is more commonly used with the *observation* data structure than with the *data set* data structure—that is, external iteration more commonly loops through *variables* within an observation, than through *observations* within a data set.

In some cases, however, in looping through variables, observations may also be affected. For example, an analyst might need to unpack the Characters variable and create a stacked data set that has a one-to-one actor-to-character mapping (across observations). The following DATA step relies on external iteration by employing the DO loop:

Sections 11.1.5 and 11.2 demonstrate external iteration that does loop over observations, relying on the END option to detect EOF

```
data expand (drop=characters i id);
   set south_park;
   length char_unpacked $20;
   do i=1 to countw(characters,',');
      char_unpacked=scan(characters,i,',');
      output;
      put actor ': ' char_unpacked;
   end;
run;
```

Although the DO loop iterates across comma-delimited elements (within the Characters character variable), one observation is generated for each element (i.e., South Park character) that is encountered—because the OUTPUT statement occurs inside the DO loop. The log demonstrates the "stacked" data saved to the Expand data set:

```
Trey Parker : Eric Cartman
Trey Parker : Stan Marsh
Trey Parker : Randy Marsh
Trey Parker : Jimmy Valmer
Trey Parker : Herbert Garrison
Matt Stone : Kenny McCormick
Matt Stone : Kyle Broflovski
Matt Stone : Gerald Broflovski
Matt Stone : Butters Stotch
Matt Stone : Tweek Tweak
Isaac Hayes : Chef
Mona Marshall : Sheila Broflovski
Mona Marshall : Wendy Testaburger
April Stewart : Sharon Marsh
April Stewart : Liane Cartman
```

In other cases, the data structure being traversed is only a temporary list or range that does not exist outside of the iteration loop. For example, the following DATA step neither creates nor reads a data set (or other persistent data structure), yet relies on the DO loop to print a message to the infamous South Park creators:

```
data _null_;
   length i $5;
   do i='Trey','and','Matt','Rock!';
      put i;
      end;
run;
```

The output follows:

```
Trey
and
Matt
Rock!
```

In this example, the literal values constitute a list—a temporary data structure that is iterated, and which exists only for the duration of the DO loop.

In a similar example, the following DATA step relies on external iteration to loop through a temporary range comprising the values one through 26—the seasons of South Park (as of 2023):

```
data _null_;
   do i=1 to 26;
      put 'South Park: season ' i;
      end;
run;
```

Similarly, the DATA step neither reads from nor writes to a data set. Rather, the iteration traverses the temporary range to produce some action a specified number of times. The abridged output follows:

```
South Park: season 1
South Park: season 2
. . .
South Park: season 25
```

```
South Park: season 26
```

External iteration is common within the SAS macro language because the SAS macro language has no built-in data structures equivalent to the data set or observation. In some cases, a DATA step may occur inside a macro, as in the WHODATVOICE macro (procedure) that iteratively searches the Characters variable to print an actor-character pairing:

```
%macro whodatvoice(character);
data _null_;
   set south_park;
   length putout $50;
   do i=1 to countw(characters,',');
      if find(scan(characters,i,','),
            "&character")>0 then do;
         putout=strip(actor) || ': ' ||
            scan(characters,i,',');
         put putout;
         end;
      end;
run;
%mend;
```

The following invocation of WHODATVOICE (which searches for any character names containing the case-sensitive "Brof") demonstrates that Matt Stone voices both Kyle Broflovski and his father, Gerald:

```
%whodatvoice(Brof);
```

The output follows:

```
Matt Stone: Kyle Broflovski
Matt Stone: Gerald Broflovski
Mona Marshall: Sheila Broflovski
```

If software requirements were updated to reflect that the WHODATVOICE macro *procedure* should be refactored into a macro *subroutine* (that contains neither the DATA step nor other step boundaries), then I/O functions called by the SAS macro language could replace the DATA step functionality.

Macro procedures and macro functions are introduced and differentiated in Sections 3.5.1 and 3.6.1, respectively

The SUB_WHODATVOICE macro subroutine produces identical results to the WHODATVOICE macro procedure; however, it does so by relying on I/O functions (OPEN, CLOSE, ATTRN, VARNAME, FETCH, and GETVARC) that are operationalized by the %SYSFUNC function:

```
%macro sub_whodatvoice(character);
%local dsid vars i varnumactor varnumcharacter
    manychars onecharacter actor close;
%let dsid=%sysfunc(open(south_park,i));
* dynamically determines the three variables are;
* ID, Actor, and Characters;
%let vars=%sysfunc(attrn(&dsid,nvars));
%do i=1 %to &vars;
    %if %eval(%upcase(%sysfunc(varname(&dsid,
        &i)))=ACTOR) %then %let varnumactor=&i;
    %else %if %eval(%upcase(%sysfunc(varname(&dsid,
        &i)))=CHARACTERS) %then %let varnumcharacter=&i;
    %end;
* loops through observations to get values;
* for Actor and Character variables that match;
%do %while(%sysfunc(fetch(&dsid))=0);
    %let manychars=%sysfunc(getvarc(&dsid,
        &varnumcharacter));
    %let actor=%sysfunc(getvarc(&dsid,&varnumactor));
    %do i=1 %to %sysfunc(countw(%bquote(&manychars),
        %str(,)));
        %let onecharacter=%scan(%bquote(&manychars),
        &i,%str(,));
        %if %sysfunc(find(&onecharacter,&character))
        %then %put &actor: &onecharacter;
        %end;
    %end;
%let close=%sysfunc(close(&dsid));
%mend;
```

The SUB_WHODATVOICE invocation produces identical output to the preceding invocation of WHODATVOICE, albeit, through very different methods:

```
%sub_whodatvoice(Brof);
```

Because SUB_WHODATVOICE does not contain a DATA step, SAS procedure, or step boundary, it can be called from within a DATA step or SAS procedure to produce output dynamically. However, it is considered a subroutine rather than a function because it does not return a value.

The first %DO loop demonstrates external iteration, in that &I iterates across the range of variables to find the respective variable positions (within the data set definition) for Actor and Character. Thus, the values for &VARNUMACTOR and &VARNUMCHARACTER are dynamically generated, which ensures that the correct variables will be identified even if the variable order of the South_Park data set is modified.

The %DO %WHILE loop demonstrates external iteration in looping through all observations in the data set, with FETCH retrieving observations until EOF. This I/O read functionality differs substantially from the internal iteration that the DATA step and SAS procedures rely on to read data sets. The exposed iteration mechanics help elucidate the work that the DATA step performs behind the scenes when we use it. Moreover, this demonstrates the simplification and readability that internal iteration provides when contrasted with functionally equivalent external iteration methods.

Within the %DO %WHILE loop, a nested %DO loop represents the third example of external iteration within SUB_WHODATVOICE. This final loop extracts individual South Park characters from the comma-delimited Characters variable. Thus, although the Characters variable has a character data type, it masquerades as a comma-delimited list. And because this comma-delimited list represents a user-defined data structure, it must be iterated and decomposed programmatically.

Although substantially more complex, the SUB_WHODATVOICE macro *subroutine* has met the stated requirements, and can now be invoked from within a DATA step or SAS procedure, providing greater flexibility than the previous WHODATVOICE macro *procedure*.

5.2.3 Implicit and Explicit Iteration Scope

Implicit iteration scope distinguishes iteration in which the scope of the iteration—that is, the extent of the data structure being iterated—is abstracted and concealed. In other words, only the data structure itself is referenced, rather than its constituent elements. This contrasts with *explicit iteration scope* in which the data structure elements themselves are visible or can be explicitly referenced via an index.

For example, the _CHARACTER_, _NUMERIC_, and _ALL_ automatic variables are the three *special SAS name lists* that represent lists of variable names; like SAS arrays, they are not true data structures, but nevertheless can be referenced as objects to provide access to the constituent variables they contain.

As a developer, I can utilize _NUMERIC_ within a program to denote all numeric variables within a specific data set, yet I am not required to know these numeric variable names, nor even how many numeric variables exist! This extreme abstraction represents implicit scope because the size of the _NUMERIC_ object is not revealed. Moreover, as variables are added to or removed from the data set, _NUMERIC_ can still be referenced.

In Section 5.2.1, two functionally equivalent DATA steps demonstrate concatenation of two variables using the CATX function:

```
* explicit iteration scope;
data concat;
   set south_park;
   length concat $500;
   concat=catx(':',actor,characters);
run;

* implicit iteration scope;
data concat;
   set south_park;
   length concat $500;
   concat=catx(':',of _character_);
run;
```

The first DATA step demonstrates explicit scope in defining the list of variables over which CATX iterates, whereas the second DATA step references these variables using implicit scope (_CHARACTER_). The resultant output is identical; however, were the South_Park data set to be modified (e.g., by the inclusion of additional character variables), the CATX function using *explicit scope* would remain unchanged, whereas the CATX function using *implicit scope* would flexibly incorporate the new character variables into the list of variables to be concatenated.

The increased flexibility that implicit iteration scope delivers might be desirable—or it might not. In the preceding example, the explicit scope would be more desirable if the South_Park data set were likely to incorporate additional character variables, and if developers would *not* want those variables incorporated into the Concat value. However, if developers *would* want those new variables incorporated (without modification of the code), the implicit scope of _CHARACTER_ would cause the CATX function to incorporate the new variables automatically.

A second example compares explicit and implicit iteration scope, in which the individual character names are extracted from the Characters variable and placed into an array comprising variables SP1 through SP10. The following DATA steps are functionally equivalent:

```
* explicit scope (range of 1 to 10);
data southparkarray (drop=i);
   set south_park;
   array sp[10] $20;
   do i=1 to dim(sp);
      sp[i]=scan(characters,i,',');
      end;
run;


* implicit scope (range over entire SP array);
data southparkarray;
   set south_park;
   array sp $20 sp1-sp10;
   do over sp;
      sp=scan(characters,_i_,',');
      end;
run;
```

Both array declarations (i.e., the ARRAY statements) define the scope as having ten elements; however, the first array is subscripted ([10]) whereas the second is not, which influences how the arrays (and their elements) can subsequently be referenced. Both the DO and DO OVER loops demonstrate external iteration, in that their looping mechanics are exposed; however, the similarities end here.

The first DATA step demonstrates *explicit iteration scope*, in that the range of variables over which the DO loop iterates is known, having been evaluated by the DIM function at the start of the loop. The array elements are subscripted, and thus require an index variable (I) to be iterated and individually referenced.

Conversely, the DO OVER loop in the second DATA step loops over SP—the array itself—rather than a numeric range (e.g., 1 to 10), thus shielding the array scope in subsequent operations. Rather than initializing subscripted array elements (e.g., SP[5]), the entire array (e.g., SP) is referenced; no counter is required. Note that the SP array is nevertheless still indexed; however, implicit iteration scope facilitates access to array elements without references to that index.

In general, *implicit* iteration scope allows software to flex more readily when the scope of a data structure changes, whereas *explicit* iteration scope allows software developers to interact more fully with individual elements within a data structure. If a program requires greater control of the iteration across some data structure (like skipping elements or re-reading elements), explicit scope is preferred because the counter within a DO loop can be modified programmatically.

Implicit iteration scope typically does not provide this flexibility; the entire data structure is iterated in sequence. For example, once the DO OVER loop is set in motion, it always iterates over each element until it either reaches the end of the data structure or a break statement (like LEAVE) is encountered.

The following DATA step demonstrates the use of LEAVE to exit the DO OVER loop after the second observation is reached, as indicated by the automatic variable (_I_) that denotes the array element number:

```
* implicit DO;
data sp_leave;
   set south_park;
   array sp $20 sp1-sp10;
   do over sp;
      sp=scan(characters,_i_,',');
      if _i_=2 then leave;
      end;
run;
```

The DATA step initializes values for SP1 and SP2 when the Characters variable contains two or more elements. However, for each observation, if the second element is encountered, the LEAVE statement exits the loop, and the remaining values (SP3 through SP10) are never initialized.

The use of LEAVE demonstrates some of the modest control that SAS practitioners have when relying on implicit iteration scope; however, where more control over looping dynamics is required, explicit iteration scope is typically a better choice.

5.3   THE EXECUTE SUBROUTINE (AKA CALL EXECUTE)

The EXECUTE built-in subroutine (aka CALL EXECUTE) is a powerful albeit woefully mismanaged tool—think Mjölnir (aka Hammer of Thor) but wielded by a three-year old. EXECUTE facilitates the iteration of a control table, in which EXECUTE is repetitively called (once for each observation within a SAS data set) and performs one or more operations, which can include the invocation of a user-defined macro. Moreover, variables in the control table can be passed as arguments (or otherwise used dynamically) by each successive call of EXECUTE.

The nomenclature of *subroutines* (vs. *CALL routines*) is discussed in Section 3.7.1

One of the primary benefits of control tables, like configuration files, is the ability to store and reuse control data, rather than having to generate them repetitively or store them within code. When all control data that relate to a specific operation are maintained within a single observation of a control table, EXECUTE is able to transform those data into dynamic instructions, and to execute those instructions immediately after the DATA step (in which EXECUTE resides) has terminated.

Data structure *persistence* is discussed in Section 9.3, including the advantages that control tables and configuration files have over parameterized arguments

For example, consider the business requirement to generate two uniquely formatted reports from the Expand data set (created in Section 5.2.2). The following two REPORT procedures demonstrate a hardcoded approach that meets these functional requirements:

```
title1 'The Incomparable Trey Parker';
proc report data=expand style(header)=
    [background=very light gray foreground=black];
  column actor char_unpacked;
  define actor / order 'Actor';
  define char_unpacked / 'Characters';
  where actor='Trey Parker';
run;

title1 'The Illustrious Matt Stone';
proc report data=expand style(header)=
    [background=black foreground=white];
```

```
column actor char_unpacked;
define actor / order 'Actor';
define char_unpacked / 'Characters';
where actor='Matt Stone';
run;
```

The output from the two REPORT procedures is demonstrated in Figure 5.1. Note that several aspects of the reports vary, including the title, header styles (background and foreground), and the Actor selection criteria. Despite this variability, the underlying "bones" of the reports are identically structured; thus, these few aspects of variability could be parameterized through the SAS macro language, and delivered through data-driven design rather than hardcoding.

The Incomparable Trey Parker

Actor	Characters
Trey Parker	Eric Cartman
	Stan Marsh
	Randy Marsh
	Jimmy Valmer
	Herbert Garrison

The Illustrious Matt Stone

Actor	Characters
Matt Stone	Kenny McCormick
	Kyle Broflovski
	Gerald Broflovski
	Butters Stotch
	Tweek Tweak

Figure 5.1 Output from REPORT Procedures

For example, the SP_REPORT macro declares four parameters—TITLE, BACK, FORE, and ACTOR—and can be saved as a SAS program file (&LOC\sp_report.sas):

```
* saved as SP_report.sas;
%macro sp_report(title= /* report title */,
    back= /* report header background color */,
    fore= /* report header foreground color */,
    actor= /* actor to be selected */);
title1 "&title";
proc report data=expand style(header)=
        [background=&back foreground=&fore];
    column actor char_unpacked;
    define actor / order 'Actor';
    define char_unpacked / 'Characters';
    where actor="&actor";
run;
%mend;
```

In a separate program file, two invocations of SP_REPORT now generate output identical to the hardcoded reports in Figure 5.1:

```
%let loc=d:\sas\;        * USER MUST CHANGE LOCATION *;
%include "&loc.sp_report.sas";

%sp_report(title=The Incomparable Trey Parker,
    back=very light gray, fore=black, actor=Trey Parker);

%sp_report(title=The Illustrious Matt Stone,
    back=black, fore=white, actor=Matt Stone);
```

Although this solution does demonstrate data-driven design, it nevertheless requires control data to be passed as arguments, and thus stored within code. Alternative data-driven design approaches could instead store these control data within a control table, such as a SAS data set, and subsequently read and interpret that control table to provide dynamic instruction.

The following DATA step creates the SP_control data set (i.e., control table) that will drive subsequent data-driven methods:

```
data sp_control;
   infile datalines delimiter=',';
   length title $50 back $50 fore $50 actor $50;
   input title $ back $ fore $ actor $;
   datalines;
The Incomparable Trey Parker, very light gray, black,
Trey Parker
The Illustrious Matt Stone, black, white, Matt Stone
;
```

The EXECUTE subroutine can be operationalized with varying degrees of abstraction to leverage this control table, as demonstrated in the following subsections.

5.3.1 Ugly EXECUTE

Unfortunately, more times than not, EXECUTE is implemented with reckless abandon in which a functional solution is achieved despite the near extinguishment of software readability—inasmuch as developer sensibility. Challenges to readability occur because each additional inclusion of a control table variable (within the EXECUTE call) requires the demarcation of variables from the code that uses them. Thus, as the points of articulation grow, so too does the unnecessary madness and morass.

Software articulation, a measure of *flexibility*, is contrasted with *abstraction* in Section 2.2.1

For example, the following functionally equivalent solution squishes the entire REPORT procedure into the EXECUTE call, with the four parameters now encased within delimiting vertical spaces:

```
data _null_;
   set sp_control;
   call execute('title1 ' || title || ';
      proc report data=expand style(header)=
            [background=' || back || ' foreground='
            || fore || '];
         column actor char_unpacked;
         define actor / order "Actor";
         define char_unpacked / "Characters";
         where actor="' || actor || '";
      run;');
run;
```

On the one hand, this use of EXECUTE does demonstrate data-driven design because the control data are extracted from an external source, the SP_control data set. On the other hand, the entire REPORT procedure is effectively passed as a single argument within the EXECUTE invocation—and this violates the best practice of hiding complexity within the *implementation* rather than brandishing it within the *invocation*. This is by far the ugliest duckling—and no, it don't become no swan!

5.3.2   EXECUTE with a User-Defined Macro

The EXECUTE call demonstrated in the previous subsection can be vastly improved by removing the majority of the *functionality* from EXECUTE's single argument, and retaining only the *control data*. That is, rather than passing the entire REPORT syntax via EXECUTE, only the control data contained within SP_control need be passed.

This improved methodology can be achieved by calling the SP_REPORT macro (defined within Section 5.3) from within EXECUTE:

```
%let loc=d:\sas\;        * USER MUST CHANGE LOCATION *;
%include "&loc.sp_report.sas";
data _null_;
    set sp_control;
    call execute('%sp_report(title=' || strip(title)
        || ', back=' || strip(back)
        || ', fore=' || strip(fore)
        || ', actor=' || strip(actor) || ');');
run;
```

This streamlined approach is beneficial for several reasons. First, note that that the SP_REPORT macro could be reused and did not require any modifications to be called from the EXECUTE subroutine. Second, note that all arguments—TITLE, BACK, FORE, and ACTOR—are now passed via a standardized method, and are no longer commingled with the prior REPORT procedure syntax. Third, because of this standardized syntax, far more readable code is achieved with far fewer opportunities to introduce unnecessary syntax errors.

This method also demonstrates a more abstract solution, as all functionality (i.e., REPORT syntax) has been removed from the EXECUTE invocation, and instead resides in the SP_REPORT macro definition. Thus, if some facet of the REPORT procedure were to require modification, this alteration could be made within the SP_REPORT macro definition—residing in a separate SAS program file—rather than directly in the EXECUTE invocation. For all these reasons, this functionally equivalent solution is far superior to the code presented in Section 5.3).

5.4   THE SYSTASK COMMAND

Whereas the EXECUTE subroutine can read a control table and perform operations in *series* (once the DATA step concludes), the SYSTASK command can read a control table and perform operations in *parallel* in real time—that is, while the DATA step continues to read the control table. SYSTASK can spawn multiple, concurrent SAS sessions (in supported SAS environments, like the SAS Display Manager), with operations running simultaneously in each session.

For example, Section 5.3.2 demonstrates an effective method to read a control table (SP_control), and generate dynamic instructions via the EXECUTE subroutine. Consider the revised requirements, however, to generate the two SAS reports in *parallel* rather than in *series*. SYSTASK can accomplish these objectives while relying on the same control table.

5.4.1   Making the SAS Report SYSTASK-Ready

In Section 5.3, the SP_report.sas program file was created, which defines the SP_REPORT macro. With only subtle modifications, this program file and macro can be revised to be called in batch mode, which enables SYSTASK to invoke the macro in a new SAS session.

The following program file (SP_report2.sas) now defines the updated SP_REPORT2 macro:

```
* saved as SP_report2.sas;
%let loc=d:\sas\;      * USER MUST CHANGE LOCATION *;
libname southprk "&loc";

%macro sp_report2(title= /* report title */,
    back= /* report header background color */,
    fore= /* report header foreground color */,
    actor= /* actor to be selected */);
ods html path="&loc" file="&actor..html";
title1 "&title";
proc report data=southprk.expand style(header)=
```

```
        [background=&back foreground=&fore];
     column actor char_unpacked;
     define actor / order 'Actor';
     define char_unpacked / 'Characters';
     where actor="&actor";
  run;
  ods html close;
%mend;
```

Note that the new SAS session (called in batch mode) requires global macro variables and other environmental settings to be reinitialized. Thus, the &LOC global macro variable must be declared.

The new SAS session similarly will have a fresh WORK library, so it will not have access to the Expand data set, which the SP_REPORT macro previously utilized. Thus, the updated REPORT procedure now relies on the SOUTHPRK.Expand data set, and the LIBNAME statement is required to initialize the SOUTHPRK library.

Finally, as the SP_REPORT2 macro is running in batch mode, its SAS session will terminate (closing the SAS application) when the macro completes. For this reason, as the output will not be viewable, the ODS HTML statement is required to save the report so that it can be viewed after SAS terminates. For simplicity, each report has been named after its respective actor, utilizing the &ACTOR argument.

5.4.2   Passing Arguments to the SAS Report (in Batch)

The SP_REPORT2 macro, defined in the previous subsection, can be run identically to its predecessor macro, SP_REPORT—that is, it can be compiled with the %INCLUDE statement within a current SAS session. However, if SP_REPORT2 is to be invoked in batch mode, its arguments must be passed from the current SAS session to a new SAS session. One method to pass these arguments is to utilize the SYSPARM option (within the SYSTASK command), which passes a single argument (a global macro variable, &SYSPARM) into the new SAS session.

The following program file (SP_report_batch.sas) interprets the &SYSPARM macro variable, and decomposes it into the four arguments that SP_REPORT2 requires—TITLE, BACK, FORE, and ACTOR:

```
* saved as SP_report_batch.sas;
* evaluate if SYSPARM exists;
```

```
%macro get_sysparm();
%local i;
%let i=1;
%do %while(%length(%scan(%quote(&sysparm),&i,','))>1);
    %let var=%scan(%scan(%quote(&sysparm),&i,','),1,=);
    %let val=%scan(%scan(%quote(&sysparm),&i,','),2,=);
    %global &var;
    %let &var=&val;
    %let i=%eval(&i+1);
    %end;
%mend;


%get_sysparm;


%let loc=d:\sas\;        * USER MUST CHANGE LOCATION *;
%include "&loc.sp_report2.sas";


%sp_report2(title=&title,
    back=&back, fore=&fore, actor=&actor);
```

Although described repeatedly as a *macro list*, note that the &SYSPARM value is, in fact, a list of key-value pairs, and thus represents a tabular data structure masquerading as a list, as discussed in Section 10.4.2

For example, the first report produced is for Trey Parker, as his observation is first in the SP_control control table (created in Section 5.3). Thus, the &SYSPARM argument that is received (for Trey Parker) resolves to the following "list" of key-value pairs:

```
title=The Incomparable Trey Parker, back=very light
gray, fore=black, actor=Trey Parker
```

The &SYSPARM value should look familiar, as it is the hardcoded, comma-delimited list of arguments initially passed to the SP_REPORT macro in Section 5.3. Thus, the GET_SYSPARM macro parses &SYSPARM, resolving this single macro variable to initialize four global macro variables—&TITLE, &BACK, &FORE, and &ACTOR. Thereafter, the program calls the SP_REPORT2 macro, and passes these newly initialized arguments.

When the SP_REPORT2 macro terminates, program control returns to the SP_report_batch program, which also terminates, causing the batch SAS session to terminate as well.

5.4.3 Controlling Parallel Processes with SYSTASK

The full syntax and functionality of the SYSTASK command far exceed the scope of this text; however, some explanation is warranted to demonstrate the complexity that parallel processing requires. Thus, with even a soupçon of sagacity, SAS practitioners can more justly weigh the benefits of faster, parallel processing against the undeniable convolution of SYSTASK and its minions. Notwithstanding this sometimes seemingly bleak miasma, to the worthy SAS practitioner who conquers SYSTASK, the largesse of far superior performance awaits and will inarguably astound.

In this example, the objective is to read the control table (SP_control) and spawn a new (parallel) SAS session for each observation that is encountered. However, as these new SAS sessions will not have access to the current WORK library, the Expand data set (on which the previous SP_REPORT macro relied) first must be saved within a permanent library that all SAS sessions can access.

The following LIBNAME statement initializes the SOUTHPRK library, and the DATA step creates the SOUTHPRK.Expand data set:

```
libname southprk "&loc";
data southprk.expand (drop=characters i id);
   set south_park;
   length char_unpacked $20;
   do i=1 to countw(characters,',');
      char_unpacked=scan(characters,i,',');
      output;
      put actor ': ' char_unpacked;
   end;
run;
```

Parallel processes, at least when spawned with SYSTASK, typically require an *engine* or *controller* program that instantiates and monitors the parallel SAS sessions. In data-driven design, a loop can iterate over a control table, extract one observation at a time, and transmit the observation's control data to a new SAS session via the SYSPARM option in the SYSTASK command. That is, the single character argument transmitted via the SYSPARM option will be initialized to the &SYSPARM automatic macro variable within the newly created SAS environment.

The CONTROLLER macro evaluates the number of observations in the control table, and iterates over the control table to spawn new SAS sessions—each of which will produce one HTML report:

```
%macro controller();
%local nobs i title back fore actor;
* evaluate control table obs;
proc sql noprint;
    select count(*) into : nobs
        from sp_control;
quit;
%do i=1 %to &nobs;
    * initialize macro variables to control data;
    proc sql noprint;
        select title, back, fore, actor
            into : title trimmed, : back trimmed,
            : fore trimmed, : actor trimmed
                from sp_control (firstobs=&i obs=&i);
    quit;
    * instantiate new SAS session;
    systask command """"%sysget(SASROOT)\sas.exe"" -
noterminal -nosplash -sysin ""&loc.sp_report_batch.sas""
-log ""&loc.sp_report_batch&i..txt"" -sysparm
""title=&title, back=&back, fore=&fore, actor=&actor"""
taskname=task&i;
    %end;
waitfor _all_
    %do i=1 %to &nobs;
        task&i
        %end;;
%mend;
```

The SYSTASK command calls sas.exe to instantiate a new SAS session. The SYSIN option directs that the SP_REPORT_BATCH program file should be run when this new session opens, and the LOG option directs that the SAS log should be saved to a text file (in which notes, warnings, and runtime errors can be reviewed). Finally, the SYSPARM option passes the required arguments—TITLE, BACK, FORE, and ACTOR—to the new

SAS session, albeit as a single, comma-delimited macro list that must be unpacked (by the GET_SYSPARM macro).

SYSTASK commands, by default, execute *asynchronously*—that is, once SYSTASK executes, the SAS processor continues running subsequent code, which can include additional SYSTASK commands. This behavior is desired—and required to foster parallel sessions—but once all sessions have been spawned, the controller program must wait for each session to complete before subsequent operations can commence.

Thus, a major component of SYSTASK is the WAITFOR statement, which instructs SAS to wait for all parallel SAS sessions to complete once they have been spawned. The TASKNAME option in the SYSTASK command uniquely names each SAS session, relying on the incrementing &I counter. The WAITFOR statement subsequently must include each of these incrementally named task names.

The CONTROLLER macro is called from the primary SAS session with a straightforward invocation:

```
%controller();
```

The SAS log from the primary (i.e., controller) session provides little insight into the parallel processing magic that has just occurred:

```
NOTE: PROCEDURE SQL used (Total process time):
      real time                0.00 seconds
      cpu time                 0.00 seconds


NOTE: PROCEDURE SQL used (Total process time):
      real time                0.00 seconds
      cpu time                 0.00 seconds


NOTE: PROCEDURE SQL used (Total process time):
      real time                0.00 seconds
      cpu time                 0.00 seconds


NOTE: Task "task1" produced no LOG/Output.


NOTE: Task "task2" produced no LOG/Output.
```

However, two new SAS reports have been generated—Matt Stone.html and Trey Parker.html. Moreover, two log files—sp_report_batch1.txt and sp_report_batch2.txt—record the SAS processes that created these two reports.

In this example, the performance benefits of parallel processing will be negligible or nonexistent because each report, even when generated in series, takes only microseconds to complete. However, where a control table might contain hundreds of observations, each of which is intended to spawn some derivative process or produce some data product, the spawning of batches of concurrent sessions could greatly improve performance, and make worthwhile the objective of mastering and implementing SYSTASK to facilitate parallel data-driven design.

5.5   ITERATING MACRO LISTS AND INDEXED MACRO LISTS

Indexed macro lists are introduced in Section 10.3, and offer greater functionality than macro lists

Neither the macro list nor the indexed macro list represents a built-in SAS data structure, and for this reason, user-defined methods must be engineered that can iterate these user-defined lists. The *macro list* is declared as a macro variable yet is operationalized as a comma-delimited (or *other*-delimited) series of values contained within a single character variable. The *indexed macro list*, conversely, is declared as a series of incrementally named macro variables (e.g., &VAR_1, &VAR_2), in which each macro variable is initialized to one value (i.e., list element).

Macro lists are introduced in Section 10.2, but control data are often better maintained within built-in data structures like SAS data sets, as shown in Section 11.1

Albeit invaluable to data-driven design, macro lists and indexed macro lists (and the user-defined iteration thereof) often cause headaches and, arguably worse, performance degradation and software inefficiency. For this reason, design considerations for their iteration and decomposition are discussed in the following subsections.

Consider the need to containerize the list of South Park voice actors in a comma-delimited list—for example, to pass to some unseen process that requires these data to be aggregated. From the South_Park data set created in Section 5.2, the following SQL procedure declares and initializes the comma-delimited &ACTORLIST macro variable:

```
proc sql noprint;
    select actor
    into : actorlist
    separated by ','
    from south_park;
quit;
```

```
%put &actorlist;
%put %sysfunc(countw(%bquote(&actorlist),','));
```

The %PUT statements print the macro list and the number of elements therein, as demonstrated in the SAS log:

```
Trey Parker,Matt Stone,Isaac Hayes,Mona Marshall,April
Stewart
5
```

User-defined macro lists, whether delimited by commas or other symbols, always must be parsed with the %SCAN macro function, which both tokenizes and iterates over list elements, facilitating list decomposition into constituent elements. For example, the following use of %SCAN extracts the third element (Isaac Hayes) from &ACTORLIST, and initializes &ELEMENT to this value:

```
%let element=%scan(%bquote(&actorlist),3,',');
%put &=element;
```

A weakness with this methodology is the requirement that all prior elements must be parsed and identified prior to any subsequent element. For example, despite our interest in *only* Isaac Hayes, accessing this third element requires that both Trey Parker and Matt Stone must first be parsed and identified. And where a macro list may contain hundreds or thousands of values, its iteration will inherently result in tremendous inefficiency.

Indexed macro lists, in contrast to *macro lists*, overcome this limitation because they are explicitly indexed. For example, an indexed macro list can also be initialized to the values of Actor. The following DATA step declares and initializes incrementally named macro variables having the base name "IDX_ACTORLIST_" and initializes &IDX_ACTORLIST_0 to 5, the total number of actors:

```
data _null_;
   set south_park end=eof;
   call symputx('idx_actorlist_' ||
      strip(put(_n_,8.)), actor, 'g');
   if eof then call symputx('idx_actorlist_0',
strip(put(_n_,8.)), 'g');
run;
```

```
%put _global_;
```

The log demonstrates &IDX_ACTORLIST_0, the macro variable containing the number of list elements, and &IDX_ACTORLIST_1 through &IDX_ACTORLIST_5, the five macro variables maintaining the list values:

```
GLOBAL IDX_ACTORLIST_0 5
GLOBAL IDX_ACTORLIST_1 Trey Parker
GLOBAL IDX_ACTORLIST_2 Matt Stone
GLOBAL IDX_ACTORLIST_3 Isaac Hayes
GLOBAL IDX_ACTORLIST_4 Mona Marshall
GLOBAL IDX_ACTORLIST_5 April Stewart
```

If the benefit of indexed macro lists is not already apparent, it will become so. Consider again the need to identify and extract the third element (Isaac Hayes) from the indexed macro list, and to initialize &ELEMENT to this value:

```
%let element=&idx_actorlist_3;
%put &=element;
```

No parsing, tokenization, or decomposition of the indexed macro list is required; the use of %SCAN is obviated because all elements (including the third element, &IDX_ACTORLIST_3) are explicitly indexed. Thus, rather than having to crawl across an entire series of delimited values (as is required when macro lists are implemented), iteration of indexed macro lists is clean and efficient.

5.5.1 *Initializing Sample Macro Lists and Indexed Macro Lists*

To demonstrate the relative performance of iterating user-defined macro lists and indexed macro lists, a larger list can be constructed, comprising 3,000 nine-character values (123456789). This list is initialized into three distinct data structures within this section, including:

1. TESTLIST – a comma-delimited macro list
2. AST_TESTLIST – an asterisk-delimited macro list
3. IDX_TESTLIST – an indexed macro list

First, the following DATA step creates a 29,999-character macro variable (&TESTLIST) that is operationalized as a comma-delimited macro list:

```
data _null_;
```

```
   length testlist $30000;
   do i=1 to 3000;
      testlist=catx(',',testlist,'123456789');
      end;
   call symputx('testlist',strip(testlist),'g');
run;
```

```
%put %substr(%bquote(&testlist),1,39);
```

The %PUT statement displays the first 39 characters of &TESTLIST in the SAS log:

```
123456789,123456789,123456789,123456789
```

Note that %BQUOTE is required to mask the commas, which comprise the user-defined delimiters in this macro list.

Second, the following DATA step creates a 29,999-character macro variable (&AST_TESTLIST) that is operationalized as an asterisk-delimited macro list:

```
data _null_;
   length ast_testlist $30000;
   do i=1 to 3000;
      ast_testlist=catx('*',ast_testlist,'123456789');
      end;
   call symputx('ast_testlist',strip(ast_testlist),'g');
run;
```

```
%put %substr(&ast_testlist,1,39);
```

The %PUT statement displays the first 39 characters of &AST_TESTLIST in the SAS log:

```
123456789*123456789*123456789*123456789
```

Note that %BQUOTE is *not* required to print the macro list; the use of asterisks to delimit macro list elements, in lieu of commas (which delimit the elements within &TESTLIST), obviates the need to mask the delimiting symbol. This removal of %BQUOTE can provide profound performance advantages, as demonstrated in subsequent subsections.

Third, the same data, comprising 3,000 nine-character elements, can be initialized within a user-defined indexed macro list. The following DATA step declares and initializes 3,000 macro variables spanning &IDX_TESTLIST_1 through &IDX_TESTLIST_3000, with an index dimension variable (&IDX_TESTLIST_0) initialized to the total number of indexed elements (3,000):

```
data _null_;
   call symputx('idx_testlist_0','3000','g');
   do i=1 to 3000;
      call symputx('idx_testlist_'
         || strip(put(i,8.)),'123456789','g');
      end;
run;


%put _global_;
```

A partial display of the SAS log demonstrates the first few macro variables (alphabetically) within the IDX_TESTLIST indexed macro list:

```
GLOBAL IDX_TESTLIST_0 3000
GLOBAL IDX_TESTLIST_1 123456789
GLOBAL IDX_TESTLIST_10 123456789
GLOBAL IDX_TESTLIST_100 123456789
GLOBAL IDX_TESTLIST_1000 123456789
GLOBAL IDX_TESTLIST_1001 123456789
GLOBAL IDX_TESTLIST_1002 123456789
```

Note that delimiting commas are no longer required, as the indexed macro list elements are intrinsically decomposed, and thus each is assigned to a unique macro variable.

The next subsections—ordered from worst performing to best performing—compare and contrast five functionally equivalent methods to iterate the comma-delimited macro list (&TESTLIST), asterisk-delimited macro list (&AST_TESTLIST), and indexed macro list (IDX_TESTLIST). Repeated tests demonstrate the following average runtimes:

1. Comma-delimited macro list %SCAN squared loop (8.7 sec)
2. Other-delimited macro list %SCAN squared loop (4.7 sec)
3. Comma-delimited macro list with single %SCAN (4.3 sec)

4. Other-delimited macro list with single %SCAN (2.3 sec)
5. Indexed macro list (0.014 sec)—The Big Winner!!!

Each example computes the runtime required to count the number of elements within the macro list or indexed macro list. Your runtimes will vary based on your SAS system resources and constraints; however, the same performance ranking will be observed across the methods, which demonstrates the clear victor, the indexed macro list, is 600 times faster!

5.5.2 Comma-Delimited Macro List %SCAN Squared Loop

Although the "%SCAN squared loop" method is never recommended, the %SCAN function is unfortunately often utilized both to increment a %DO loop counter and to identify and extract constituent elements from a macro list. Within the COUNT_LIST1 macro, note the two occurrences of %SCAN—the first of which is unnecessary:

```
%macro count_list1(list /* comma-delim list [REF] */);
%local cnt element;
%let cnt=1;
%do %while(%length(%scan(%bquote(&&&list),
    &cnt,','))>1);
  %let element=%scan(%bquote(&&&list),&cnt,',');
  %let cnt=%eval(&cnt+1);
  %end;
%eval(&cnt-1)
%mend;
```

The following invocation of COUNT_LIST1 demonstrates that the macro takes approximately 8.7 seconds to count (i.e., iterate across) the 3,000 elements within the comma-delimited macro list:

```
%let start=%sysfunc(datetime());
%put Elements: %count_list1(testlist);
%put Runtime: %sysevalf(%sysfunc(datetime())-&start);
```

The primary inefficiency stems from the first %SCAN, which can be replaced with the COUNTW function. For example, within COUNT_LIST1, the %DO %WHILE loop must repeatedly evaluate the &&&LIST value (which resolves to the &TESTLIST macro list in this invocation).

The second inefficiency stems from the use of commas to delimit the user-defined macro list. Because commas must be masked within SAS macro functions (like %SCAN) or Base SAS functions (like COUNTW), %BQUOTE must be repeatedly implemented within COUNT_LIST1, which further slows its performance.

Despite this second inefficiency, the use of commas (as delimiters) still may be warranted based on technical requirements, including data structure readability requirements. Moreover, in far shorter macro lists, this performance inefficiency will be negligible. Regardless, savvy SAS practitioners should be aware that built-in masking functions (such as %BQUOTE) can incur a significant performance cost.

5.5.3 Other-Delimited Macro List %SCAN Squared Loop

In the previous subsection, the "%SCAN squared loop" method is introduced and operationalized to iterate a comma-delimited macro list. Although never recommended, the %SCAN squared loop method is again utilized here, albeit to iterate an asterisk-delimited macro list. Within the COUNT_LIST2 macro, note the two occurrences of %SCAN—the first of which is unnecessary:

```
%macro count_list2(list /* ast_delim list [REF] */);
%local cnt element;
%let cnt=1;
%do %while(%length(%scan(&&&list,&cnt,*))>1);
   %let element=%scan(&&&list,&cnt,*);
   %let cnt=%eval(&cnt+1);
   %end;
%eval(&cnt-1)
%mend;
```

The following invocation of COUNT_LIST2 demonstrates that the macro takes approximately 4.7 seconds to count (i.e., iterate across) the 3,000 elements within the asterisk-delimited macro list:

```
%let start=%sysfunc(datetime());
%put Elements: %count_list2(ast_testlist);
%put Runtime: %sysevalf(%sysfunc(datetime())-&start);
```

The primary inefficiency stems from the first %SCAN, which can be replaced with the COUNTW function. For example, within COUNT_LIST2, the %DO %WHILE loop must repeatedly evaluate the &&&LIST value (which resolves to the &TESTLIST macro list in this invocation).

However, note that %BQUOTE has now been removed from the macro, as it is no longer required to mask delimiting commas. Thus, because asterisks now delimit list elements, the COUNT_LIST2 macro takes far less time to complete than COUNT_LIST1, nearly halving the runtime to process the comma-delimited macro list.

As stated in the previous subsection, however, technical requirements and software readability requirements should also drive the definition of any user-defined data structure (including the selection of delimiter symbols). This is to say that the user-defined, comma-delimited macro list should not be excluded from your toolbelt solely because it is evaluated more slowly than macro lists having funkier delimiters.

5.5.4 Comma-Delimited Macro List with Single %SCAN

Abandoning the "%SCAN squared loop" debacle (demonstrated in the previous two subsections), a preferred, functionally equivalent method to iterate macro lists instead relies on the built-in COUNTW function. Thus, rather than relying on a %DO %WHILE loop to repeatedly evaluate the macro list during each iteration, the COUNTW method (aka, "single %SCAN" method) evaluates list size only once, and thereafter loops until that dimension threshold has been met.

Within the COUNT_LIST3 macro, note the single occurrence of COUNTW and the single occurrence of %SCAN:

```
%macro count_list3(list /* comma-delim list [REF] */);
%local cnt element;
%do cnt=1 %to %sysfunc(countw(%bquote(&&&list),','));
   %let element=%scan(%bquote(&&&list),&cnt,',');
   %end;
%eval(&cnt-1)
%mend;
```

The following invocation of COUNT_LIST3 demonstrates that the macro takes approximately 4.3 seconds to count (i.e., iterate across) the 3,000 elements within the comma-delimited macro list:

```
%let start=%sysfunc(datetime());
%put Elements: %count_list3(testlist);
```

```
%put Runtime: %sysevalf(%sysfunc(datetime())-&start);
```

As discussed in the preceding two subsections, some inefficiency is incurred by the use of commas to delimit the user-defined macro list. Because commas must be masked within macro functions (like %SCAN) or SAS functions (like COUNTW), %BQUOTE must be repeatedly implemented within COUNT_LIST3, which slows its performance.

5.5.5   Other-Delimited Macro List with Single %SCAN

Some inefficiency present in the previous iteration method can be eliminated by replacing a comma-delimited macro list with a macro list that defines a non-comma delimiter (such as the asterisk). Within the COUNT_LIST4 macro, note the single occurrence of %SCAN, and note the removal of the %BQUOTE masking function:

```
%macro count_list4(list /* ast-delim list [REF] */);
%local cnt element;
%do cnt=1 %to %sysfunc(countw(&&&list,*));
    %let element=%scan(&&&list,&cnt,*);
    %end;
%eval(&cnt-1)
%mend;
```

The following invocation of COUNT_LIST4 demonstrates that the macro takes approximately 2.3 seconds to count (i.e., iterate across) the 3,000 elements within the asterisk-delimited macro list:

```
%let start=%sysfunc(datetime());
%put Elements: %count_list4(ast_testlist);
%put Runtime: %sysevalf(%sysfunc(datetime())-&start);
```

This stellar performance nears the upper limits of tokenization and iteration of user-defined macro lists. However, far greater performance can be achieved through *indexed macro lists*, as demonstrated in the next subsection.

5.5.6   Iterating Indexed Macro Lists

The IDX_TESTLIST *indexed macro list* is created in Section 5.5.1; it contains the same sample data as both the comma-delimited macro list (&TESTLIST) and the asterisk-delimited macro list (&AST_TESTLIST), yet distributes elements across incrementally named macro variables, rather than within a single macro variable. This user-defined data structure (insofar as a collection of separate macro variables can arguably be termed a *data structure*—which is a debate for a subsequent edition) is advantageous for many operations, especially data structure iteration.

Of note, within this text, indexed macro lists are referenced without a preceding ampersand (unlike macro lists) because indexed macro lists always must be passed by reference, not value. For example, the IDX_TESTLIST indexed macro list includes the macro variables &IDX_TESTLIST_0 and &IDX_TESTLIST_1, the list's dimension variable and the list's first element, respectively. However, because no macro variable &IDX_TESTLIST is ever declared, the indexed macro list aggregate is consistently referenced as IDX_TESTLIST—not &IDX_TESTLIST.

Because indexed macro lists are never truly containerized (within a single data structure), no tokenization or decomposition is required to identify, reference, or operationalize their constituent elements. Moreover, the explicit indexing facilitates immediate access to any list element. Finally, list dimensions (i.e., total number of elements) are known at the time of list initialization, so these dimensions can be initialized as the "0" element of the indexed macro list, thus eliminating any subsequent need to count an indexed macro list.

For example, the functionally equivalent IDX_COUNT_LIST1 macro resolves to the number of elements within an indexed macro list:

```
%macro idx_count_list1(list /* indexed list [REF] */);
&&&list._0
%mend;
```

The following invocation of IDX_COUNT_LIST1 demonstrates that the macro takes approximately 0 seconds to count (i.e., iterate across) the 3,000 elements within the asterisk-delimited macro list:

```
%let start=%sysfunc(datetime());
%put Elements: %idx_count_list1(idx_testlist);
%put Runtime: %sysevalf(%sysfunc(datetime())-&start);
```

However, this could be considered cheating, given that the total number of elements does not need to be counted—because the &IDX_TESTLIST_0 macro variable is initialized to the count of total elements. Notwithstanding, it demonstrates the significant performance improvement in evaluating the size of an indexed macro list.

For a fairer comparison, the IDX_COUNT_LIST2 macro does iterate the IDX_TESTLIST indexed macro list, and iteratively initializes the &ELEMENT macro variable to each of the list's 3,000 constituent elements:

```
%macro idx_count_list2(list /* indexed list [REF] */);
%local cnt tot element;
%let tot=&&&list._0;
%do cnt=1 %to &tot;
    %let element=&&&list._&cnt;
    %end;
%eval(&cnt-1)
%mend;
```

Despite the iteration evinced by IDX_COUNT_LIST2, the invocation of IDX_COUNT_LIST2 nevertheless completes in less than 0.014 seconds:

```
%let start=%sysfunc(datetime());
%put Elements: %idx_count_list2(idx_testlist);
%put Runtime: %sysevalf(%sysfunc(datetime())-&start);
```

This runtime is more than 150 times faster than the fastest method of iterating an equivalent macro list, demonstrated by the COUNT_LIST4 macro in Section 5.5.5, and more than 600 times faster than the slowest method of iterating a macro list!!! This tremendous performance advantage occurs because no tokenization of delimiters is required—either to define or parse the indexed macro list—so the explicitly indexed values can be directly referenced and utilized.

In many cases, user-defined *macro lists* can be supplanted by user-defined *indexed macro lists* that can yield noticeable performance improvement without compromising functionality. Moreover, data structure versatility and robustness is typically improved because masking of list delimiters is no longer required.

5.6 SUMMARY

Iteration traverses data structures to perform some action or set of actions repeatedly. Iteration is essential as developers design reusable modules that leverage data structures; especially where user-defined data structures are employed, the methods that iterate and decompose these structures into their constituent elements often must be engineered. And because *iteration* denotes that some operation or action is occurring repetitively, it is essential that iteration be accurate, reliable, and meet performance objectives—because any flaws will be multiplied.

This chapter introduced software design concepts that differentiate iteration, including *internal iteration, external iteration, implicit iteration scope,* and *explicit iteration scope.* Internal iteration abstracts and hides looping mechanics from view, simplifying code and making it more concise and readable. External iteration, conversely, relies on various DO loops to perform operations repetitively.

Implicit iteration scope hides the scope of the data structure being iterated, whereas explicit iteration scope reveals the scope, requiring elements to be referenced through counters or subscripted indexes.

Design concepts were contrasted through techniques that rely on internal and external iteration to parse data structures, including data sets, SAS arrays, user-defined macro lists, and user-defined indexed macro lists. The EXECUTE subroutine was introduced as a method to iterate over a control table in *series,* and the SYSTASK command was introduced as a method that can support spawning *parallel* data-driven operations in separate SAS sessions.

Chapter 6.

PROCEDURAL COMMUNICATION

This chapter has the following objectives:

- ❖ Demonstrate the importance of the procedural *signature* in defining a module's parameters (inputs) and return values (outputs).

- ❖ Demonstrate the components of a *signature*, including parameter name, order, data type, identification method, and call method.

- ❖ Disambiguate parameters, arguments, variables, and values.

- ❖ Discuss *positional* and *keyword* parameters.

- ❖ Introduce *call-by-value* and *call-by-reference* methods of passing arguments.

- ❖ Discuss the VARARGS option in supporting multi-element arguments within the FCMP procedure, and the PARMBUFF option in supporting multi-element macro arguments.

- ❖ Demonstrate the use of returning *return values* and *return codes* from called modules.

Procedural communication facilitates the dynamic functionality for which procedural abstraction is often sought. Yes, abstract design does support dynamic functionality—it's right there on the book cover! However, *procedural communication* describes the dynamic inputs to callable software modules that engender dynamic output, as well as the return values and return codes produced by callable modules and evaluated by calling programs. And just as procedural abstraction more generically describes the abstraction of *all* callable software modules (including applications, procedures, functions, and subroutines), procedural communication and its methods, too, should be generalized.

Procedural communication imbues software with configurability and flexibility, but not in a limitless sense. During software design, SAS practitioners must evaluate (and sometimes prioritize) in which ways a procedure is intended to flex, and often must describe the format or range of acceptable input, as well as that of *exceptional* (i.e., invalid) input. In so doing, a *signature* is born, which describes the required (or optional) inputs for a callable module, as well as the outputs that may be produced. Input and output represent control data, with the former telling a called module *how to behave*, and the latter telling the calling module how the called module *did behave*.

Even after selecting specific control data that should be passed to a module, a multitude of design considerations can abound. For example, consider the requirement of passing a SAS data set name to a user-defined function. The data set name could be passed as a string literal—or as a data set variable—or as macro variable—or as the name of a macro variable (that holds the data set name)—or as a value in a configuration file. Each option can support data-driven design, and each has design consequences that should be understood and evaluated.

The sometimes conflated terms *parameter, argument, variable,* and *value* are defined, discussed, and demonstrated in Section 6.3

This chapter explores various methods of passing control data to callable modules, including distinguishing keyword from positional parameters, and call-by-reference from call-by-value methods. Collection parameters are also explored, which can pass multiple, similarly typed elements to a single parameter, further supporting scalability of control data.

Parameter design concepts are universal within SAS data-driven design, irrespective of the type or format of control data being referenced by a software module. That is, whether passing an argument, list, array, or table, you will need to make decisions about whether those control data should be passed by value or by reference, and whether they should be passed singly (as a scalar) or as a collection that must be iterated. Concepts are demonstrated using both user-defined macros and user-defined FCMP functions and subroutines.

6.1   PROCEDURAL ABSTRACTION IS NOT ENOUGH

Procedural abstraction alone should not be misconstrued as a tell-tale indicator of data-driven design, as procedural abstraction is evident in even the most egregiously hardcoded of callable software modules; neither should procedural abstraction be confused with software flexibility. For example, the following code produces static results each time it is executed:

Section 13.3.2 includes a user-defined function that demonstrates procedural abstraction despite abominably hardcoded design

```
%macro beetlejuice();
%local i;
%do i=1 %to 3;
   %put Beetlejuice!;
   %end;
%mend;


%beetlejuice;
```

The BEETLEJUICE macro demonstrates procedural abstraction, in that Beetlejuice is conjured when he is thrice summoned, as displayed in the SAS log:

```
Beetlejuice!
Beetlejuice!
Beetlejuice!
```

Although this procedural abstraction could be considered beneficial, in that it is more efficient to type %BEETLEJUICE once rather than "Beetlejuice!" three times, the macro nevertheless lacks data-driven design; no control data are passed, and no communication occurs between the calling and the called module—aside from the macro function call itself.

Section 6.7 demonstrates data-driven design in which dynamic inputs are supplied by the system or environment, not by the calling program

Additional software modularity can be achieved by saving the BEETLEJUICE macro to a separate program file:

```
* saved as d:\sas\beetlejuice.sas;
%macro beetlejuice();
%local i;
```

```
%do i=1 %to 3;
   %put Beetlejuice!;
   %end;
%mend;
```

However, despite now calling BEETLEJUICE from a separate program, which demonstrates software modularity, the invocation still passes no control data to the macro:

```
%let loc=d:\sas\;      * USER MUST CHANGE LOCATION *;
%include "&loc.beetlejuice.sas";
%beetlejuice;
```

No dynamic input equates to *no dynamic output*, so BEETLEJUICE will produce identical results each time it is run. This is not necessarily *poor* design, and could meet software technical requirements; however, it does not represent *data-driven* design.

Conversely, just as it is possible to have software that demonstrates procedural abstraction yet lacks data-driven design, it is also possible to attain data-driven design that lacks procedural abstraction—by statically referencing an external control file within the code.

However, when parameters are defined within a procedure or other module, and dynamic inputs are passed, procedural abstraction can support data-driven design—facilitating software flexibility and configurability through dynamic functionality. As the quintessential communicator in data-driven design, this flow of control data can include not only dynamic inputs (arguments) being passed *to* software modules, but also dynamic outputs (return codes and return values) being returned *from* these modules.

6.2   IT ALL STARTS WITH A SIGNATURE

Signatures are defined in Section 3.1.2

A *signature* lives inside a procedural implementation and defines (i.e., declares) the parameters that can be passed to a software module. Signatures ensure that only prescribed parameters in predetermined formats can be passed to modules, thus restricting the flow of control data into modules. As software modules are often conceptualized as black boxes, having known functionality yet concealed methods, signatures define the pinholes through which control data can permeate modules to instruct software.

For each parameter that is defined, the signature should define the following attributes:

- **Name** – the name of the parameter, with which its argument will also be referenced.
- **Identification Method** – the method (i.e., positional or keyword) through which the argument is identified.
- **Position** – the order of the parameter, with respect to other parameters that are defined.
- **Call Method** – the method (i.e., call by value or call by reference) through which arguments are passed, with the former being the default for passing variables and the latter being the default for passing data objects such as SAS data sets.
- **Data Type** – the data type (i.e., character or numeric).
- **Data Format** – the built-in or user-defined SAS format an argument must exhibit before it is passed.

> Section 4.3.1 demonstrates the refactoring of a user-defined macro procedure to modify a parameter's data type and format to facilitate a more readable invocation

Procedural communication does not exist without parameters, and parameters do not exist without signatures, so the signature constitutes the most important component of callable software modules—at least where data-driven design is concerned. The signature is first conceptualized within design specs, and should be defined early in the software development life cycle (SDLC). Although the signature is ultimately prescribed within code (i.e., within a module's implementation), the signature is also abstractly represented in a module's specification—the documentation that instructs developers how to invoke and interact with the module.

Where straightforward procedures and functions are defined within code rather than within external documentation, such as is common within user-defined macros, functions, and subroutines, the signature itself—the literal code—may belong to the implementation but be borrowed by the specification. Figure 3.1 demonstrates this end-user development paradigm, showing the signature at the intersection of the implementation and the specification.

The following sections contrast methods in which parameters can be designed, and in which arguments can be passed. In all cases, the signature defines and declares all parameters, and arguments follow suit. First, some disambiguation of terms will facilitate this exploration.

6.3   PARAMETERS, ARGUMENTS, VARIABLES, & VALUES

Parameters are the lifeblood of procedures because they supply the dynamic inputs that *flexible* procedural abstraction requires. They allow end users or calling processes to whisper into the ears of applications, procedures, functions, subroutines, macros, and other software modules, providing dynamic instruction to effect dynamic functionality.

The terms *parameter* and *argument* are often conflated or used interchangeably, so some introduction and detangling is warranted. In many circles and for many purposes, using *parameter* (or *argument*) to refer broadly to both parameters and arguments will not dilute the concept being conveyed, and might even be considered acceptable. Within a procedural abstraction discussion, however, the very specific definitions of these distinct terms, as well as their relation to *variable* and *value*, must preface any further dialog.

The International Organization for Standardization (ISO) defines a *parameter* as a "constant, variable, or expression that is used to pass values between software modules."[49] ISO similarly defines a *formal parameter* as a "variable used in a software module to represent data or program elements that are to be passed to the module by a calling module."[50] Both *parameter* and *formal parameter* are commonly used to denote the variable(s) declared within a callable module's signature, with preference given within this text to *parameter* because it is far more common in SAS literature.

Parameters *prescribe* the data type, position, and other characteristics to which corresponding input (arguments) must adhere. They are the conduits through which arguments are passed to software modules—from the *invocation* to the *implementation*. And whereas parameters are *defined* within a procedural implementation, they are *described* within the procedural specification—the documentation that conveys usage, functionality, context, and caveats to end users.

Procedural specification, implementation, and invocation are introduced in Sections 3.2, 3.3, and 3.4, respectively

ISO defines an *argument* as a "constant, variable, or expression used in a call to a software module to specify data or program elements to be passed to that module."[51] Literature denoting *formal parameters* (in lieu of *parameters*) typically denotes *actual parameters* (in lieu of *arguments*), and any reader who has ever suffered through even a single chapter alternately referencing *formal parameters* and *actual parameters* understands the clear decision to adopt the parameter-argument distinction herein!

Whereas parameters are declared and exist solely within a callable software module, arguments are the messages passed from the calling module. When arguments are passed *by value*, those messages are unidirectional, from the calling to the called module; however, passing arguments *by reference* allows the called module to modify the arguments it receives, after which the modified values have also been changed within the calling module.

Call by value and *call by reference*, two methods of passing arguments, are defined and discussed in Sections 6.5.1 and 6.5.2, respectively

Arguments can vary substantially in scope, with some directing entire software applications and others influencing only a procedure or a function. But in all cases, software modularity must first have encapsulated and defined that scope—as an application, program, procedure, or other module. This modularity facilitates the data independence pillar of data-driven design, by allowing arguments to live outside of software modules while influencing the code therein.

Within a procedure, parameters initialize variables—either to a value passed from an argument or to a default value (if no argument is passed). ISO defines a *variable* as a "data item whose value can change during program execution."[52] Variables provide variability within software modules through data abstraction; however, only those variables initialized from parameters facilitate the procedural abstraction that data-driven design requires, by linking the dynamic arguments *outside* a procedure to the dynamic values *inside* it.

The LEAKYPETE macro, demonstrated in Section 6.7, illustrates the design flaw that occurs when variables are referenced, yet not parameterized, by macros and other modules

In each of the following four functionally equivalent examples, the &INIT macro variable is initialized to the value "Hello"; however, the examples differ in whether parameters are declared, and in whether arguments are passed.

Within the NOPARAMS macro, no *parameters* are declared; the %LOCAL statement declares the &INIT local macro *variable*, and the %LET statement initializes &INIT to the *value* "Hello":

```
%macro noparams();
%local init;
%let init=Hello;
%put &init;
%mend;


%noparams;
```

NOPARAMS demonstrates procedural abstraction because its functionality is hidden inside its definition, but does not demonstrate data-driven design, as no control data are passed; the macro cannot receive instruction from calling modules, so its functionality is concrete and cannot be varied.

In a functionally equivalent macro definition and invocation, the INIT *parameter* is declared and initializes the &INIT local macro *variable* to the default *value* "Hello" (when no argument is passed):

```
%macro noargs(init=Hello);
%put &init;
%mend;


%noargs;
```

Note that by default, NOARGS declares &INIT as a local macro variable (having scope only inside NOARGS while it executes), without the necessity to declare &INIT using the %LOCAL statement. In this example, passing a Null value (i.e., calling NOARGS without arguments) still conveys information and alters macro functionality, so this demonstrates configurability.

In a third, functionally equivalent example, the ONEARG macro invocation passes the INIT *argument* "Hello" to the INIT *parameter* (inside the ONEARG macro), where the INIT *parameter* initializes the &INIT local macro *variable* to the *value* "Hello":

```
%macro onearg(init=);
%put &init;
%mend;


%onearg(init=Hello);
```

Note that the INIT parameter is a *keyword* parameter; thus, the parameter name (INIT) as well as its argument "Hello" must appear in the macro invocation, delimited by an equal sign.

In a fourth, functionally equivalent example, the ONEARG macro invocation passes the INIT *argument* "Hello" to the INIT *parameter* (inside the ONEARG macro), where the INIT *parameter* initializes the &INIT local macro *variable* to the *value* "Hello":

```
%macro onearg(init);
%put &init;
%mend;


%onearg(Hello);
```

This example differs in that the INIT parameter has been changed from a keyword parameter to a positional parameter. The parameter name (INIT) is no longer included in the macro invocation, nor is the equal sign required in the %MACRO statement's declaration of INIT.

In the last three examples, a one-to-one relationship exists between parameters and arguments, so a developer commingling terms (between *parameter* and *argument*) would likely cause neither panic nor confusion. As arguments increase in complexity, however, such as modules in which multi-element parameters (i.e., *collections*) are declared, the use of accurate nomenclature for these distinct constructs becomes more important.

6.4 PARAMETER IDENTIFICATION

Control data that cannot be universally and unambiguously identified lack value because they cannot be trusted to be interpreted and operationalized accurately. Configuration files, for example, often rely on *key-value pairs* to ensure that values are mapped to their corresponding variables. Arguments, similarly, must be able to be identified as belonging to a specific parameter, especially where a module's signature defines multiple parameters.

Key-value pairs are discussed in Section 16.3.5

In general, control data are distinguished through one of two methods—*position* or *keyword*. That is, you either know *where* to look for a specific value, or you know *how* to search for that specific value. Both methods provide equivalent argument-passing functionality, and both keyword and positional parameters can be declared within the same SAS macro; however, all positional parameters always must precede all keyword parameters. FCMP functions and subroutines do differ (from SAS macros) in that they support only positional parameters.

Section 11.1.3 demonstrates a user-defined macro that declares both keyword and positional parameters

6.4.1 Positional Parameters

Positional parameters are favored when only one or a few arguments must be passed. Built-in functions and subroutines rely almost exclusively on positional parameters, as they typically declare no more than a handful.

Positional arguments always must appear (within the invocation) in the order in which their respective parameters are declared within the module's signature.

For example, the macro function CONVERT transforms a temperature value from Fahrenheit to Celsius:

```
* converts fahrenheit to celsius;
* provides 3 decimal precision;
%macro convert(f /* fahrenheit temp */);
%sysfunc(putn(%sysevalf((&f-32)*(5/9)),8.3))
%mend;


%put %convert(212);
```

The single argument (212) does not risk misidentification because no other parameters are defined; thus, there is no need to specify the F parameter by keyword within the invocation. Also note that because the F parameter is declared as a positional parameter, no equal sign is required after its declaration (within the %MACRO statement).

But what happens when a new analyst decides to extend the functionality of CONVERT so that it can additionally convert Celsius to Fahrenheit? This expanded functionality (CONVERT_EXP) follows:

```
* converts fahrenheit to celsius;
* or celsius to fahrenheit;
* provides 3 decimal precision;
* only F or C param can be specified;
%macro convert_exp(f /* fahrenheit temp */,
    c /* celsius temp */);
%if (%length(&f)>0 and %length(&c)>0)
    or (%length(&f)=0 and %length(&c)=0) %then %return;
%if %length(&f)>0 %then %do;
    %sysfunc(putn(%sysevalf((&f-32)*(5/9)),8.3))
    %end;
%else %do;
    %sysfunc(putn(%sysevalf((&c*(9/5)+32)),8.3))
    %end;
%mend;
```

The overhaul succeeds, and CONVERT_EXP now converts Fahrenheit and Celsius interchangeably; supplying an argument to the first parameter converts Fahrenheit to Celsius, and supplying an argument to the second parameter converts Celsius to Fahrenheit. Some exception handling has been added, so if *both* F and C are specified, or if *neither* F nor C are specified, the %RETURN statement will terminate the macro.

However, the invocation to convert 100°C to 212°F is not straightforward because end users must remember the order in which the measurement systems must be specified:

```
%put %convert_exp(,100);
```

A preferred alternative would be to create a new function that converts Celsius to Fahrenheit or, if both functionalities *must* be combined into a single function, to designate the arguments with keyword parameters to ensure that the temperature systems are not confused.

A separate requirement illustrates a better use of an additional positional parameter—the need to make CONVERT more flexible so that the number of decimal degrees can be specified by the end user. The FTOC (Fahrenheit to Celsius) macro function now demonstrates this configurability, in which the optional DIG parameter has been added:

```
* converts fahrenheit to celsius;
* F required, quits with error if missing or non-num;
* DIG [OPT] specifies decimals, defaults to integer;
%macro ftoc(f /* fahrenheit temp */,
    dig /* [OPT] decimal digits 1 to 9 */);
%if %length(&f)=0 %then %do;
    %let syscc=4;
    %put ERROR: First argument (temp) missing;
    %return;
    %end;
%else %if %sysfunc(findc(&f,-.,DK)) %then %do;
    %let syscc=4;
    %put ERROR: First argument (temp) must be a number;
    %return;
    %end;
%if %length(&dig)=0 %then %let dig=0;
%else %if %sysfunc(notdigit(&dig)) %then %do;
```

```
    %let syscc=4;
    %put ERROR: Second argument (decimals) must be a
number;
    %return;
    %end;
%else %if %sysevalf(&dig<1) %then %do;
    %let dig=1;
    %put NOTE: DIG parameter set to lowest value (1);
    %end;
%else %if %sysevalf(&dig>9) %then %do;
    %let dig=9;
    %put NOTE: DIG parameter set to highest value (9);
    %end;
%sysfunc(putn(%sysevalf((&f-32)*(5/9)),15.&dig))
%mend;
```

FTOC now defines one required argument (temperature in degrees Fahrenheit) and one optional argument (number of decimals precision). Additional exception handling now terminates the macro with a runtime error (&SYSCC set to 4) if the F argument is missing, or if either the F or DIG arguments contain non-numeric characters. An additional note is printed to the SAS log if the DIG argument is not between one and nine.

The following four functional tests show the FTOC invocation and log, demonstrating functionality when valid arguments are supplied:

```
* no decimals;
%put %ftoc(36);
2

* decimals in temperature;
%put %ftoc(98.6);
37

* brrrrrr below zero;
%put %ftoc(-22.3);
-30

* 3 decimals;
```

```
%put %ftoc(36,3);
2.222
```

The use of inequivalent parameters—the first, a temperature, and the second, the number of decimal places of precision—represents a far superior use of positional parameters than the aborted attempt (CONVERT_EXP) that declared two temperature parameters (for Fahrenheit and Celsius). The placement of the required parameter in the first position and optional parameter in the second position also represents a best practice, as all required parameters should precede optional ones (if possible).

Equally important in functional testing is a demonstration of what software does under *exceptional* conditions—when invalid inputs are supplied. The following five tests show the FTOC invocation and log, demonstrating functionality when invalid arguments are supplied or the first (i.e., required) argument is omitted:

```
* too few decimals;
%put %ftoc(36,0);
NOTE: DIG parameter set to lowest value (1)
2.2


* too many decimals;
%put %ftoc(36,10);
NOTE: DIG parameter set to highest value (9)
2.222222222


* missing temperature;
%put %ftoc();
ERROR: First argument (temp) missing


* nonnumeric temperature;
%put %ftoc(thirty-six,5);
ERROR: First argument (temp) must be a number


* nonumeric decimals;
%put %ftoc(36,five);
ERROR: Second argument (decimals) must be a number
```

The use of log messages that are prefaced with "ERROR:," "NOTE:," or "WARNING:" aids in manual log review because the SAS application highlights these messages by default—with notes shown in blue, warnings in green, and runtime errors in red. Moreover, the &SYSCC automatic macro variable is set to 4 when the corresponding ERROR messages are printed, enabling developers to detect runtime errors programmatically.

Positional parameters are common in functions and other less complex modules that require few parameters to be defined. However, as the complexity of a signature grows, and especially when several optional arguments may be missing (in which case, extra commas must be added as placeholders), the use of keyword parameters is recommended.

Positional identification of arguments maintained within configuration files is demonstrated in Section 16.3.4

6.4.2 Keyword Parameters

Keyword parameters identify arguments by name (or a representation thereof) to the end user calling a software module. They are beneficial when arguments represent equivalent constructs (e.g., two temperatures, as depicted in Section 6.4.1), or when the number of arguments could cause confusion—for example, requiring a developer to "count the commas" to identify to which parameter a specific argument maps.

Refactoring the CONVERT_EXP macro function from Section 6.4.1, keyword parameters can aid in the development of a single macro that converts Fahrenheit and Celsius temperatures interchangeably:

```
* converts fahrenheit to celsius;
* or celsius to fahrenheit;
* provides 3 decimal precision;
* only F or C param can be specified;
%macro convert_exp(f= /* fahrenheit temp */,
   c= /* celsius temp */);
%if (%length(&f)>0 and %length(&c)>0)
   or (%length(&f)=0 and %length(&c)=0) %then %return;
%if %length(&f)>0 %then %do;
   %sysfunc(putn(%sysevalf((&f-32)*(5/9)),8.3))
   %end;
%else %do;
   %sysfunc(putn(%sysevalf((&c*(9/5)+32)),8.3))
   %end;
%mend;
```

The following invocations and output demonstrate converting from Fahrenheit to Celsius and vice versa:

```
%put %convert_exp(f=98.6);
37.000
```

```
%put %convert_exp(c=100);
212.000
```

The inclusion of the F and C parameters now clarifies the CONVERT_EXP invocation, ensuring that developers never mistakenly apply the wrong conversion. Moreover, the second invocation of CONVERT_EXP with 100°C no longer requires a Null value (representing the F argument) to precede the C argument.

Built-in functions and subroutines almost exclusively rely on positional rather than keyword parameters because these modules provide specific, concise functionality. After all, functional discretion boasts that a function should do "one and only one thing." This explains why the FCMP procedure supports the declaration of positional parameters only—not keyword—because FCMP exclusively creates user-defined functions and subroutines.

However, when the number of parameters grows beyond a fistful, as is especially common when invoking a software application (like SAS) or calling a procedure (like SORT), keyword parameters are more common. For example, when the SAS application (sas.exe) is launched from the command prompt or a batch file, only keyword parameters can be specified.

The following invocation of the SAS application (from the command prompt) specifies that the MEMSIZE system option should be set to 8GB, the SORTSIZE system option set to 4GB, and the FULLSTIMER system option activated:

Section 16.2 demonstrates use of the SAS configuration file (sasv9.cfg), which also can be used to specify SAS system options at initialization of the SAS application

```
c:\progra~1\sashome\sasfoundation\9.4\sas.exe -memsize
8g -sortsize 4g -fullstimer
```

Note the varied format within the system options, with SORTSIZE and MEMSIZE each requiring an argument, but FULLSTIMER requiring only the parameter name (i.e., FULLSTIMER) itself. Many parameters for which only two valid values exist (e.g., FULLSTIMER and NOFULLSTIMER) can be passed in this latter format. Also note that only relevant system options were referenced; thus, there is no need for an endless train of commas, as would be required were SAS system options conveyed positionally.

If it is unknown, the location of the SAS application (sas.exe) can be shown by querying the SASROOT environmental variable:

```
%put %sysget(SASROOT);
C:\Program Files\SASHome\SASFoundation\9.4
```

When the new SAS session opens, its updated system options can be demonstrated using the following statements:

```
* demonstrates the 8g memsize;
%put %sysfunc(getoption(memsize));
8589934592


* demonstrates the 4g sortsize;
%put %sysfunc(getoption(sortsize));
4294967296


* demonstrates FULLSTIMER activation;
%put %sysfunc(getoption(fullstimer));
FULLSTIMER
```

Where the parameter landscape is vast and complex, as is especially common for applications and procedures, keyword parameters simplify invocation, and ensure arguments are passed (bound) to the correct parameters.

6.5   CALL METHOD IDENTIFICATION

Callable software modules are executed using an invocation or *call*, which ISO defines as the "transfer of control from one software module to another, usually with the implication that control will be returned to the calling module."[53] Within a procedural signature, the *call method* describes how an argument is passed to the module.

Call by value (also *pass by value*) passes a copy of the argument, whereas *call by reference* (also *pass by reference*) passes only the argument name (or a reference thereto). Because call by value always passes a copy, the original argument (e.g., the literal value, constant, or variable) cannot be altered in the calling program—even if the called module modifies the argument. However, when an argument is passed by reference, changes made to the argument within a called module are available in the calling module; the original—not a copy—has been modified.

Thus, call by reference is sometimes considered to be riskier (than call by value) because the arguments themselves—the procedural input—can be modified. In this bilateral communication, the input essentially also operates as output. However, call by reference is often more efficient because no copying of an argument is required. For example, when passing a collection argument (like a lengthy list or an array), you would not want to copy hundreds or thousands of elements unnecessarily, so call by reference is typically employed. Similarly, data object complexity can dictate that call by reference be used—for example, by passing a data set *name* to a SAS procedure, in lieu of copying the *actual data* maintained within the data set.

Both Base SAS and the SAS macro language support user-defined call-by-value and call-by-reference methods; however, these are operationalized uniquely, with far more formalized methods existing for FCMP functions and subroutines than for user-defined macros. Within the FCMP procedure, arguments are passed by value by default, whereas the OUTARGS statement enumerates arguments passed by reference. Although FCMP subroutines are more often associated with call by reference and the ability to modify arguments (within the calling program), this reputation is a bit of #fakenews, as both FCMP functions and subroutines equally support call-by-value and call-by-reference methods.

Call-by-value and call-by-reference methods are not officially defined within the SAS macro language, although they can be mimicked with ease; passing a macro variable (&ARG) passes the argument by value, whereas passing a macro variable *name* (ARG) passes the argument by reference. Greater argument complexity, such as a lengthy macro variable list or a macro variable containing special characters, often dictates that a user-defined macro should pass an argument by reference, not by value.

Each call method delivers distinct functionality, and in the end, SAS practitioners will need to choose the right tool for each challenge. Many user-defined functions or subroutines even require a mix of both call-by-value and call-by-reference parameters to be declared to meet some functional objective. The following subsections further explore and contrast call-by-value and call-by-reference methods, as demonstrated in both Base SAS (i.e., the FCMP procedure) and the SAS macro language.

6.5.1   Call by Value

ISO defines *call by value* as "a method of passing parameters, in which the calling module provides to the called module the actual value of the parameter to be passed."[54] As introduced in Section 6.5, call-by-value methods pass a local copy of the argument to a module, and because the called module uses only a *copy* to deliver its functionality, the called module lacks the ability to modify the argument in the calling program.

Call by value is typically used when arguments contain scalar values or simple structures. Thus, user-defined functions and subroutines created using the FCMP procedure pass all arguments by value by default.

The following FTOC (Fahrenheit to Celsius) function converts Fahrenheit temperatures to Celsius:

```
proc fcmp outlib=sasuser.myfuncs.temps;
    function ftoc(f);
        c=(f-32)*(5/9);
        return(c);
        endfunc;
quit;
```

The reality that user-defined macro functions *resolve* rather than *return* values is discussed in Section 3.6.1

The FUNCTION statement declares the FTOC function, and the F parameter is implicitly declared as call by value. The C variable is initialized to the Celsius value, and is subsequently returned to the calling process by the RETURN function. At no point is the FTOC function able to modify the F variable in the calling program.

The following DATA steps create the Templist data set that contains Fahrenheit temperatures, after which FTOC is called to convert these values from Fahrenheit (45°F and 36°F) to Celsius (7.22°C and 2.22°C):

```
options cmplib=sasuser.myfuncs;

data templist;
    length fahrenheit 8;
    format fahrenheit 8.2;
    fahrenheit=45; output;
    fahrenheit=36; output;
run;
```

```
data newtemps;
   set templist;
   length celsius 8;
   format celsius 8.2;
   celsius=ftoc(fahrenheit);
run;
```

As invoked within the second DATA step, FTOC passes a copy of Fahrenheit (as an argument) to the F parameter. Thus, FTOC has no access to the Fahrenheit variable; it can read F but can modify only C.

Call methods are less formalized in the SAS macro language than in the FCMP procedure, but call by value can be operationalized by passing a macro variable (e.g., &VAR) to a macro. Whereas the FCMP procedure *prescribes* (with the OUTARGS statement) which variables are passed by reference, SAS macros can only implicitly convey call method based on how arguments are utilized within a macro. Thus, it becomes critical that SAS practitioners describe within SAS macro comments (or other documentation) the call method employed by macro parameters, lest users be relegated to scouring the code for contextual queues. The [REF] comment is demonstrated in this text as a method of identifying call-by-reference parameters in a macro signature.

The ONEARG macro declares the INIT parameter, after which ONEARG is invoked, and &MSG is passed by value:

```
%macro onearg(init);
%put &init;
%mend;

%let msg=Hello!;
%onearg(&msg);
```

The log displays the parameterized message Hello! But here's where things get wonky within the SAS macro language. Despite having passed &MSG "by value," ONEARG could nevertheless still modify &MSG because it is a global macro variable—having scope both inside and outside the ONEARG macro. Thus, the SAS macro language can only *approximate* call by value.

For example, the updated code now reinitializes &MSG within the ONEARG macro:

```
%macro onearg(init);
%let msg=Goodbye!;
%put &init;
%mend;

%let msg=Hello!;
%onearg(&msg);
%put &=msg;
```

The log demonstrates that Hello! is still passed to ONEARG and printed within the macro, but when ONEARG terminates, the reinitialized &MSG is printed to the log:

```
%onearg(&msg);
Hello!
%put &=msg;
MSG=Goodbye!
```

This reinitialization would be impossible in true call-by-value methods. Thus, even local macro variables will continue to have scope when nested macros are called, and can be modified (by called processes) even when passed in this manner. SAS documentation describes this inherited scope:

> "Scopes can be nested, like boxes within boxes. For example, suppose you have a macro A that creates the macro variable LOC1 and a macro B that creates the macro variable LOC2. If the macro B is nested (executed) within the macro A, LOC1 is local to both A and B. However, LOC2 is local only to B."[55]

Consider the CALLING_PGM macro, which declares, initializes, and passes the local macro variable &GREETING; because ONEARG is nested within (i.e., invoked by) CALLING_PGM, ONEARG is able to modify the value of &GREETING in both the called (ONEARG) and calling (CALLING_PGM) macros:

```
%macro onearg(init);
%let greeting=Goodbye!;
%put &init;
%mend;
```

```
%macro calling_pgm();
%local greeting;
%let greeting=Hello!;
%onearg(&greeting);
%put &=greeting;
%mend;


%calling_pgm();
```

The log demonstrates that once again, ONEARG is able to modify &GREETING—the argument that was passed "by value:"

```
%calling_pgm();
Hello!
GREETING=Goodbye!
```

The ability to change arguments in the calling program is not typical of call-by-value methods; thus, these examples only *approximate* call methods in the SAS macro language. Nevertheless, call by value remains the most common method of passing arguments to SAS macros.

However, as argument complexity or volume increases, call by reference often becomes a more tenable call method than call by value, and is supported by both Base SAS (i.e., the FCMP procedure) and the SAS macro language.

6.5.2   Call by Reference

ISO defines *call by reference* (also *call by location* or *call by address*) as "a method for passing parameters, in which the calling module provides to the called module the address of the parameter to be passed."[56] Call-by-reference methods pass a reference or pointer (of a variable or object) to the software module rather than passing a copy of the argument. Because the software module has access to the actual data object, not a copy, when the data object is modified *inside* the module, it is also modified *outside* the module—in the calling program.

Call by reference is relied upon when a called module needs to modify the arguments it is passed. In Section 6.5.1, the FTOC function does not modify the temperature it is passed, but rather makes a copy, uses that copy within the function, and returns the result as a separate return value. That return value is subsequently initialized to a new variable within the calling program; thus, both the Fahrenheit and Celsius temperatures are retained.

To achieve similar functionality, a subroutine could be defined in lieu of a function. The FCMP procedure in Section 6.5.1 has been amended to declare the SUB_FTOC subroutine:

```
proc fcmp outlib=sasuser.myfuncs.temps;
    function ftoc(f);
        c=(f-32)*(5/9);
        return(c);
        endfunc;
    subroutine sub_ftoc(f, c);
        outargs c;
        if n(f) then c=(f-32)*(5/9);
        endsub;
quit;
```

SUB_FTOC requires that two arguments—representing Fahrenheit and Celsius temperatures—be passed, with the OUTARGS statement specifying C is passed by reference. When a Fahrenheit value is passed, its missing Celsius equivalent value is computed, but when F is missing, C is not computed.

For example, the following DATA step reads the Templist data set (created in Section 6.5.1) that contains only Fahrenheit values, and calls SUB_FTOC to convert Celsius values and save them in the Celsius variable:

```
options cmplib=sasuser.myfuncs;

data _null_;
    set templist;
    length celsius 8;
    call sub_ftoc(fahrenheit, celsius);
    put fahrenheit= celsius=;
run;
```

The log demonstrates the successful conversion:

```
NOTE: Variable celsius is uninitialized.
fahrenheit=45.00 celsius=7.2222222222
fahrenheit=36.00 celsius=2.2222222222
```

If the "variable is uninitialized" note is particularly vexing to you, the MISSING subroutine eliminates the note by initializing Celsius to a missing value:

```
data _null_;
   set templist;
   length celsius 8;
   call missing(celsius);
   call sub_ftoc(fahrenheit, celsius);
   put fahrenheit= celsius=;
run;
```

Note that the invocation of SUB_FTOC, which passes Celsius as an argument, requires that Celsius first be declared as a new variable in the DATA step. This differs from functions, which can be used to initialize a variable that has never been declared.

This difference is even starker when user-defined functions and subroutines are called in the SAS macro language, using the %SYSFUNC function and %SYSCALL statement, respectively.

For example, the FTOC function can be invoked directly by %SYSFUNC and can pass a literal as an argument to convert 45° Fahrenheit to 7.22° Celsius:

```
%put %sysfunc(FTOC(45));
```

Alternatively, the &F macro variable could be initialized and passed to FTOC to produce the same result:

```
%let f=45;
%put %sysfunc(FTOC(&f));
```

However, %SYSCALL cannot similarly call user-defined subroutines because %SYSCALL only accepts arguments that are macro variable names—that is, macro variables stripped of their ampersands. Thus, to use the SUB_FTOC subroutine to convert 45° Fahrenheit to 7.22° Celsius, the following convolution—the explicit declaration of &F and &C—is required:

```
%let f=45;
%let c=.;
%syscall sub_ftoc(f,c);
%put &=f &=c;
```

Note that &C must be initialized to a period (.), which represents a numeric missing value. Despite these differences, both FTOC (which demonstrates call by value) and SUB_FTOC (which demonstrates call by reference) convert the temperatures, and both can be called within the DATA step or through the SAS macro language.

Three methods of passing tabular data via arguments are demonstrated in Section 10.4, although Section 11.1 demonstrates the often preferred method of maintaining tabular data as a SAS data set

Call by reference is required when you need to modify the value of arguments (in the calling program), as demonstrated in the previous FCMP examples; however, call by reference is also the call method of choice for passing complex or voluminous data—and this is true of both built-in and user-defined modules.

Section 6.5.1 introduces the ONEARG macro that is used to print a message to the log, as passed by an argument. But what occurs when even a modicum of complexity is added to that argument, such as a comma? This modification follows:

```
%macro onearg(init);
%put &init;
%mend;


%let msg=Hello, my name is Pinky! Have you seen my
sparkly shoes?;
%onearg(&msg);
```

The log demonstrates the failure, in that &MSG could not be passed, as SAS interpreted the comma as a delimiter token rather than part of the message:

```
%onearg(&msg);
ERROR: More positional parameters found than defined.
```

The macro facility has interpreted "Hello" as the first argument and "my name is Pinky! Have you seen my sparkly shoes?" as the second—believing the comma to fall betwixt arguments rather than between a salutation and an introduction. The simple solution is to pass the macro variable's name (MSG)—not its value (&MSG)—to the macro, thereby removing comma complexity from the invocation:

```
%macro onearg(init /* [REF] */);
%put &&&init;
```

```
%mend;

%let msg=Hello, my name is Pinky! Have you seen my pink
nails?;
%onearg(msg);
```

In *referring* to the macro variable's name (MSG), the ONEARG invocation simulates call by *reference* within the SAS macro language. Inside the ONEARG macro, &INIT now resolves to "MSG," so three ampersands (&&&INIT) are required to resolve the value of the &MSG macro variable—the message to be printed. Thus, calling by reference in the SAS macro language effectively adds a level of abstraction, in that the macro facility first tokenizes &&&INIT (which resolves to &MSG), and next tokenizes &MSG.

Abstraction levels are discussed in Section 2.2

As discussed in Section 6.5.1, call methods are an inexact discipline within the SAS macro language, and to reiterate, global macro variables demonstrate global scope in that they can be modified within both calling and called modules. Notwithstanding, far more complex data can be passed by reference to SAS macros. For example, exhausted by passing dozens of configurable arguments to a user-defined macro, a savvy SAS practitioner might instead opt to pass a single argument—*by reference*—that names a configuration file that contains equivalent control data, stored in key-value pairs.

Equivalent methods of storing key-value pairs within configuration files are demonstrated in Section 16.3.5

Throughout SAS literature, macro arguments are more commonly passed by value than by reference; this text adopts the nomenclature that call by value is assumed, whereas an inline [REF] comment in a signature denotes call by reference. Thus, the [REF] comment in ONEARG alerts SAS practitioners that the INIT parameter is expecting a macro variable name—not the macro variable itself—when the argument is passed.

In general, wherever ambiguity could arise, a macro's signature should specify the passing method for arguments—whether by value or by reference. This documentation will help ensure that control data are maintained and supplied in the correct format and at the correct abstraction level.

6.6 POLYANDROUS PARAMETERS

Some parameters just can't be satisfied with a single argument, so they take a couple—or a few—or a bushel. And this is OK within procedural abstraction, with these player parameters more officially known as *collections*. A collection comprises one or more same-type *elements* (i.e., values), and common collections include lists and arrays. Thus, it is not so much that multiple *arguments* are passed to a single parameter, but rather that multiple *elements* are passed.

As a multi-element parameter that supports a variable number of inputs, a collection facilitates scalability of control data, which in turn facilitates greater reusability and configurable. Myriad callable modules require this flexibility because the number of elements (being passed) may not be known until software execution, and this number may change from one execution to the next, and from one user to the next.

For example, the built-in MIN function evaluates the minimum value within a series of values (which can include constants, variables, and literals), and this flexibility enables MIN to operate on ten or ten thousand inputs. In the second DATA step, both invocations of MIN pass the same collection of five elements:

```
data somedata;
    length var1-var5 8;
    var1=16;
    var2=54;
    var3=4;
    var4=97;
    var5=21;
run;

data _null_;
    set somedata;
    m=min(var1, var2, var3, var4, var5);
    n=min(of var1 - var5);
    put m= n=;
run;
```

Thus, Var1, Var2, Var3, Var4, and Var5 are SAS variables that are passed collectively as a single, composite argument. Note the two functionally equivalent methods of defining this collection—the first initializes M and explicitly lists all elements, and the second initializes N and more abstractly lists the range of elements. The log demonstrates that both methods evaluate the minimum value to be 4:

m=4 n=4

But consider a postapocalyptic world in which the SAS MIN function does not exist. Faced with an expandable series of numeric values, how would you find the smallest? A hardcoded prototype can be engineered to evaluate the variables in Somedata.

A SAS array is a type of collection that can reference multiple variables as elements. Thus, one method of mimicking MIN functionality could define an array, and iterate across it until the minimum value is revealed:

> SAS arrays are introduced in Section 4.4.3, and are further explored in Section 10.1

```
data _null_;
    set somedata;
    array minarray[*] var:;
    length m 8;
    do i=1 to dim(minarray);
        if missing(m) or minarray[i]<m
            then m=minarray[i];
        end;
    put m=;
run;
```

The DATA step produces the desired functionality but is neither modular nor reusable; both the array declaration and the DO loop would need to be repeated wherever this functionality was needed. Thus, the benefit of passing a collection to a user-defined module is that a limitless number of values can be passed while complexity is hidden within the implementation of the macro, FCMP function, or FCMP subroutine.

Both Base SAS and the SAS macro language support multi-element collection parameters, operationalized by FCMP array parameters and the %MACRO statement PARMBUFF option, respectively.

6.6.1   FCMP Procedure Array Parameters

Within the FCMP procedure, both character and numeric array parameters can be declared within either the FUNCTION or the SUBROUTINE statement. A bracketed asterisk ([*]) follows the array parameter name in its declaration, and denotes that a multi-element collection (often referenced as "multi-argument") can be passed (bound) to the parameter.

The declaration of an array parameter *inside* a function further requires that a corresponding array must be declared *outside* the function—that is, within the calling program, prior to the function's invocation. In other words, an array is the only type of collection that can be passed to a user-defined function, and multiple constants, variables, or literals cannot be passed to a user-defined function—as they readily can be to built-in functions.

For example, the user-defined MINMIN function mimics the functionality of the built-in MIN function, and declares the MINARRAY numeric array parameter:

```
proc fcmp outlib=sasuser.myfuncs.num;
   function minmin(minarray[*]);
      m=.;
      do i=1 to dim(minarray);
         if missing(m) or minarray[i]<m
            then m=minarray[i];
         end;
      return(m);
      endfunc;
quit;
```

Note that MINMIN contains the same DO loop logic, borrowed from the previous DATA step in Section 6.6. User-defined functions and subroutines often can be created with little effort by reusing statements from equivalent DATA steps.

In the following DATA step, the built-in MIN function is called (on the Somedata data set, created in Section 6.6), after which the user-defined MINMIN function is called:

```
data _null_;
   set somedata;
   m=min(of var1 - var5);
   array minarray[*] var1 - var5;
   n=minmin(minarray);
   put m= n=;
run;
```

The log demonstrates identical results for MIN and MINMIN:

m=4 n=4

Note the substantial limitation of array parameters—that all variables must be passed as an array. For example, the following two invocations of MINMIN both fail—the first because it contains numeric literals, and the second because it contains variable names:

```
data min;
   set somedata;
   length min 8;
   min=minmin(1,2,3,4,5);
   min=minmin(var1,var2,var3,var4,var5);
run;
```

The log demonstrates these failures:

```
data min;
   set somedata;
   length min 8;
   min=minmin(1,2,3,4,5);
   min=minmin(1,2,3,4,5);
       ------
       72
ERROR 72-185: The minmin function call has too many
arguments.

min=minmin(1,2,3,4,5);
       ------
       707
ERROR 707-185: Expecting array for argument 1 of the
minmin subroutine call.

min=minmin(var1,var2,var3,var4,var5);
       ------
       72
       707
ERROR 72-185: The minmin function call has too many
arguments.
```

```
ERROR 707-185: Expecting array for argument 1 of the
minmin subroutine call.


run;


NOTE: The SAS System stopped processing this step
because of errors.
WARNING: The data set WORK.MIN may be incomplete.  When
this step was stopped there were 0
          observations and 6 variables.
WARNING: Data set WORK.MIN was not replaced because this
step was stopped.
```

Despite their limitations, where multiple same-type elements must be passed, array parameters can facilitate the development of reusable user-defined functions and subroutines.

6.6.2   %MACRO PARMBUFF Option

The PARMBUFF option can be applied to the %MACRO statement during the declaration of a user-defined macro, and similar to FCMP array parameters, allows a multi-element argument to be passed to a user-defined callable module. When the PARMBUFF option is specified, SAS initializes the &SYSPBUFF automatic macro variable to the collection of elements that are passed, after which the macro can be directed to iterate, tokenize, decompose, or otherwise operationalize the individual elements within the collection.

For example, consider the need to find the lowest number occurring in a comma-delimited macro variable (that contains a list of values). One method (that does not require PARMBUFF) could pass the macro variable by reference, iterate over the macro list, and return the minimum value. The following code initializes the &NUMLIST macro variable, and declares and calls the MIN1 macro function:

```
%let numlist=16,54,4,97,21;


%macro min1(listname /* [REF] macro name */);
%local i min num;
%let min=;
```

```
%do i=1 %to
%sysfunc(countw(%bquote(&&&listname),%str(,)));
    %let num=%scan(%bquote(&&&listname),&i,%str(,));
    %if %length(&min)=0 or %sysevalf(&num<&min)
        %then %let min=&num;
    %end;
&min
%mend;
```

```
%put %min1(numlist);
```

The &NUMLIST macro variable is initialized to the same values found in the Somedata data set (created in Section 6.6), so the log demonstrates that 4 is again evaluated to be the lowest number:

4

Although &NUMLIST can be anecdotally referred to as a macro list, &NUMLIST is in fact *defined* (or *prescribed*) as a macro character variable, and is only *described* as a comma-delimited macro list. For this reason, logic must be developed to tokenize &NUMLIST "elements" by scanning for commas—the user-defined delimiter.

The MIN1 macro is a functional solution that determines the lowest number; however, it passes a scalar (i.e., single-element) argument rather than a collection of elements. A functionally equivalent solution can instead rely on the PARMBUFF option to pass a collection of elements to a macro. But first, basic PARMBUFF functionality can be demonstrated.

The INTHEBUFF macro declares one parameter (PLAYER), and specifies the PARMBUFF option, after which both &PLAYER and &SYSPBUFF are printed to the log:

```
%macro inthebuff(player) / parmbuff;
%put PLAYER: &player;
%put SYSPBUFF: &syspbuff;
%mend;
```

```
%inthebuff(one, two, three);
```

The PARMBUFF option causes all three elements (one, two, and three) to be initialized into the *parameter buffer*—the automatic macro variable

> The *prescription-description* gap is described in Sections 4.5.2 and 9.6

> Section 11.1.3 demonstrates use of PARMBUFF within a user-defined macro that accepts a variable number of search terms

&SYSPBUFF. However, only the first element (one) is initialized into the &PLAYER macro variable. The log also demonstrates the parentheses in which &SYSPBUFF is always enclosed:

PLAYER: one

SYSPBUFF: (one, two, three)

Somewhat anticlimactically, however, identical functionality can be achieved by masking the commas (between the values) by supplying an extra pair of parentheses:

```
%macro nobuff(player);
%put PLAYER: &player;
%mend;


%nobuff((one, two, three));
```

The log demonstrates that despite not relying on PARMBUFF, the same three-element argument was successfully passed to the macro—by value, albeit masked by within parentheses:

PLAYER: (one, two, three)

Returning to the need to select the minimum value in a comma-delimited macro variable, the following MIN2 macro now utilizes PARMBUFF to deliver functionality equivalent to MIN1:

```
%macro min2(listname /* [VAL] macro variable */)
   / PARMBUFF;
%local i min num;
%let min=;
%let listname=%substr(%bquote(&syspbuff),2,
   %sysevalf(%length(&syspbuff)-2));
%do i=1 %to
%sysfunc(countw(%bquote(&listname),%str(,)));
   %let num=%scan(%bquote(&listname),&i,%str(,));
   %if %length(&min)=0 or %sysevalf(&num<&min)
      %then %let min=&num;
   %end;
&min
%mend;
```

MIN2, unlike MIN1, relies on call by value (not reference), so the macro variable (&NUMLIST) is passed, not the macro variable name (NUMLIST):

```
%put %min2(&numlist);
```

Thus, MIN2 can accommodate the equivalent invocation using literal values, whereas the MINMIN function (created in Section 6.6.1 using the FCMP procedure) is unable to pass literals:

```
%put %min2(16,54,4,97,21);
```

These examples demonstrate that the MIN2 solution (with PARMBUFF) is longer and more complex than the equivalent MIN1 solution that instead passes the macro list by reference. Thus, for many purposes, passing a macro variable by reference will be the most straightforward solution when passing a multi-element argument to a macro.

PARMBUFF is especially useful when passing a multi-element argument to a macro, where the argument comprises literal values. Thus, passing by reference to a macro requires that only the macro variable name be passed, and that the macro variable has already been declared. PARMBUFF overcomes these limitations.

6.7 PARAMETER-LESS PROCEDURES AND FUNCTIONS

Data-driven design maximizes software flexibility and configurability through control data that drive dynamic functionality. In some cases, however, a procedure or function will be created that relies on control data not passed from an end user or process, but rather obtained from the system or environment.

Modules intended to interact with environmental variables or read-only automatic macro variables can still demonstrate data-driven design, despite the end user often not having the ability to modify these variables. For example, the SAS automatic macro variable &SYSSCP denotes the operating system (OS) on which SAS is running:

Parameter-less functions are introduced in Section 3.6

```
%put SYSSCP: &sysscp;
SYSSCP: WIN
```

Try as you might, &SYSSCP is an immutable, read-only macro variable, and you will not be able to modify it. However, this should not stop you from utilizing it within data-driven design. And because read-only automatic macro variables and environmental variables can be accessed from within any SAS software module, they do not need to be parameterized or passed through arguments.

The GETPATH macro function evaluates the SAS instance on which SAS is running (for three common Windows-based systems), and dynamically evaluates the file path of the current named program:

```
/* returns path of the current NAMED program
portable to:
- Enterprise Guide, SAS Studio, SAS Display Manager */
%macro getpath();
%local path pathfil;
%if %symexist(_clientapp) %then %do;
    %if &_clientapp='SAS Enterprise Guide' %then %do;
        %let pathfil=%sysfunc(dequote(&_sasprogramfile));
        %let pathno=
            %index(%sysfunc(reverse("&pathfil")),\);
        %let path=%substr(&pathfil,1,%eval
            (%length(&pathfil)-&pathno+1))\;
        %end;
    %if &_clientapp='SAS Studio' %then %do;
        %let pathfil=%sysfunc(dequote(&_sasprogramfile));
        %let pathno=
            %index(%sysfunc(reverse("&pathfil")),/);
        %let path=%substr(&pathfil,1,%eval
            (%length(&pathfil)-&pathno+1))\;
            %let path=%sysfunc(tranwrd(&path,/,\));
        %end;
    %end;
%else %if &sysscp=WIN %then %do;
    %let path=%sysget(sas_execfilepath);
    %let path=%substr(&path,1,%length(&path)-
        %length(%scan(&path,-1,\)));
    %end;
%else %let path=UNK;
&path
%mend;
```

GETPATH declares no parameters, and instead relies on automatic macro variables (e.g., &SYSSCP) and environmental variables (e.g., _SAS_EXECFILEPATH) to generate &PATH. The following invocation demonstrates the path that is dynamically evaluated for some named program file (e.g., d:\sas\my_sas_program.sas):

```
%put %getpath;
D:\SAS\
```

Some built-in SAS functions operate similarly and do not declare parameters; for example, the DATE function retrieves the current date, relying on the system to provide this information:

```
%put %sysfunc(date());
%put %sysfunc(putn(%sysfunc(date()),mmddyy10.));


21150
07/04/2019
```

In assessing whether a built-in function or procedure declares parameters, consider the specification first, but also consider the possibility that undocumented parameters exist—perhaps those that are used only by developers or quality assurance engineers during software testing or for other internal purposes. For example, it is possible (albeit unlikely) that the built-in DATE function accepts one or more super-secret arguments that are not documented publicly, but which SAS Institute uses for testing.

In other cases, user-defined modules may define no parameters due to poor coding practices. For example, the LEAKYPETE macro declares no parameters, yet relies on the &DSN user-defined global macro variable—a core dependency:

```
%let dsn=somedata;


%macro leakypete();
proc print data=&dsn;
run;
%mend;


%leakypete;
```

Although modularity objectives aim to reduce coupling between software modules, all modules will have some dependencies—external interactions that should be defined and documented. Thus, LEAKYPETE is not poorly constructed because it relies on &DSN—it is poorly constructed because it leaks, relying on a dependency (&DSN) that is neither declared in its signature (i.e., the %MACRO statement) nor documented elsewhere.

The functionally equivalent UNLEAKYPETE macro now passes the &DSN global macro variable through the GLOBALDSN parameter:

```
%macro unleakypete(globaldsn= /* dsn */);
proc print data=&globaldsn;
run;
%mend;
```

```
%unleakypete(globaldsn=&dsn);
```

UNLEAKYPETE succeeds because it exhibits appropriate *information hiding*, as discussed in Section 8.4.1

The result is a macro whose dependencies (i.e., its reliance on the &DSN global macro variable) are now declared in its signature—which can be viewed by SAS practitioners if they need to reuse the macro, and upon which the macro's specification (i.e., documentation) should be based. LEAKYPETE and UNLEAKYPETE have identical functionality—that is, until someone attempts to call LEAKYPETE without having first declared or initialized &DSN, at which point it will unceremoniously fail. For this reason, declaring all dependencies—including user-defined global macro variables—is considered a best practice.

6.8 PROCEDURAL OUTPUT

Procedural communication goes both ways—or at least it should. Procedures, functions, and subroutines exist to deliver some functionality; in general, SAS procedures perform one or more operations, SAS functions return a value, and SAS subroutines perform some action or modify one or more arguments. Whereas dynamic *inputs* passed to a called module can demonstrate data-driven design and facilitate dynamic functionality, dynamic *outputs* can provide equal value, by conveying functional results, performance metrics, or both.

When callable software modules are invoked (i.e., *called*), and their execution subsequently terminates, they *return*, which ISO defines as "to transfer control from a software module to the module that called it."[57] Thus, at some point, procedural abstraction must conclude, and the calling module resumes at the point of invocation. And because the calling module is likely dependent on the functionality or results of the called module, this information must be returned from the called module.

The next two subsections introduce *return values* and *return codes*, both of which transmit data or information from the called to the calling module. Usage of the terms can vary by software language (even between Base SAS and the SAS macro language), personal preference, and other factors; however, in general, *return values* are returned by called modules and comprise data or control data, and *return codes* comprise control data that describe the success, failure, or other characteristics of the called module's execution or completion status. In this sense, return codes represent the subset of return values that convey status—not substance.

6.8.1   Return Values

ISO defines a *return value* as "a value assigned to a parameter by a called module for access by the calling module."[58] Most commonly, when a function has transformed data or performed some action, the return value captures the transformed output or the completion status of that action. All functions must return a single value, with user-defined FCMP functions relying on the RETURN function to transmit data back to the calling module.

For example, Section 6.6.1 demonstrates calls to the built-in MIN function and the user-defined MINMIN function, both of which return a value representing the lowest number among a series of values. These functions return *domain data*, in that the output (i.e., each return value) is equivalent to the input (i.e., the data that are passed to the functions).

Control data and domain data are defined and contrasted on Page 4

In other cases, the return values produced by functions instead represent *control data*, and describe the completion status or other characteristics of the function's execution. For example, the built-in OPEN function opens a SAS data set; it returns 0 if the function fails, and returns a positive integer (incremented from 1) if the function succeeds. The OPEN function still produces a *return value* (because all functions generate a return value), but the OPEN function can more precisely be said to produce a *return code* because the value that is returned describes the execution or completion status. Thus, it would not be incorrect to describe the 0 returned from OPEN as either a return value or a return code, although the latter term is favored as it more specifically describes the nature of the data.

User-defined FCMP subroutines, on the other hand, do not support the RETURN function (as FCMP functions do). However, subroutines can modify one or more arguments (in the calling program) when the parameters are enumerated in the optional OUTARGS statement. OUTARGS declares parameters to be passed by reference to a subroutine (or function), and when these arguments are modified inside the callable module, their values are correspondingly changed in the calling program.

Return values and return codes are fairly straightforward within FCMP functions and subroutines, owing principally to the RETURN function and OUTARGS statement. Far murkier, however, is the distinction between return values and return codes generated in the SAS macro language. Thus, just as *user-defined macro functions* and *user-defined macro subroutines* must be anecdotally (and somewhat arbitrarily) defined, so too must the values they generate.

For example, as discussed in Section 3.6.1, user-defined macro functions do not actually *return* a value—they *resolve* a value. Notwithstanding this trifling technicality, user-defined macro functions are often anecdotally (even within this text) said to *return* a value.

The HOWBIG user-defined macro function determines the number of observations in a SAS data set, and generates both return values and return codes:

```
data test;
   length iter 3;
   do iter=1 to 100;
      output;
      end;
run;


%macro howbig(dsn /* data set name */);
%local dsid close nobs;
%let dsid=%sysfunc(open(&&dsn));
%if &dsid>0 %then %do;
   %let nobs=%sysfunc(attrn(&dsid,nobs));
   %let close=%sysfunc(close(&dsid));
   &nobs
   %end;
%mend;
```

```
%put %howbig(work.test);
```

When the %PUT statement (representing the calling program) executes, the HOWBIG macro invocation resolves to 100, which is printed to the log:

```
100
```

Anecdotally, however, HOWBIG is often said to have a "return value" of 100—because the macro *resolves* to 100 when it executes. Within the macro, however, two actual return codes are generated by the OPEN and CLOSE functions, as discussed in the next subsection.

6.8.2 Return Codes

A return code is a type of return value that returns control data from a called module. ISO defines a *return code* as "a code used to influence the execution of the calling module following a return from a called module."[59] Thus, all return codes are return values (that communicate control data), but not all return values are return codes. Where the data returned from a called module represent both a return value and a return code, either term can be used, although this text more precisely references *return code.*

In the previous subsection, two built-in functions—OPEN and CLOSE—generate return codes. It is for this reason that when OPEN is called, its results—the return code—must be initialized to a macro variable:

```
%let dsid=%sysfunc(open(&&dsn));
```

In this example, &DSID is initialized to 0 if the data set cannot be opened and to a positive integer if the data set can be opened. Thereafter, the macro's logic dictates that if a data set cannot be opened, no attempt will be made to evaluate or return the observation count. The &DSID macro variable is considered to be *control data* because its value dynamically directs program control during execution. Similarly, user-defined callable modules can be designed to generate intelligent return codes that can be used to drive subsequent program operation.

A refactored HOWBIG macro now generates a return value representing observation count under normal conditions; however, under exceptional conditions, -1 is returned if the data set is missing, and -2 is returned if the data set is exclusively locked or otherwise fails to open:

```
* returns number of obs under normal conditions;
* returns -1 for missing data set;
* returns -2 for failure during opening;
%macro howbig(dsn /* data set name */);
%local dsid close nobs;
%if %sysfunc(exist(&dsn))=0 %then %do;
    -1
    %end;
%else %do;
    %let dsid=%sysfunc(open(&&dsn));
    %if &dsid>0 %then %do;
        %let nobs=%sysfunc(attrn(&dsid,nobs));
        %let close=%sysfunc(close(&dsid));
        &nobs
        %end;
    %else %do;
        -2
        %end;
    %end;
%mend;
```

For example, when HOWBIG is called on the nonexistent Gone_fishin data set, it returns a value—a *return code*—of -1:

```
%put %howbig(gone_fishin);
-1
```

This communication paradigm represents *in-band signaling*, in which *either* a return value or a return code—that is, either domain data or control data (or, as sometimes described, *either data or metadata*)—can be returned through the same pathway. In this instance, in-band-signaling is possible because observation count is always zero or a positive integer. Thus, all negative numbers can be used to represent various exceptional conditions, with specific numbers (i.e., return codes) corresponding to specific issues or exceptions.

When the calling program (not depicted) receives a zero or positive number, it intuits that HOWBIG has completed successfully, and can utilize that return value in subsequent processes. However, if the calling program instead receives a negative number, it understands that HOWBIG has failed, and can follow exception handling routines based on the specific return code that was generated.

In other cases, *out-of-band* signaling is required to communicate a return code, such as when a valid return value can contain the set of all alphanumeric characters and symbols. Within the SAS macro language, a global macro variable is typically declared inside a macro, and this return code (having global scope) will be available to the calling program.

For example, HOWBIG is refactored one final time, and now declares the &HOWBIG_RC global macro variable return code:

```
%macro howbig(dsn /* data set name */);
%global howbig_rc;
%let howbig_rc=;
%local dsid close nobs;
%if %sysfunc(exist(&dsn))=0 %then %let howbig_rc=-1;
%else %do;
    %let dsid=%sysfunc(open(&&dsn));
    %if &dsid>0 %then %do;
        %let nobs=%sysfunc(attrn(&dsid,nobs));
        %let close=%sysfunc(close(&dsid));
        &nobs
        %end;
    %else %let howbig_rc=-2;
    %end;
%mend;
```

The return code (&HOWBIG_RC) is made available to the calling program, and can be utilized within exception handling routines. For example, when HOWBIG executes without exception, &HOWBIG_RC is initialized to a missing value, and when an exception does occur, &HOWBIG_RC is initialized to -1 or -2, and the HOWBIG macro will resolve to a Null value. In both cases—normal and exceptional—results can be evaluated programmatically in real-time to drive program flow.

6.9 SUMMARY

This chapter introduced procedural communication, which accompanies procedural abstraction to facilitate data-driven design. Dynamic inputs— declared as *parameters* within the callable module, but passed as *arguments* from the calling program—make dynamic functionality possible. Less common are those instances in which data-driven software modules receive all input from the operating environment, system, or application—but these examples do exist in which no parameters are declared.

The procedural *signature* was introduced, including its role in declaring parameters and their characteristics. Parameter identification defines whether parameters are identified *positionally* or by *keyword*, and call methods include *call by value* and *call by reference*. Call by value is more commonly observed, both within Base SAS and the SAS macro language, whereas call by reference is more typically used to pass complex or large data to a software module, and permits the called module to modify arguments within the calling module.

Although less common, polyandrous parameters were discussed, which support passing multi-element arguments (i.e., collections) to modules. Array parameters within the FCMP procedure and the PARMBUFF option within the %MACRO statement facilitate declaring and accessing these composite arguments.

Finally, it must be recognized that procedural communication does not comprise inputs alone, but also includes output produced by called modules. *Return values* were distinguished as data produced by called modules that are made available to the calling module. *Return codes* were distinguished as the subset of return values that report the execution or completion state of a module, and which comprise control data intended to drive subsequent dynamic functioning in the calling module.

Chapter 7.

STAKEHOLDERS AND THE SDLC

This chapter has the following objectives:

- ❖ Introduce common stakeholders in software development, including product owners, developers, and end users.

- ❖ Demonstrate how data-driven programming objectives, priorities, and benefits differ based on stakeholder perspective.

- ❖ Introduce the software development life cycle (SDLC), including planning, design, development, testing, and operations and maintenance (O&M) phases.

- ❖ Demonstrate how data-driven design benefits product owners and developers through the design and development phases.

- ❖ Demonstrate how data-driven design improves end user experience and software maintainability during the O&M phase.

Thus far, data-driven design has been presented primarily from the perspective of the SAS practitioner—the developer writing SAS software or, in some cases, the end user running SAS programs. But data-driven programming can look very different depending on whose chair you occupy and where in the software development life cycle (SDLC) you sit. This chapter explores these two dynamics—the *who* and *when*—to expose a broader perspective of data-driven programming.

Depending on your vantage point, data-driven programming will appear very different. To the developer implementing data-driven design, you spend your time in the technical weeds, so this book is for you, as it explores data-driven design best practices in SAS. For the project manager, product owner, or stakeholder managing or funding a software project, the weeds may be irrelevant; you want to know how data-driven design will improve software quality while reducing project workload and cost (so please continue reading this chapter). And, for the end user or customer running SAS software, you want to understand how data-driven design will improve your ability to configure software, and achieve greater dynamic functionality.

The SDLC, whether implemented within an Agile (e.g., Scrum, Lean, Extreme Programming) or a Waterfall (boo!!!) environment, also influences the focus and objectives of data-driven design. For example, SAS practitioners focused on software design and development might prioritize methods that help meet specific functional requirements. Meanwhile, developers who are instead focused on "keeping the lights on" in the software operations and maintenance (O&M) phase might prioritize software configurability as well as methods that reduce the frequency of software upgrades (such as future-proofing). Both are valid pursuits, so unless resources are unlimited, a balance must be struck based on competing, albeit worthy, priorities and business need.

7.1 STAKEHOLDERS

An endless array of stakeholders could be assembled, all of whom would have some vested interest in functional, quality software. Many stakeholders have overlapping roles across teams, so inclusion in one stakeholder group should never imply exclusion from others. Within end-user development environments, for example, a SAS practitioner writes software, tests software, validates software, uses software, and refactors or upgrades software when maintenance or modification is needed. End-user developers often wear multiple hats simultaneously throughout the SDLC.

For this brief foray, however, stakeholders are aggregated into three distinct groups: product owners, developers, and end users. *Product owners* represent an assemblage of the leadership, management, and moneybags who spawn, sponsor, and direct software. *Developers* design, develop, test, and maintain software. *End users* utilize software and, especially within a data-driven design paradigm, are responsible for modifying data structures and supplying control data to drive dynamic software functionality. What ties these stakeholders together is their shared desire that software meet stakeholder needs and technical specifications, and that it deliver stated functional and performance requirements.

7.1.1 Product Owners

Product owners represent the stakeholders who are ultimately directing that software be bought or built to meet some business need, and who are ultimately prioritizing the functionality and performance that a successful solution must incorporate. They may have software development knowledge and experience—or they may not. For example, even product owners well-versed in statistics or data analytics may conduct the breadth of their analytic endeavors through point-and-click interfaces rather than programmable, repeatable code.

Arguably worse may be those product owners who *believe* they are technical, and who may have some script-kiddy creds, but who lack an understanding of (or interest in) software quality. Notwithstanding one's ability to *write* software, however, it is still incumbent on all product owners (of software projects) to understand how to *valuate* software, including how to evaluate the costs and benefits of functionality, performance, and quality, as well as the risks of the lack thereof.

Regardless of technical prowess, a product owner's focus typically lies with delivering software that satisfies but does not distend the *golden triangle*—a software product's budget, schedule, and scope—where *scope* comprises both functionality and quality. Thus, during planning, design, and development, product owners are interested in reducing the production time and cost of software while ensuring that the released product meets functional requirements and delivers the necessary quality (including both dynamic and static performance requirements).

Product owners need to understand that data-driven design can facilitate software that is faster to build—because software modules as well as user-defined data structures (and their respective operations) can be reused more readily. Especially over time, as a team consistently embraces data-driven design across projects, newer software endeavors often will be able to reuse and implement older components (such as user-defined callable modules)—because those modules will have been built with reusability, configurability, and extensibility in mind, each of which promotes flexibility of use.

In other cases, data-driven design can facilitate faster development because it promotes specialization and division of labor. Especially where data-driven design pulls complex analytic models or business rules out of code, and places these instead inside external data structures, this bifurcation enables SAS developers to focus on writing code while business analysts and SMEs focus on creating and updating data models and structures. These two, discrete development processes—for code and for control data—can often proceed in parallel, inflicting little interference on each other while maximizing development productivity.

But development speed alone is worthless unless functional software is produced that meets stated quality requirements. Whereas hardcoded methods can typically deliver equivalent *functionality* as that produced through data-driven programming, these concrete methods typically cannot deliver the required *quality*—especially when quality requirements comprise characteristics such as reusability, configurability, and maintainability. That is, if performance requirements state that a callable module must be readily configured through a user-defined configuration file, there is no hardcoded solution that can deliver this stated requirement; data-driven design must be implemented.

Checkpoints and *checkpoint tables* are demonstrated in Section 14.2

The benefits of data-driven design do not end once software is constructed and released. Within the O&M phase, software recoverability is improved where checkpoints (within a control table) can be used to restore functionality more quickly after a failure has occurred. Software maintainability is also typically improved, allowing both adaptive and corrective maintenance to be performed more efficiently when software must be modified. For example, in some cases, these modifications can be made by altering only external data structures—that is, favoring *configuration* over *customization*—while leaving code untouched.

To product owners, budget is often the bottom line. Where data-driven design can reduce software's time to market while improving software quality, software development costs are often commensurately reduced. Thus, a developer may muse "Data-driven design helps me do my job more efficiently, and to produce better software," whereas a product owner hearkens "Data-driven design improves customer satisfaction and, ultimately, profit margin."

7.1.2 Developers

Developers represent the stakeholders interacting with software on a technical level, and are responsible for planning, designing, developing, testing, validating, and releasing software. Once production software has been released, developers are responsible for software maintenance and upgrades during the O&M phase, and may work with end users to solicit and understand future business needs and functionality, and to incorporate these into subsequent software releases.

In some teams, the same developers perform the breadth of this work, whereas in other cases, one developer might build software, a second might peer review the code, a third (a quality assurance engineer) might test it, and a fourth might deploy it. Regardless of where developers fall in the sausage assembly line, they are still integral to cranking out that sweet meat—and sausage-making requires technical know-how.

Developers are typically focused on satisfying technical requirements because we are responsible for implementing and testing those requirements, as well as for validating to product owners that requirements have been fulfilled. But developers are also a creative bunch who would prefer to be solving intriguing problems rather than painstakingly rehashing a problem we have thrice before solved.

To combat this mental fatigue, data-driven design, spurred by abstraction, empowers developers to build software modules that are more readily reused. This internal software flexibility might never be seen (much less understood) by nontechnical product owners or end users, but it increases the productivity of developers by allowing us to use, reuse, and repurpose (i.e., extend) software modules and data structures.

Configurability is the objective of data-driven design most closely associated with end users, as it empowers them to alter software functionality dynamically through arguments and data structures. However, configurability also aids developers because it makes end users

> Software *extensibility* describes the repurposing or extending of software functionality, and is demonstrated in Section 10.2.4

Configuration and *customization* are defined and contrasted in Section 16.1

responsible for configuring many of the dynamic aspects of software that developers would otherwise be required to customize through maintenance. Thus, as end users are empowered, developers are freed from customization tasks, and can pursue more rewarding design and development, as well as the often forsaken testing and documentation.

One of the most rewarding activities (for many developers) is *refactoring*—taking a functional software component, and refining it to improve performance while not altering functionality. A refactored software module does the same thing as before—it just does it *better*—where *better* could be faster, more reliable, more configurable, or all or any of the above. Where *static* performance characteristics, as opposed to *dynamic* performance characteristics, have been improved, *better* could be code that runs equivalently but is more organized, more modular, more readable, and thus more maintainable—each of which can be a refactoring goal.

Section 10.2.4 demonstrates backward compatibility as user-defined modules are refactored

Section 7.2.1 defines and contrasts dynamic and static performance characteristics

Data-driven design embraces procedural abstraction, which enables a module's implementation to be refactored while its specification and invocation are untouched. This refactoring and backward compatibility often promotes software that can be upgraded with ease and without awareness by (or disruption) to end users.

7.1.3   End Users

End users comprise the stakeholders who utilize or rely on software, including developers, product owners, analysts, and other users. In some cases, end users may not be SAS practitioners or may not even have access to the SAS application. Data-driven design is especially beneficial in these cases, as well as in all cases in which end users have less technical expertise than the developers who produced the software—because software configurability objectives can empower end users to modify control data independently (i.e., without developer intervention or overwatch) to alter software functionality.

"Codeless" software is so called because end users can modify software functionality without having to alter code. Through graphical user interfaces (GUIs), application parameters, configuration files, and other control files, end users are able to achieve dynamic functionality. Especially where control data are maintained within user-defined configuration files, end users can additionally save personalized settings for future software use, as well as maintain different versions of the same configuration file for functional testing and comparison purposes.

Codeless Software

Codeless software (aka, *code-free, no-code, low-code, faux-code* software) describes software in which end users are able to configure software without (or with minimal) development. Professional codeless software applications typically have well-formed GUIs that allow end users to navigate and modify configuration items, and which validate control data as they are entered. Thus, codeless software is merely the end user perspective of highly configurable, data-driven software.

Codeless software maximizes procedural abstraction, relying on parameters and other control data to drive dynamic functionality. However, only those abstractions that are forward-facing (i.e., with which end users interact) contribute to the *codeless software* description. Thus, SAS software that espouses data-driven design is nevertheless typically not considered *codeless* because end users are still required to interact with the underlying code to execute SAS programs.

Rather, true codeless software is often facilitated by coalescing configuration items into a single interface. However, as GUIs are uncommonly implemented within user-defined SAS modules, this same consolidation of control data is typically accomplished (in SAS) though the development of user-defined configuration files. Thereafter, users interact with SAS software *only* through these files—the interface.

This text demonstrates data structures such as parameters, control tables, and configuration files that drive dynamic software functionality. Professional codeless software interacts with these same data structures, albeit while providing data quality control methods that validate user entry and prevent catastrophic failure that can result from invalid control data. User-defined codeless software, too, should enforce data quality controls, especially where nontechnical end users are interacting directly with data structures and control data that drive core functionality.

SAS software development most commonly occurs within an end-user development paradigm, in which SAS practitioners both develop and utilize software; thus, the *codeless* moniker is uncommonly applied in the SAS world. However, data-driven methods can facilitate highly configurable software, in which much maintenance burden is alleviated from developers as end users are empowered to configure their own software.

Reusability is a natural sequela of flexible, data-driven software, albeit a benefit that will go unnoticed to nontechnical end users. That is, only developers inspecting software will understand the extent to which software components have been reused to bolster productivity and reliability. Configurability, conversely, is salient to end users because they can perceive this software flexibility, and this salience helps promote configurability as an objective over less visible software requirements.

Configurable software allows different end users to select and personalize settings, but it also facilitates comparative analysis by the same user who wishes to supply varied control data to the same program or process. For example, an analyst might be testing comparative hypotheses, and rather than maintaining multiple copies of complex formulas or data models within separate programs, these hypotheses could be represented within multiple instances of the same data structure.

Thus, rather than having to modify and save twenty versions of a program, the analyst could maintain a single program that is capable of interpreting and operationalizing the twenty control files. Moreover, when the analyst compares analytic models with colleagues (who are themselves relying on different data models), all are assured that the underlying program is consistent because only the data models—operationalized through external data structures—have been modified.

End users might never be aware that they are using software developed through data-driven methods; however, they will be aware of salient benefits like configurability, achieved through data-driven design. This increased software flexibility endows commensurately increased customer satisfaction, and that is something for which all stakeholders—from product owners on down—should strive.

7.2   THE SDLC

The *software development life cycle* (SDLC) broadly describes the phases—from cradle to grave—through which software passes as it is conceptualized, built, tested, utilized, and decommissioned. In general, a business need exists; requirements are generated; software planning commences; software is designed, developed, tested, and documented; software is validated against functional and performance requirements; software is released; software is utilized by end users while it is maintained by developers; and at some point (unless the software is running on an aged DoD mainframe), the software is decommissioned.

This longwinded description might appear to elapse over months if not years, and in many cases, *months or years* aptly describes a software's lifespan. However, in other cases, a developer might traverse these same SDLC phases within a single day—conceptualizing an analytic program in the morning that will answer some burning question, writing code throughout the day, and producing a terminal data product before happy hour that evening. Thus, phases of the SDLC can be used to structure and drive software development and operations, irrespective of the software development methodology that is espoused (e.g., Agile, Waterfall), and irrespective of the length of the software's intended lifespan.

The objectives and benefits of data-driven design will vary throughout the SDLC, just as Section 7.1 demonstrates that stakeholders will have different perspectives on data-driven design based on their respective vantage points, roles, and responsibilities. The following subsections introduce data-driven design throughout phases of the SDLC; they aim not to describe SDLC phases, but rather the role that data-driven programming can play in each.

7.2.1 Planning

Planning is generally regarded as being *needs-focused*, whereas later phases of the SDLC, especially design and development, are *solutions-focused*. In software development, one of the most critical aspects of planning is the discussion and creation of accurate technical requirements. Technical specifications should prescribe both functional and performance requirements, and ideally describe other tangible deliverables, such as software documentation and project artifacts (e.g., communication plans, project charters, risk registers) that will be required.

As data-driven design is not appropriate for all software products, technical requirements should be evaluated (during later design and development phases) to establish whether and how data-driven design could benefit a proposed software product or project. To make this evaluation, however, business needs must be understood, and accurate requirements must have been established.

Besides requirements gathering, another relevant discussion could include the way in which stakeholders envision software utilization, including a description of probable end users and other stakeholders who will interact with the software. For example, if software is intended to be utilized internally (by the developers building it), greater flexibility and reusability might be prioritized. However, if software is instead intended to be utilized by nontechnical end users, configurability might be a primary objective—to ensure that software supports the variability of its diverse user base.

For example, SAS developers likely would be more comfortable (and commensurately competent) interacting with code (e.g., to modify arguments), whereas less technical end users might instead prefer to modify an external control table or configuration file. Either method could supply the same control data to software, but the latter method would provide additional security because alteration of control data would not risk accidental modification of the underlying code that interprets it. Thus, the intended and prospective end users always should be discussed when data-driven design is being considered.

Another key discussion during planning should uncover the software's intended lifespan—is it conceptualized as a robust system that will endure through the ages, or an ephemeral, fly-by-night job? Either objective may be appropriate, but this decision can only be made through requirements gathering. In general, because data-driven programming requires more complex design (than functionally equivalent code-driven programming), the appropriateness and value of data-driven design increases as the intended lifespan of software commensurately grows. That is, if your software is going to be hanging out for a while, you likely will want to embrace data-driven design because it will facilitate more manageable maintenance over the years.

Where formalized software requirements are generated and documented, an unfortunate trend is the disproportionate focus on *dynamic performance requirements* (e.g., reliability, availability, recoverability, speed, efficiency, configurability) to the detriment of *static performance requirements* (e.g., maintainability, modularity, data independence, readability, reusability, extensibility). *Data Analytic Development: Dimensions of Software Quality* (aka, the author's first child) extols the virtues of performance requirements for more than 600 pages, and should be consulted for more in-depth commentary—as well as for life-altering chicken bus anecdotes![60]

Dynamic performance requirements are those that can be evaluated through software execution. For example, when technical specifications state the speed with which a software module must execute, this metric can be tested, evaluated, and observed by running the software. This salience makes dynamic performance requirements more observable (than static performance requirements) to developers, product owners, and anyone else watching software run.

Static performance requirements, on the other hand, are those that can be evaluated only through code inspection rather than software execution. They are more difficult to demonstrate to product owners and other key stakeholders, and are typically invisible to nontechnical stakeholders who have no access to the underlying code. For example, software modularity, a pillar of data-driven design, can be demonstrated only by inspecting how code is written and organized, and can be difficult to evaluate quantitatively, unlike dynamic characteristics like speed or efficiency.

Because of this disproportionality and favor of *dynamic* performance requirements, stakeholders at the planning table must ensure that *static* performance requirements are equally considered, discussed, and prioritized. Armed with accurate software requirements (including both functional and performance requirements), SAS practitioners are well-positioned to make informed decisions about whether and how data-driven design should be implemented within software.

7.2.2   Design and Development

Developers receive their marching orders from software requirements and technical specifications that originate in the planning phase. They should also receive context about the software product, such as its intended lifespan, user base, and acceptable performance levels. With this information, developers can begin to shift from *needs-focused* to *solutions-focused* attitudes and activities.

As demonstrated throughout this text, code that espouses data-driven design techniques is often more complex and longer than functionally equivalent code that is concrete. The abstraction that facilitates software flexibility requires an interpreter to parse and operationalize control data; software modularity requires developers to decompose software into chunks; and data independence relies on external data structures to house control data, and separate modules to interpret these control data.

> Data-driven design and code-driven design are contrasted in Section 1.2

Thus, data-driven methods should be implemented to meet specific software requirements, including both functional and performance requirements. However, the methods through which requirements are met can vary greatly and should be explored throughout the software design phase. For example, developers may be faced with choices such as whether to utilize a built-in data structure (like the SAS data set) or to design and develop a user-defined data structure (like a macro list).

During the design and development phases, developers also discuss which software components must be built, which can be borrowed or pilfered from external sources, and which can be reused from internal sources such as previous software projects or software reuse libraries. This conversation is similar to the initial build-versus-buy decision that often occurs in the planning phase, in which stakeholders discuss whether in-house software should be built, purchased, or contracted out for development by a third party.

Where a team or organization has consistently prioritized data-driven design and the development of flexible, modular software, developers often will have a substantial reuse library on which they can rely, and whose components can be implemented—often with little to no modification—in the current software product. Thus, components including code modules, user-defined data structures, and their respective operations can be built, catalogued, and reused for subsequent, unrelated software products. Software reuse can tremendously increase the productivity of a development team because not only design and development phases, but also subsequent testing and validation phases, can be greatly reduced.

For some software projects, the software modularity and data independence embraced by data-driven design provide an added benefit—development *fast-tracking*, in which software components are developed in parallel rather than in series. Although not always possible (or prudent), fast-tracking can occur when requirements for procedural and other specifications are clearly defined, enabling different developers to build different software modules simultaneously. Data structures, too, can often be developed in parallel with code, so long as the interfaces through which they will interact have been clearly defined. Fast-tracking does not necessarily make a software project more efficient, and can increase risk, but it can reduce time to completion when implemented judiciously.

The procedural *signature* describes parameterized inputs, and is discussed in Section 6.2; the procedural *specification* and *implementation* are introduced in Sections 3.2 and 3.3, respectively

For example, during the design phase, a new macro might be conceptualized, and its specification defined. That is, developers discuss and determine what inputs the macro will require (i.e., its *signature*), what outputs it will produce (i.e., data products, return values, return codes), and what overall functionality it will deliver. Thereafter, while one developer builds the macro *implementation* (that does the work), a separate developer can build modules that interact with the macro—either supplying its inputs or utilizing its outputs—because these components have been explicitly defined in the macro's *specification* during the software design phase. A third developer (operating in a business analyst role) might simultaneously build the data structure(s) that will supply control data to the macro.

This example helps illustrate the specialization and division of labor that data-driven design can facilitate, and which can contribute to software that can be developed at a faster pace—both because more stakeholders can simultaneously work toward the same objectives, and because each stakeholder is working in his area of expertise.

7.2.3   Testing

Software *testing*, in the most basic sense, validates software functionality and performance against software functional and performance requirements. It aims to demonstrate that software is doing what it should do, and equally important, *not* doing what it *should not* do. Thus, testing uncovers software *errors*—human failures—that are causing or could cause functional or performance failures in software.

Section 6.4.1 demonstrates functional testing of the user-defined FTOC macro

Data-driven design can both complicate and simplify software testing. Where parameters, control tables, configuration files, and other data structures maintain control data, these structures must be afforded the same scrutiny during testing as other software components, principally code. This can complicate testing because developers should test procedures and other data-driven components with various data inputs to demonstrate how software operates with *valid* control data, as well as with *invalid* control data.

But where flexible data-driven software modules have been developed in the past and can be reused in developing a current software product, time and effort expended toward testing and validation (of the current product) can be greatly reduced because functional testing, unit testing, and other basic testing will have already been completed.

To be clear, integration testing will likely be required to demonstrate how the reused component operates in its new environment; however, the new module itself often will not need to be independently tested. Especially where software comments and other documentation adequately describe software functionality, vulnerabilities, usage caveats, and a formalized test plan with test cases and test results, software modules are more likely to be reused, thus reducing workload and improving developer productivity.

7.2.4 Operations and Maintenance (O&M)

Operations and maintenance (O&M) may constitute a single temporal phase, but its name intimates a very real duality—that live software must be maintained and modified. Thus, once software has been released into production, developers maintain, modify, and update the software while end users utilize the software. Within more formalized software development environments, these separate activities are performed independently by end users and developers, with the former doing the O and the latter providing the M.

As SAS practitioners, however, we often operate within end-user development environments and wear simultaneous developer and end user hats. In these environments, when we detect a software failure, or desire new or varied functionality, we—rather than some unseen force of Silicon Valley stooges—provide this maintenance. Notwithstanding the overlap of responsibilities that many SAS practitioners have across developer and end user roles, data-driven design provides distinct benefits to both developers and end users.

From the developer's perspective, whose responsibility it is to maintain software in a production environment, *maintainability* and *recoverability* are two of the most desirable software performance requirements because they collectively limit the "down time" that software experiences, even during scheduled upgrades or outages. Both performance characteristics can be improved through data-driven design.

Maintainability speaks to a developer's ability to modify and maintain software with ease. When software requires an upgrade, maintainability helps us make those changes faster because we can efficiently comprehend the software and make necessary modifications. Data-driven design supports maintainability, in part because of its reliance on modularity and data independence, in which complex business rules and other dynamic elements are removed from code and maintained in external data structures. Thus, developers can focus on managing the code—unimpeded by control data, which have been extracted.

In other cases, the pith lies not in the code but in those data structures. In code-driven design, when software functionality must be modified, this always entails altering code. Within data-driven design, however, only associated data structures may need to be modified to alter software functionality. Thus, within data-driven programming, maintainability is also increased when only data structures must be modified (by developers), and especially when dynamic functionality can be achieved through end user (rather than developer) configuration of data structures. In highly configurable, data-driven design, developer maintenance responsibilities may be substantially curtailed because end users are empowered to configure software to meet their own needs.

Recoverability, another performance objective associated with data-driven design, reflects the ability of software or a system to recover after a failure. When software requires modification before it can be restarted (after some failure), it can be modified more readily when components are modular and where data structures have abstracted complex logic, thus improving software readability.

Software *checkpoints* also facilitate recoverability objectives, and enable software to recover from the point of last known success. Checkpoints facilitate more autonomous, recoverable software because discrete processes can be validated for completion and correctness, after which metadata (describing those process successes) are updated in a *checkpoint table*—a control table that archives process or program completion status and other metrics. If a program or process subsequently fails, the software can autonomously rerun only the failed module at a later time—often without developer intervention—and can bypass the program modules that had succeeded and did not need to be rerun.

> *Checkpoints* and *checkpoint tables* are demonstrated in Section 14.2

From the end user perspective (where end users do *not* also wear a developer's hat), the O&M phase is the only phase that exists; users use software. Their perception of software is informed by the software's functionality and performance—what it does and how well it does it, which should align with software requirements and business need.

Nontechnical end users benefit from data-driven design because it affords them more flexible, configurable software. If a nontechnical business analyst can modify a *configuration* file to effect necessary formatting and stylistic changes within a SAS report, he will be overjoyed—especially if he once had had to consult SAS developers to request equivalent report *customization*. Highly configurable software, coupled with apt documentation and instruction, empowers nontechnical end users to learn how to fish, rather than their relying on developers to spoon feed them fish after endless fish in a cavalcade of requests for software customization.

> Section 16.5.2 demonstrates how end users can use CSS files to control dynamic stylistic attributes for data products

7.3 SUMMARY

The *data-driven design* discussed and demonstrated throughout this text is predominantly focused on building software that is run by SAS practitioners—those who use SAS software. But even SAS practitioners can vary dramatically in their technical expertise, from hardcore developers to those who run programs that others have built for them. This is in no way intended to shame the less technical, but rather to note that data-driven design will appear different based on your role and responsibilities, as well as where in the SDLC you are operating.

This chapter introduced various stakeholders in software development and lumped these into three broad categories: product owners, developers, and end users. The awareness of other perspectives throughout the SDLC can facilitate more comprehensive requirements gathering and better overall design. Moreover, the awareness that not all objectives of data-driven design (e.g., reusability, modularity) will be patently visible to nontechnical stakeholders can help developers shape and justify their arguments at the planning and design table to emphasize and incorporate static performance requirements.

This chapter also introduced the SDLC and various phases thereof that are often conceptualized, including planning, design, development, testing, software release, and O&M. Irrespective of the size of the software project and the size of the development team, adoption of a formalized SDLC can facilitate more accurate software requirements, as well as the production of higher-quality software. Throughout the SDLC, data-driven design can facilitate the attainment of specific functional and performance requirements.

Chapter 8.

DATA-DRIVEN UNDERPINNINGS

This chapter has the following objectives:

- ❖ Discuss disciplines that intersect with and facilitate data-driven design.

- ❖ Introduce table-driven design.

- ❖ Describe master data management (MDM) and the concept of the *golden record* single source of truth.

- ❖ Discuss a *business rules approach*, in which business rules are abstracted to an external data structure, and interpreted by a *business rules engine (BRE)*.

- ❖ Introduce object-oriented programming (OOP), including the concepts of *classes*, *objects*, *inheritance*, *information hiding*, and *software modularity*.

S ome may view data-driven concepts and methods and remark, "But this is all recycled information!" And this is true! Data-driven design does not embody *new* concepts, but rather an amalgam of *old*. From various disciplines and methodologies, it assembles and interweaves concepts, principles, patterns, components, and techniques—knowledge and tools for which developers can reach to deliver increased software flexibility, configurability, reusability, and maintainability. That is, data-driven design can imbue software with quality.

The disciplines discussed in this chapter are not intended to be an exhaustive list of contributors, but rather represent primary influencers of data-driven design. Many are coevals whose origins are contemporaneous with the development of computers themselves. This chapter aims not to explore these disciplines fully, but rather to pluck the choicest of morsels in which data-driven design is embodied.

Just as data-driven design describes software that lies at the nexus of code and control data, these disciplines, too, lie on a continuum—from code-focused to data-focused. Master data management (MDM), for example, describes a philosophy for managing, coordinating, and governing enterprise data. Although central to software development, its essence lies closest to data modeling and to design. For this reason, MDM is typically presented in a programming language-agnostic format that focuses on data structures, data relationships, data governance, and data federation. Developers are often familiar with MDM concepts but may not have fully explored the MDM knowledge domain.

Other disciplines, such as object-oriented programming (OOP), lie closer to the code-focused end of the spectrum. Although OOP languages such as C++, Java, and Python do interact with and manipulate data and data structures, their instruction is often focused on the design and development of code, with less attention paid to data. Finally, at center stage lies table-driven design, the closest kissing cousin to data-driven design, and an excellent place to begin the foray into these disciplines to which data-driven design owes its humble existence.

8.1 TABLE-DRIVEN DESIGN

Table-driven design (also *table-oriented design* or *database-driven design*) describes software functionality that is driven by tables, in which business rules, conditional logic, and other dynamic elements are contained within tables rather than code. Sound familiar? It should—because table-driven design is the primordial ancestor of data-driven design. The International Organization for Standardization (ISO) defines a *table-driven method* as a "scheme that lets a program look up information in a table rather than using logic statements."[61] Schemery aside, table-driven design has been a pretty stand-up character in relational database community for decades.

Table-driven design espouses the same objectives as data-driven design, but limits itself in decrying that "only tables" drive software, whereas data-driven design encompasses a fuller view of *control data*, in asserting that not only tables but also parameters, linear data structures (e.g., lists), hierarchical data structures (e.g., XML), and other data structures (e.g., configuration files) abstractly instruct software to deliver dynamic functionality.

Thus, in a table-driven design paradigm, the only control data of import are those maintained within tabular data structures having rows and columns—or, in SAS parlance—*data sets* having *observations* and *variables*. Notwithstanding the reduced scope, table-driven design evolved out of the same need for more flexible and configurable software, including the desire to shift basic configuration permissions and responsibilities from developers (interacting with code) to end users (interacting with control tables).

Tanya Kolosova and Samuel Berestizhevsky wrote the eponymous *Table-Driven Strategies for Rapid SAS® Application Development* in 1995, more than a quarter century ago, yet its sage advice endures.[62] They expertly introduce the advantages of configurable software, likening it to codeless software in describing how table-driven design changes the focus of the development team:

> "Code-free design changes the role of the programmer. The programmer is no longer responsible for implementation of the specific application, and he or she is independent from any changes in the application's requirements or application design. Instead, the programmer builds an environment in which the specific application will be generated."[63]

An ancillary limitation of table-driven design results from its dependence on only tables—predominantly proprietary table structures, such as SAS data sets or Oracle tables. Somewhat ironically, despite pursuing greater configurability, table-driven design can reduce interoperability where end users are required to modify software functionality only through these proprietary data structures. This effectively restricts table update activities to only those personnel with access to (and familiarity with) the proprietary software. To overcome this limitation and expose nontechnical end users to data structures, a graphical user interface (GUI) often must be constructed to provide a medium—that is, an *abstraction*—through which control data can be indirectly accessed and modified.

Abstraction levels are introduced and discussed in Section 2.2

Data-driven design, on the other hand, espouses a much more comprehensive view of the spectrum of control data that can drive software, as well as the types of end users—many of whom may not be developers or have access to development applications—who will need to modify control data. Notwithstanding its reduced scope, table-driven design evinces only the noblest of ideals, and provides excellent guidance for the manipulation of control data within SAS data sets and other tabular data structures.

8.2   MASTER DATA MANAGEMENT (MDM)

Master data management (MDM) broadly describes the management of *master data*, which ISO defines as "data held by an organization that describes the entities that are both independent and fundamental for an enterprise that it needs to reference in order to perform its transaction."[64] *Independence* speaks to master data originality and uniqueness, whereas *fundamentality* speaks to the criticality of master data within an enterprise. Synthesizing these terms, *master data* are elements that are *unique*, and thus should be represented only once by data, and *important*, in that organizations and developers should invest in doing master data right.

MDM principles are demonstrated in Section 16.5.2, in which cascading style sheets (CSS) files maintain global stylistic definitions

Although MDM references comprehensive strategies and methods that prescribe data management and data governance operations, MDM is commonly distilled down to a single aphorism—*maintaining a single version of the truth*. This concept is also known as the *golden record*, in which all attributes for an object or element are maintained within a single (golden) record, and in which all derivative references to that object (or its attributes) must obtain their information from that golden record. Thus, when a golden record is added, deleted, or modified, all derivative references to (and uses of) that record are correspondingly (and automatically) modified to reflect the change; data synchronization across an enterprise is achieved.

Reliance on golden records combats the often perceived need to maintain redundant copies of tables, lookup tables, and other data sources within and across an organization. This redundancy often occurs when stakeholders do not trust (or understand) extract-transform-load (ETL) processes that validate, clean, or transform data, and thus choose to maintain their own "version" of some third-party data. Golden records eliminate the data integrity nightmare that occurs when multiple, decentralized, unsynchronized versions of data exist.

Alex Berson and Larry Dubov capture this golden record distillation in defining *MDM* as "the framework of processes and technologies aimed at creating and maintaining an authoritative, reliable, sustainable, accurate, and secure data environment that represents a "single version of the truth," an accepted system of record used both intra- and interenterprise across a diverse set of application systems, lines of business, and user communities."[65] Note the far-reaching implications of MDM, in that the golden record should effectively become the watering hole for the entire community, quenching the respective thirsts of all the critters who require access to the master data it contains.

David Loshin defines MDM as "a collection of best data management practices that orchestrate key stakeholders, participants, and business clients in incorporating the business applications, information management methods, and data management tools to implement the policies, procedures, services, and infrastructure to support the capture, integration, and subsequent shared use of accurate, timely, consistent, and complete master data."[66] Despite not referencing the golden record concept, he captures another hallmark of the scope of MDM—that its implementation takes a village. Stakeholders from the top down must be committed to identifying and verifying golden records, updating records, removing duplicate records, and ensuring that all derivative data products and processes reference only golden records.

MDM is central to data-driven design because control data, too, should be held to MDM exacting standards. For example, a company might rely on a control table that includes ZIP codes and their respective cities and states for its website, marketing, and other business processes. In lieu of the company maintaining separate instances of the same or similar tables across the organization, MDM principles prescribe that a single (golden) table be maintained for all use cases. This is not to suggest that all dependent processes should directly access the ZIP table, but rather that they must directly or indirectly be fed data from that single source of truth.

Master control tables are discussed and demonstrated in Sections 13.3, 13.4, and 13.5, in which a single data model is maintained and updated

As ZIP code definitions are modified over time, these changes should be made only in the ZIP master table, after which the updated data can be made available to all dependent processes. For example, the company's website might use the ZIP table as a lookup table to populate city and state names automatically when a user enters a ZIP code in a data entry field. A separate marketing department might use the ZIP table to validate its mass mailing campaign. Finally, the single instance of the ZIP table could facilitate the company's decision to contract out this data management responsibility to a third-party vendor who could supply updated ZIP data on a periodic or as-needed basis. This shift in data ownership (or stewardship) could be performed more efficiently if all ZIP data were to reside in one table in a standardized format.

Section 2.2.3 discusses how the principle of least privilege can help guard the integrity of control data

The flipside of maintaining master data is that when a golden record is accidentally deleted, modified, or corrupted, these errors can ripple throughout an entire organization. Because of this increased risk, MDM always prioritizes data governance objectives and activities that aim to ensure master data accuracy, uniqueness, and integrity. Thus, a common practice is to restrict master data access to read-only (for all but a few required users or operations). In doing so, subordinate data remain synchronized with master data, yet do not risk corrupting them.

CNTLIN is demonstrated in Sections 13.3.1, 13.4.3, and 13.5.2, in which formats are used to validate, clean, and categorize data

Within data-driven design, data models (including lookup tables and data mappings) commonly benefit from an MDM approach. Values for user-defined SAS formats and informats can be maintained within an external control table or hierarchical structure, ingested into a SAS data set, and ported into a user-defined SAS format or informat using the FORMAT procedure CNTLIN option.

Hierarchical data models, maintained as master control files, are discussed and demonstrated throughout Chapter 15

Moreover, the same master table can be ingested into a SAS data set or hash object, and used as a validation lookup table. The key is to maintain a single, external data structure in a format that supports the varied uses and software applications for which the control data are intended. This interoperability promotes reuse of master data, and ensures that even the most remote recesses of an organization do not waste time recreating, cleaning, or maintaining a duplicate copy of the same control data.

8.3   A BUSINESS RULES APPROACH

In a business sense, far removed from the realm of software, a *business rule* defines the systematic evaluation of conditions, constraints, and calculations to reach a repeatable decision or conclusion. That is, given the same real-world inputs, a business rule should reliably and repeatedly produce the same result or output. Business rules are used across industries and organizations to make sense of the world, to make business decisions, and to automate these processes.

For example, a residential rental agency might have business rules that define acceptance criteria for tenants. One business rule might state that prospective tenants having credit scores below 400 are automatically rejected. A second business rule might specify that annual household income must be greater than 40 times the monthly rent. Although many prospective tenants will need further examination based on other criteria, these business rules can expedite the application review process by automatically eliminating unfavorable applicants, and can help agency staff to reach reliable, repeatable, justifiable decisions regarding the acceptance or denial of applicants.

Business rules define real-world rules used by businesses, but stepping back into the software realm, a *business rule* also describes the conditional logic and other dynamic processing implemented within software to operationalize *real-world* business rules. That is, to a developer, business rules (within software) help model (or abstract) *real-world* business rules.

> Sections 1.3.2 and 1.3.3 demonstrate Social Security Administration business rules that prescribe eligibility requirements

For example, if the rental agency hosts a website on which prospective tenants can complete an online application, the analytic software behind that website could filter the incoming applicants into three bins: automatically accepted, automatically rejected, and those who require manual review. Moreover, based on income, credit rating, and additional criteria, the analytic software could rank the "manual review" candidates so that agency employees could evaluate the "best" candidates first. The software would be performing (and automating) the otherwise manual function of screening applicants, relying on business rules within software.

Business rules are critical to software because they effectively model (and automate) real-world business operations and decision-making. In *Clean Architecture*, Robert C. Martin boasts that "Business rules are the reason a software system exists. They are the core functionality. They carry the code that makes, or saves, money. They are the family jewels."[67] He goes on to decry that "Business rules should be the most independent and reusable code in the system."

Sounds like Uncle Bob would be a fan of data-driven design—because one of the most effective ways to make business rules "independent and reusable" is to extricate them from code, and to maintain them within external data structures. This data independence of business rules provides several advantages over the hardcoded alternative.

First, business rule independence promotes transparency because developers, subject matter experts (SMEs), and other stakeholders can more readily understand rules that have been decoupled and removed from code.[68] This readability can be improved where rules are maintained in standardized, interoperable data structure formats. For example, decision tables and decision trees are tabular data structures that transparently maintain business rules.[69]

Decision tables are demonstrated in Section 14.1, in which business rule constraints and outcomes are modeled within a decision table

Second, independent business rules (maintained in external data structures) facilitate data entry and modification by nontechnical stakeholders. Especially where SMEs are not developers, business rules can nevertheless be modified without reliance on programmers.[70] For example, the employees of the rental agency might have no software development experience, making them a poor choice to build or maintain business rules within code. However, when those rules are instead maintained within a user-friendly spreadsheet, suddenly the employees take ownership and are able to maintain and modify the business rules skillfully, facilitating dynamic software functionality. For example, if the rental agency wanted to increase the credit rating threshold from 400 to 500, this change could be made by nontechnical employees within a spreadsheet—without modification of the underlying code interpreting that spreadsheet.

Third, where SMEs are able to modify and take ownership of business rules, this onus is lifted from developers. This is advantageous because developers, despite being software SMEs, may not be knowledge domain experts as well. For this reason, Malcolm Chisholm unapologetically decries "What cannot be disputed is that IT professional should not define business rules."[71] In truth, many SAS practitioners *do* wear dual hats of software developer and knowledge domain expert, and in these end-user environments, SAS practitioners *absolutely* should define business rules—because they expertly understand the business.

Like all control data abstractly maintained within external data structures, where there is abstraction, there must also be interpretation of that abstraction to facilitate actionable software instruction. Akin to data-driven design and table-driven design, a business rules approach requires that developers shift their focus from writing hardcoded business rules and other conditional logic statements to writing programs that interpret the data structures in which business rules are maintained.

Business rules engines (BREs) typically represent commercial software applications in which business rules are both maintained and interpreted. These systems often promote codeless software in which users can interact with business rules—independent of code—through GUIs. BREs are not further discussed in this text; however, when SAS practitioners build interpreters that parse control data, and especially business rules, they are effectively building user-defined BREs.

> Codeless software is discussed in Section 7.1.3

The extent to which user-defined interpreters can be flexibly reused increases the value of the associated user-defined data structures that are interpreted—because developers can reuse the structures yet do not have to rebuild their interpreters. For example, the same rental agency might also maintain real-world business rules that prescribe how annual rent increases are calculated. Had a flexible data structure been developed, it (and its interpreter) could be reused to interpret the unrelated control data that prescribe rent increases.

> The user-defined macros that interpret user-defined data dictionaries, demonstrated in Section 12.5, represent reusable, user-defined BREs

Of course, there may be exceptions—outliers in which business rules are better suited for hardcoding than addition to an existing data structure. Scott Miller notes that in "a particularly nasty and complex edge case," it may be more desirable to treat a business rule separately, whether maintained in code or in a data structure.[72]

Many texts contrast *business rules* and *data quality rules* (also *data integrity constraints*). Data quality rules focus on aspects such as data uniqueness, validity, standardization, accuracy, and completeness.[73] David Loshin makes the distinction that a data quality rule might describe a set of valid values for a field, yet provide "no insight into why the value must be in that form."[74]

Thus, a *software* business rule should always represent an abstraction of a *real-world* business rule. If a business rule is violated within software, this represents that its corresponding real-world business rule was violated. For example, if a realtor accepts a tenant having a credit score below 400, he breaks a real-world business rule—a policy established by his company by which he is bound. Thus, a software business rule that detects a 350-point credit score (i.e., an unacceptably low score for a successful applicant) is not finding invalid or inaccurate *data*, but rather that some invalid business operation has transpired that violated the associated real-world business rule. On the other hand, when a data quality rule is violated, this indicates that the data are invalid or inaccurate, in which case they do not represent the real-world construct they aim to model.

Despite the distinction in terms, *data quality rules* and *business rules* are often operationalized through identical software development methods, and in some cases, even a single rule. For this reason, although these terms should be differentiated by discerning developers, they can at times be used interchangeably.

For example, the rental agency's online rental application includes an input field in which applicants enter their credit score. The internal software subsequently has a rule that validates the credit score to ensure it exceeds 400, but in so doing, the rule also intrinsically validates that a number—the required data type—has been entered. The rule is a *business rule*, because it models the real-world business rule that the minimum credit score threshold is 400, but is also a *data quality rule*, because the rule would exclude non-numeric values as being invalid (i.e., possessing the wrong data type).

These composite rules can be effective, but in this example, one risk is that an applicant would be removed from consideration because he had typed a character value in the credit score field, and thus appeared to fail to meet the minimum credit score threshold. For this reason, data quality rules are often applied to data prior to business rules to ensure that all data referenced by the business rules are of the correct data type, structure, and format, after which business rules can be applied. Within data-driven design, both data quality rules and business rules are best maintained apart from code within external data structures, thus supporting control data independence.

The necessity to validate or clean data prior to subsequent transformation (including business rules application) is discussed in Sections 13.2 and 13.4

8.4 OBJECT-ORIENTED PROGRAMMING

Object-oriented programming (OOP) relies on *objects*, which represent both data and their respective operations. OOP software is essentially built by linking objects together, like building blocks, and facilitating their communication. OOP rose to prominence in the 1980s and 1990s, due in part to the development of C++, which extended the C language with the addition of classes.

ISO defines a *class* as a "static programming entity in an object-oriented program that contains a combination of functionality and data."[75] And this sounds remarkably similar to *data abstraction*, on which OOP is

Data abstraction is introduced in Section 2.1.1, and is defined and discussed throughout Chapter 4

heavily dependent. Classes represent the reusable templates in which developers define what data types, structures, and operations will be bundled together. Once a class is defined, it can be instantiated repeatedly to create different objects—copies of itself that can contain and operate on varied data. ISO defines an *object* as the "encapsulation of data and services that manipulate that data."[76]

Despite the SAS language being a procedural fourth-generation language (4GL) that is not object-oriented (with the exception of its dabble with DS2 and hash object methods), it can nevertheless benefit from OOP concepts, a standout cast of characters, some of whom include abstraction, software modularity, encapsulation, information hiding, and inheritance.[77]

When an object is instantiated, it contains the same data operations—*methods*, in OOP parlance—as its superordinate *class*. The object's methods, however, are able to interact with the data that are unique to that object. Thus, a class is likened to a data structure template that defines how data will be structured, what data will be supported, and what operations can be performed on those data. An object represents a specific instance of that data structure and its data, and will boast the same methods that were defined in its class.

Although a 4GL like the SAS language will never approach the full functionality of a third-generation language (3GL) in its ability to support true classes and objects, highly flexible and reusable SAS software can be constructed by defining and reusing user-defined data structures, as well as their respective operations.

8.4.1 *Encapsulation and Information Hiding*

Encapsulation contains, protects, and hides data and functionality, effectively placing a *black box* around a software module, and separating it from other components. This also enables the contents of the box to be referenced collectively as an object. The Institute of Electrical and Electronics Engineers (IEEE) defines *encapsulation* as a "software development technique that consists of isolating a system function or a set of data and operations on those data within a module and providing precise specifications for the module."[78]

> *Specification* is introduced in Section 2.1.2, and is defined and demonstrated in Section 3.2

The "precise specification" is key, without which a module would be secure (in that no other process could call or access it), as well as rendered useless. Thus, the specification defines parameters through which software can call a module, as well as outputs that will be produced or returned—

essentially poking tiny holes in the black box so that prescribed messages in predetermined formats can be passed to and from modules.

One aspect of encapsulation is *information hiding* (also *data hiding*), which ISO defines as a "software development technique in which each module's interfaces reveal as little as possible about the module's inner workings and other modules are prevented from using information about the module that is not in the module's interface specification."[79] Various languages and authors espouse varying views as to the degree of sameness or separation that exists between *encapsulation* and *information hiding*. For example, within Python, attributes can be marked as PRIVATE or PROTECTED to hide their information.[80] In a discussion about SAS software, conversely, the terms can often be used interchangeably.

Encapsulation is commonly achieved through procedural abstraction, in which user-defined procedures or functions are created. A procedure's specification will document its functionality, inputs, outputs, return codes, return values, and known vulnerabilities or usage caveats. Thereafter, a SAS practitioner can invoke a user-defined procedure or function with confidence, guided by its specification, and without having to understand the intricacies of how the procedure was built or how it functions.

8.4.2 Modularity

Modularity breaks software into bite-sized chunks that are sometimes described as being "functionally discrete and loosely coupled." In this anecdotal definition, a module should "do one and only one thing" and should not have unnecessary external dependencies. Modularity has also been described as expressing "high module cohesion and low module coupling." This us-versus-them mentality is less restrictive than the *functionally discrete* moniker because it groups like-minded (rather than *single-minded*) functionality inside a module, with other functionality held outside.

Software modularity is introduced in Section 1.3.2

ISO defines *modularity* as the "degree to which a system or computer program is composed of discrete components such that change to one component has minimal impact on other components."[81] This definition speaks to the two primary advantages of modularity—to make software more stable and more secure. Although not explicitly called out in the definition, software reusability and extensibility are also facilitated through modularity because smaller, discrete chunks of code having fewer dependencies are more likely to be reused or repurposed.

Modularity promotes software stability because only the software module being surgically operated on must be splayed open, not the entire body of software. Thus, where corrective maintenance is required on one user-defined function, other functions and modules do not have to be accessed or modified. This, in turn, increases the security and integrity of software because what has not been touched is not at risk of accidental corruption, and does not need to be retested, revalidated, and rereleased into production. Some integration testing or regression testing may nevertheless be required (to test how the modified module interacts with other software components), but the risk of other modules having been accidentally corrupted is mitigated.

Modularity promotes software reuse because smaller chunks of code have less functionality and fewer dependencies, and are more readily integrated into new and existing software products. Although modularity is often pursued in its own right, it exists as one of the natural sequelae of OOP programming; because OOP relies on concepts like procedural abstraction, data abstraction, encapsulation, and information hiding, object-oriented software is more likely to be naturally decomposed into smaller pieces than equivalent procedural software. SAS software, too, however, can be improved where modular design is embraced.

> Software modularity promoting software reuse is demonstrated in Section 10.4.3

8.4.3 Inheritance

Inheritance is the final OOP concept discussed, which IEEE defines as the "semantic notion by which the responsibilities (properties and constraints) of a subclass are considered to include the responsibilities of a superclass, in addition to its own, specifically declared responsibilities."[82] Without wading too far into the marshlands, OOP languages allow subclasses to be spawned from classes—and this is beneficial because class methods and attributes do not need to be redefined.

This user-defined inheritance is unavailable in the SAS language; however, when SAS practitioners are building a user-defined data structure, they should consider what attributes are being inherited from its superordinate data structure or file type. For example, SAS arrays are defined only within data set data structures, and despite the utility of arrays, they are limited by the same rules that define and govern SAS data sets. Similarly, when a user-defined configuration file is maintained within a text file, its data structure must conform to characteristics that it inherits from the text file type, including both functionality and limitations.

> SAS arrays are introduced in Section 4.4.3, and user-defined configuration files in Section 16.3

As a 4GL, the SAS language operates at a higher level of abstraction than 3GL OOP languages. This abstraction removes complexity and allows SAS practitioners to focus on the business of all things data. This abstraction also removes functionality and flexibility innately available in 3GLs that birthed OOP, its concepts, classes, methods, and madness. Although core OOP concepts like encapsulation, information hiding, modularity, and inheritance may appear far different when operationalized within the SAS language, these concepts can nevertheless spur more flexible, reusable SAS software through data-driven design.

Data structure inheritance is introduced in Section 4.5.2, and is discussed in Sections 9.5 and 9.6

8.5 SUMMARY

This chapter introduced various disciplines and methodologies from which data-driven design borrows its concepts and principles, and with which it overlaps. Rather than lying in contrast to these related disciplines, data-driven design represents an amalgam—a diverse toolkit from which developers can select design patterns and development techniques that deliver more flexible, configurable, reusable software.

Table-driven design was described, including its centrality in data-driven design. MDM concepts introduced the *golden record*—the single source of truth that can eliminate redundancy that too often occurs when multiple versions of control data are maintained within a team or organization.

A business rules approach was described, in which business rules are extracted from code and maintained within external data structures to promote maintainability and configurability. Data quality rules were contrasted with business rules, in that the latter should model real-world business rules that exist outside of software. Finally, OOP was introduced, including the concepts of abstraction, modularity, encapsulation, information hiding, and inheritance—each of which can support data-driven design.

Part II
Control Data

Chapter 9.

CONTRASTING CONTROL DATA

This chapter has the following objectives:

- ❖ Introduce several axes along which control data and their data structures can be compared and contrasted.

- ❖ Discuss control data stewardship and role-based responsibilities in maintaining control data.

- ❖ Define built-in and user-defined data structures, and describe the benefits of each.

- ❖ Describe control data persistence and its benefit in versioning software during development, in troubleshooting failed software, and in evaluating and contrasting data models.

- ❖ Demonstrate how characteristics of superordinate files and data structures are inherited by the user-defined data structures defined within them.

- ❖ Describe the importance of intrinsic *element decomposition*, and why it should influence the decision to select built-in over user-defined data structures.

- ❖ Discuss control data communication, including bidirectional communications in which control data not only drive software but also are modified by software.

Control data come in all shapes, sizes, and formats, their commonality being their love for bossing around software, and telling it what to do. Control data complexity can vary from single arguments that are passed to procedures and functions, to hierarchical control tables and complex configuration files; from data maintained only in memory, to data structures saved in diverse file types; from control data accessed only by software processes, to control data maintained by administrators, developers, and even nontechnical end users. This chapter introduces several axes along which control data can be identified and differentiated.

Control data always represent abstraction—the levers that you push or pull to effect some representative movement within software. And because the point of *having* control data is to be able to *modify* those control data, the data structures that maintain control data must be sufficiently adaptable to accommodate control data variability, and sufficiently strict to ensure control data do not violate the house rules of the containers in which they live. Focus and flexibility—the Yin and Yang that define and drive software abstraction.

This chapter introduces subsequent control data chapters, whose collective objective is to model the use of built-in data structures that store invaluable control data, and to demonstrate how user-defined data structures can be built to be sufficiently robust, flexible, and reusable. To this end, these control data axes explore dynamics that SAS practitioners should consider when deciding how and where to maintain control data to meet specific software requirements.

9.1 CONTROL DATA AXES AND CLASSIFICATIONS

The following axes differentiate control data, and are described in subsequent sections:

- **Control Data Stewardship** – Data stewards are the stakeholders (or processes) responsible for accessing, updating, validating, and maintaining control data.
- **Persistence** – Persistent control data are stored on disk (e.g., control files, configuration files), whereas ephemeral control data exist only in memory (e.g., in-memory arguments, in-memory hash objects).

- **Built-in vs. User-Defined** – *Built-in* data structures are native to a software application, whereas *user-defined* data structures are designed, developed, and documented by developers.
- **File Type** – Persistent control data can be stored in various file types (e.g., SAS data sets, spreadsheets, text files).
- **Data Structure** – The general structure of control data can vary greatly, and include scalar (e.g., simple arguments), linear (e.g., lists), tabular (e.g., data sets), hierarchical (e.g., XML files), and complex structures (e.g., non-tabular configuration files).
- **Tokenization and Element Decomposition** – Where a data structure includes multiple elements (i.e., values), it must be parsed, tokenized, and decomposed, and this can occur intrinsically or require user-defined programmatic methods.
- **Communication Directionality** – *Unidirectional communication* describes control data read by software processes, whereas *bidirectional communication* describes software processes that can additionally alter those control data.

Given the many axes along which control data can independently vary, it would be difficult, if not impossible, to select a single axis with which to differentiate *all* control data. Within this text, however, *data structure* is used as a proxy classification, with chapters in Part II focusing on specific data structures:

- **Lists** – SAS does not define a built-in list data structure, although user-defined lists can be operationalized both within Base SAS and the SAS macro language. One-dimensional SAS arrays, a linear quasi-data structure, are also discussed alongside lists.
- **Control Tables** – Tables arrange data in same-format columns (i.e., variables) and rows (i.e., observations), and built-in tables include SAS data sets and hash objects. User-defined methods can also operationalize spreadsheets, XML files, and other files within tabular structures.
- **Hierarchical Structures** – A hierarchical or relational structure (e.g., XML) must be denormalized before it can be represented in tabular format.
- **Configuration Files** – This catch-all classification captures complex, non-tabular data structures that are primarily maintained within text files.

Although subsequent chapters are organized around data structure classification, data structure is typically *not* the first design consideration when planning control data that will drive some application or software module. For example, control data stewardship—comprising the authority, accountability, and responsibility for data design, maintenance, and utilization—is often a prior consideration. Moreover, are the control data envisioned as being ephemeral, or should they be stored in code or in some external data structure? And must the control data be archived to support software versioning, or other policy or legal considerations?

Thus, file type and data structure, despite being most emblematic of a specific housing in which control data are maintained, are more commonly determined through a process of elimination during which functional and performance requirements for the control data, as well as other implications, are discussed during software planning and design. Yes, there are times when *prima facie* you will "just know" that you need a control table for a specific task; however, other instances will necessitate more careful consideration of control data and data structure options.

9.2   DATA STEWARDSHIP

Control data represent the "data" in data-driven programming, and similar to any driver behind the wheel, control data should be expected to provide varied, dynamic input. That is, although some control data (like a lookup table enumerating U.S. state names and their respective abbreviations) may be set once and never be modified, control data must be able to be altered when necessary. In other cases, such as when arguments are passed to called modules, control data may be in near-constant flux, differing each time they are passed. In all cases, however, someone (i.e., a stakeholder) or something (i.e., a process) must possess access and ability to modify control data; this responsibility falls to the control data steward.

Control data stewards can be software developers, but they do not have to be. The data independence espoused by data-driven design aims to separate control data from the code that interprets and operationalizes them. One benefit of maintaining external data structures is to allow developers to relinquish maintenance responsibilities for control data, and to cede responsibility to those most familiar with the data, who understand the underlying business, business rules, and business processes.

Thus, as SAS practitioners shift from a code-driven to a data-driven design paradigm, new opportunities for data stewardship arise, including

---

The adoption of external business rules can shift some data stewardship responsibilities from developers to end users, as discussed in Section 8.3

Data independence is introduced as a data-driven pillar in Section 1.3.3, and is further discussed in Section 4.6

not only a diverse array of stakeholders, but also co-parenting (i.e., shared responsibility) patterns in which multiple stakeholders simultaneously maintain separate control data for a single software product. This sharing of control data responsibilities facilitates two objectives—the cybersecurity principle of *least privilege*, in which stakeholders' accesses are minimized to limit their threat to a system, and the concept of domain knowledge expertise, in which subject matter experts (SMEs) manage only the control data within their respective domains.

> Various stakeholders are described in Section 7.1, and their roles in sharing responsibilities for managing control data is discussed in Section 2.2.3

For example, a single program might have built-in control data that are maintained by a system or SAS administrator, such as access to the SAS configuration file, the autoexec.sas file, or the SAS registry. Sensitive user-defined data structures, such as user-defined configuration files, also might be brought under the purview of an administrator to ensure they are safeguarded and not accidentally modified.

SAS developers, meanwhile, could be granted access to less critical control data that drive software modules, or to data models that drive data product formatting. Where data model expertise lies not with developers but with business analysts, product owners, or other SMEs, these stakeholders—despite having varying degrees of technical expertise—could be handed the keys to maintain the data structures whose content (and control data) they know best.

Finally, in highly configurable data-driven design, nontechnical end users often maintain control data that drive the style and formatting for reports and other data products, as well as other less critical aspects of software functionality. End users gain the ability to *configure* reports, so developers do not have to *customize* reports—*configuration* representing the modification of only control data, and *customization* representing actual software development to effect an equivalent change in functionality.

> *Customization* and *configuration* are defined and differentiated in Section 16.1

The other data stewards in this diverse field are the non-human ones—the processes that supply or maintain control data for us. Their autonomy and performance can be mesmerizing—so much so that we can forget they are even pulling strings behind the scenes. For example, a control table built to record and archive process completion metrics could be used to drive software recoverability. That is, when software fails, it can automatically recover to the *checkpoint* that demonstrates the point of last known success, rather than having to rerun processes that had previously completed successfully.

> *Checkpoints* are introduced and demonstrated in Section 14.2

9.3   PERSISTENCE

The degree of control data persistence describes whether data are available only during program or process execution, or are maintained thereafter. In some cases, a temporary control table (like a SAS data set) may be created as software executes. However, if that data set is not saved in a permanent SAS library, and persists only in a SAS temporary library (WORK), the data structure is not considered to be persistent. Thus, persistent control data represent those data that will be available (for some implied or stated duration) after software terminates.

Persistent control data provide several benefits over their ephemeral counterparts, including the ability to version software as it is being developed, to audit failed processes, and to run competing or contrasting instances of software modules using different data models (or other control data). Conversely, arguments—including those that drive procedures, functions, subroutines, and applications—are often specified at runtime by developers or other end users, in which case they are not archived and cannot be interrogated after program termination (including failure). One exception occurs when batch jobs contain application initialization arguments, thus memorializing application control data.

SAS logs, too, often can capture the arguments and other control data passed ephemerally to SAS programs and processes, where no other mechanism exists to record control data. However, logs first must be saved to log files; not all control data may be shown in logs; and control data will typically need to be extricated from system notes and other log information to isolate them for further analysis. In general, where there is any chance that a SAS log will need to be scrutinized later to decipher with which control data some program was run, it is best to have purposefully written control data to the log with PUT or %PUT statements to ensure they can be unambiguously identified and interpreted.

As software is developed, it is often *versioned*, in which copies of the software are archived at notable points in time. Versioning practices differ by programming language, development tool, environment, local policy, developer preference, and a host of other factors, but a common goal of versioning is to maintain working copies of software to which a team can "roll back," if necessary, to return to a functional state after software failure. Even a SAS practitioner coding alone in a dank, dark, grue-infested basement may save copies of a program as it is being constructed, and this, too, describes a home-grown form of versioning.

More structured versioning can support change management and release management policies, in which versions represent functional, validated software states that have passed the rigors of software testing and acceptance. These versions are typically documented, with notes declaring what functionality was added or modified, what performance was enhanced, or which defects were corrected. This more formalized versioning may even be required within some industries (e.g., pharmaceutical, clinical trials) for which policy, professional standards, or government regulations prescribe the archival of production software.

Control data are software, too, as discussed in Section 1.5

Even within less restrictive environments, versioning is often used to create functional software baselines that support software restoration— both because a production environment can roll back to a prior, functional version of the software, and because prior versions of code can provide a baseline against which to compare the current, dysfunctional software during troubleshooting. Within a code-driven design paradigm, the solution is simple, or at least simple to describe—review the code; find the error; fix the error; and rerun the program. That is, hardcoded software typically fails because of issues with *code*—because hardcoded software comprises only code.

Yet, within a data-driven design paradigm, software comprises both code and control data. Thus, software versioning must similarly maintain and archive both control data and the underlying code that interprets and operationalizes them. Versioning only code would not allow data-driven software to roll back, nor would it accurately capture the state in which software had been run. Where control data represent external files, in facilitating greater control data independence, both program files and control files are commonly packaged, zipped, and archived for posterity.

Data independence, a pillar of data-driven design, is introduced in Section 1.3.3, and is further discussed in Section 4.6

Finally, SAS is often the application of choice in support of *data analytic development*, in which ultimate business value is conferred not through the production, release, or sale of software itself, but rather through some resultant data product or data-driven decision that SAS software facilitates. For example, Base SAS might be selected for use in developing complex, competing financial models that rely on SAS programs, but which do not directly derive business value from those programs.

Data-driven design facilitates data analytic development where competing data models can be maintained within separate, external *control files*—not separate, competing versions of *code*. For example, if two econometricians are evaluating and testing their respective economic world views, and those models are hardcoded into SAS programs, then two separate streams of software must be tested, maintained, updated, and so forth. When a SAS developer supporting the econometricians wants to upgrade and add functionality to one program, he is relegated to modifying both competing software streams.

The data-driven alternative, of course, is to wrest the data model from the code, and maintain it instead within an external data structure. In doing so, the data model alone can be versioned, with each version representing an updated or competing model that is being evaluated. Moreover, as econometricians want to compare their respective data models with those of their peers, they can do so by sharing only the external data structures, rather than having to share the underlying code that interprets them—because the code remains consistent.

Thus, data models should be competing, but software versions should not! *Versioning* is intended to describe the serialized progression of software over its lifespan, with only one version reigning supreme at any single point in time, and the rest relegated to archival status. Where developers or other stakeholders attempt to maintain multiple, competing, production versions of one software product, linear versioning is vacated, and at worst, versioning can devolve into a reticulated fracas of frayed functionality that actively stymies future software enhancements.

Data-driven design instead maintains only one version of production software at any point in time, as dynamic functionality is wrought by control data, not code. For example, a single software product could support both econometricians, with each maintaining a respective data model within a separate control file. This data independence empowers stakeholders to modify their respective data models over time at their discretion. At the same time, SAS developers could separately improve the underlying code throughout its lifespan to incorporate functional and performance enhancements—because only one version of the SAS code is being maintained.

Control data persistence is not always required. User-defined functions, subroutines, and other modules that lack complexity often parameterize all control data without untoward effect. However, where software auditing or archival is necessary, or where multiple versions of complex data models or other control data need to be maintained or compared, control data persistence can facilitate these objectives.

9.4 BUILT-IN VS. USER-DEFINED

Built-in data types, data structures, and their associated operations are those that ship (or download) with a commercial software application. Within the SAS language, character and numeric built-in data types can be declared, and these two types constitute all variables defined within the primary built-in data structure, the SAS data set. *User-defined* data structures describe the structures that SAS practitioners design and develop, such as macro lists, indexed macro lists, data dictionaries, lookup tables, and configuration files.

Built-in data structures tend to be structurally sound, well defined, and well documented. Hundreds of hours of design, development, testing, and validation will have produced a reliable, robust structure that can be confidently used with diverse data. User-defined data structures, conversely, often lack this rigorous testing and validation, may be undocumented (or under-documented), and may be intended for use with only a specific program or a specific use case. Thus, user-defined data structures often lack the flexibility and reusability inherent in built-in data structures.

One of the most structurally integral aspects of any data structure is element decomposition, in which a linear, tabular, or other data structure is parsed and tokenized into its constituent elements. Built-in data structures typically handle this decomposition intrinsically; thus, developers do not need to build parsing, iteration, or extraction operations. Intrinsic decomposition is one of the principal factors elevating built-in data structures over their user-defined counterparts.

Despite actual or perceived shortcomings, user-defined data structures and their respective operations are invaluable because they effectively extend the functionality of software beyond its native offering. In some unfortunate instances, however, SAS practitioners painstakingly recreate functionality already provided by the SAS application and its built-in data structures and associated operations. These instances can only be avoided by fully understanding the breadth of built-in software capabilities—including those of both data structures and their operations.

> Data structure decomposition into constituent elements is more fully discussed in Section 9.6

In other cases, SAS practitioners do need to create user-defined data structures to meet some need not delivered through built-in functionality. Developers can design more enduring, flexible, reusable data structures by modeling data structure design after built-in data structures, to include how they facilitate data abstraction, procedural abstraction, and iteration abstraction—all of which at some point may be required.

Despite the "versus" in the section title, built-in and user-defined data structures often overlap more than they contrast. After all, user-defined data structures must be built upon some substrate. For example, a control table maintained within a SAS data set will represent a SAS data set—plain and simple. Additional data quality rules or business rules may *describe* how those control data should be maintained within the data set, as well as the type and format of data they can contain, but these rules must be enforced programmatically through user-defined methods—or else they will remain *descriptions*, not *prescriptions*.

Inheritance is introduced within an OOP paradigm in Section 8.4.3, and data structure inheritance is discussed and demonstrated in Section 4.5.2

Similarly, where increased interoperability or flexibility (of control data) is required, text files represent a common, canonical file format in which user-defined, subordinate data structures can be built. For example, cascading style sheets (CSS) and other configuration files are maintained in text files. But even the plainest text files must follow the ANSI standard that prescribes file characteristics such as end-of-line (EOL) and end-of-file (EOF) markers. Thus, all user-defined data structures inherently inherit both functionality and limitations from the superordinate file type and data structure in which they are maintained.

Where a built-in data structure will not suffice, and the decision is made to adopt or design a user-defined data structure, planning for that use must incorporate not only the intended *structure* but also the *associated operations* that the data structure will support. Bear in mind, however, that in many cases, a built-in data structure can deliver requisite functionality if only new, user-defined operations are built to operationalize the existing structure.

9.5 FILE TYPE

Persistent data structures can embody any number of file types, including SAS data sets, spreadsheets, canonical text files (e.g., CSV, XML, CSS), user-defined configuration files, and a host of others. When the decision has been made to persist control data, the next design considerations are often *in what file type* and *with what data structure* should I intern my data?

These decisions are often made together, as file type and data structure are tightly bound, if not inseparable.

In some cases, the data structure is indistinguishable from the underlying file type, as is common in proprietary file types like SAS data sets. In these cases, when a developer chooses to maintain control data in a SAS7BDAT *file*, he is simultaneously selecting the SAS data set *data structure*—they are inseparable. For example, the SAS7BDAT file type will always represent a tabular data set; it will never represent a complex structure like a CSS file or hierarchical XML file.

In other cases, file type may prescribe certain (but not all) characteristics that are inherited by the underlying data structure. For example, intrinsic in all spreadsheets is the notion of the *cell*—a defined element that can contain data, but which is universally and unambiguously separated from all other cells within the spreadsheet. Although all spreadsheets contain cells, the ways in which they can be arranged is limitless; thus, the data structures that Excel supports will also be more varied than those supported by proprietary tables (like SAS data sets and Oracle tables).

Text files add even more flexibility to data structures, and thus also add distance between file type definitions and the data structures they contain. Thus, text files can support an endless variety of canonical and user-defined subordinate data structures. Canonical data structures include CSS, XML, and others, and prescribe a data structure that is enforced not by the text file itself, but rather by parsers that interpret the canonical data structures within the text file.

For example, "malformed XML"—the ubiquitous error that signals something has gone awry—results from data that are *valid* within the text file (file type definition), yet *invalid* within the XML file (data structure definition). You will never see a "malformed SAS data set" error because there is no distance between the SAS7BDAT file type and the SAS data set data structure—they are one in the same.

When selecting a file type in which to maintain control data, one of the implied decisions being made also selects the inherited characteristics— from the file type to the underlying data structure. For example, SAS data sets intrinsically decompose observations into variables, so control tables maintained as SAS data sets will also share this benefit. Similarly, control data maintained within spreadsheets will inherit the "cell" structure, and those maintained within text files, the EOL and EOF markers.

Although all SAS data sets are totally tabular all day every day, some hierarchical and relational data can be normalized and stored in data sets, as demonstrated in Sections 15.1 and 15.2

In the end, and like the selection of a data structure, the selection of a file type (in which to maintain control data) will reflect the requisite balance of flexibility and functionality, with built-in file types providing the greatest functionality and breadth of associated built-in operations, and canonical file types (including text files) providing varying degrees of flexibility and functionality, dependent largely on the subordinate data structure in which control data are maintained.

9.6   DATA STRUCTURE

Data structures and *data types* are defined and contrasted in Section 4.2, and *atomic types* are introduced in Section 4.3

Section 9.1 introduces the data structure classification for control data, around which content in Part II of this text is organized. The structure of control data can vary widely from scalar arguments representing a single value, to linear structures that represent multiple same-type values, to tables and other multi-dimensional or complex structures. In this sense, *data structure* is used generically to represent *all the ways* of containerizing control data—even the simplest, such as when an argument passes a numeric or character scalar value to a process.

As discussed in Section 9.5, control data file type and the underlying data structure are irrevocably linked, and in some cases (such as with proprietary file formats like the SAS data set), they are one in the same. Where a file type can support multiple and varying data structures, data structure flexibility is facilitated. However, this flexibility also inherently creates a gap between file type *prescription* and data structure *description*.

This gap, known as the *prescription-description gap* (or the *definition-description gap*) dictates that although *file type integrity* will be enforced automatically (through built-in methods), *data structure integrity* will need to be enforced programmatically through operations specific to that data structure. Wherever a user-defined data structure is defined, this gap will exist, and the breadth of user-defined operations that must be designed will vary based on the required functionality, the degree of robustness and validation that is sought, and the relative distance between the subordinate user-defined data structure and its superordinate file type.

Similarly, a user-defined data structure can be designed within a built-in data structure or data type. This, too, can inherently create a gap between the subordinate user-defined data structure being *described* and the superordinate built-in data structure or data type being *defined*. For example, all macro variables are declared as character data type; numeric macro variables do not exist. However, when a macro parameter is declared and its usage requires only numeric data to be passed, this numeric restriction must be enforced programmatically through user-defined data quality rules—because a gap exists between the character definition and the numeric description.

Thus, selection of a data structure—whether built-in or user-defined—must include an awareness of the functionality, limitations, and other characteristics of all superordinate file types and data structures. Considering a CSS file to maintain control data that describe style elements for a report? This is a fantastic solution, but you'd better understand the characteristics of text files, as well as how SAS interprets them—because the CSS data structure is defined within text files. Considering creating a custom control table within a spreadsheet? Well, then you need to understand how SAS imports and interprets spreadsheets or CSV files.

The use of CSS files, as leveraged by the PROC REPORT CSSSTYLE option, is demonstrated in Section 16.5

In general, as the prescription-description gap increases for a selected data structure, so too will development effort commensurately increase—with SAS practitioners required to build methods that enforce and interpret the data structure rules that are being *described* yet not *prescribed*. Still, the juice is worth the squeeze when the selected data structure and its associated operations deliver the required functionality.

Linear data structures represent a common method of containerizing multiple control data elements. Within the SAS language, common linear data structures include observations, whose variables can be referenced as an array, and user-defined macro lists and indexed macro lists. A character variable can also be described as a user-defined list, in which user-specified delimiters separate values that are interpreted as constituent elements of the variable. Such user-defined, multi-element data structures are not intrinsically decomposed (into their constituent elements), so user-defined operations must be developed to parse, tokenize, and iterate the structures; this necessity is discussed in the next section.

Tabular data structures include SAS data sets, SAS hash objects, non-SAS tables, and other file types (such as spreadsheets) that can be operationalized in tabular form. For example, control data can be used to generate SAS formats and informats, and are often stored within tables that support both *mapping* (i.e., one-to-one) and *multimap* (i.e., many-to-one) formats.

Data mappings and multimaps are defined in Section 4.3.3

Hierarchical structures include data structures that are non-tabular, but which sometimes can be denormalized into a table. For example, XML can represent hierarchical data without the redundancy that an equivalent table would require; thus, parent elements may be included only once within an XML structure, yet apply to all subordinate child elements. In addition to being highly interoperable, XML files can represent some control data more efficiently than tabular structures.

Finally, complex data structures represent the big bucket in which all other data structures are subsumed within this text. These structures principally include canonical data structures (e.g., CSS) and user-defined data structures (e.g., configuration files) that are maintained within text files.

This duality of data abstraction, which comprises not only structure but also functionality, is introduced in Section 2.1.1, and discussed in Section 4.5

As SAS practitioners are selecting data structures in which to maintain control data, including the decision of whether to use a built-in or user-defined data structure, the availability of associated operations should heavily influence this decision. Central to data abstraction, a data structure's definition includes not only its structure and format but also the operations that interact with it. The accoutrement of available operations, inasmuch as the innate characteristics of a data structure, often sways the decision in selecting one structure over another.

9.7   TOKENIZATION AND ELEMENT DECOMPOSITION

Most data structures are containers comprising multiple elements, with each element representing a value. Thus, *element decomposition* describes the ability to decompose a data structure into its constituent elements, by universally and unambiguously identifying and separating elements. *Intrinsic* decomposition further describes the parsing of a data structure in which built-in (rather than user-defined) operations perform this decomposition. For example, a SAS array is indexed and thus can leverage built-in operations to access individual array elements. However, a macro list instead relies on user-defined operations to iterate over and extract individual list elements.

Section 10.2 defines the macro list, and Section 5.5 illustrates some complexities of parsing user-defined data structures like macro lists

Element decomposition also occurs intrinsically whenever a SAS data set is divided into observations and variables—which is all the time, every time. You never open a SAS data set to find that a value has quantum-leaped itself from one observation to another, or from one variable to another. As SAS practitioners, we may at times experience difficulty in initially ingesting data from a raw source into a SAS data set, but once the data have landed, they are there to stay—or until we command otherwise.

This paradigm differs substantially from data structures in which elements are *not* intrinsically defined and decomposed. For example, when a character variable contains a comma-delimited list of values, it can be conceptualized as a user-defined data structure—anecdotally, a *user-defined list*. The variable type is *defined* as character, yet user-defined rules *describe* that commas delimit values (i.e., elements) within the variable. This *prescription-description* gap is discussed in the previous section.

User-defined SAS lists are introduced in Section 10.5, and are explored in Section 4.5

Whenever delimitation rules are user-defined, associated user-defined operations must be built to tokenize the data structure into its constituent elements, to iterate across elements, and to extract values therefrom. This can be a straightforward task, where control data do not contain special characters; however, the complexity of the control data contained within user-defined data structures commensurately increases the complexity of the operations that must parse and otherwise interact with those data.

Section 4.5.5 demonstrates the coding complexity to read a user-defined list that contains quotation marks

Intrinsic element decomposition is one of the primary rationales for selecting built-in data structures, such as SAS data sets, over user-defined data structures. The ability of an application or programming language to parse a data structure natively into its constituent elements is not only powerful, but also represents built-in functionality that developers will not have to engineer through user-defined operations.

9.8   COMMUNICATION DIRECTIONALITY

Control data *drive* software; this much is clear, but control data can also be *driven by* software. Control data comprise the arguments, lists, tables, configuration files, and other control files that provide dynamic input which produce dynamic functionality. But in some instances, control data are listening as much as they are speaking. And in these cases, control data themselves can be considered to be as much a part of dynamic output as dynamic input.

At the most rudimentary level, control data are passed as arguments to applications or called processes; the data are ingested, and dynamic functionality is pooped out. This unidirectional communication (of control data) is also common when control tables and configuration files are read by software; the control data are stored persistently, but they nevertheless interact with software through equivalent procedural abstraction, and the control files are not modified by software execution.

In other cases, the control data themselves can be modified by a process through bidirectional communication. For example, SAS subroutines can modify the arguments they are passed, which can include domain data or control data. The SORTC subroutine sorts a series of

Section 3.7 introduces built-in and user-defined subroutines variables (horizontally, not vertically like the SORT procedure), after which the values of each variable have been reassigned to other variables, and rearranged in ascending order. SORTC can similarly be utilized to sort the values contained in SAS array elements.

User-defined operations can manifest bidirectional communication by relying on *call-by-reference* invocations. Within the SAS macro language, a global macro variable can be effectively passed by reference by parameterizing and passing its variable *name* rather than *value*. In so doing, a macro receives the global macro variable *name* (as an argument), modifies that global macro variable *value*, and terminates, after which the value of the global macro variable remains altered in the calling program. The FCMP procedure similarly supports bidirectional communication (of parameters) in both functions and subroutines, leveraged by the OUTARGS statement.

Call by reference and *call by value* are discussed and contrasted in Section 6.5

More complex bidirectional communication can be achieved through control tables and other control files that are modified by processes. In some cases, the same processes both read data from and write data to a control file, whereas in other cases, one process will write data to a control file while another process reads data from that control file. Where multiple processes (or users) are anticipated to modify the same data set or other control file, appropriate file-locking protocols should be emplaced to ensure functional failures do not occur from concurrent attempts to access the same locked data set or control file.

Checkpoints are introduced and demonstrated in Section 14.2

Checkpoint tables are one example of control tables that support bidirectional communication. They contain process metadata that record the successful (or unsuccessful) completion status of processes, and which support software recoverability objectives. They enable software to recover more rapidly and efficiently—from the point of last known success, rather than from the start of an often lengthy workflow. Thus, successful tasks that preceded some failure are recognized as having completed, and can be skipped rather than redundantly rerun.

For example, when a slew of serialized processes exists, checkpoints record (in real-time) the successful completion of each process, and upon recovery from a failure, facilitate autonomous return to the process that should be rerun. Checkpoints facilitate software that recovers more quickly, efficiently, and autonomously because processes are modularized, and because their completion statuses are recorded within a control table.

Checkpoint tables embody bidirectional communication because processes are both recording their successful (or failed) completion statuses and querying the same control table to ensure that prerequisite processes have completed successfully. Within the SAS language, checkpoint tables are most commonly operationalized within SAS data sets.

Where data-driven design has been adopted to facilitate software configurability objectives, graphical user interfaces (GUIs) can be utilized to facilitate indirect access to control data, especially by nontechnical end users. GUIs typically provide data entry constraints, thus enforcing that only valid data types and formats can be entered. Behind the scenes, GUIs are interacting with control tables or configuration files; however, they provide safer, indirect access for end users than direct access to the underlying control data. Highly configurable software is often described as *codeless* when all dynamic functionality is configured through a GUI.

Codeless software is discussed in Section 7.1.3

GUIs are uncommon, however, within SAS development environments, which are often teeming with highly technical end users who maintain and modify control data directly. Within this end-user development paradigm, control files are less likely to be modified by software, and more commonly represent unidirectional communication in which control data give orders to—but do not take orders from—software.

9.9 SUMMARY

Control data can be differentiated along a number of axes, several of which were discussed in this chapter. In selecting how to best operationalize control data within data types and data structures, SAS practitioners will often need to evaluate these axes to ensure that control data are appropriately represented, and that they include the requisite balance of functionality and flexibility.

In making this decision, control data stewardship should be considered, which describes the ownership or shared ownership of control data maintenance responsibilities, and which can include people or processes. Control data persistence, which describes the degree to which data are maintained after process or software termination, should also be considered, with objectives such as software rollback, versioning, archival, and auditing facilitated by persistent control data.

File type and data structure are two of the most salient considerations when selecting a data structure. Built-in data structures afford the reliability and robustness of commercial software, as well as myriad built-in operations designed to interact with built-in data structures. User-defined data structures, conversely, can at times provide more flexibility than their built-in counterparts, but often require associated parsing, iteration, and other operations to be designed. Ultimately, the decision of how to maintain control data is an important and enduring one, so choose wisely!

Chapter 10.

LISTS

This chapter has the following objectives:

- ❖ Demonstrate the creation and parsing of user-defined lists within SAS character variables.

- ❖ Define and differentiate between (unindexed) macro lists and indexed macro lists, and demonstrate the clear advantages of the latter.

- ❖ Introduce user-defined operations that can support and extend the functionality of user-defined macro lists.

- ❖ Illustrate the complexities that spaces, commas, symbols, and other special characters can cause during list definition, creation, iteration, and decomposition.

- ❖ Demonstrate how espousing backward compatibility can achieve longer-lasting user-defined data structures.

- ❖ Introduce use cases for which tables, rather than user-defined lists, represent a more appropriate data structure in which to maintain control data.

L ists commence where scalars conclude, and are invaluable when you cannot pack sufficient information into a single variable, value, or argument—or if packing and pancaking information is doable yet yields an inscrutable, inseparable, unhealthy mass. Lists both collect and containerize; as a *collection*, lists hold a series of discrete elements, and as a *container*, they facilitate data abstraction by enabling users and processes to reference all list elements in aggregate as a cohesive data structure.

The International Organization for Standardization (ISO) defines a *list* as a "set of data items, each of which has the same data definition."[83] Many software languages define a built-in list data type or data structure that may have additional functionality or limiting characteristics, such as the requirement that list elements not be repeated or the requirement that lists be ordered. For example, the Institute of Electrical and Electronics Engineers (IEEE) defines a *list* as a "collection class that contains no duplicates and whose members are ordered."[84] Within this text, however, the least restrictive definition of *list* has been adopted—*a series of same-type values*.

Neither Base SAS nor the SAS macro language defines a list built-in data structure, although the built-in SAS array most closely resembles the list ADT, and is discussed in this chapter. Notwithstanding this deficiency, generations of SAS practitioners have bedazzled and bastardized their way to begetting user-defined lists, most commonly operationalized within the SAS macro language. And though we honor their hutzpah, the sometimes golem-like creations that have been animated in the name of "list making" bear no resemblance to software design best practices—data-driven or otherwise. May these monsters rest in peace.

Abstract data types (ADTs) are introduced and discussed in Section 4.1

This chapter aims to illustrate some decision points in list design, such as delimiter selection and tokenization, and stresses the importance of effective list decomposition. That is, because any SAS list represents a user-defined data structure, and because that data structure comprises a collection of discrete elements, some programmatic method must be engineered to reliably parse, iterate over, and extract individual list elements so they can be utilized by software.

Finally, data-driven design stresses the benefits of building reusable data structures and the reusable operations that support and operationalize them. In defining and documenting a data structure more fully, its likelihood for reuse is increased—even when filled with unrelated control data, and supporting unrelated software products or projects.

Thus, this chapter demonstrates the benefits of standardizing *your* definition of the "list data structure," of building associated operations that interpret that data structure, and of striving for backward compatibility as the data structure and its functionality are maintained and potentially expanded over time.

10.1 SAS ARRAYS

As described in Section 4.4.3, SAS documentation explicitly admonishes that SAS arrays are *not* data structures; they exist solely as pointers that temporarily reference a series of variables during a DATA step. Notwithstanding, these so-called second-class SAS citizens sure do pull their weight in optimizing and streamlining code. No, a SAS array will never make your program run faster, but it will make your code more efficient to write, more readable, and thus more maintainable.

Arrays are included in a chapter about linear data structures because, although SAS does support multi-dimensional arrays, the one-dimensional variety is most commonly declared. That is, a single index incrementally references a series of array elements, starting from 1 (by default in the SAS language) and continuing until the elements are exhausted.

The full functionality of arrays far exceeds the focus of this text, but their introduction demonstrates the gravitas of element decomposition, in that although arrays are not data structures, as built-in *quasi*-data structures, their elements are nevertheless intrinsically decomposed. Thus, despite having vast limitations (as compared with arrays in other languages), SAS arrays remain extremely useful, and far more reliable than equivalent user-defined data structures like SAS lists and macro lists.

Section 9.7 introduces intrinsic element decomposition, a typical characteristic of built-in data structures

It also must be stressed that any data structure—built-in or user-defined—is only as strong as its associated operations. The SAS array also excels here through the myriad built-in functions that support arrays, as well as the built-in OF operator that can operationalize a series of values by referencing their array name. Moreover, and although not discussed, the FCMP procedure supports passing arrays both by reference and by value, so arrays can be both read and modified by user-defined functions and subroutines.

Containerizing variables within a SAS array will not empower you to perform feats of strength not possible through other means—but arrays do facilitate effecting these feats through far smaller and far more agreeable code. Moreover, the SAS array archetype demonstrates data structure finesse and functionality that should be mimicked when designing a user-defined linear data structure. Finally, arrays are often a more appropriate solution to programmatic challenges that too often are lazily solved using hackneyed SAS macro solutions. Hip hip h-array!!!

10.1.1 Array Declaration

The following DATA step creates the Grades data set, which declares the numeric variables Grades1, Grades2, and Grades3, representing three months of schoolhouse grades for the first three U.S. presidents:

```
data grades;
    infile datalines dsd;
    length fname $20 lname $20 grades1-grades3 8;
    input fname $ lname $ grades1-grades3;
    datalines;
George, Washington, 97, 92, 95
John, Adams, 89, 92, 95
Thomas, Jefferson, 96, 95, 92
;
```

Arrays can similarly declare a series of variables within a DATA step. For example, a functionally equivalent DATA step declares Grades1 to Grades3 using the ARRAY statement in lieu of the LENGTH statement:

```
data grades;
    infile datalines dsd;
    length fname $20 lname $20;
    array grades[3] 8;
    input fname $ lname $ grades[*];
    datalines;
George, Washington, 97, 92, 95
John, Adams, 89, 92, 95
Thomas, Jefferson, 96, 95, 92
;
```

Use of [*] array subscripting is further demonstrated in Section 5.2.1

Note that the INPUT statement subscripts the Grades array with an asterisk (i.e., Grades[*]) to reference all array elements.

In addition to declaring, initializing, and interacting with groups of variables, arrays can also interact with individual elements—the constituent variables (or values) inside an array. Element-level interaction, when bundled inside array functionality, can dramatically reduce and simplify the code required to iterate over a series of variables—especially when the number or names of variables are unknown during software development, or are expected to vary from one execution to the next.

Section 14.1 demonstrates the use of arrays in defining a scalable, reusable decision table data structure

10.1.2 Arrays vs. Metaprogramming

Where a process or operation must be repeated multiple times, once for each variable (or value) in a series, metaprogramming and array processing often provide two alternative solutions. Each method has strengths and weaknesses, so SAS practitioners should understand when to reach for one tool over the other. Both methods, however, are superior to the concrete alternative, in which an operation is coded statically, once for each element (or operation) in a series.

Sections 11.1.5 and 11.2 demonstrate the prowess of SAS temporary arrays to load and maintain entire control tables

Consider the need to create a new variable (Gradescnt) that counts the number of non-missing grade values for each observation (i.e., student) in the Grades data set (created in Section 10.1.1). To build a DATA step that will accommodate a year's worth of grades, the variables Grades1 through Grades12 (if they exist) will need to be evaluated.

This painfully concrete DATA step delivers the required functionality by generating counts for each observation, and saving them to the Gradescnt variable:

```
data gradescum;
   set grades;
   length gradescnt 8 grades1-grades12 8;
   gradescnt=0;
   if n(grades1) then gradescnt+1;
   if n(grades2) then gradescnt+1;
   if n(grades3) then gradescnt+1;
   if n(grades4) then gradescnt+1;
   if n(grades5) then gradescnt+1;
   if n(grades6) then gradescnt+1;
   if n(grades7) then gradescnt+1;
   if n(grades8) then gradescnt+1;
   if n(grades9) then gradescnt+1;
   if n(grades10) then gradescnt+1;
   if n(grades11) then gradescnt+1;
```

This repetitive pattern is an indication that iteration abstraction, as discussed throughout Chapter 5, should be used to simplify the redundant code

```
    if n(grades12) then gradescnt+1;
run;
```

Note that the built-in N function returns a 1 when a variable is not missing, and a 0 when a variable is missing. Thus, Gradescnt generates the correct count even when some months have no grades; however, a SAS note will be printed to the log when a variable contains no data, although the built-in MISSING subroutine can eliminate this pesky note.

The MISSING subroutine is demonstrated in Section 6.5.2

Many SAS practitioners instinctively turn toward the SAS macro language whenever they need to replicate a process and remove redundancy, such as the endless IFs in the previous DATA step.

Metaprogramming describes "code that writes code," and within SAS, is typically operationalized through the SAS macro language. Macro iterations can dynamically generate repetitive DATA step statements and other code to reduce redundancy, thus improving software readability and maintainability through decreased code complexity.

The GRADESCUM macro refactors the previous DATA step using a metaprogramming approach that requires far fewer lines of code:

```
%macro gradescum(months= /* number of months */);
data gradescum;
    set grades;
    length gradescnt 8 grades1-grades&months 8;
    gradescnt=0;
%do i=1 %to &months;
    if n(grades&i) then gradescnt+1;
    %end;
run;
%mend;


%gradescum(months=12);
```

When the %DO loop executes, the macro facility generates the twelve IF statements shown in the previous example. Thus, although the two examples are coded differently, each DATA step ultimately runs identical code, with the first example hardcoded and the second example generated dynamically. This metaprogramming does not increase performance or efficiency, but rather implements iteration that improves code readability, as well as the ease with which code can be written and mainainted.

Despite the improvements facilitated through metaprogramming, a preferred solution instead relies on a SAS array to deliver iteration abstraction. The ARRAY statement declares Grades as a numeric array having twelve elements (variables Grades1 through Grades12). The DO loop iterates across the array while the N function evaluates whether a grade is present, and if the value is not missing, increments the Gradescnt counter:

```
data gradescum (drop=i);
   set grades;
   array grades[12] 8;
   length gradescnt 8;
   gradescnt=0;
   do i=1 to dim(grades);
      if n(grades[i]) then gradescnt+1;
      end;
run;
```

The DO loop demonstrates *external iteration*, in that its loop mechanics are exposed. The DO loop also demonstrates *explicit iteration scope*, in that the range of the array being iterated is visible; thus, the counter (I) references each array element individually. Explicit array indexing (i.e., *subscription*) is supported because the array declaration includes bracketed dimensions ([12]), thus Grades[I] can be subsequently referenced.

External and *internal iteration abstraction, and explicit and implicit iteration scope,* are defined and discussed in Section 5.2

A second, functionally equivalent solution demonstrates *external iteration* and *implicit iteration scope*; the array is still indexed, but individual array elements can be referenced without inclusion of the index. Thus, the array scope is *implicit* because the DO OVER statement and the N function reference the array object (Grades)—not its subscripted elements (Grades[I]):

```
data gradescum;
   set grades;
   array grades 8 grades1-grades12;
   length gradescnt 8;
   gradescnt=0;
   do over grades;
      if n(grades) then gradescnt+1;
      end;
run;
```

In this example, the array is not subscripted; thus, the upper dimension of the array does not need to be calculated using the DIM function, and the DO OVER loop iterates the actual array rather than the range thereof (as a DO loop does).

The final, functionally equivalent solution demonstrates *internal iteration* and *implicit iteration scope*. The iteration is *internal* because no looping mechanics are accessible; the OF operator iterates through the entire array in one statement, evaluating whether each element (i.e., variable within the array) is missing.

The iteration scope is *implicit* because the individual elements within the array are never referenced; only the array name (Grades) is referenced throughout the DATA step:

The colon (:) in the ARRAY statement is used in Section 10.1.2 to restrict array element scope to only existent variables

```
data gradescum;
    set grades;
    array grades[*] grades:;
    length gradescnt 8;
    gradescnt=n(of grades[*]);
run;
```

Similarly, the N function references the array name rather than an individual (i.e., subscripted) array element (i.e., Grades[I]). Note that the colon within the ARRAY statement prescribes that only current variables (already defined within the Grades data set) starting with "Grades" (i.e., Grades1 through Grades3) will be included in the array. Thus, unlike the previous example, the ARRAY statement does not create variables that do not already exist (i.e., Grades4 through Grades12).

Of these five functionally equivalent solutions, the last is the slickest, showcasing internal iteration with implicit scope—iteration abstraction at its finest, as all iteration complexity is concealed from view! However, this is not a data-driven solution, as it declares no parameters, nor does it access any control data. Sometimes the effortless solution is neither data-driven nor macro-based!

10.1.3 Arrays Supporting Data-Driven Design

So, how could data-driven design benefit the preceding example? The possibilities are endless but should be driven by requirements. Consider the scenario in which you need additional flexibility (and abstraction) to be able to count not only presidential grades, but *any* series of similarly named variables within *any* data set. Data-driven design *can* deliver this configurability, as demonstrated in the COUNTSOMETHING macro:

```
%macro countsomething(dsnin= /* data set to read */,
    dsnout= /* data set to create */,
    varbase= /* base of var to be counted */,
    varcnt= /* variable name of count */);
data &dsnout;
    set &dsnin;
    array &varbase[*] &varbase:;
    length &varcnt 8;
    &varcnt=0;
    &varcnt=n(of &varbase[*]);
run;
%mend;
```

For example, the following invocation of COUNTSOMETHING generates identical results to the preceding DATA step:

```
%countsomething(dsnin=grades, dsnout=gradescum,
    varbase=grades, varcnt=gradescnt);
```

As demonstrated, arrays provide a convenient method to containerize a series of variables, and to refer to and operate on them singly or as a collection of elements. Moreover, as a built-in quasi-data structure, the SAS array showcases some of the functionality for which we should strive when designing user-defined linear data structures, such as SAS lists, macro lists, and indexed macro lists. These user-defined data structures are demonstrated and contrasted throughout the remainder of this chapter.

10.2 SAS MACRO LISTS

Within this text, the SAS *macro list* describes a macro variable operationalized as a collection of values, having one or more user-specified symbols that delimit elements in a series. As a user-defined data structure, every macro list must rely on data structure rules that describe list format—for example, delimiter symbols, masking symbols, termination symbols, supported characters or data types, and symbols or data types that are *not* supported. As SAS practitioners, we have endless design options when defining *our* macro lists.

Unnecessary metaprogramming is demonstrated in Section 11.1.4, and replaced with array design in Section 11.1.5, whereas necessary metaprogramming is demonstrated in Section 11.3

However, this diversity can become a double-edged sword, as limitless flexibility in data structure construction can bathe us in redundant user-defined data structures, and we can find ourselves having to build (and maintain) user-defined operations to support our accrescent data structure brood. For example, if you have software that is utilizing three different *types* of macro lists (e.g., comma-delimited, asterisk-delimited, and space-delimited), and you need to build a macro function to count macro list elements, you may have to develop three separate macros—one to support each user-defined data structure definition. This excessive overwork is unnecessary.

The following subsections introduce the SAS macro list, demonstrate various definitions thereof, and advocate for standardizing the fewest number of *macro list* definitions—with one being ideal. In standardizing the macro list data structure, focus and effort can instead support expanding list functionality through user-defined operations. And should data complexity overwhelm macro list functionality, consider replacing macro list usage with indexed macro lists or built-in data structures like the SAS data set.

Indexed macro lists are introduced in Section 10.3, and control tables are the focus of Chapters 11 through 14

10.2.1 Diversity of the SAS Macro List

The following four %LET statements initialize &LIST1, &LIST2, &LIST3, and &LIST4, which represent (in varying degrees of precision and format) the first three federal holidays in 2022:

```
%let list1=JAN FEB MAY;
%let list2=1 2 5;
%let list3=01/17/2022, 02/21/2022, 05/30/2022;
%let list4=January 17, 2022*February 21, 2022*May 30,
2022;
```

Despite their unique constructions, because each macro variable represents a series of elements, it nevertheless can be referred to as a *macro list*. Thus, &LIST1 is a space-delimited list of month abbreviations; &LIST2 is a space-delimited list of month order (that requires numeric values); &LIST3 is a comma-delimited list of dates in MMDDYY10 format; and &LIST4 is an asterisk-delimited list of dates in WORDDATE20 format.

Abstract data types (ADTs) are introduced in Section 4.1

That is, macro lists, as user-defined data structures, can exhibit widely divergent functionality and formats, despite nevertheless still modeling the list ADT. This variability demonstrates the necessity to define the full functionality and structure of all user-defined data structures—list or otherwise. For example, commas in &LIST3 represent delimiting symbols, whereas commas in &LIST4 denote data—the information being conveyed. Thus, SAS practitioners must consider whether and how symbols such as commas should be interpreted within a user-defined data structure that is being designed.

Even more "list" variability can be demonstrated when data masking is required or implemented to filter specific symbols within a data structure. For example, because &LIST4 values can contain commas, a non-comma delimiter (i.e., the asterisk) has been selected. However, if the &LIST4 data structure definition *required* commas to represent both delimiters *and* data, then masking could support this objective.

The following DATA step creates the Pres data set that lists the first eight U.S. presidents, their dates in service, and their vice president(s):

```
data pres;
    infile datalines dsd;
    length fname $20 lname $20 num 3 dt1 8 dt2 8
        vp $100;
    input fname $ lname $ num dt1 : mmddyy10.
        dt2 : mmddyy10. vp $;
    format dt1 dt2 mmddyy10.;
    label fname='First Name' lname='Last Name'
        num='Number' dt1='Term Start' dt2='Term End'
        vp="President's VPs";
    datalines;
George, Washington, 1, 04/30/1789, 03/04/1797, John
Adams
John, Adams, 2, 03/04/1797, 03/04/1801, Thomas Jefferson
Thomas, Jefferson, 3, 03/04/1801, 03/04/1809, "Aaron
Burr, George Clinton"
James, Madison, 4, 03/04/1809, 03/04/1817, "George
Clinton, Elbridge Gerry"
James, Monroe, 5, 03/04/1817, 03/04/1825, Daniel
Tompkins
John, Adams, 6, 03/04/1825, 03/04/1829, John Calhoun
Andrew, Jackson, 7, 03/04/1829, 03/04/1837, "John
Calhoun, Martin Van Buren"
```

```
Martin, Van Buren, 8, 03/04/1837, 03/04/1841, Richard
Johnson
;
```

The following SQL procedure reads Pres and creates the &FNAME_LIST macro variable, a space-delimited list of presidential first names:

```
proc sql noprint;
   select fname into : fname_list separated by " "
      from pres;
quit;


%put &=fname_list;
```

The log demonstrates that the space character is an appropriate delimiter because no presidential first names include a space:

```
FNAME_LIST=George John Thomas James James John Andrew
Martin
```

However, if a separate macro list of presidential *last names* is later required, President Van Buren poses a challenge—either a non-space delimiter must be defined or the space in his last name must be masked (so as not to be interpreted as a delimiter). For example, the following SQL procedure fails to produce the desired results:

```
proc sql noprint;
   select lname into : lname_list separated by " "
      from pres;
quit;


%put &=lname_list;
```

The log shows that "Van" and "Buren" now appear as two separate last names:

```
LNAME_LIST=Washington Adams Jefferson Madison Monroe
Adams Jackson Van Buren
```

But what happens when America elects Conan O'Brien, her first late-night talk show host president? Hilarity ensues, naturally, but also semantic ambiguity, as SAS interprets the apostrophe in his last name as an unmatched quote that requires masking.

Thus, as the complexity of data maintained within a macro list increases, so too must the complexity of the definition of the corresponding list data structure.

For example, by enclosing all values in quotes, a space can still delimit *between* last names, so long as spaces *within* last names (like Van Buren) are masked:

```
proc sql noprint;
   select quote(strip(lname))
      into : lname_list separated by " "
         from pres;
quit;


%put &=lname_list;
```

The &LNAME_LIST macro list demonstrates the successful masking of the space symbol—allowing it to represent both data and the delimiter:

```
LNAME_LIST="Washington" "Adams" "Jefferson" "Madison"
"Monroe" "Adams" "Jackson" "Van Buren"
```

Each macro list—&FNAME_LIST and &LNAME_LIST—maintains valid control data that can drive dynamic functionality, but the variability in macro list definition and structure demonstrates a key challenge in user-defined data structures. That is, where multiple user-defined data structures are designed to model a single ADT (such as the list), redundant operations that act upon those structures also must be designed, tested, and maintained.

For example, consider the requirement to count the number of elements in &FNAME_LIST, which the COUNT_MACRO_LIST macro function performs:

```
%macro count_macro_list(mac /* [REF] macro var */);
%sysfunc(countw(&&&mac))
%mend;


%put %count_macro_list(fname_list);
```

The &FNAME_LIST macro list is passed (by reference) to COUNT_MACRO_LIST, which evaluates that the list contains eight elements. However, COUNT_MACRO_LIST cannot evaluate &LNAME_LIST because the macro function does not accommodate the double quotes or the masked space in the macro list.

Thus, were these two, separate definitions of *macro list* maintained, dueling macro functions to count the respective list types would also need to be developed and maintained. This demonstrates the importance and advantage of standardizing user-defined data structures, so SAS practitioners can instead focus on building our armies of user-defined operations that support an elite band of user-defined data structures.

10.2.2 Defining the SAS Macro List Business Need

Macro lists are most commonly utilized to facilitate *metaprogramming*—code that writes code—in which a series of actions is performed, or objects are created or modified. Thus, if you want to create a repeatable, configurable process that can be run on a variety of data sets, variables, or other objects or elements, data-driven design, facilitated by macro lists, can support this objective.

For example, consider the requirement to create "error variables" that accompany a data set, and which can be used to indicate whether data quality rules or business rules have been violated. Thus, for each variable, a correspondingly named error variable could be created—by either prefacing or suffixing "ERR"—and these variables could be used to drive subsequent exception reporting. Each error variable could be declared as a numeric data type, with various numeric error codes applied to denote when specific data rules had been broken.

> Data quality rules and business rules are introduced and contrasted in Section 8.3

The following DATA step demonstrates a hardcoded solution that declares and appends these error variables using the LENGTH statement:

```
data pres_err;
   set pres;
   length fname_err lname_err num_err dt1_err dt2_err
      vp_err 8;
run;
```

But to generate error variables dynamically, you could use a space-delimited macro list (of variable names), thus allowing the macro list to be passed at runtime by a user, or generated by a preceding process:

```
%let var_list=fname_err lname_err num_err dt1_err
   dt2_err vp_err;
data pres_err;
   set pres;
   length &var_list 8;
run;
```

Note that the usage of &VAR_LIST requires neither iteration nor parsing; it can simply be dropped into the LENGTH statement "as is." However, the list is statically declared in the code, so it fails to demonstrate data-driven design.

A reusable macro could dynamically generate the &VAR_LIST macro variable, thus allowing error variables to be generated for *any* data set. The FINDVARS macro function, defined in Section 3.3, can be called to generate a space-delimited list of all variables within any data set:

FINDVARS is refactored in Section 10.3.1 into a macro subroutine that initializes an indexed macro list, rather than returning a space-delimited list

```
%macro findvars(dsn= /* data set name */,
   type= /* CHAR or NUM [ALL for CHAR and NUM] */);
%local varlist dsid vars vartype i close;
%let varlist=;
%let dsid=%sysfunc(open(&dsn,i));
%let vars=%sysfunc(attrn(&dsid,nvars));
%do i=1 %to &vars;
   %let vartype=%sysfunc(vartype(&dsid,&i));
   %if %upcase(&type=ALL) or (&vartype=N and
      %upcase(&type)=NUM) or (&vartype=C and
      %upcase(&type)=CHAR) %then %let
      varlist=&varlist %sysfunc(varname(&dsid,&i));
   %end;
%let close=%sysfunc(close(&dsid));
&varlist
%mend;
```

The MAKE_ERROR_DSN macro calls FINDVARS, and subsequently uses its output to dynamically write the LENGTH statement:

```
%macro make_error_dsn(dsn /* data set name */,
   dsn_out /* error data set created */);
%local varlist i;
```

```
%let varlist=%findvars(dsn=&dsn);
data &dsn_out;
   set &dsn;
   length
   %do i=1 %to %sysfunc(countw(&varlist));
      %scan(&varlist,&i,,S)_err
      %end;
      8;
run;
%mend;
```

```
%make_error_dsn(pres, pres_err);
```

Note that whereas the &VAR_LIST macro list in the previous DATA step could be dropped into the code, the &VARLIST macro list in the MAKE_ERROR_DSN macro must be iterated so that elements can be extracted. That is, after the LENGTH statement, a %DO loop must decompose &VARLIST into its constituent variable names so that "_err" can be appended to compose the error variable names.

The log demonstrates that the Pres_err data set was created, as parameterized in the DSN_OUT argument, but also records numerous "variable uninitialized" notes:

```
NOTE: Variable fname_err is uninitialized.
NOTE: Variable lname_err is uninitialized.
NOTE: Variable num_err is uninitialized.
NOTE: Variable dt1_err is uninitialized.
NOTE: Variable dt2_err is uninitialized.
NOTE: Variable vp_err is uninitialized.
NOTE: There were 8 observations read from the data set
WORK.PRES.
NOTE: The data set WORK.PRES_ERR has 8 observations and
12 variables.
```

The notes occur because no error conditions (i.e., data quality rules) have yet been defined, so the error variables are unused. The MISSING subroutine (aka CALL MISSING) initializes one or more variables to a missing value, and is the recommended method to eliminate these notes.

For example, the following statement can be added to the DATA step to remove all notes:

```
call missing(fname_err, lname_err, num_err, dt1_err,
dt2_err, vp_err);
```

However, to generate this statement dynamically, the &VARLIST macro must be parsed a second time, which requires a second %DO loop:

```
%macro make_error_dsn(dsn /* data set name */,
    dsn_out /* error data set created */);
%local varlist i;
%let varlist=%findvars(dsn=&dsn);
data &dsn_out;
    set &dsn;
    length
    %do i=1 %to %sysfunc(countw(&varlist));
        %scan(&varlist,&i,,S)_err
        %end;
        8;
    call missing(
    %do i=1 %to %sysfunc(countw(&varlist));
        %if &i^=1 %then %do;
            ,
            %end;
        %scan(&varlist,&i,,S)_err
        %end;
        );
run;
%mend;


%make_error_dsn(pres, pres_err);
```

When MAKE_ERROR_DSN is invoked again, the log is clean, and the "uninitialized" notes no longer appear. At this point, a user-defined data structure has been defined as a space-delimited list. This is a fantastic data structure to hold SAS variables, data set names, and other values that cannot contain spaces or special characters because of SAS naming conventions. However, note the limitations of the space-delimited macro list—that spaces, single and double quotes, and other special characters cannot appear as list values without further data masking or other programmatic operations.

10.2.3 Developing Macro List Operations

At this point, the space-delimited list has been defined, and is used both as output from the FINDVARS user-defined macro function and inside the MAKE_ERROR_DSN macro. In other cases, however, you will want to design functions and other callable modules that evaluate or transform macro lists—and thus require passing lists *to* the user-defined module.

For example, consider a new requirement that the error variable names should appear in alphabetical order within the data set. This requires that the DT1_err variable be declared first in the LENGTH statement, and the VP_err variable be declared last. The following static DATA step represents the code that must be generated dynamically:

```
data pres_err;
   set pres;
   length dt1_err dt2_err fname_err lname_err num_err
      vp_err 8;
run;
```

Subroutines are introduced in Section 3.7, and do not produce a return value

To achieve this order dynamically, a macro list sorting subroutine can be developed, which passes the list as an argument. A user-defined subroutine is selected (as opposed to a function) because the argument itself (i.e., the macro list) needs to be modified within the calling program, and because no return value is required. The modification of arguments within the calling program requires arguments to be passed by reference, not by value.

Call by reference is introduced and demonstrated in Section 6.5.2

The SORTLIST macro subroutine passes the macro list by reference—that is, the macro variable name (LIST) as opposed to the macro variable itself (&LIST):

```
* SORTLIST (subroutine) sorts a space-delim macro list;
* MACROVAR is the list name passed by reference;
%macro sortlist(macrovar /* [REF] global macro
      variable */);
%local cnt i zzvarlist start by;
%let cnt=%sysfunc(countw(&&&macrovar));
```

```
%do i=1 %to &cnt;
   %local var&i;
   %let var&i=%scan(&&&macrovar,&i,,S);
   %if &i=1 %then %let zzvarlist=var1;
   %else %let zzvarlist=&zzvarlist, var&i;
   %end;
%syscall sortc(&zzvarlist);
%let &macrovar=;
%do i=1 %to &cnt;
   %if &i=&start %then %let &macrovar=&&&var&i;
   %else %let &macrovar=&&&macrovar &&&var&i;
   %end;
%mend;
```

For example, consider the following code, which first prints the natural order of the Pres variables, and then prints the variables alphabetically:

```
%let list=%findvars(dsn=pres);
%put &=list;
LIST=fname lname num dt1 dt2 vp


%sortlist(list);
%put &=list;
LIST=dt1 dt2 fname lname num vp
```

With SORTLIST engineered, the macro subroutine can be inserted into the MAKE_ERROR_DSN macro to sort the error variables that are being created dynamically:

```
%macro make_error_dsn(dsn /* data set name */,
   dsn_out /* error data set created */);
%local varlist i;
%let varlist=%findvars(dsn=&dsn);
%sortlist(varlist);
data &dsn_out;
   set &dsn;
   length
   %do i=1 %to %sysfunc(countw(&varlist));
      %scan(&varlist,&i,,S)_err
```

```
        %end;
        8;
    call missing(
    %do i=1 %to %sysfunc(countw(&varlist));
        %if &i^=1 %then %do;

            ,
            %end;
        %scan(&varlist,&i,,S)_err
        %end;
        );
    run;
    %mend;
```

When MAKE_ERROR_DSN is invoked on the Pres data set, the resultant Pres_err data set reveals that the error variables now appear alphabetically:

```
    %make_error_dsn(pres, pres_err);
```

However, note that MAKE_ERROR_DSN now *always* creates error variables in alphabetical order, and this rigidity (and shift from legacy functionality) might be undesirable. Thus, a more flexible approach is demonstrated in the next subsection.

10.2.4 Extensibility and Backward Compatibility

It is not uncommon for software requirements to change over the course of a software product's lifespan; this is not to say that requirements are drifting aimlessly, but rather that new or modified functionality has been considered and ultimately included. For example, a callable module like a function may start its life with relatively few user options, yet over time, grow to support more diverse configuration options. This flexibility ultimately aims to improve the user experience, but does so while limiting the introduction of *new* functions, with deference to updating *existent* functions.

For example, in the previous subsection, MAKE_ERROR_DSN was modified to include a single line of code that calls the SORTLIST macro subroutine:

```
    %sortlist(varlist);
```

However, in making this modification, all historic calls to MAKE_ERROR_DSN now alphabetize the list of error variables—even if that alphabetization is not always desired. Thus, when extending functionality of reusable modules, backward compatibility should be considered. Often, the desired solution is to impart the new functionality through a parameter or configuration item that can be specified at invocation.

Backward compatibility is introduced as a data-driven design principle in Section 1.4, and applies not only to code but also to data structures, as discussed in Section 4.5.5

For example, the MAKE_ERROR_DSN macro can be modified to only call SORTLIST if the optional parameter ORDER is specified:

```
%macro make_error_dsn(dsn /* data set name */,
    dsn_out /* error data set created */,
    order /* [OPT] ASC to sort ascending */);
%local varlist i;
%let varlist=%findvars(dsn=&dsn);
%if %upcase(&order)=ASC %then %do;
    %sortlist(varlist);
    %end;
data &dsn_out;
    set &dsn;
    length
    %do i=1 %to %sysfunc(countw(&varlist));
        %scan(&varlist,&i,,S)_err
        %end;
        8;
    call missing(
    %do i=1 %to %sysfunc(countw(&varlist));
        %if &i^=1 %then %do;
            ,
            %end;
        %scan(&varlist,&i,,S)_err
        %end;
        );
    run;
%mend;
```

MAKE_ERROR_DSN retains its original usage and functionality, in that historic calls that pass only two arguments—DSN and DSN_OUT— create error variables in the order in which the variables appear in the data set. However, if the optional ORDER argument is specified, SORTLIST will be conditionally called to alphabetize the error variables.

To provide a second example in which extensibility can support backward compatibility, consider the teammate who has successfully used the SORTLIST subroutine for months on various software projects, but who now has a requirement to sort a space-delimited macro list in *reverse* order. SORTLIST functionality cannot be swapped to always sort in reverse, as that would invalidate the countless current programs that rely on SORTLIST. Thus, the teammate has two options—extend the functionality of SORTLIST to include the newfangled reverse sorting, or construct a new subroutine that performs only reverse sorts.

With relative ease, the SORTLIST macro can be modified (i.e., *extended*) to accommodate the additional functionality—that is, the configurable option to sort a macro list in reverse. By adding the optional ORDER parameter, "desc" can be specified to denote a reverse sort. Thus, by default, SORTLIST will continue to sort alphabetically, but when ORDER is optionally specified, a descending sort will be performed:

SORTLIST is refactored in Section 10.3.3 to sort indexed macro lists

```
* SORTLIST (subroutine) sorts a space-delim macro list;
* MACROVAR is the list name passed by reference;
* ORDER [OPT] sorts the MACROVAR list in descending;
%macro sortlist(macrovar /* [REF] global macro
        variable */,
    order /* [OPT] DESC to sort descending */);
%local cnt i varlist start by;
%let cnt=%sysfunc(countw(&&&macrovar));
%do i=1 %to &cnt;
    %local var&i;
    %let var&i=%scan(&&&macrovar,&i,,S);
    %if &i=1 %then %let varlist=var1;
    %else %let varlist=&varlist, var&i;
    %end;
%syscall sortc(&varlist);
%let &macrovar=;
%if "%upcase(&order)"="DESC" %then %do;
    %let start=&cnt;
    %let cnt=1;
    %let by=-1;
```

```
    %end;
%else %do;
    %let start=1;
    %let by=1;
    %end;
%do i=&start %to &cnt %by &by;
    %if &i=&start %then %let &macrovar=&&&var&i;
    %else %let &macrovar=&&&macrovar &&&var&i;
    %end;
%mend;
```

The descending sort functionality is added by recognizing that iteration can go both ways—that is, rather than counting from one to the total number of elements within the macro list, the %DO loop performs a reverse count (iterating by -1) when the ORDER argument (DESC) is specified.

Note that as SORTLIST functionality has expanded, the subroutine's specification must be updated, including both preceding comments and %MACRO statement inline comments. Also note that the [REF] comment denotes to users that the MACROVAR parameter is passed by reference.

> The *procedural specification* is introduced in Section 3.2, and the [REF] notation is described in Section 6.5.2

The added functionality can be tested by printing three variable lists to the log—the natural order of variables within the Pres data set, the alphabetized order, and the reverse order:

```
%let list=%findvars(dsn=pres);
%put &=list;
LIST=fname lname num dt1 dt2 vp

%sortlist(list);
%put &=list;
LIST=dt1 dt2 fname lname num vp

%sortlist(list, desc);
%put &=list;
LIST=vp num lname fname dt2 dt1
```

In both macros, MAKE_ERROR_DSN and SORTLIST, the original functionality has been preserved through the definition of optional parameters, so legacy invocations of these macros will not be invalidated. Thus, extensible solutions extend while preserving functionality.

10.3 SAS INDEXED MACRO LISTS

Indexed macro lists represent macro variables that are incrementally named, and thus are explicitly indexed. Whereas a macro list must be parsed to find the Nth element, an indexed macro list requires neither iteration nor decomposition to extract its constituent elements. This not only yields faster, more efficient processing, but also enables embedded spaces, commas, and other special characters to be more readily stored.

For example, the FINDVARS macro is defined in Section 10.2.2, and creates a space-delimited list containing all variables within a data set:

```
%let list=%findvars(dsn=pres);
%put &=list;
```

```
LIST=fname lname num dt1 dt2 vp
```

However, you could instead store each list element within a separate macro variable, and increment macro variable names so they could be collectively (and predictably) referenced. For example, the following six %LET statements initialize six macro variables (&LIST_IDX_1 to &LIST_IDX_6) having identical values as the &LIST macro list:

```
%let list_idx_1=fname;
%let list_idx_2=lname;
%let list_idx_3=num;
%let list_idx_4=dt1;
%let list_idx_5=dt2;
%let list_idx_6=vp;
```

It is often beneficial to know the size of a data structure, so the zero-index position is initialized to the data structure dimensions—the highest incremented macro variable name (i.e., &LIST_IDX_6):

```
%let list_idx_0=6;
```

Because indexed macro lists require multiple, successive initializations, they are sometimes referred to as *vertical lists*, whereas macro lists are contrasted as *horizontal lists*, as they can be initialized with a single line of code.

Indexed macro lists are faster to parse than macro lists because macro lists inherently require some delimiter character that must be tokenized;

note the spaces between elements in the &LIST macro variable. Indexed macro lists never require this decomposition because each macro variable contains a single value.

The HUGE performance advantages of iterating indexed macro lists over macro lists are demonstrated in Section 5.5

This simplification also removes the design challenge of deciding how to delimit a macro list—because indexed macro lists do not require delimiters. Thus, indexed macro lists can support a wider array of data while minimizing the code required to process those data. For example, President Van Buren posed a conundrum in Section 10.2.1 because his last name contains a space, and cannot appear within a space-delimited list unless his space is masked.

Placing "Van Buren" within an indexed macro list, however, is straightforward because no delimiter is required:

```
%let lname_idx_8=Van Buren;
```

The next subsections further demonstrate the indexed macro list, and illustrate some of its advantages over (unindexed) macro lists.

10.3.1 Initializing Indexed Macro Lists

As demonstrated in the previous section, whereas a macro list can be created with a single initialization statement, an indexed macro list requires a separate %LET statement to initialize each list element. For this reason, indexed macro lists are typically created dynamically by callable processes.

FINDVARS_IDX is considered to be a macro subroutine because it initializes variables, yet does not return (or resolve) a value, as discussed in Section 3.7

For example, the FINDVARS macro function is defined in Section 10.2.2, and generates a space-delimited list of all variables within a data set. The macro can be refactored into the FINDVARS_IDX macro *subroutine*, however, to initialize an indexed macro list:

```
* this version outputs an indexed macro list;
* places results in an indexed macro list;
%macro findvars_idx(dsn /* data set name */,
   mac /* [REF] macro base for indexed list */,
   type /* CHAR or NUM [ALL for CHAR and NUM] */);
%local dsid vars vartype i close;
%global &mac._0;
%if %length(&type)=0 %then %let type=ALL;
%let dsid=%sysfunc(open(&dsn,i));
%let vars=%sysfunc(attrn(&dsid,nvars));
%let &mac._0=&vars;
```

```
%put _local_;
%do i=1 %to &vars;
    %let vartype=%sysfunc(vartype(&dsid,&i));
    %if %upcase(&type=ALL) or (&vartype=N and
        %upcase(&type)=NUM) or (&vartype=C and
        %upcase(&type)=CHAR) %then %do;
            %global &mac._&i;
            %let &mac._&i=%sysfunc(varname(&dsid,&i));
            %end;
    %end;
%let close=%sysfunc(close(&dsid));
%mend;
```

FINDVARS_IDX can be invoked on the Pres data set using the following call:

```
%findvars_idx(pres, pres_vars_idx);
%put _global_;
```

This invocation creates the PRES_VARS_IDX indexed macro list, which comprises &PRES_VARS_IDX_0, representing the total number of list elements (6), and &PRES_VARS_IDX_1 through &PRES_VARS_IDX_6, representing each element—the variables found in the Pres data set:

```
GLOBAL PRES_VARS_IDX_0 6
GLOBAL PRES_VARS_IDX_1 fname
GLOBAL PRES_VARS_IDX_2 lname
GLOBAL PRES_VARS_IDX_3 num
GLOBAL PRES_VARS_IDX_4 dt1
GLOBAL PRES_VARS_IDX_5 dt2
GLOBAL PRES_VARS_IDX_6 vp
```

In other cases, you might need to transfer the *values* (not *variables*) of a data set to an indexed macro list; this can be a far riskier endeavor. SAS variable names must adhere to standardized SAS variable-naming conventions, which exclude spaces, commas, and most special characters, and thus pose no threat to macro list inclusion. Data set character *values*, on the other hand, might include single quotes, double quotes, unmatched quotes, and other special characters, so—as is the case with all user-defined data structures—an understanding of the type and diversity of values being maintained is required.

The FINDVALS_IDX_TEMP macro declares and initializes an indexed macro list from the values of any variable within a data set:

```
%macro findvals_idx_temp(dsn /* data set name */,
    var /* variable to be exported to list */,
    mac /* [REF] macro base for indexed list */);
data _null_;
    set &dsn end=eof;
    call symputx("&mac._" || strip(put(_n_,8.)),
        &var, 'g');
    if eof then call symputx("&mac._0",
strip(put(_n_,8.)), 'g');
run;
%mend;
```

The DSN parameter represents the data set name; the VAR parameter represents the variable name; and the MAC parameter represents the base name to be used to construct the indexed macro list name. For example, the following invocation transfers the contents of the Lname variable (within the Pres data set) to the LNAME_IDX indexed macro list:

```
%findvals_idx_temp(pres, lname, lname_idx);
%put _global_;
```

Thereafter, a partial listing of global macro variables demonstrates the macro variables that have been created:

```
GLOBAL LNAME_IDX_0 8
GLOBAL LNAME_IDX_1 Washington
GLOBAL LNAME_IDX_2 Adams
GLOBAL LNAME_IDX_3 Jefferson
GLOBAL LNAME_IDX_4 Madison
GLOBAL LNAME_IDX_5 Monroe
GLOBAL LNAME_IDX_6 Adams
GLOBAL LNAME_IDX_7 Jackson
GLOBAL LNAME_IDX_8 Van Buren
```

One downfall of the FINDVALS_IDX_TEMP implementation, however, is its reliance on the DATA step to initialize the macro variables in the indexed macro list. This step boundary prevents FINDVALS_IDX_TEMP from being called from within a SAS procedure or DATA step; thus, FINDVALS_IDX_TEMP represents a macro *procedure* rather than a macro *subroutine*.

FINDVALS_IDX, a functionally equivalent yet more versatile user-defined macro *subroutine*, is now defined, and *can* be called from within a SAS procedure or DATA step, as the subroutine contains no step boundary:

User-defined macro *procedures* are introduced in Section 3.5.1, and are considered to be any macro that does not meet definition criteria for a macro *function* or macro *subroutine*

```
%macro findvals_idx(dsn /* data set name */,
    var /* variable to be exported to list */,
    mac /* [REF] macro base for indexed list */);
%local dsid vars i vartype val close;
%global &mac._0;
%let dsid=%sysfunc(open(&dsn,i));
%let vars=%sysfunc(attrn(&dsid,nvars));
%do i=1 %to &vars;
    %if %upcase(%sysfunc(varname(&dsid,
            &i)))=%upcase(&var) %then %do;
        %let vartype=%sysfunc(vartype(&dsid,&i));
        %let j=0;
        %do %while(%sysfunc(fetch(&dsid))=0);
            %let j=%eval(&j+1);
            %if %upcase(&vartype)=C %then
                %let val=%sysfunc(getvarc(&dsid, &i));
            %else %let val=%sysfunc(getvarn(&dsid, &i));
            %global &mac._&j;
            %let &mac._&j=&val;
            %end;
        %let &mac._0=&j;
        %end;
    %end;
%let close=%sysfunc(close(&dsid));
%mend;


%findvals_idx(pres, lname, lname_idx);
```

When FINDVALS_IDX is invoked, it again initializes the LNAME_IDX indexed macro list to the values of the LNAME variable.

10.3.2 Iterating Indexed Macro Lists

One of the first operations often developed to support a user-defined data structure is a counting function that returns the *dimensions*—the number (and sometimes arrangement) of elements in a data structure. However, when indexed macro lists hold list dimensions in the zero-index position, no counting function is required because the dimensions are known. For example, the &FNAME_LIST macro list was previously initialized:

```
%let fname_list=George John Thomas James James John
Andrew Martin
```

The ITER_MACRO_LIST macro iterates over a macro list, passed by reference, and prints each constituent value to the log:

```
%macro iter_macro_list(mac /* [REF] macro list */);
%local i;
%do i=1 %to %sysfunc(countw(&&&mac));
   %put %scan(&&&mac,&i,,S);
   %end;
%mend;


%iter_macro_list(fname_list);
```

The macro prints the first names of the first eight U.S. presidents to the log:

```
George
John
Thomas
James
James
John
Andrew
Martin
```

However, ITER_MACRO_LIST requires the COUNTW function to evaluate the total number of list elements, and requires the %SCAN function to decompose the list and extract each element.

Iterating an indexed macro list is more straightforward and more efficient because neither counting nor decomposition is required. The functionally equivalent ITER_IDX_MACRO_LIST macro iterates and prints the elements within an indexed macro list:

```
%macro iter_idx_macro_list(mac /* [REF] idx list */);
%local i;
%do i=1 %to &&&mac._0;
    %put &&&mac._&i;
    %end;
%mend;


%iter_idx_macro_list(lname_idx);
```

The last names of the first eight U.S. presidents are again printed to the log:

```
Washington
Adams
Jefferson
Madison
Monroe
Adams
Jackson
Van Buren
```

Thus, as indexed macro lists are explicitly indexed, there is no need to decompose and extract individual elements; all values are stored as they will be used—even spacey Van Buren.

This benefit of indexed macro lists is made even more apparent when a specific list element is needed rather than the series of all list elements. For example, consider the requirement to extract only the seventh element, representing Andrew Jackson, from the &FNAME_LIST macro list and the LNAME_IDX indexed macro list.

The revised ITER_MACRO_LIST_N macro now declares a second parameter (ELEMENT) that corresponds to the list element that should be printed. The following macro prints "Andrew" to the log:

```
* just the 7th element;
%macro iter_macro_list_n(mac /* [REF] macro list */,
```

```
    element /* list element to print */);
%put %scan(&&&mac,&element,,S);
%mend;


%iter_macro_list_n(fname_list, 7);
```

By evaluating a specific element in the list, the %DO loop (demonstrating *external iteration*) can be removed from the macro. However, the %SCAN function is required to parse the first six elements—tokenizing space delimiters along the way—until it arrives at the seventh element that is printed. Thus, despite being coded simply, this logic is terribly inefficient, albeit our best option where user-defined macro lists must be evaluated.

Compare the preceding macro with the functionally equivalent ITER_IDX_MACRO_LIST_N that prints a single element from an indexed macro list:

> Internal and external iteration are defined and demonstrated in Sections 5.2.1 and 5.2.2, respectively

```
* just the 7th element;
%macro iter_idx_macro_list_n(mac /* [REF] idx list */,
    element /* list element to print */);
%put &&&mac._&element;
%mend;


%iter_idx_macro_list_n(lname_idx, 7);
```

Because indexed macro lists are explicitly indexed, neither external nor internal iteration is required to parse and extract the seventh element. Thus, this invocation prints "Jackson" to the log without reliance on the inefficient %SCAN function.

The performance and efficiency improvement of iterating indexed macro lists (as opposed to macro lists) will be negligible for smaller lists. However, where list elements begin to number in the hundreds or thousands, real differences will emerge. Section 5.5.1 demonstrates an indexed macro list parsed more than 600 times faster than the equivalent macro list!!!

10.3.3 Developing Indexed Macro List Operations

The _GLOBAL_ automatic list demonstrates one of the few pitfalls of the otherwise glamorous indexed macro lists—the sheer number of macro variables that can be created. Consider the partial output of _GLOBAL_ that results from those indexed macro lists created in Sections 10.3 and 10.3.1:

```
%put _global_;
GLOBAL LIST_IDX_0 6
GLOBAL LIST_IDX_1 fname
GLOBAL LIST_IDX_2 lname
GLOBAL LIST_IDX_3 num
GLOBAL LIST_IDX_4 dt1
GLOBAL LIST_IDX_5 dt2
GLOBAL LIST_IDX_6 vp
GLOBAL LNAME_IDX_0 8
GLOBAL LNAME_IDX_1 Washington
GLOBAL LNAME_IDX_2 Adams
GLOBAL LNAME_IDX_3 Jefferson
GLOBAL LNAME_IDX_4 Madison
GLOBAL LNAME_IDX_5 Monroe
GLOBAL LNAME_IDX_6 Adams
GLOBAL LNAME_IDX_7 Jackson
GLOBAL LNAME_IDX_8 Van Buren
GLOBAL PRES_VARS_IDX_0 6
GLOBAL PRES_VARS_IDX_1 fname
GLOBAL PRES_VARS_IDX_2 lname
GLOBAL PRES_VARS_IDX_3 num
GLOBAL PRES_VARS_IDX_4 dt1
GLOBAL PRES_VARS_IDX_5 dt2
GLOBAL PRES_VARS_IDX_6 vp
```

Thus, one of the first user-defined operations to be designed to support the indexed macro list could be a subroutine that deletes unnecessary indexed macro lists. The DEL_IDX_MACRO_LIST subroutine first confirms that both the zero and first element exist (in the parameterized indexed macro list name), after which the entire indexed macro list is deleted:

```
%macro del_idx_macro_list(mac /* [REF] idx list */);
%local i j;
%if %symexist(&mac._0) and %symexist(&mac._1) %then %do;
   %let j=&&&mac._0;
   %put &=j;
```

```
    %symdel &mac._0;
    %do i=1 %to &j;
        %symdel &mac._&i;
        %end;
    %put NOTE: Macro variables %upcase(&mac._0) through
%upcase(&mac._&j) were successfully deleted.;
    %end;
%else %do;
    %put WARNING: Macro variable(s) %upcase(&mac._0)
and/or %upcase(&mac._1) were not found.;
    %end;

%mend;
```

A note to the log denotes the range of macro variables that were deleted, or if unsuccessful, a warning reports that one or both of the macro variables (occupying the zero- and first-index positions) could not be found.

For example, the following invocation deletes the redundant LIST_IDX indexed macro list, including &LIST_IDX_0 through &LIST_IDX_6, as indicated in the log:

```
%del_idx_macro_list(list_idx);
NOTE: Macro variables LIST_IDX_0 through LIST_IDX_6 were
successfully deleted.
```

Alternatively, if a non-existent indexed macro list is passed (as LIST_NOT does not exist), a warning is displayed:

```
%del_idx_macro_list(list_not);
WARNING: Macro variable(s) LIST_NOT_0 and/or LIST_NOT_1
were not found.
```

An operation like DEL_IDX_MACRO_LIST is *beneficial* if you want to keep a tidy macro symbol table, but is *required* if you intend to reuse indexed macro list names. For example, overwriting an existent indexed macro list with new values (and presumably a new quantity of values) could result in a mismatch between the list dimensions (i.e., the zero-index value) and the actual number of list elements.

In Section 10.2.3, the SORTLIST macro was defined, which sorts a space-delimited macro list, and in Section 10.2.4, SORTLIST functionality was extended to incorporate reverse sorting. An equivalent SORTLIST_IDX macro subroutine sorts indexed macro lists with far fewer statements:

```
%macro sortlist_idx(mac /* [REF] idx macro list */,
    order /* [OPT] DESC to sort in reverse */);
%local i varlist;
%if %upcase(&order)=DESC %then %do;
    %do i=&&&mac._0 %to 1 %by -1;
        %if &i=&&&mac._0 %then
            %let varlist=&mac._&&&mac._0;
        %else %let varlist=&varlist, &mac._&i;
        %end;
    %end;
%else %do;
    %do i=1 %to &&&mac._0;
        %if &i=1 %then %let varlist=&mac._1;
        %else %let varlist=&varlist, &mac._&i;
        %end;
    %end;
%syscall sortc(&varlist);
%mend;
```

SORTLIST_IDX is less cumbersome than SORTLIST (which sorts *macro lists*) because SORTLIST must transform a parameterized space-delimited macro list into an indexed macro list (internally) so that SORTC can sort these individual macro variables. SORTLIST_IDX foregoes this extra step because it is directly passed an indexed macro list.

Note the convoluted &mac._&&&mac._0 reference that is required to reverse the list of macro variables. For example, if LNAME_IDX is passed to the MAC parameter, then the &MAC macro variable will resolve to LNAME_IDX within the macro. Thus, in its first pass, the macro facility resolves this value to LNAME_IDX_&LNAME_IDX_0, and because &LNAME_IDX_0 resolves to 8, in its second pass, the macro facility resolves the convoluted value to LNAME_IDX_8—the final element in the indexed macro list. Triple ampersands (&&&) are a hallmark of macro variables that are passed by reference to macros.

To demonstrate SORTLIST_IDX, the LNAME_IDX indexed macro list is initialized by invoking the FINDVALS_IDX macro (defined in Section 10.3.1):

```
%findvals_idx(pres, lname, lname_idx);
```

```
%put _global_;
```

The SAS log demonstrates the indexed macro list values:

```
GLOBAL LNAME_IDX_0 8
GLOBAL LNAME_IDX_1 Washington
GLOBAL LNAME_IDX_2 Adams
GLOBAL LNAME_IDX_3 Jefferson
GLOBAL LNAME_IDX_4 Madison
GLOBAL LNAME_IDX_5 Monroe
GLOBAL LNAME_IDX_6 Adams
GLOBAL LNAME_IDX_7 Jackson
GLOBAL LNAME_IDX_8 Van Buren
```

The LNAME_IDX indexed macro list can be sorted in ascending order using the following invocation:

```
%sortlist_idx(lname_idx);
%put _global_;
```

The log shows the presidents' last names have been alphabetized:

```
GLOBAL LNAME_IDX_0 8
GLOBAL LNAME_IDX_1 Adams
GLOBAL LNAME_IDX_2 Adams
GLOBAL LNAME_IDX_3 Jackson
GLOBAL LNAME_IDX_4 Jefferson
GLOBAL LNAME_IDX_5 Madison
GLOBAL LNAME_IDX_6 Monroe
GLOBAL LNAME_IDX_7 Van Buren
GLOBAL LNAME_IDX_8 Washington
```

A second invocation of SORLIST_IDX with the optional ORDER argument (DESC) now sorts the indexed macro list in reverse:

```
%sortlist_idx(lname_idx, desc);
%put _global_;
```

The SAS log demonstrates that the presidents' last names have been sorted in reverse alphabetical order:

```
GLOBAL LNAME_IDX_0 8
GLOBAL LNAME_IDX_1 Washington
```

```
GLOBAL LNAME_IDX_2 Van Buren
GLOBAL LNAME_IDX_3 Monroe
GLOBAL LNAME_IDX_4 Madison
GLOBAL LNAME_IDX_5 Jefferson
GLOBAL LNAME_IDX_6 Jackson
GLOBAL LNAME_IDX_7 Adams
GLOBAL LNAME_IDX_8 Adams
```

The SORTLIST and SORTLIST_IDX macro subroutines, which operate on macro lists and indexed macro lists, respectively, demonstrate the importance of selecting and standardizing user-defined data structures wherever possible. When fewer data structures must be maintained, greater emphasis and effort can be afforded to building user-defined operations that support these structures.

10.3.4 Complex Indexed Macro List Values

Some of the complexity involved in adapting a user-defined data structure (the list) to incorporate new special characters (quotation marks) is demonstrated in Section 4.5.5

As stated throughout this text, the definition of any user-defined data structure requires an understanding of the data type and format of expected values, and should explicitly enumerate types, characters, or symbols that are disallowed. This subsection explores how indexed macro lists can handle not-so-infrequent Null values, unmatched quotes, and ampersands.

Consider the need to dynamically generate a list containing all labels occurring within a SAS data set. The Complex data set can be derived from the Pres data set (created in Section 10.2.1), and includes variables having labels with an apostrophe (VP), a Null value (Nolabel), and an ampersand (Amplabel):

```
data complex;
    set pres (drop=dt1 dt2);
    length nolabel amplabel 8;
    label amplabel='this & that';
run;
```

Table 10.1 demonstrates the first observation of Complex. Variable labels are shown for all variables (except Nolabel, which lacks a label, and instead displays the variable name), demonstrating that both VP and Amplabel labels contain special characters.

First Name	Last Name	Number	President's VPs	nolabel	this & that
George	Washington	1	John Adams	.	.

Table 10.1 Complex Data Set Labels and First Observation

The FINDVARS_IDX macro, created in Section 10.3.1, can be extended to initialize three indexed macro lists—one that includes all variable names within a data set, a second that includes the corresponding variable lengths, and a third that includes the corresponding variable labels.

VARS_LENS_LABELS_IDX now declares three parameters—MAC, LEN, and LAB—that denote the base variable names for the three indexed macro lists that will be initialized:

```
%macro vars_lens_labels_idx(dsn /* data set name */,
    mac /* [REF] idx macro list of variable names */,
    len /* [REF] idx macro list of variable lengths */,
    lab /* [REF} idx macro list of variable labels */,
    type /* CHAR or NUM [ALL for CHAR and NUM] */);
%local dsid vars vartype i close;
%global &mac._0 &len._0 &lab._0;
%if %length(&type)=0 %then %let type=ALL;
%let dsid=%sysfunc(open(&dsn,i));
%let vars=%sysfunc(attrn(&dsid,nvars));
%let &mac._0=&vars;
%let &len._0=&vars;
%let &lab._0=&vars;
%do i=1 %to &vars;
    %let vartype=%sysfunc(vartype(&dsid,&i));
    %if %upcase(&type=ALL) or (&vartype=N and
        %upcase(&type)=NUM) or (&vartype=C and
        %upcase(&type)=CHAR) %then %do;
            %global &mac._&i &len._&i &lab._&i;
            %let
&mac._&i=%nrbquote(%sysfunc(varname(&dsid,&i)));
            %if &vartype=N %then %let
&len._&i=%nrbquote(%sysfunc(varlen(&dsid,&i)));
```

```
        %else %let
&len._&i=%nrbquote($%sysfunc(varlen(&dsid,&i)));
        %let
&lab._&i=%nrbquote(%sysfunc(varlabel(&dsid,&i)));
        %end;
    %end;
%let close=%sysfunc(close(&dsid));
%mend;
```

Once the OPEN function accesses the data set, the VARNAME function extracts the variable name, and the VARLABEL function extracts the variable label. The %NRBQUOTE macro function masks special characters such as unmatched single quotes, unmatched double quotes, the ampersand, and the percent sign. Thus, %NRBQUOTE facilitates the initialization of macro variables that contain these special characters.

For example, the following invocation of VARS_LENS_LABELS_IDX on the Complex data set initializes three indexed macro lists—PRES_VARS_IDX (representing variable names), PRES_LENS_IDX (representing variable lengths), and PRES_LABS_IDX (representing variable labels):

```
%vars_lens_labels_idx(complex, pres_vars_idx,
    pres_lens_idx, pres_labs_idx);
%put _global_;
```

A partial listing of the log demonstrates the PRES_LABS_IDX indexed macro list of variable labels:

```
GLOBAL PRES_LABS_IDX_0 6
GLOBAL PRES_LABS_IDX_1 First Name
GLOBAL PRES_LABS_IDX_2 Last Name
GLOBAL PRES_LABS_IDX_3 Number
GLOBAL PRES_LABS_IDX_4 President's VPs
GLOBAL PRES_LABS_IDX_5
GLOBAL PRES_LABS_IDX_6 this & that
```

The indexed macro list has been successfully initialized with special characters; however, how will the legacy indexed macro list operations (like SORTLIST_IDX, defined in Section 10.3.3) perform? Spoiler ahead—not well!

The following invocation of SORTLIST_IDX intends to sort the PRES_LABS_IDX indexed macro list alphabetically:

```
%sortlist_idx(pres_labs_idx);
%put _global_;
```

However, SORTLIST_IDX fails because the macro was not designed to handle missing values, and the fifth element (&PRES_LABS_IDX_5), representing the label of the Nolabel variable, has no label:

```
ERROR: In a call to the SORT function or routine,
argument 1 and argument 5 have different data types.
ERROR: An error occurred while executing function SORTC
referenced by the %SYSFUNC or %QSYSFUNC macro function.
```

The failure occurs because %SYSCALL evaluates the missing element (&PRES_LABS_IDX_5) to have a character data type. Moreover, the built-in SORTC subroutine also fails to accommodate the special characters that were masked during initialization of the indexed macro list. However, this is not to suggest that the current indexed macro list definition (that supports special characters) should be abandoned—only that it must be understood and well defined before associated operations can be built.

For example, consider the requirement to create a data set dynamically by inheriting variable names, lengths, and labels from a primary data set. Multiple solutions exist in both Base SAS and the SAS macro language; however, one relies on the initialization of indexed macro lists to hold variable metadata, after which these lists can be iterated within a DATA step to write dynamic statements.

The DYNO_DATA macro function dynamically creates LENGTH and LABEL statements based on three parameters—VAR, an indexed macro list of variable names, LEN, an indexed macro list of variable lengths, and LAB, an indexed macro list of variable labels:

```
%macro dyno_data(var /* [REF] idx macro list of variable
      names */,
   len /* [REF] idx macro list of variable lengths */,
   lab /* [REF] idx macro list of variable labels */);
   length
      %do i=1 %to &&&var._0;
         &&&var._&i &&&len._&i
```

```
            %end;
            ;
      label
         %do i=1 %to &&&var._0;
            &&&var._&i = "&&&lab._&i"
            %end;
            ;
%mend;
```

DYNO_DATA is considered to be a macro *function* because it resolves to a single value, which comprises the dynamically generated LENGTH and LABEL statements. Thus, DYNO_DATA can be called from within a DATA step:

```
options mprint;
data dynamic;
    %dyno_data(pres_vars_idx,
        pres_lens_idx, pres_labs_idx);
run;
options nomprint;
```

The MPRINT system option reveals the metaprogramming mechanics within the SAS log, demonstrating the code that is dynamically written by the DYNO_DATA call:

```
data dynamic;
    %dyno_data (pres_vars_idx, pres_lens_idx,
pres_labs_idx);
MPRINT(DYNO_DATA):   length fname $20 lname $20 num 3 vp
$100 nolabel 8 amplabel 8 ;
MPRINT(DYNO_DATA):   label fname = "First Name" lname =
"Last Name" num = "Number" vp =
"President's VPs" nolabel = "" amplabel = "this & that"
;
run;
```

The benefits of data masking are apparent, in that missing values, ampersands, unmatched quotes, and other special characters can often be maintained within macro lists or indexed macro lists, as demonstrated by the PRES_LABS_IDX indexed macro list. However, although DYNO_DATA operates with this masking, other user-defined operations—or even built-in modules like SORTC—will not, and may require substantial overhaul.

Various built-in macro functions support data masking, including %BQUOTE, %NRBQUOTE, %QUOTE, %NRQUOTE, %STR, %NRSTR, and %SUPERQ, although their usage lies beyond the scope of this text. In general, where masking acrobatics are required to initialize or utilize macro lists or indexed macro lists, reliance on a built-in data structure like a SAS data set is a preferred solution.

Section 11.1.5 shows how special characters can be parsed without *data masking when control data are maintained within SAS data sets*

10.4 PASSING TABULAR CONTROL DATA AS LISTS

A tell-tale sign that you may be storing data or control data within a less-than-optimal data structure is the maintenance of tabular data within a non-tabular structure, such as a list, macro list, or indexed macro list. *Parallel macro lists* (including *parallel indexed macro lists*) describe two or more lists that are (and must remain) synchronized with each other, and *nested keyword arguments* describe a structure in which subordinate key-value pairs are maintained within an argument. Each can be used to maintain tabular data, although the use cases (and functionality) of each are limited as compared with those of actual control tables. This is not to say that these user-defined data structures should *always* be avoided, only that their caveats and alternatives should be understood.

One of the primary rationales for reliance on parallel macro lists and nested keyword arguments is the in-code configurability they provide to end users. Especially where control data are passed *by value*, arguments can be modified "on the fly" within the SAS application while invoking a called software module. In other cases, parallel macro lists can be passed *by reference*, and the macro list declaration (and initialization) is placed preveniently in a point of prominence—like a program header or a macro header.

Irrespective of the call method through which they are passed, however, maintaining these control data within the code itself, although not evincing control data independence, does prevent SAS practitioners from having to vacate our code windows to edit some exterior control table or other control file—and this expedience can be invaluable especially during development, rapid prototyping, testing, and debugging. In general, however, you would not find these pseudo-tabular, user-defined data structures implemented within production software.

Phases of the SDLC are discussed within a data-driven design paradigm in Section 7.2

10.4.1 Parallel Macro Lists

Parallel lists decompose a tabular data structure into columns (or rows), with each column (or row) represented by a separate macro list. Parallel lists are useful when each list contains only a few data elements because end users can visually inspect parameters, and validate that macro list arguments are appropriately formatted and have the same number of values.

Consider the BUILD_DATA user-defined macro function that dynamically generates a LENGTH statement for a DATA step:

```
%macro build_data(varlist= /* space-delim var names */,
    lenlist= /* space-delimited lengths */);
%local i;
    length
    %do i=1 %to %sysfunc(countw(&varlist));
        %scan(&varlist,&i,,S) %scan(&lenlist,&i,,S)
        %end;

        ;
%mend;
```

In truth, user-defined macro functions *resolve* rather than *return* values, as discussed in Sections 3.6.1 and 6.8.1

BUILD_DATA is considered to be a macro *function* because it does not contain a step boundary, and because it returns a value (i.e., the dynamically generated LENGTH statement). Note this distinguishing feature between user-defined *macro* functions (defined in the SAS macro language) and user-defined functions (defined in the FCMP procedure), in that macro functions can return entire *statements*, whereas FCMP functions can return only *values*. It is for this reason that BUILD_DATA is able to resolve to a value that includes the entire LENGTH statement and trailing semicolon.

A sample invocation of BUILD_DATA creates the Somedata data set having two variables, Var1 and Var2:

```
data somedata;
    %build_data(varlist=var1 var2,
        lenlist=8 $12);
run;
```

The VARLIST and LENLIST parameters represent space-delimited macro lists that contain variable names and variable lengths, respectively.

They are considered to be *parallel* macro lists because they are tidally locked, in that Var1 must correspond to the first element in LENLIST, and Var2 must correspond to the second element in LENLIST.

Within BUILD_DATA, the %DO loop iterates over only the &VARLIST macro list (and *not* &LENLIST) because both &VARLIST and &LENLIST *should* have the same number of elements. Thus, the single counter (&I) can be used to extract elements from both lists (using the %SCAN function).

Parallel macro lists can scale to accommodate tabular data, so long as the number of elements remains consistent across all lists. For example, the following updated macro call adds a new value to both the VARLIST and LENLIST arguments:

```
data somedata;
   %build_data(varlist=var1 var2 var3,
      lenlist=8 $12 $20);
run;
```

Parallel macro lists can grow unwieldy as the tabular data structures they represent increase in scope (i.e., additional variable names, in this example). Where software demands greater robustness, exception handling can be implemented (within called modules) to validate that parallel macro lists contain the identical number of elements.

Parallel macro lists facilitate extensibility and scalability, in that as additional attributes (i.e., data dictionary metadata) are added, each attribute is neatly placed in its own macro list. For example, if BUILD_DATA functionality is extended to generate FORMAT and LABEL statements dynamically, these additional attributes can be declared as two more parameters (FMTLIST and LABLIST).

Thus, the BUILD_DATA_BETTER macro function now dynamically generates LENGTH, FORMAT, and LABEL statements:

```
%macro build_data_better(varlist= /* space-delim var
      names */,
   lenlist= /* space-delimited lengths */,
   fmtlist= /* space-delimited formats */,
   lablist= /* asterisk-delimited labels */);
%local i;
   length
   %do i=1 %to %sysfunc(countw(&varlist));
```

```
        %scan(&varlist,&i,,S)  %scan(&lenlist,&i,,S)
        %end;
        ;
    format
    %do i=1 %to %sysfunc(countw(&varlist));
        %scan(&varlist,&i,,S)  %scan(&fmtlist,&i,,S).
        %end;
        ;
    label
    %do i=1 %to %sysfunc(countw(&varlist));
        %scan(&varlist,&i,,S)="%scan(&lablist,&i,*)"
        %end;
        ;
%mend;
```

Note that three %DO loops are now required to generate the LENGTH, FORMAT, and LABEL statements dynamically. As before, each loop iterates over only the &VARLIST macro list, which *should* have the same number of elements as the other three macro lists.

Also note that although these parallel macro lists must remain synchronized (in element count and position), no prohibition exists against the inclusion of differently defined macro lists. Thus, because SAS labels can contain spaces, LABLIST has been defined as an asterisk-delimited parameter so it can accommodate spaces in label values (e.g., "Some Date"). That is, the three parallelized macro lists now comprise three space-delimited macro lists and one asterisk-delimited macro list.

A sample invocation again builds the Somedata data set, but now prescribes variable lengths, formats, and labels:

```
data somedata;
    %build_data_better(varlist=var1 var2 var3,
        lenlist=8 $12 $20,
        fmtlist=mmddyy10 $12 $20,
        lablist=Some Date*Var 2*Var 3);
run;
```

The inclusion of two distinct macro list definitions does add some degree of complexity to the invocation, as end users are now responsible for supplying list data through two separate macro list data structure formats—space-delimited and asterisk-delimited. However, the asterisk-delimited macro list data structure affords an additional benefit—the ability to maintain and pass Null values.

For example, what happens if the second element in each of the FMTLIST and LABLIST arguments is removed? When these middle metadata vanish, the invocation fails because the space-delimited FMTLIST (unlike the asterisk-delimited LABLIST) has no method of holding or passing missing elements:

```
data somedata;
   %build_data_better(varlist=var1 var2 var3,
      lenlist=8 $12 $20,
      fmtlist=mmddyy10    $20,
      lablist=Some Date* *Var 3);
run;
```

Madness ensues in the log, demonstrating the chaos caused when parallel macro lists do *not* possess a consistent number of elements:

```
NOTE: Line generated by the invoked macro
"BUILD_DATA_BETTER".
ERROR 85-322: Expecting a format name.
ERROR 200-322: The symbol is not recognized and will be
ignored.
ERROR 76-322: Syntax error, statement will be ignored.


NOTE: The SAS System stopped processing this step
because of errors.
WARNING: The data set WORK.SOMEDATA may be incomplete.
When this step was stopped there were 0
         observations and 3 variables.
WARNING: Data set WORK.SOMEDATA was not replaced because
this step was stopped.
```

Parallel macro lists inherently face the limitation that although their arguments may be represented as keyword parameters, their elements are positional and can tend to be overwhelmed by complexity. Notwithstanding, when lists are brief, and the elements they contain cannot be missing, parallel macro lists represent a viable alternative for passing tabular data.

On a final note, the BUILD_DATA_BETTER macro purports to be "better" because it does more than its predecessor, BUILD_DATA, by generating additional DATA step statements. But is more functionality always better? Or, more aptly queried, should that additional functionality always be coupled to existent functionality? No.

In other words, BUILD_DATA_BETTER is not functionally discrete because it generates multiple, unrelated DATA step statements, and this effectively requires that all data dictionary metadata must be passed in an all-or-nothing fashion, which diminishes software reusability. This design may meet software requirements, but consider the scenario in which you only need to generate LENGTH and LABEL statements dynamically. BUILD_DATA_BETTER fails at this pursuit because it now always requires a parallel macro list to be created that maintains a list of formats—and you may have no interest in formats. Thus, greater modularity (and functional discretion) is demonstrated in the DYNO_LENGTH and DYNO_LABEL macro functions in Section 10.4.3.

10.4.2 Nested Keyword Arguments

Nested keyword arguments comprise keyword arguments contained within superordinate keyword arguments. Whereas parallel macro lists (including parallel indexed macro lists) identify elements *positionally*, nested keyword arguments identify elements *nominally*—that is, by keyword. This methodology can require passing a greater quantity of data (to convey identical information as parallel lists) because key-value pairs—not just values—must be passed. However, nested keyword arguments excel where missing values are valid because only non-missing elements must be specified (and passed).

For example, consider the following *single argument* that is passed to a single macro parameter (DATADICT):

```
%build_nest(datadict=
   (var=var1, len=8,   fmt=mmddyy10, lab=Some Date /
    var=var2, len=$12, fmt=$12,      lab=Var 2 /
    var=var3, len=$20, fmt=$20,      lab=Var 3))
```

Although useful in limited cases, this hot mess does violate the data-driven design principle of hiding complexity in the implementation, introduced in Section 1.4

Yes, you heard correctly—one argument. Thus, DATADICT is *declared* as a macro variable, but within the macro implementation, it is *described* as comprising tabular data—and this description must be operationalized programmatically within the macro's implementation. Just as macro lists often must be decomposed into their constituent *linear* elements, the DATADICT data structure must be decomposed into its *tabular* elements.

Parentheses mask the internal structure of the DATADICT argument, and facilitate the complexity within, including keys for VAR (variable name), LEN (variable length), FMT (variable format), and LAB (variable label). Consecutive keys are mapped to the same variable, with the slash symbol delimiting one variable's definition from the next. Thus, DATADICT effectively defines four delimiters—parentheses demarcate the beginning and end of the internal structure; slashes delimit variables; commas delimit keys; and equal signs delimit key-value pairs!

The BUILD_NEST macro function interprets the DATADICT tabular structure, and dynamically generates LENGTH, FORMAT, and LABEL statements:

This user-defined tabular data structure represents the ultimate *prescription-description gap*, discussed in Section 9.5

```
%macro build_nest(datadict= /* subparameters
    VAR, LEN, FMT, LAB */);
* VAR (req) subpar must be specified first;
* LEN (req) subpar can be in any order;
* FMT (opt) subpar can be any order (no period);
* LAB (opt) subpar can be any order (no quotes);
%local lenlist fmtlist lablist i j list;
%let datadict=%sysfunc(compress(%bquote(&datadict),
    %nrstr(%))%nrstr(%(),));
%do i=1 %to %sysfunc(countw(%bquote(&datadict),/));
    %let list=%scan(%bquote(&datadict),&i,/);
    %do j=1 %to %sysfunc(countw(%bquote(&list),
            %str(,)));
        %let assign=%scan(%bquote(&list),&j,%str(,));
        %if %lowcase(%scan(&assign,1,=))=var
            %then %let var=%scan(&assign,2,=);
        %else %if %lowcase(%scan(&assign,1,=))=len
            %then %let lenlist=
            &lenlist &var %scan(&assign,2,=);
        %else %if %lowcase(%scan(&assign,1,=))=fmt
            %then %let fmtlist=
            &fmtlist &var %scan(&assign,2,=).;
        %else %if %lowcase(%scan(&assign,1,=))=lab
            %then %let lablist=
```

```
            &lablist &var="%scan(&assign,2,=)";
        %end;
    %end;
    length &lenlist;
    format &fmtlist;
    label &lablist;
    %mend;
```

As a macro function, BUILD_NEST can be invoked from inside a DATA step to generate these statements dynamically:

```
data nested;
    %build_nest(datadict=
        (var=var1, len=8,    fmt=mmddyy10, lab=Some Date /
         var=var2, len=$12, fmt=$12,      lab=Var 2 /
         var=var3, len=$20, fmt=$20,      lab=Var 3));
run;
```

BUILD_NEST is functionally equivalent to BUILD_DATA_BETTER (defined in Section 10.4.1), although its key-value pairs are arguably more readable than passing positional elements. BUILD_NEST also readily accommodates passing missing values because elements can be excluded from the invocation.

For example, the following invocation creates the Empty_nest data set, in which some variable attributes have been omitted:

```
data empty_nest;
    %build_nest(datadict=
        (var=var1, len=8, /
         var=var2, len=$12,                    lab=Var 2 /
         var=var3, len=$20, fmt=$20,           lab=Var 3));
run;
```

Despite the missing format and length values for the first variable, and missing format value for the second variable, BUILD_NEST flexibly creates the LENGTH, FORMAT, and LABEL statements.

10.4.3 Parallel Indexed Macro Lists

In Section 10.3.4, the VARS_LENS_LABELS_IDX macro initializes three indexed macro lists that represent a data set's variable names, variable lengths, and variable labels. The three lists are considered *parallel* because the number of elements they contain must remain consistent among all three lists, and because the order of elements for each list similarly must be identical.

Parallel indexed macro lists can also be created, in which each of the zero-index values (that convey an indexed macro list's dimensions) must be identical:

```
%put &=pres_vars_idx_0;
%put &=pres_lens_idx_0;
%put &=pres_labs_idx_0;


PRES_VARS_IDX_0=6
PRES_LENS_IDX_0=6
PRES_LABS_IDX_0=6
```

Similarly, a specific indexed element within one list must correspond to the identically indexed elements in all associated parallel lists. For example, the second element in PRES_VARS_IDX represents the Lname variable, so the second elements in both the PRES_LENS_IDX and PRES_LABS_IDX indexed macro lists also must correspond to Lname:

```
%put &=pres_vars_idx_2;
%put &=pres_lens_idx_2;
%put &=pres_labs_idx_2;


PRES_VARS_IDX_2=lname
PRES_LENS_IDX_2=$20
PRES_LABS_IDX_2=Last Name
```

Despite the ability of parallel indexed macro lists to maintain tabular control data such as these, in most cases, tabular data are better maintained within a control table, as depicted in Table 10.2, which shows the Var_len_lab data set. Within the data set—a *data dictionary*—each variable represents one parallel indexed macro list, and each observation represents a variable characteristic (like length or format) that spans each of the respective indexed macro lists. This construction is far superior to attempting to maintain multiple, parallel user-defined lists that can become unsynchronized, and additionally affords all the built-in functionality that SAS data sets provide.

Data dictionaries, including both built-in and user-defined, are the focus of Chapter 12

	Variable Name	Length	Label
1	fname	$20	First Name
2	lname	$20	Last Name
3	num	3	Number
4	vp	$100	President's VPs
5	nolabel	8	
6	amplabel	8	this & that

Table 10.2 Var_len_lab Data Dictionary

For example, the Var_len_lab data set contains the same control data as the three indexed macro lists, and can be generated using the following hardcoded DATA step:

```
data var_len_lab;
    infile datalines dsd;
    length var $32 len $10 lab $50;
    input var $ len $ lab $;
    label var='Variable Name' len='Length' lab='Label';
    datalines;
fname, $20, First Name
lname, $20, Last Name
num, 3, Number
vp, $100, "President's VPs"
nolabel, 8,
amplabel, 8, this & that
;
```

The Var_len_lab data set prescribes the structure and content of a data set, capturing variable attributes like name, length, and label. These control data could be used to validate the structure of a data set—for example, if a transactional data set were received from a third-party source—or to generate a data set dynamically.

Rather than being maintained in multiple indexed macro lists, these control data can be maintained within a single control table. And for many use cases, the control data can be operationalized without the need to transform them into macro lists or indexed macro lists.

For example, the DYNO_LENGTH macro function dynamically generates a LENGTH statement based on the Var (variable name) and Len (variable length) values in the data dictionary:

```
%macro dyno_length(dsn /* control table name */,
   var /* var name holding variable names */,
   len /* var name holding variable lengths */);
%local dsid i close;
%let dsid=%sysfunc(open(&dsn,i));
length
   %do %while(%sysfunc(fetch(&dsid))=0);
      %sysfunc(getvarc(&dsid, %sysfunc(varnum(&dsid,
%upcase(&var))))) %sysfunc(getvarc(&dsid,
%sysfunc(varnum(&dsid, %upcase(&len)))))
      %end;
   ;
%let close=%sysfunc(close(&dsid));
%mend;
```

The %DO %WHILE loop iterates as long as the FETCH function returns a new observation, and the contents of that observation are resolved in the calling program when the last observation is reached. Neither macro lists nor indexed macro lists are initialized.

Similarly, the DYNO_LABEL macro function dynamically generates a LABEL statement based on the Var (variable name) and Label (variable label) values in the data dictionary:

```
%macro dyno_label(dsn /* control table name */,
   var /* var name holding variable names */,
   lab /* var name holding variable labels */);
%local dsid i close;
%let dsid=%sysfunc(open(&dsn,i));
label
   %do %while(%sysfunc(fetch(&dsid))=0);
      %sysfunc(getvarc(&dsid, %sysfunc(varnum(&dsid,
%upcase(&var))))) = "%sysfunc(getvarc(&dsid,
%sysfunc(varnum(&dsid, %upcase(&lab)))))"
      %end;
   ;
%let close=%sysfunc(close(&dsid));
%mend;
```

The Dos_dynos data set, which is identical to the Dynamic data set created in Section 10.3.4, can be created using calls to DYNO_LENGTH and DYNO_LABEL macro functions:

```
data dos_dynos;
    %dyno_length(var_len_lab, var, len);
    %dyno_label(var_len_lab, var, lab);
run;
```

Although the functionality of DYNO_LENGTH and DYNO_LABEL could have been packed into a single user-defined function, the two-function approach facilitates greater reuse through software modularity. For example, you might want to create a data set that relies on a dynamically generated LENGTH statement, but which defines no variable labels—and in this instance, you could call only DYNO_LENGTH.

Whereas this chapter focuses on linear data structures, Chapter 11 introduces control tables (like the Var_len_lab data dictionary) that can maintain control data, and the methods through which they can be accessed. For example, although DYNO_LENGTH and DYNO_LABEL rely on various input/output (I/O) functions (e.g., OPEN, ATTRN, FETCH, GETVARC, VARNUM) to retrieve control data from the data set, other methods exist to parse and extract data from control tables. These metadata could have been retrieved using the built-in SET subroutine (aka CALL SET), or by accessing the built-in SAS Dictionary tables.

> The SAS Dictionary tables are discussed in Section 12.4

Thus, regardless of the method selected to operationalize tabular control data, the savvy SAS practitioner should understand that tabular data structure options exist, and often provide greater reliability and built-in functionality than parallel macro lists and parallel indexed macro lists.

10.5 SAS LISTS

Within this text, a *SAS list* represents a series of same-type, delimited values maintained within a character variable. SAS lists are discussed extensively in Section 4.5, in which a comma-delimited list is defined and used to containerize a series of character values—vice president names.

To be clear, lists are present throughout both Base SAS and the SAS macro language, and are used extensively as input to built-in statements, options, functions, and subroutines. However, as SAS does not define a list data structure, SAS practitioners have no ability to maintain our own data in these "lists" that we commonly utilize.

For example, the following brief DATA step demonstrates multiple lists, including both space-delimited and comma-delimited lists:

```
data lists (drop=n1 n2 n3);
   length c1 c2 c3 $20 n1 n2 n3 8;
   label c1='uno' c2='dos' c3='tres';
   c1='one';
   c2='two';
   c3='three';
   call sortc(c1, c2, c3);
   cat=catx(',',c1,c2,c3);
run;
```

The DROP option specifies a space-delimited *list* of variables to be excluded from the Lists data set. The LENGTH statement declares a space-delimited *list* of variables. The SORTC subroutine sorts a comma-delimited *list* of variables. The CATX function concatenates a comma-delimited *list* of variables. And the LABEL statement accepts a *list* of key-value pairs that are delimited with equal signs! Notwithstanding all the ways that SAS practitioners pass lists to effect built-in functionality, we are not able to maintain our own data within a list data structure—because the list data structure does not exist in Base SAS.

User-defined SAS lists vary in complexity and capability, but as collections of elements, always must define some method of delimiting values. For example, in the preceding DATA step, the Cat variable is initialized to the following comma-delimited list of values:

one,three,two

Thus, Cat is *prescribed* as a character variable with a length of 20, but is *described* as a comma-delimited list of character values. This gap—between syntactical prescription and user-defined description—must be overcome programmatically through operations that interpret, parse, decompose, extract, and utilize SAS list elements.

Section 9.5 discusses this prescription-description gap

SAS lists excel at scalability, as an undetermined number of values can be stored in a single character variable, so long as the variable length is not exceeded. In practice, SAS lists are implemented far less frequently than SAS macro lists, and thus occupy a relatively fainter footprint within this text. Notwithstanding, they are powerful allies of SAS practitioners in need of flexible control data.

10.6 SUMMARY

The SAS language defines no built-in list data structure. Notwithstanding this limitation, generations of SAS practitioners have cobbled together kludgy yet clever user-defined list data structures in both Base SAS and the SAS macro language to facilitate greater scalability, readability, flexibility, and configurability. Lists represent a form of data abstraction in which a containerized series of data can be referenced (and operationalized) either as a cohesive unit or as a collection of elements—depending on the operations that are performed.

This chapter introduced the SAS array, a built-in quasi-data structure that nevertheless delivers powerful built-in functionality, and which can be leveraged by myriad built-in operations like the OF operator. With regard to data-driven design, arrays are especially useful for maintaining and evaluating business rules and data quality rules, and can sometimes replace unnecessary metaprogramming that leverages the SAS macro language.

The SAS macro list was introduced, in which a series of values are stored within a macro variable. The requirement that values be delimited, and the complexity that can result from storing values having special characters, was discussed. The SAS indexed macro list was also introduced, and is often a preferred alternative to SAS macro lists—because indexing delivers more efficient parsing of lists, and because indexing does not require list decomposition into constituent elements.

Regardless of what rules are implemented to design a user-defined list, macro list, or indexed macro list, a user-defined data structure is only as strong as the user-defined operations that support and operationalize it. Thus, the importance of judiciously designing list data structures was stressed, as well as the prioritization of backward compatibility—both when modifying data structure design and when refactoring or modifying associated user-defined operations.

Finally, the reality was demonstrated that macro lists commonly model *tabular* not *linear* data. Although built-in tabular data structures (such as the SAS data set or hash object) provide greater functionality where tabular data must be maintained, methods were demonstrated that support the creation of user-defined data structures that maintain tabular data—including both parallel macro lists and nested keyword arguments.

Chapter 11.

CONTROL TABLES

This chapter has the following objectives:

❖ Define control tables and distinguish them from other control files, such as configuration files.

❖ Demonstrate how the increasing complexity of control data can require a shift from arguments and lists to control tables.

❖ Contrast *external control tables* (i.e., non-SAS tables) and *internal control tables* (i.e., SAS data sets that may represent external tables).

❖ Demonstrate how control tables can be used to drive software operations.

❖ Contrast methods of iterating control tables, including macro metaprogramming and SAS arrays.

❖ Introduce various methods of *preloading* data quality rules and business rules into data sets to drive dynamic rule processing.

❖ Discuss the importance of maintaining tabular data within control tables rather than within user-defined data structures, such as macro lists.

Control tables represent the subset of control files that store control data in tabular form—that is, in rows and columns, or in SAS parlance, observations and variables. Like all control files, control tables provide dynamic instruction to software to effect dynamic change. Within SAS literature, control tables are sometimes referred to as *control data sets*; however, this text adopts the more inclusive reality that tabular control data can be maintained not only within SAS data sets but also within other tabular data structures and file types.

Parallel macro lists and *nested keyword arguments* are discussed and demonstrated in Sections 10.4.1 and 10.4.2, respectively

IEEE defines a *table* as "functionally related data elements, grouped together into a single data structure for transport as defined by ANSI C12.19."[85] Although user-defined data structures like *parallel macro lists* and *nested keyword arguments* can represent tabular control data, both of these "data structures" are, in truth, plain old macro variables. Thus, excluding those rare instances in which SAS practitioners need to parameterize and pass tabular data *by value*, tabular data are typically better maintained in a SAS data set (or other built-in control table), and passed *by reference* to the modules or processes that rely on them.

Call methods are introduced in Section 6.5

Control tables can originate as spreadsheets, comma-separated values (CSV) files, extensible markup language (XML) files, configuration files, and other data structures. Within the SAS application, non-SAS control tables are often first converted to SAS data sets so they can more readily interact with SAS operations. In these instances, both the *external* file (i.e., non-SAS) and the *internal* table (i.e., SAS data set) are referred to as control tables, with the external table indirectly driving software functionality, and the internal data set directly driving functionality.

In contrast with parameterized control data that are passed as arguments, control tables—like all control files—facilitate the persistence, maintenance, and archival of control data. Control tables also enable control data to be modified without accessing code, whereas passing arguments requires that control data be modified at the point of invocation of some program or callable module. Control data archival can facilitate testing, validation, and debugging efforts where the configuration settings capture the state in which a module is operating.

Where control tables are maintained in canonical file formats, such as XML or CSV, software configurability can be maximized because control data can be modified without access to the SAS application. That is, even nontechnical end users can modify control data within control tables to alter software functionality.

A tradeoff of increased interoperability, however, is often a reduction in data structure integrity and robustness. For example, once a control table is maintained as a SAS data set, *element decomposition* is intrinsically supported, and variable data types, lengths, and formats are defined and enforced. However, the equivalent control table maintained as a spreadsheet has less restrictive data definitions, and may require validation or transformation before the spreadsheet can be imported into a SAS data set. Data validation is a recommended best practice when importing external control tables.

> Section 9.7 discusses element decomposition operations that typically must be designed when user-defined data structures are utilized

This chapter introduces control tables and methods that can be operationalized in Base SAS and the SAS macro language. Given that control tables commonly store data rules, including data quality rules and business rules, examples demonstrate how these tabular control data can interact with and operate on domain data.

11.1 FROM MACRO LISTS TO CONTROL TABLES

Although control tables prescribe a tabular structure, the control data they maintain often can be represented through other data structures, such as macro lists, parallel macro lists, nested arguments, or configuration files. In many instances, the need for a control table grows incrementally as other data structures—especially user-defined data structures—become less suited for supporting control data. This can occur as the complexity or scale of control data increases during development or over the lifespan of a software product, or as a more rigorous data structure format is required to enforce control data rules.

In this incremental design paradigm, control data might first be represented by arguments that are passed *by value* to some process. Over time, however, this functionality might be refactored to pass the same control data instead *by reference* to a control table to accommodate greater complexity. The following five subsections demonstrate the progression that could occur from static, hardcoded logic to a more dynamic, configurable approach that maintains control data within control tables.

> *Call by value* and *call by reference* are discussed in Sections 6.5.1 and 6.5.2, respectively

To facilitate this expedition, the following SAS program (etl.sas) can be saved in a user-specified folder:

```
* program saved as d:\sas\etl.sas;
data etl;
   set pres;
```

```
        length fullname $50 term 8 numVPs 8;
        format term 8.2;
        fullname=catx(' ',fname,lname);
        term=round((dt2-dt1)/365.25,.01);
        numVPs=countw(vp,',');
run;

proc sort data=etl;
    by num;
run;

proc means data=etl;
    var term numVPs;
run;

proc freq data=etl;
    tables term numVPs;
run;

PROC FREQ data=etl;
    tables lname;
run;

%macro sample();
%put Today is
%sysfunc(putn(%sysfunc(date()),mmddyy10.));
%mend;


%sample;
```

Consider the need to assess the frequency with which specific built-in SAS procedures (aka PROCs) are utilized within a team or organization's codebase. For example, a company might want to analyze SAS development trends to determine if its SAS practitioners are utilizing procedures belonging to more specialized (and costly) SAS application modules like SAS/OR that lie beyond the bounds of the Base SAS license. This evaluation could enable the company to reduce its licenses for certain SAS modules, redirecting those funds toward expenditures having greater return on investment (ROI).

The first step in this analysis involves conceptualizing software that can open a SAS program file, interrogate its contents, and generate frequency counts of procedures of interest. This functional requirement is explored in the following five subsections, with various functionally equivalent solutions demonstrated from least to most attractive.

11.1.1 The Concrete Approach

A hardcoded approach to software design is sometimes warranted, especially during early design and development, when various methods are being explored, contrasted, and tested. In limiting or eliminating software abstraction, developers can focus code-and-fix development on delivering specific (rather than generalized) software functionality.

Unfortunately, in some cases, as soon as a preliminary *functional* solution is achieved, focus and priorities shift immediately to the next *functional requirement* (or even to another program or project), rather than to the *performance requirements* that remain unfulfilled. Stakeholders can help combat this tendency by ensuring that software technical specifications comprise not only functional but also performance requirements (e.g., maintainability, configurability, flexibility). In this scenario, the initial solution will be incrementally refactored through data-driven design until it is sufficiently configurable, flexible, and maintainable.

Dynamic and static performance requirements are discussed in Section 7.2.1

The following DATA step concretely demonstrates how the SORT and FREQ procedures can be programmatically identified within the etl.sas program (created in Section 11.1):

```
%let loc=d:\sas\;      * USER MUST CHANGE LOCATION *;
data metrics;
   length line 8 contents $500 keyword $50;
   infile "&loc.etl.sas" truncover end=eof;
   input contents $500.;

   * first hardcoded condition;
   if find(upcase(contents),'PROC SORT') then do;
      line=_n_;
      keyword="PROC SORT";
      output;
```

```
    end;

* second hardcoded condition;
if find(upcase(contents),'PROC FREQ') then do;
    line=_n_;
    keyword="PROC FREQ";
    output;
    end;
run;
```

The INFILE statement identifies the SAS program file to be ingested, and the INPUT statement iteratively ingests each line into the Metrics data set. Two conditional (IF-THEN) logic blocks use the FIND function to search the data stream for instances of SAS procedures. For example, the first block searches the program file for "PROC SORT" and the second block searches for "PROC FREQ," with only positive results saved to the Metrics data set.

The Metrics data set (shown in Table 11.1) has three observations, demonstrating that the SORT procedure was identified once and the FREQ procedure twice, within lines 11, 19, and 23 of the code, respectively. This program might be constructed as a proof of concept during initial development to test the search syntax, or perhaps to test runtime performance if executed iteratively on a larger sample of program files (beyond just etl.sas).

When the dynamic performance requirement of *scalability* is sought, iteration methods, discussed in Chapter 5, can help meet this objective

However, too often, a manager or even the SAS practitioner developing the code will abandon further design opportunities at the onset of a functional solution. For example, the initial requirements are intended to search for a large selection of SAS procedures, and although it would be syntactically possible to add separate conditional logic blocks for each procedure (beyond SORT and FREQ), this less-than-scalable solution would be inadvisable, if not infeasible.

	line	contents	keyword
1	11	proc sort data=etl;	PROC SORT
2	19	proc freq data=etl;	PROC FREQ
3	23	PROC FREQ data=etl;	PROC FREQ

Table 11.1 Metrics Data Set

11.1.2 Adding Iteration Abstraction

With the success of the first implementation in the preceding section, the developer could refactor the DATA step to include iteration that loops over a comma-delimited list of procedure names. This iteration, a form of abstraction, enables the functionality within each IF-THEN block to be coded only once albeit executed multiple times—once for each list element.

A functionally equivalent DATA step follows, in which a DO loop now iterates over a comma-delimited list of SAS procedures:

```
%let loc=d:\sas\;        * USER MUST CHANGE LOCATION *;
data metrics;
    length line 8 contents $500 keyword $50;
    infile "&loc.etl.sas" truncover end=eof;
    input contents $500.;
    do keyword='PROC SORT','PROC FREQ';
        if find(upcase(contents),strip(keyword))
            then do;
            line=_n_;
            output;
            end;
        end;
run;
```

> The DO loop demonstrates *external iteration*, discussed in Section 5.2.2, because its looping mechanics are revealed

The Keyword variable is also initialized as the DO loop iterates, so the explicit keyword initialization has also been removed, further shortening the code. In becoming more scalable, this DATA step also increases the productivity of SAS practitioners *writing* it, because far less code must be written, and *maintaining* it, because far less code must be parsed when modifications are required.

For example, the addition of a new search term (PROC MEANS) now only requires modifying the comma-delimited list within the DO loop—rather than adding an entire IF-THEN block:

```
    do keyword='PROC SORT','PROC FREQ','PROC MEANS';
```

> The solution lacks *modularity* and *data independence*, two pillars of data-driven design, introduced in Sections 1.3.2 and 1.3.3, respectively

This solution is more scalable but does not represent data-driven design because any modifications to the list of keywords must be made in the code, rather than within a separate data structure.

11.1.3 Adding Procedural Abstraction

Procedural abstraction further enhances the previous DATA step, encapsulating it within a SAS macro that can be saved as a separate SAS program file, and called repeatedly. This modularity facilitates software reuse because user-defined macros can be maintained independently, and used to support future software projects or products.

The FINDKEYWORDS macro (findkeywords.sas) should be created and saved:

```
* saved as d:\sas\findkeywords.sas;
%macro findkeywords(keywordlist /* comma-delim */,
    pgmfile= /* SAS program file name to parse */)
    / parmbuff;
%local i keyword findpos;
* remove the outer parentheses and PGMFILE argument;
%let findpos=%index(%upcase(&syspbuff),PGMFILE);
%let syspbuff=%substr(&syspbuff,2,%eval(&findpos-2));
data metrics;
    length line 8 contents $500 keyword $50;
    infile "&pgmfile" truncover end=eof;
    input contents $500.;
%do i=1 %to %sysfunc(countw(%bquote(&syspbuff),
        %str(,)));
    %let keyword=%scan(%bquote(&syspbuff),
        &i,%str(,));
    if find(upcase(contents),
            strip("%upcase(&keyword)")) then do;
        line=_n_;
        keyword="&keyword";
        output;
        end;
    %end;
run;
%mend;
```

FINDKEYWORDS defines two parameters—KEYWORDLIST, which specifies a comma-delimited list of SAS procedures, and PGMFILE, which specifies the name of the SAS program file to be parsed. Note that the KEYWORDLIST parameter is a multi-element positional parameter, in that the PARMBUFF option enables multiple, comma-delimited values to be passed to the &SYSPBUFF automatic macro variable inside the macro.

Also note that because &SYSPBUFF is enclosed within parentheses, these extraneous characters must be stripped before &SYSPBUFF can be parsed in subsequent statements. And because &SYSPBUFF still contains comma-separated values, these commas must be masked using %BQUOTE.

The design pattern also demonstrates metaprogramming, in which DATA step DO loops (which had previously iterated over the list of keywords) have been replaced with SAS macro %DO loops. These %DO loops dynamically write DATA step statements (conditional IF-THEN blocks), so despite representing data-driven design, the resultant code that is executed by SAS more closely resembles the DATA step in Section 11.1.1 than the DATA step (having the DO loop) demonstrated in Section 11.1.2.

The %INCLUDE statement compiles the FINDKEYWORDS macro, and the subsequent FINDKEYWORDS invocation produces the identical Metrics data set:

> The %MACRO statement *PARMBUFF* option and *&SYSPBUFF* automatic macro variable are introduced in Section 6.6.2

> *Metaprogramming* is introduced in Section 10.1.2

```
%let loc=d:\sas\;        * USER MUST CHANGE LOCATION *;
%include "&loc.findkeywords.sas";
%findkeywords(PROC FREQ,PROC SORT,
   pgmfile=&loc.etl.sas);
```

With its use of procedural abstraction, the FINDKEYWORDS macro represents the first data-driven design approach to these three functionally equivalent solutions. For example, the arguments passed in the FINDKEYWORDS invocation can now be modified without the need to modify the underlying FINDKEYWORDS macro.

The FINDKEYWORDS macro represents a successful end of the road for many SAS practitioners because a reusable, modular solution has been engineered, facilitated by iteration and procedural abstraction. However, as the scope or complexity of control data increases, passing control data by value can become arduous.

Consider the requirement that all SAS procedures (or at least a significant number) should be included in the list of search terms. The FINDKEYWORDS invocation now includes all two-, three-, four-, and five-character SAS procedure names:

```
%let loc=d:\sas\;        * USER MUST CHANGE LOCATION *;
%include "&loc.findkeywords.sas";
%findkeywords(PROC DS,PROC S3,PROC DS2,PROC DTB,
    PROC ETB,PROC LUA,PROC SQL,PROC STB,PROC XSL,
    PROC YZB,PROC COPY,PROC CORR,PROC FCMP,PROC FREQ,
    PROC HTTP,PROC JSON,PROC OLAP,PROC PLOT,PROC PLUA,
    PROC RANK,PROC SOAP,PROC SORT,PROC SPDO,PROC TSPL,
    PROC ZBLD,PROC ACCES,PROC CALEN,PROC CDISC,
    PROC CHART,PROC CLASS,PROC COMPA,PROC CONVE,
    PROC CV2VI,PROC DATEK,PROC DBCST,PROC DBLOA,
    PROC DELET,PROC EXPLO,PROC EXPOR,PROC FMTC2,
    PROC FORMS,PROC FSLIS,PROC GENFM,PROC GENKE,
    PROC HADOO,PROC IMAGE,PROC IMPOR,PROC INFOM,
    PROC IOMOP,PROC IOTST,PROC LOCAL,PROC MBSCO,
    PROC MEANS,PROC METAB,PROC METAC,PROC METAD,
    PROC METAI,PROC METAL,PROC METAO,PROC METAR,
    PROC METAS,PROC MIGRA,PROC NICKN,PROC ODBCS,
    PROC OLAPC,PROC OLAPO,PROC OPTSA,PROC PLOT1,
    PROC PMENU,PROC POLAP,PROC PRESE,PROC PRINT,
    PROC PRODU,PROC PROTO,PROC PRTDE,PROC PRTEX,
    PROC PRTTO,PROC PSCOR,PROC PWENC,PROC QUNIV,
    PROC QUTIL,PROC REGIS,PROC RENDE,PROC REPMN,
    PROC REPOR,PROC REPWD,PROC SASAF,PROC SASDS,
    PROC SASE7,PROC SASEB,PROC SASFM,PROC SASMS,
    PROC SASOO,PROC SASRM,PROC SASSD,PROC SASXB,
    PROC SASXN,PROC SASYH,PROC SASYP,PROC SASYR,
    PROC SASZU,PROC SCHED,PROC SGDES,PROC SGPAN,
    PROC SGPLO,PROC SGREN,PROC SGSCA,PROC SORTT,
    PROC SPELL,PROC STAND,PROC TABUL,PROC TEMPL,
    PROC TIMEP,PROC TKBUG,PROC TOOLB,PROC TRANT,
    PROC TREPO,PROC TSOPE,PROC TSPLT,PROC TSSQL,
    PROC XCOPY,PROC ZCATL,PROC ZFORM,PROC ZIMGF,
    PROC ZLIST,PROC ZVARL,pgmfile=&loc.etl.sas);
```

The data-driven design principles of passing simple invocations and hiding complexity in the implementation, introduced in Section 1.4, are both violated in this call

	line	contents	keyword
1	11	proc sort data=etl;	PROC SORT
2	15	proc means data=etl;	PROC MEANS
3	19	proc freq data=etl;	PROC FREQ
4	23	PROC FREQ data=etl;	PROC FREQ

Table 11.2 Updated Metrics Data Set (with PROC MEANS)

The invocation of KEYWORDS regenerates the Metrics data set, shown in Table 11.2. Note that because MEANS was added to the list of keywords, the Metrics data set now contains four (rather than three) observations.

Yes, the *called* module (i.e., the FINDKEYWORDS macro program file) remains uncluttered, but now the *calling* module (in which the FINDKEYWORDS invocation is made) has diminished readability, as it passes all control data by value. Hundreds of arguments or values within an invocation is off-putting to most developers; thus, a control table could maintain the list of SAS procedures, and in lieu of passing a cavalcade of PROCs, only the table name could be passed by reference to the macro.

As discussed throughout Chapter 10, control tables can be warranted not only when control data become more voluminous, but also when control data become more complex, such as encompassing special characters that require masking. To be clear, the *tabular* nature itself is not the panacea, but rather the *built-in* data structure (the SAS data set), which delivers greater functionality and reliability.

For example, consider an additional software requirement specifying that macro statements (such as %MACRO, %MEND, %DO, and %LET) need to be added to the list of searchable keywords. The following sample invocation fails because these keywords are not correctly parsed (by the SAS macro facility) because they (and their percent signs) are unmasked:

```
%let loc=d:\sas\;       * USER MUST CHANGE LOCATION *;
%include "&loc.findkeywords.sas";
%findkeywords(%MACRO,%MEND,%DO,%LET,
    pgmfile=&loc.etl.sas);
```

If you are wont to create Frankenstein's monster, various macro functions (e.g., %BQUOTE, %NRSTR, %SUPERQ) could be painstakingly patched together to mask these macro statement keywords further. However, the macro statement keywords would still cause failure within the macro call, and would require masking there as well. And because masking within the macro call would violate the data-driven design principle of hiding complexity within the implementation, a far superior alternative is to forego masking altogether, and instead store these pesky data within a data set rather than a comma-delimited list of values.

11.1.4 Adding a Control Table (via Macro List)

Given the requirement that the FINDKEYWORDS macro support potentially hundreds of keyword values, maintaining these control data within a control table is a recommended solution. The following DATA step creates the Terms data set, which readily scales to incorporate an endless list of search terms—only three of which (SORT, FREQ, and MEANS) are included in this abbreviated representation:

```
data terms;
    infile datalines delimiter=',' dsd;
    length term $32;
    input term $;
datalines;
PROC SORT
PROC FREQ
PROC MEANS
;
```

The FINDKEYWORDS macro from Section 11.1.3 is refactored into FINDKEYWORDSCTRL, which now defines the CTRL parameter in which the Terms data set name can be passed by reference. The SQL procedure within FINDKEYWORDSCTRL creates the comma-delimited macro list (&CTRL), which is utilized by the subsequent DATA step to query the SAS program file (etl.sas).

Also note that because CTRL now passes the keyword list by reference (rather than as a series of comma-delimited values), the PARMBUFF option is no longer required.

The FINDKEYWORDSCTRL macro follows:

```
* saved as d:\sas\findkeywordsctrl.sas;
%macro findkeywordsctrl(ctrl= /* control table */,
    pgmfile= /* SAS program file name to parse */);
* get observation count;
%local keywordlist keyword i;
```

```
proc sql noprint;
    select term into : keywordlist
    separated by ',' from &ctrl;
quit;
data metrics;
    length line 8 contents $500 keyword $50;
    infile "&pgmfile" truncover end=eof;
    input contents $500.;
    %do i=1 %to %sysfunc(countw(%bquote(&keywordlist),
        %str(,)));
        %let keyword=%scan(%bquote(&keywordlist),
            &i,%str(,));
        if find(upcase(contents),
                strip("%upcase(&keyword)")) then do;
            line=_n_;
            keyword="&keyword";
            output;
            end;
    %end;
run;
%mend;
```

The following invocation is simplified, and now remains stable, irrespective of the number of keyword terms that are defined within the Terms data set:

```
%let loc=d:\sas\;       * USER MUST CHANGE LOCATION *;
%include "&loc.findkeywordsctrl.sas";
%findkeywordsctrl(ctrl=terms, pgmfile=&loc.etl.sas);
```

The invocation recreates the Metrics data set, demonstrated in Table 11.2. However, were macro statements (e.g., %MACRO, %MEND, %DO) to be included in the control table, the FINDKEYWORDSCTRL macro would fail because these macro keywords are not masked. At issue here, as in the previous subsection, is the unnecessary iteration over macro lists to access a collection of control data elements.

Thus, the macro needlessly ports control data from a built-in data structure (i.e., the Terms data set) to a less desirable, user-defined data structure (i.e., the comma-delimited macro list &CTRL) that does not

Maintaining control data within built-in data structures (whenever possible) is a data-driven design principle, enumerated in Section 1.4, and discussed in Section 4.4

support intrinsic element decomposition. Coupled with the new requirement that control data must contain macro keywords (having special characters), SAS practitioners are left with two options—waste effort designing operations that mask special characters, or design a more versatile solution that can leave control data in the original Terms SAS data set (where they belong). The preferred solution is obvious.

11.1.5 Adding a Control Table (the Right Way)

In Section 11.1.4, the FINDKEYWORDSCTRL macro is defined, which enables a variable number of keyword arguments to be maintained within a control table that drives subsequent search operations within a user-specified SAS program file. However, the solution suffers in that complex keywords such as %MACRO and %MEND are not supported because FINDKEYWORDSCTRL unnecessarily converts the control table (Terms data set) into a comma-delimited macro list.

The required keyword complexity can be demonstrated by redefining the Terms data set to include more complex search terms:

```
data terms;
    infile datalines delimiter=',' dsd;
    length term $32;
    input term $;
datalines;
PROC SORT
PROC FREQ
PROC MEANS
%MACRO
%MEND
%DO
%LET
;
```

The refactored KEYWORDSFINAL macro now contains a single DATA step that reads both the control table (Terms) and the SAS program file (etl.sas).

Internal iteration and external iteration are discussed in Sections 5.2.1 and 5.2.2, respectively

The DATA step initially reads the control table, relying on *external iteration* of the DO loop to initialize the Arrkey temporary array with keywords from Terms. When the end-of-file (EOF) marker is detected, the DO loop exits, and the DATA step subsequently reads the SAS program file (etl.sas), relying on internal iteration (in which the iteration mechanics are concealed) to read each line of code.

The second DO loop iterates through the SAS array, and assesses whether each keyword is found within each line of the program file being evaluated. At no point do the control data leave the sanctity of the SAS data set, a built-in data structure, thus overcoming the limitations of all previous solutions.

The KEYWORDSFINAL macro follows:

```
* saved as d:\sas\keywordsfinal.sas;
%macro keywordsfinal(ctrl /* control table (DSN) */,
    pgmfile= /* SAS program file name to parse */);
* get observation count;
%local nobs;
proc sql noprint;
    select count(*) into : nobs
    from &ctrl;
quit;
data metrics (drop=i term);
    if _n_=1 then do;
        i=0;
        do until(eof);
            i=i+1;
            set &ctrl end=eof;
            array arrkey[&nobs] $32 _temporary_;
            arrkey[i]=strip(term);
        end;
    end;
    length line 8 contents $500 keyword $50;
    infile "&pgmfile" truncover end=eof;
    input contents $500.;
    do i=1 to dim(arrkey);
        if find(upcase(contents),
              strip(upcase(arrkey[i]))) then do;
            line=_n_;
            keyword=arrkey[i];
            output;
```

> Arrays are introduced in Section 4.4.3, and further described in Section 10.1

```
        end;
      end;
   run;
   %mend;
```

The KEYWORDSFINAL macro demonstrates the *preloading* of data rules—that is, the initial ingestion of one or more control tables that precedes a subsequent ingestion of domain data with which the control data interact dynamically. By loading the control table into temporary arrays (in lieu of comparable macro lists), the control data can be evaluated without leaving the sanctity of their control table. Various preloading methods are explored in Section 11.2.

KEYWORDSFINAL can be called (from within a separate program), and relies on the same parameters—PGMFILE and CTRL—that were utilized by the FINDKEYWORDSCTRL macro:

```
%let loc=d:\sas\;        * USER MUST CHANGE LOCATION *;
%include "&loc.keywordsfinal.sas";
%keywordsfinal(ctrl=terms, pgmfile=&loc.etl.sas);
```

The resultant Metrics data set is represented in Table 11.3. Note that the more complex keywords %MACRO and %MEND can now be passed without failure, and without unnecessarily creating user-defined data structures, iteration mechanics, or data masking acrobatics. In this solution, as is often the case when control data interact with domain data, the control data should remain in a SAS data set, if at all possible.

If you gain nothing else from this text, please resist the unhealthy urge to convert control data to macro lists and other user-defined data structures *unless the solution requires it.*

	line	contents	keyword
1	11	proc sort data=etl;	PROC SORT
2	15	proc means data=etl;	PROC MEANS
3	19	proc freq data=etl;	PROC FREQ
4	23	PROC FREQ data=etl;	PROC FREQ
5	27	%macro sample();	%MACRO
6	29	%mend;	%MEND

Table 11.3 Metrics Data Set of (Complex) Discovered Keywords

11.2 PRELOADING DATA RULES

The International Organization for Standardization (ISO) defines a *rule* as a "constraint on a system specification."[86] Data rules, including data quality rules and business rules (where these concepts are differentiated), interact with data to effect dynamic functionality. Data rules comprise three components—input data, criteria or conditions that define logic, and the dependent result or outcome.

The first rules component—*input*—describes the data on which rules are applied. Within SAS data analytic development, these data typically describe *domain data*, the data of principal business value. Thus, within the SAS language, business rules most commonly act upon SAS data sets; however, any data source (such as text files or spreadsheets) can also provide this domain data substrate.

The second rules component—*criteria*—evaluates inputs by applying data rules to those inputs. ISO defines *criteria* as the "specific data items identified as contents of information items for appraising a factor in an evaluation, audit, test or review."[87] In a code-driven design paradigm, criteria might be defined through conditional IF-THEN-ELSE logic or similar hardcoded methods. Within a data-driven design paradigm, however, data rules are instead abstractly defined within external data structures (such as control tables). For example, a *business rules engine* (BRE) describes the interpretive software that ingests dynamic business rules to produce dynamic outcomes.

Business rules and *business rules engines (BREs)* are introduced in Section 8.3

The third rules component—*output*—describes the dynamic functionality that rules produce. For example, data rules might be applied to a SAS data set to identify, validate, clean, or transform values, or to produce other functionality or outcomes. Within SAS programming, data rules are often applied to manipulate data residing in SAS data sets. For example, data quality rules might apply a SAS format to standardize a variable, or business rules might consult a lookup table to validate business processes.

Within a data-driven design paradigm, data rules can be *preloaded* by ingesting a control table, and by subsequently ingesting the domain data to which the rules are being applied. A single DATA step can often ingest both domain data and data rules thereof, as demonstrated in the next four subsections. In some cases, however, preliminary processes first should have ingested and validated the structure and integrity of the domain data or the control data—especially where those data originate from user-defined data structures or third-party sources.

Control tables are often represented by SAS data sets or CSV files, which are commonly imported from spreadsheets. Domain data are most commonly maintained within SAS data sets; however, in some cases, they constitute text files. For example, when software dynamically parses SAS log files or SAS program files, these text files constitute domain data.

Four data-driven design examples demonstrate the diversity and intersections of control table file type and domain data file type, each of which is demonstrated in subsequent subsections:

1. **Control table maintained in a SAS data set, and domain data maintained in text file**. For example, Section 11.1.5 demonstrates a SAS data set containing SAS reserved keywords (i.e., control data) that are applied to evaluate a SAS program file.

2. **Control table maintained in a text file, and domain data maintained in a text file**. For example, a CSV file might contain SAS reserved keywords (i.e., control data) that are applied to evaluate a SAS program file.

3. **Control table maintained in a SAS data set, and domain data maintained in a SAS data set**. For example, a SAS data set might contain data quality rules (i.e., control data) that are applied to a second SAS data set (i.e., domain data) to clean or validate those data.

4. **Control table maintained in a text file, and domain data maintained in a SAS data set**. For example, a CSV file might contain data quality rules (i.e., control data) that are applied to a second SAS data set (i.e., domain data) to clean or validate those data.

Subsequent subsections rely on the Termstable control table, which includes the SAS language keywords being searched for, as well as keyword categories ascribed to each keyword:

```
data termstable;
    infile datalines delimiter=',' dsd;
    length term $32 cat $32;
    input term $ cat $;
datalines;
PROC SORT,Procedure: Base
```

```
PROC FREQ,Procedure: Stats
PROC MEANS,Procedure: Stats
%MACRO,Macro Statement
%MEND,Macro Statement
%DO,Macro Statement
%LET,Macro Statement
;
```

Spreadsheets are commonly used as control tables because of their interoperable format. Additionally, stakeholders who may not have access to (or familiarity with) the SAS application are empowered because they can modify control data in a more ubiquitous format with which they are comfortable. Spreadsheets are often exported as CSV files, and the ingestion of a CSV control file mimics this transfer of control data from Excel to the SAS application.

The Termstable data set should also be saved as a CSV file (termstable.csv) to demonstrate how control tables can be stored outside of the SAS application:

```
PROC SORT,Procedure: Base
PROC FREQ,Procedure: Stats
PROC MEANS,Procedure: Stats
%MACRO,Macro Statement
%MEND,Macro Statement
%DO,Macro Statement
%LET,Macro Statement
```

Each subsequent subsection parses the ETL program (etl.sas) created in Section 11.1 to search for SAS keywords. Control data are *preloaded* using the "IF _N_=1" criterion, in which a group of statements is executed only during the first observation of some data set or file that is being ingested. This enables the entire control table to be ingested, and its values assigned to one or more temporary arrays, before the subsequent domain data are ingested.

Thus, as the second file is processed, the arrays (which contain control data) apply rules to the domain data. SAS temporary arrays (declared with the _TEMPORARY_ keyword) facilitate this design pattern because they are automatically retained across observations, and are deleted when the DATA step terminates.

The following subsections demonstrate and contrast four array-based methods that apply data rules (stored in control tables) to domain data (stored in text files or SAS data sets). In each example, control data are maintained in control tables throughout the process, eliminating the undesirable design pattern in which control tables are unnecessarily transformed into user-defined macro lists.

11.2.1 SAS Control Data and Text Domain Data

In this first paradigm, the control table is maintained as a SAS data set, and interacts with a text file, such as a SAS log or SAS program file. The data rules from the control table are preloaded into the DATA step using an initial DO loop that creates a temporary array of all control data. The DATA step subsequently reads and parses the SAS program file, applying the data rules to the domain data.

The CTRL_DSN_DOMAIN_TEXT macro follows and should be saved as ctrl_dsn_domain_text.sas:

```
* saved as d:\sas\ctrl_dsn_domain_text.sas;
%macro ctrl_dsn_domain_text(ctrl= /* ctrl tab DSN */,
    domain= /* SAS program file name to parse */,
    case= /* SENSITIVE to do case-sensitive search */);
* facilitate case-insensitive FIND;
%if "%upcase(&case)"="SENSITIVE" %then %let case=;
%else %let case=,'i';
* get observation count;
%local nobs;
proc sql noprint;
    select count(*) into : nobs
    from &ctrl;
quit;
data metrics (drop=i term);
    if _n_=1 then do;
        i=0;
        do until(eof);
            i=i+1;
            set &ctrl end=eof;
            array arrkey[&nobs] $32 _temporary_;
            arrkey[i]=strip(term);
```

```
        array arrcat[&nobs] $32 _temporary_;
        arrcat[i]=strip(cat);
        end;
     end;
  length line 8 contents $500 keyword $32 cat $32;
  infile "&domain" truncover end=eof;
  input contents $500.;
  do i=1 to dim(arrkey);
     if find(contents,strip(arrkey[i])&case) then do;
        line=_n_;
        keyword=arrkey[i];
        cat=arrcat[i];
        output;
        end;
     end;
  run;
%mend;
```

The macro is nearly identical to the KEYWORDSFINAL macro defined in Section 11.1.5, with the exception of the CASE parameter, which now specifies whether the FIND function should default to case-insensitive, or optionally perform a case-sensitive search.

A sample invocation first initializes the &LOC global macro variable to the folder in which both the CTRL_DSN_DOMAIN_TEXT macro and the program (etl.sas) are saved. Thereafter, the %INCLUDE statement compiles the macro, and the invocation specifies the default case-insensitive search:

```
%let loc=D:\sas\;      * USER MUST CHANGE LOCATION *;
%include "&loc.ctrl_dsn_domain_text.sas";
%ctrl_dsn_domain_text(ctrl=termstable,
   domain=&loc.etl.sas, case=);
```

When the macro executes, the Metrics data set (shown in Table 11.4) is created with six observations, identifying the line numbers in which SAS language keywords (maintained within the control table) were discovered within the SAS program file. Altering the CASE argument to "SENSITIVE" (not shown) yields a Metrics data set with only one observation—the single uppercase keyword (PROC FREQ) found in line 23 of etl.sas.

	cat	line	contents	keyword
1	Procedure: Base	11	proc sort data=etl;	PROC SORT
2	Procedure: Stats	15	proc means data=etl;	PROC MEANS
3	Procedure: Stats	19	proc freq data=etl;	PROC FREQ
4	Procedure: Stats	23	PROC FREQ data=etl;	PROC FREQ
5	Macro Statement	27	%macro sample();	%MACRO
6	Macro Statement	29	%mend;	%MEND

Table 11.4 Metrics Data Set with Keyword Category

Note that because the Termstable control table (unlike the Terms control table, created in Section 11.1.4) contains two variables, two ARRAY statements (and subsequent array initialization statements) are required within the DATA step. Similarly, within the second DO loop, both Keyword and Cat must be separately initialized.

Thus, as control tables grow in scope (i.e., number of variables), the number of required arrays will increase, and as control tables grow in size (i.e., observations), the number of required array elements will increase. Arrays enable control tables to be represented natively—as tables—and for this reason are preferred to functionally equivalent metaprogramming facilitated through macro lists.

Arrays are contrasted with metaprogramming in Section 10.1.2

11.2.2 Text Control Data and Text Domain Data

In some instances, both the control table containing data rules and the domain data being evaluated are maintained within text files. For example, were the Termstable data set housed within a spreadsheet, the resulting CSV file—an *external control table*—could be used to evaluate domain data.

The CTRL_TEXT_DOMAIN_TEXT macro preloads the external control table into two arrays (Arrkey and Arrcat) through an initial DO loop. Thereafter, the SAS program file (etl.sas) is ingested and evaluated using the dynamic data rules. Note that because the control table is now a CSV file (as opposed to a data set, as before), it must be read twice—first to determine its observation count (&NOBS), and next to declare arrays and initialize them with control data.

The CTRL_TEXT_DOMAIN_TEXT macro should be saved as ctrl_text_domain_text.sas:

```
* saved as d:\sas\ctrl_text_domain_text.sas;
%macro ctrl_text_domain_text(ctrl= /* ctrl tab CSV */,
    domain= /* SAS program file name to parse */,
```

```
      case= /* SENSITIVE to do case-sensitive search */);
* facilitate case-insensitive FIND;
%if "%upcase(&case)"="SENSITIVE" %then %let case=;
%else %let case=,'i';
* get observation count;
%local nobs;
data _null_;
   infile "&ctrl" truncover end=eof;
   input line $500;
   if eof then call
      symputx('nobs',strip(put(_n_,8.)),'l');
run;
data metrics (drop=i term);
   if _n_=1 then do;
      i=0;
      infile "&ctrl" truncover end=eof dsd
            delimiter=',';
      do until(eof);
         i=i+1;
         length term $32 cat $32;
         input term $ cat $;
         array arrkey[&nobs] $32 _temporary_;
         arrkey[i]=strip(term);
         array arrcat[&nobs] $32 _temporary_;
         arrcat[i]=strip(cat);
         end;
      end;
   length line 8 contents $500 keyword $32;
   infile "&domain" truncover end=eof;
   input contents $500.;
   do i=1 to dim(arrkey);
      if find(contents,strip(arrkey[i])&case) then do;
         line=_n_;
         keyword=arrkey[i];
         cat=arrcat[i];
         output;
```

```
            end;
        end;
    run;
    %mend;
```

A sample invocation creates the identical Metrics data set, shown in Table 11.4:

```
%let loc=D:\sas\;        * USER MUST CHANGE LOCATION *;
%include "&loc.ctrl_text_domain_text.sas";
%ctrl_text_domain_text(ctrl=&loc.termstable.csv,
    domain=&loc.etl.sas, case=);
```

The CTRL_TEXT_DOMAIN_TEXT macro demonstrates that a single DATA step can ingest both control data and domain data. However, is this necessarily prudent, as opposed to ingesting the control table first into a SAS data set?

For example, the following DATA step converts termstable.csv (created in Section 11.2) into the Termstable data set:

```
data termstable;
    infile "&loc.termstable.csv" delimiter=',' dsd;
    length term $32 cat $32;
    input term $ cat $;
run;
```

Once the Termstable data set has been created, a SAS practitioner could utilize the CTRL_DSN_DOMAIN_TEXT macro (in lieu of CTRL_TEXT_DOMAIN_TEXT), which poses some advantages.

First, the SAS application maintains data set metadata within the SAS Dictionary tables, which can drive dynamic processing. For example, for all data sets, these metadata include variable names, lengths, formats, informats, labels, and other attributes. None of these metadata are available when an external (i.e., non-SAS) control table is being ingested, such as a CSV file or other text file.

SAS Dictionary tables are introduced in Section 12.4

Second, when control data are maintained in external files, they may not have strict structural or data quality standards imposed on them. For example, a CSV file exported from Excel could have character data in a numeric field (i.e., a column or cell *described* as having numeric data), which could trigger a failure when ingested into SAS with the INPUT statement. Thus, in some cases, data cleaning, manipulation, or transformation of control data may be required before those control data can be used to evaluate domain data (or otherwise drive software).

These benefits of SAS data set processing should not preclude stakeholders from maintaining control tables within Excel and other external sources; rather, the added flexibility that interoperable formats provide may dictate that data validation occur when external control tables are converted to internal SAS control tables. A macro such as CTRL_TEXT_DOMAIN_TEXT will always be the most direct method to apply data rules (maintained in a text file) to a separate text file; however, in many cases, a preliminary import of an external control table into a data set will be warranted to first vet those data.

11.2.3 SAS Control Data and SAS Domain Data

In this paradigm, both the control table and the domain data being evaluated are maintained within SAS data sets. The following DATA step converts the program being searched (etl.sas) to the Programfile data set:

```
data programfile;
    infile "&loc.etl.sas" delimiter=',' dsd;
    length contents $500;
    input contents $;
run;
```

In this design paradigm, two SET statements are required to ingest two parameterized data sets—the first to preload the control table, and the second to ingest the domain data.

The CTRL_DSN_DOMAIN_DSN macro should be saved to ctrl_dsn_domain_dsn.sas:

```
* saved as d:\sas\ctrl_dsn_domain_dsn.sas;
%macro ctrl_dsn_domain_dsn(ctrl= /* ctrl tab DSN */,
    domain= /* SAS data set to parse (DSN) */,
    case= /* SENSITIVE to do case-sensitive search */);
* facilitate case-insensitive FIND;
%if "%upcase(&case)"="SENSITIVE" %then %let case=;
%else %let case=,'i';
* get observation count;
%local nobs;
```

```
proc sql noprint;
    select count(*) into : nobs
    from &ctrl;
quit;
data metrics (drop=i term);
    if _n_=1 then do;
        i=0;
        do until(eof);
            i=i+1;
            set &ctrl end=eof;
            array arrkey[&nobs] $32 _temporary_;
            arrkey[i]=strip(term);
            array arrcat[&nobs] $32 _temporary_;
            arrcat[i]=strip(cat);
            end;
        end;
    length line 8 keyword $32;
    set &domain;
    do i=1 to dim(arrkey);
        if find(contents,strip(arrkey[i])&case) then do;
            line=_n_;
            keyword=arrkey[i];
            cat=arrcat[i];
            output;
            end;
        end;
run;
%mend;
```

A sample invocation generates an identical Metrics data set, shown in Table 11.4:

```
%let loc=D:\sas\;        * USER MUST CHANGE LOCATION *;
%include "&loc.ctrl_dsn_domain_dsn.sas";
%ctrl_dsn_domain_dsn(ctrl=termstable,
    domain=programfile, case=);
```

Of the four paradigms represented in these subsections, this paradigm is most commonly associated with data quality rules and business rules that are applied to SAS data sets. For example, a data dictionary might be maintained as a data set, and subsequently used to enforce data quality rules that apply to a separate data set. Data rules similarly could clean, transform, or otherwise modify domain data. The next subsection demonstrates a corresponding paradigm, which differs only in that the control table is maintained as a text file.

11.2.4 Text Control Data and SAS Domain Data

The fourth and final paradigm demonstrates a control table that is maintained within a text file (i.e., CSV), which applies data rules to a SAS data set. Similar to the preceding subsection, this is a common paradigm for data quality rules and business rules validation, in which the control table is maintained within a spreadsheet, or is exported to a CSV file.

Data-driven design pillars, principles, and methods can be applied to most programming languages, so although *domain data* will commonly be maintained, transformed, and analyzed within proprietary data structures (like SAS data sets), *control data*, conversely, often can be maintained within more interoperable formats. Text files, including canonical data structure standards like CSV, JSON, and XML, inherently ensure that control data can be leveraged by as many programming languages and applications as possible—far beyond the SAS bubble.

Thus, even for a development or analytics team that relies primarily on SAS, the maintenance of control data (such as data quality rules or business rules) within external, non-SAS data structures can be beneficial—for example, when that team or organization has other uses for those control data (unrelated to SAS functionality), or when they eventually transition from SAS to an open-source solution like Python.

The CTRL_TEXT_DOMAIN_DSN macro should be saved as ctrl_text_domain_dsn.sas:

```
* saved as d:\sas\ctrl_text_domain_dsn.sas;
%macro ctrl_text_domain_dsn(ctrl= /* ctrl tab CSV */,
    domain= /* SAS program file name to parse (DSN) */,
    case= /* SENSITIVE to do case-sensitive search */);
* get observation count;
* facilitate case-insensitive FIND;
```

```
%if "%upcase(&case)"="SENSITIVE" %then %let case=;
%else %let case=,'i';
%local nobs;
data _null_;
   infile "&ctrl" truncover end=eof;
   input line $500;
   if eof then call
      symputx('nobs',strip(put(_n_,8.)),'l');
run;
data metrics (drop=i term);
   if _n_=1 then do;
      i=0;
      infile "&ctrl" truncover end=eof dsd
         delimiter=',';
      do until(eof);
         i=i+1;
         length term $32 cat $32;
         input term $ cat $;
         array arrkey[&nobs] $32 _temporary_;
         arrkey[i]=strip(term);
         array arrcat[&nobs] $32 _temporary_;
         arrcat[i]=strip(cat);
         end;
      end;
   length line 8 keyword $32 cat $32;
   set &domain;
   do i=1 to dim(arrkey);
      if find(contents,strip(arrkey[i])&case) then do;
         line=_n_;
         keyword=arrkey[i];
         cat=arrcat[i];
         output;
         end;
      end;
   run;
   %mend;
```

A sample invocation generates the Metrics data set, shown in Table 11.4:

```
%let loc=D:\sas\;        * USER MUST CHANGE LOCATION *;
%include "&loc.ctrl_text_domain_dsn.sas";
%ctrl_text_domain_dsn(ctrl=&loc.termstable.csv,
    domain=programfile, case=);
```

Where a control table is maintained external to the SAS application, this represents the most direct method to apply data rules to a SAS data set. That is, the interoperable format is directly leveraged by SAS. Similar to the solution demonstrated in Section 11.2.2, however, this paradigm could be modified to ingest the CSV file into a SAS data set prior to the DATA step; the degree of prerequisite control data massaging and validation will help determine whether the CSV file should be evaluated prior to (or in conjunction with) the subsequent domain data ingestion.

For example, CTRL_TEXT_DOMAIN_DSN relies on the first DATA step only to evaluate the number of lines in the CSV control table; thereafter, the second DATA step *expects* that only two columns—Term and Cat—will be found in the control table. But what if more columns exist, or fewer, or the wrong columns? And because text files are more flexible, and CSV files do not enforce a tabular structure, it is entirely possible that a "corrupted" CSV file could be ingested, having an inconsistent number of columns across its rows.

Given all these potential risks to the data integrity of an external control table, validation of its structure and content could occur within the first DATA step, or within a process that precedes the invocation of CTRL_TEXT_DOMAIN_DSN. This is all to say that although you *can* read both control data and domain data using a single DATA step, as demonstrated throughout the last four subsections, non-trivial reasons exist for why you *should not* want to do this. Ultimately, the required robustness of your software, including the degree to which you expect to validate your control data and domain data, will drive this design decision.

11.3 CONTROL TABLES CONTROLLING CODE

The preceding examples in this chapter demonstrate the use of control tables in evaluating data; in all examples, however, the control data themselves are *equivalent* (e.g., in data type, knowledge domain) to the domain data being analyzed. That is, the control data (i.e., SAS language keywords) in the Terms and Termstable data sets (generated in Sections 11.1 and 11.2, respectively) are the very values that are being searched for (within a SAS program file) in the subsequent DATA step. This equivalency makes arrays an appropriate container for control data because those arrays can equivalently interact with the domain data within the DATA step.

However, in other cases, control data are not equivalent to domain data, but rather to code itself. For example, the CTRL_TEXT_DOMAIN_DSN macro (defined in Section 11.2.4) has the following invocation:

```
%ctrl_text_domain_dsn(ctrl=&loc.termstable.csv,
    domain=programfile, case=SENSITIVE);
```

The CASE argument (SENSITIVE) does not describe domain data, but rather prescribes whether the case-insensitive modifier (I) should be applied to the FIND function. Thus, the CASE parameter is speaking to the *code*— not to the *domain data*.

For this reason, whereas the control table can be transformed into one or more SAS arrays for evaluation in subsequent DATA step statements, the CASE parameter instead directs *metaprogramming*—code that writes code—within the DATA step. Thus, the &CASE macro variable is dynamically initialized from the CASE argument, after which &CASE is used within the FIND function to denote either a case-insensitive or a case-sensitive search:

```
if find(contents,strip(arrkey[i])&case) then do;
```

Because the CASE parameter is directing code, not domain data, this use of metaprogramming is appropriate, as opposed to the unnecessary metaprogramming demonstrated in Sections 11.1.3 and 11.1.4. It is also robust, given that any argument other than "SENSITIVE" initializes &CASE to instruct FIND to perform a case-insensitive search.

A common example of control tables controlling code occurs when control tables represent data dictionaries that prescribe variable attributes (rather than values). Because the variable values and variable attributes are inequivalent, metaprogramming must be used to bridge this gap, as demonstrated in the DICT_INGEST macro in Section 12.5.3.

11.4 SUMMARY

This chapter introduced control tables—control files that have a tabular data structure. Single-column control tables can be used to supplant linear data structures, like arrays, lists, and macro lists, and can be useful where control data volume or complexity favors a built-in data structure. Control tables primarily, however, describe two-dimensional, tabular data having multiple rows and columns. Built-in control tables leveraged by SAS are typically constructed within SAS data sets, but also include in-memory hash objects.

Where software leverages non-SAS control tables, including more interoperable data structures and file types like spreadsheets and XML files, both external and internal representations of a single control table may exist. End users may directly modify the external control table, whereas SAS practitioners and SAS software may access only an internal version that has been imported into SAS. Where SAS operations directly access an external control table, or a control table maintained by third-party stakeholders, validation of control data may be warranted prior to their operationalization by SAS software.

The versatility and robustness of built-in control tables and their associated operations were demonstrated throughout the chapter. SAS arrays were demonstrated as a preferred method of interacting with control data that are *equivalent* to the domain data being processed or analyzed, whereas SAS I/O functions (operationalized through the SAS macro language) were demonstrated as a preferred method of interacting with *inequivalent* control data that dynamically write code.

Both methods espouse data-driven design, however, and demonstrate the benefits of relying on built-in data structures (and their associated operations), in lieu of having to design a slew of user-defined operations to support user-defined data structures like macro lists and indexed macro lists.

Chapter 12

Control Tables: Data Dictionaries

This chapter has the following objectives:

- ❖ Introduce the SAS Dictionary tables, the built-in data dictionaries that are automatically created in all SAS environments.

- ❖ Contrast *descriptive* data dictionaries and *prescriptive* data dictionaries, and demonstrate the clear advantages of the latter.

- ❖ Demonstrate how to generate user-defined data dictionaries automatically from SAS data sets and other data structures.

- ❖ Discuss the importance of designing a flexible, user-defined data structure that can be reused to maintain various data dictionaries.

- ❖ Demonstrate different methods for reading data dictionaries, including the SQL procedure, the DATA step, and built-in I/O functions leveraged through the SAS macro language.

- ❖ Illustrate how data dictionaries can be used to facilitate data integrity through quality control processes and exception reporting.

Data dictionaries describe data and data structures, but beyond this empty epitaph, the nuances of their structures, stakeholders, functionality, quality, and implementation are as varied as the data they represent. Embodying data abstraction, a data dictionary captures the essence of some data object, and communicates the pith thereof to humans, machines, or both.

ISO defines a *data dictionary* as a "collection of information about data such as name, description, creator, owner, provenance, translation in different languages, and usage."[88] Data dictionaries are not definitively tables; however, they are represented in tabular form so exclusively that no other construction is discussed in this text. Each row of a data dictionary represents some data element, and each column represents some characteristic of that data element, with the data elements maintained typically having equivalent structure, status, or hierarchy.

For example, a data dictionary describing a single table might have rows representing unique variables, and columns representing unique variable characteristics, such as variable name, format, label, description, and whether the variable is required or optional. At a higher hierarchical level, a data dictionary describing a catalog (or collection of tables) might have rows representing unique tables, and columns representing unique table characteristics, such as table name, label, number of rows, table sorting criteria, or owner.

Some data dictionaries expand beyond this single-level construction, and additionally define relationships between the data elements they describe. For example, a simple definition for a categorical character variable might reflect its name and length only, whereas a more complex definition might prescribe the specific subset of values that the variable can contain. In doing so, the variable's definition effectively maintains referential integrity and operates as a lookup table—irrespective of whether those values are maintained as string literals or within a logical table. This more complex usage also demonstrates how some data dictionaries can additionally model data quality rules and business rules.

However, just as data dictionaries themselves are not definitively tables, neither must the data structures they describe be tabular. Thus, it is not uncommon for XML files, configuration files, and other non-tabular data structures to rely on data dictionaries that describe their contents—either at the data object or element level.

In some lax environments, a *data dictionary* can denote a whiteboard or notebook on which data attributes are scribbled—and this definition may be accurate, albeit describing a less useful artifact. But the standardization of data object metadata within data dictionaries supports communication to not only stakeholders but also processes. Some systems, especially relational database management systems (RDBMS), and including the SAS application, rely on *active* data dictionaries to store data object metadata, and to grant and facilitate access to data objects.

This chapter introduces built-in, active data dictionaries maintained by the SAS system, commonly known as the *SAS Dictionary tables* (and views). These built-in tables can be leveraged through the SQL procedure, as well as through more than a dozen input/output (I/O) functions, and allow SAS practitioners to extract metadata about our data sets. And in case you're wondering...Kirk Paul Lafler *owns* SAS Dictionary tables—he owns them like Michael Scott owns *"That's what she said!"*

Modeling built-in SAS Dictionary tables, SAS practitioners can build our own user-defined data dictionaries—with *descriptive* data dictionaries lazily documenting data attributes for human consumption only, and more useful *prescriptive* data dictionaries driving software, dynamically writing code, munging data sets, and validating data products. This chapter describes the latter reality, in which data dictionaries act as not only documentation but also control data that can be leveraged by data-driven processes to effect dynamic functionality.

12.1 ACTIVE VS. PASSIVE DATA DICTIONARIES

The *active-passive* data dictionary distinction is an old one, wrought from the days of punch cards and megalithic mainframes—in other words, largely irrelevant to today's SAS practitioners. However, understanding the benefits of active data dictionaries, and appreciating that SAS Dictionary tables are active, helps us better discuss and model the user-defined data dictionaries that we design.

An *active data dictionary* is an integral component that is both synchronized with and essential to the operation of a system or application; it is live, and actively coordinates access to and use of the data it describes.[89] Leong-Hong and Plagman remark that a data dictionary is active *"if and only if* that program or process is dependent [on the data dictionary] for its metadata."[90] For example, a procedure querying or otherwise opening a data set could rely on an active data dictionary to evaluate the size and structure of the data set. Moreover, changes made to a data object—at least to those data elements that are under dictionary governance—are updated and reflected *in real-time* within an active data dictionary. This ensures synchronization of the data object and the metadata that describe it.

As a central repository for data object metadata, an active data dictionary must be carefully controlled to ensure its data are not compromised.[91] Data dictionary records should represent unique *golden records*, and per master data management (MDM) objectives, must be guarded against accidental or malicious modification or destruction. For example, SAS protects its SAS Dictionary tables by enforcing read-only access for all users and processes, as is common practice.

Active data dictionaries are essential to operations because they can prevent misuse of data objects, by prescribing data rules about object inclusion and other characteristics. For example, if an active data dictionary defines the variables maintained within a data set, and if a variable's data type is specified (and within SAS, it always is), this prohibits all data *not* matching this type from being stored; invalid data are excluded.

Passive data dictionaries describe less-than-active dictionaries; they are logical data dictionaries (so no whiteboard renderings or Word documents allowed), but they are either not integral or not integrated. The active-passive distinction is somewhat fluid, and broadly represents how central a role a data dictionary plays in the system, application, operations, and data it models and supports.

Apropos data-driven design, the active-passive distinction means that user-defined active data dictionaries cannot be built in SAS. Notwithstanding this understandable limitation, SAS practitioners can design user-defined data dictionaries that facsimile—and even expand—SAS Dictionary table construction and content. And although we lack the ability to build real-time processes that facilitate or guarantee synchronization (as active data dictionaries do), we can rely on user-defined data dictionaries to validate data before (or as) they are ingested, and to validate data sets, data objects, and other input and output.

Thus, *prescriptive data dictionaries*, introduced in the next section, are the viable and valuable next best thing to the active data dictionaries that we as SAS practitioners are unable to construct or implement. And just as data-driven design relies heavily on active SAS Dictionary tables, so, too,

MDM objectives, including the *golden record* concept, are discussed in Section 8.2

should our data-driven processes leverage the not-quite-active user-defined data dictionaries that we cast in their likenesses.

12.2 PRESCRIPTIVE VS. DESCRIPTIVE DATA DICTIONARIES

Prescriptive data dictionaries are user-defined data dictionaries that model tables and other data objects, that prescribe the characteristics of those objects through data quality rules and other business rules, and that can be queried by processes to compare the data object to the dictionary metadata that abstract it. Thus, in the SAS ecosystem, a prescriptive data dictionary is a logical table—maintained in a SAS data set, spreadsheet, or other tabular format—that can be used to validate elements and characteristics of some data object, like a SAS data set, CSV file, or a SAS report that is generated.

Similar to active data dictionaries, prescriptive data dictionaries can describe data objects and elements at varying hierarchical levels—for example, one dictionary representing the contents of a folder at the control table (or data set) level, and a lower-level dictionary representing the contents of a control table (or data set) at the column (or variable) level. Examples in this text, however, depict only prescriptive data dictionaries that describe the variables or columns within a control table or data set. Thus, when operationalized within a SAS data set, a prescriptive data dictionary will have one observation for each variable or column it describes, and one variable for each characteristic, attribute, or rule it models.

Prescriptive data dictionaries can work in conjunction with the SAS Dictionary tables, and extend their functionality in three significant ways. First, they can expand the type of data objects that are brought under dictionary governance. Second, they can expand the type of characteristics that are maintained for each variable. Third, they can expand the type of interaction and associations that can be modeled.

SAS Dictionary tables describe the characteristics of only internal SAS data sets; they maintain no metadata for external data objects, such as spreadsheets, CSV files, or other control files. For example, as soon as you create a SAS data set, its variables and their attributes are immediately described in the DICTIONARY.Columns table. Thus, the Columns table can be queried programmatically to determine the names of variables in the data set, and their respective data types, formats, labels, and other attributes. However, this functionality does not exist for non-SAS data objects, but can be mimicked by designing prescriptive data dictionaries that similarly include metadata for these non-SAS objects.

SAS Dictionary tables contain *data rules*, such as prescribing that a specific variable has a character data type, or has a format of $20, but they do not prescribe more complex *business rules*. Prescriptive data dictionaries, on the other hand, can additionally model interaction among multiple fields, or model the relationship between a field and an external data object or element. Even the environment or system state itself can be leveraged to build dynamic data rules, with the extent of rules limited only by the creativity of their designers and developers.

For example, a rule might dynamically reference the current date or some past date to validate a field. Consider a startup gaming company that manages human resources (HR) records in SAS, and that allowed FIRSTNAME@infocom.com to represent employee emails early in its inception. However, after years of success and grue-spurred growth, the company might have adopted FIRST.LAST@infocom.com for new employees. This shift in requirements could be modeled in a single business rule that references hire date to determine email address validity, thus "grandfathering in" the inaugural employees' abbreviated email accounts.

As a second example, the same data dictionary might describe the Department variable in the HR data set, which denotes the team for which an employee works. In addition to prescribing that the Department variable must be a character variable of format $20, a dictionary could specify the list of valid values that Department can contain—either by enumerating string literals, or by referencing a data object where the list of values is maintained. In so doing, prescriptive data dictionaries can enforce *referential integrity* of categorical variables.

Dictionary governance describes the bailiwick over which a specific data dictionary has jurisdiction, and in the case of an active data dictionary that describes a specific data set, all variables in that data set will be brought *under governance*—that is, represented as metadata within the associated active data dictionary—because all data set elements must remain synchronized with the active data dictionary. Thus, active data dictionaries typically only model the here and now—the current state of the data object they represent.

User-defined data dictionaries, on the other hand, can be implemented in a far more flexible fashion than active data dictionary counterparts. For example, you can incrementally build a user-defined data dictionary—while it is in production—by incrementally adding new variables over time, and by incrementally bringing new variables under dictionary governance. Thus, you might start with a data dictionary that only models three of ten variables in a data set—but three is better than none, and next week you might add the fourth and fifth variables, thereby expanding the range of variables over which the dictionary has governance and can validate through data-driven processes.

User-defined data dictionaries similarly can model variables that are no longer extant—for example, when past transactional data sets include a variable, but current data sets omit it. A column in the data dictionary can indicate whether a variable is "current," and thus allow past variable definitions to persist. This aids SAS practitioners reviewing the dictionary (by providing historical context of extinct elements or objects) while ensuring that SAS processes only evaluate current variables. Active dictionaries typically lack this historical chronology.

At the other end of the spectrum, *descriptive data dictionaries* are user-defined data dictionaries that are not designed to drive dynamic processing, to interact with the data objects they model, or to interact with the processes that operationalize those data objects. Descriptive data dictionaries exist solely to communicate dictionary metadata to stakeholders. At one extreme, descriptive data dictionaries may be Word documents, cocktail napkin scratches, or other physical or logical documents that maintain data in a purely human-readable format.

At a more useful middle ground, descriptive data dictionaries may be spreadsheets or logical tables that maintain dictionary metadata in a rigorously standardized format. These descriptive data dictionaries may be structured identically to active and prescriptive data dictionaries, with the only difference being their lack of interaction with dynamic processes that rely on these dictionaries. That is, with a little finagling, well-bred descriptive data dictionaries can be transitioned into prescriptive data dictionaries that drive processing and validate data objects.

One of the primary objectives of prescriptive data dictionaries is to communicate simultaneously to people and processes. At some point in a data object's lifetime, some coworker or end user or other stakeholder will ask to see the specs on a data set, spreadsheet, or other data object—at which point the primary artifact you want to convey is the object's data dictionary. By standardizing the dictionary format, such that SAS processes can also read these metadata, and by committing to update the data dictionary to ensure it remains synchronized (with the data object it describes), SAS practitioners can build prescriptive data dictionaries that both prescribe and describe the data they model.

12.3 A TALE OF TWO DICTIONARIES

Data dictionaries, like many software artifacts, often grow organically throughout the lifespan of the software or data object they model, with complexity increasing commensurate to the complexity of the functionality or data represented. In data-driven design, however, data dictionaries also grow in complexity (and value) as developers understand the breadth of automated processes that can be driven by a prescriptive data dictionary.

This is to say that once the benefits of operationalizing built-in active data dictionaries and user-defined prescriptive data dictionaries are understood, SAS practitioners will want to implement these artifacts sooner in the software development life cycle (SDLC), and will want to model even those data objects lacking complexity.

> The SDLC is introduced from a data-driven design perspective in Section 7.2

It is not uncommon for a user or team to fail to maintain a data dictionary for some data object at its outset. Over time, as requirements are cobbled together, a *descriptive* data dictionary may be born, in which attributes representing a data set are documented for stakeholders.

Consider Rey's Tamales, a small-town tamale and taco vendor that maintains its purchase history of ingredients within a spreadsheet. In an attempt to standardize data entry for purchases, Rey defines the following data rules, and communicates them to his staff in a memo; these rules constitute a *descriptive data dictionary*:

- Item –the item purchased, such as tomatoes, beans, or rice
- Quantity –the number of items purchased
- Unit –the unit of the item, such as pounds, ounces, or liters
- Cost –the cost of the item, without a dollar sign
- Store –the store where the item was purchased

An abridged purchase history, demonstrated in Table 12.1, can be created and saved as a CSV file (purchases.csv):

```
Item,Quantity,Unit,Cost,Store
tomato,3,lbs,5.6,Ralph's
tomatos,100,,10.2,
tomatoes,5,lbs,6.32,Target
```

```
cilantro,1,lb,$2.23 ,Costco
cebolla,2,lbs,3.41,Cosco
```

Note that although the descriptive data dictionary might be useful in conveying to workers the type of data that should be entered in each spreadsheet column, it does nothing to enforce data integrity, and some obvious turmoil in tamale data is immediately apparent.

For example, the second observation is missing the Store value; the third observation is missing the Unit value; and the fifth observation has a dollar sign in the Cost value. Moreover, variability in all categorical variables is noted—for example, "tomato" versus "tomatoes," "lb" versus "lbs," and "Costco" versus "Cosco."

The preferred method of enforcing data integrity is always to validate data entry at the point of user input—for example, using the Excel Data Validation tab to restrict values to those in a list or lookup table. However, if user input cannot be restricted or validated, then data must be scrubbed as part of the extract-transform-load (ETL) process.

For example, without this data validation and standardization, it would be difficult to analyze the purchase data to evaluate the average cost of tomatoes—because of the variability in Item spelling, as well as in Unit.

The remainder of this chapter relies on Rey's Tamales' purchase history (purchases.csv), and demonstrates the respective roles that two data dictionaries—including a built-in SAS Dictionary table and user-defined prescriptive data dictionary—can play in developing data-driven processes. In all cases, the principal objective is to enforce and demonstrate data integrity for those data objects and data elements brought under data dictionary governance.

	A	B	C	D	E
1	Item	Quantity	Unit	Cost	Store
2	tomato	3	lbs	5.6	Ralph's
3	tomatos	100		10.2	
4	tomatoes	5	lbs	6.32	Target
5	cilantro	1	lb	$2.23	Costco
6	cebolla	2	lbs	3.41	Cosco

Table 12.1 Purchase History of Ingredients (Purchases.csv)

12.4 BUILT-IN SAS DICTIONARY TABLES

The *SAS Dictionary tables* (often *SAS DICTIONARY tables*) are the read-only, built-in tables maintained in the DICTIONARY library of all SAS environments and instances. They are active data dictionaries, as discussed in Section 12.1, and thus remain synchronized at all times with the data objects they describe. The DICTIONARY.Dictionaries table is the catalog for all tables in the DICTIONARY library, and can be queried to reveal the list of tables and the respective columns they contain.

The following SQL procedure and DATA step print the list of all SAS Dictionary tables to the log:

```
proc sql noprint;
   create table dicts as
      select unique memname
         from dictionary.dictionaries;
quit;
data _null_;
   set dicts;
   put _n_ @4 memname;
run;
```

The SAS Dictionary tables include the following members of the DICTIONARY library:

1 CATALOGS
2 CHECK_CONSTRAINTS
3 COLUMNS
4 CONSTRAINT_COLUMN_USAGE
5 CONSTRAINT_TABLE_USAGE
6 DATAITEMS
7 DESTINATIONS
8 DICTIONARIES
9 ENGINES
10 EXTFILES
11 FILTERS
12 FORMATS
13 FUNCTIONS
14 GOPTIONS

```
15  INDEXES
16  INFOMAPS
17  LIBNAMES
18  LOCALES
19  MACROS
20  MEMBERS
21  OPTIONS
22  PROMPTS
23  PROMPTSXML
24  REFERENTIAL_CONSTRAINTS
25  REMEMBER
26  STYLES
27  TABLES
28  TABLE_CONSTRAINTS
29  TITLES
30  VIEWS
31  VIEW_SOURCES
32  XATTRS
```

Although the DICTIONARY library contains 32 tables, only the Columns table, which describes variable-level metadata for each SAS data set, is discussed in this text. As soon as a data set comes into existence, because the SAS Dictionary tables are *active*, the tables are synchronized with that data set's metadata.

For example, the following DATA step ingests the purchase history (purchase.csv) and creates the Purchases data set:

```
%let loc=D:\sas\;        * USER MUST CHANGE LOCATION *;

data purchases;
    infile "&loc.purchases.csv" truncover dsd
        delimiter=',' firstobs=2;
    length item $30 quantity 8 units $20 cost 8
        store $30;
    input item $ quantity units $ cost store $;
    format item $30. quantity 8. units $20.
        cost dollar8.2 store $30.;
    label item='Item' quantity='Quantity' units='Units'
```

```
        cost='Cost' store='Store';
run;
```

Once Purchases has been created, its metadata are automatically loaded into the SAS Dictionary tables, and can be queried. The following SQL procedure creates the Tamale_dict data set, which contains all tamale-related metadata within the DICTIONARY.Columns table:

```
proc sql noprint;
    create table tamale_dict as
        select * from dictionary.columns
            where libname='WORK' and memname='PURCHASES';
quit;
```

DICTIONARY.Columns cannot be opened directly in the SAS application (either viewed manually or referenced by a DATA step), but the SQL procedure copies the records that match the library (WORK) and data set (Purchases) of WORK.Purchases. Note that SAS Dictionary tables use LIBNAME and MEMNAME to reference SAS libraries and data sets, respectively.

Table 12.2 demonstrates the first several columns of the Tamale_Dict data set, built from the DICTIONARY.Columns table. These include the library (WORK), data set (Purchases), data object type (SAS data set, as opposed to SAS view or SAS catalog), variable name, variable data type, variable length, and numerous attributes that are not depicted.

Note that the columns and values mirror the variable names, data types, and lengths defined in the previous DATA step, in which the Purchases data set was created. Thus, SAS Dictionary tables provide a method to view the structure and contents of a data set without having to open the data set itself.

	Library Name	Member Name	Member Type	Column Name	Column Type	Column Length
1	WORK	PURCHASES	DATA	item	char	30
2	WORK	PURCHASES	DATA	quantity	num	8
3	WORK	PURCHASES	DATA	units	char	20
4	WORK	PURCHASES	DATA	cost	num	8
5	WORK	PURCHASES	DATA	store	char	30

Table 12.2 Tamale_Dict Data Set (from DICTIONARY.Columns Table)

The following SQL procedure and DATA step print the list of all metadata variables (and their labels) in the DICTIONARY.Columns table:

```
proc sql noprint;
   create table columns_dict as
      select * from dictionary.dictionaries
         where memname='COLUMNS';
quit;
data _null_;
   set columns_dict;
   put _n_ @4 name @16 label;
run;
```

The DICTIONARY.Columns table contains the following variables:

```
 1  LIBNAME     Library Name
 2  MEMNAME     Member Name
 3  MEMTYPE     Member Type
 4  NAME        Column Name
 5  TYPE        Column Type
 6  LENGTH      Column Length
 7  NPOS        Column Position
 8  VARNUM      Column Number in Table
 9  LABEL       Column Label
10  FORMAT      Column Format
11  INFORMAT    Column Informat
12  IDXUSAGE    Column Index Type
13  SORTEDBY    Order in Key Sequence
14  XTYPE       Extended Type
15  NOTNULL     Not NULL?
16  PRECISION   Precision
17  SCALE       Scale
18  TRANSCODE   Transcoded?
19  DIAGNOSTIC  Diagnostic Message from File Open Attempt
```

Thus, SAS Dictionary tables can support data-driven design because processes can query these tables programmatically to evaluate the structure and contents of a data set. The next subsections demonstrate how the DICTIONARY.Columns table and its metadata can be leveraged by data-driven processes.

12.4.1 Programmatically Pulling Dictionary Data

Data-driven programming relies on the programmatic extraction of metadata from SAS Dictionary tables, so printing a list of tables or columns to the log, as demonstrated in the previous section, is great for exploring dictionary content—but not so useful for extracting meaningful data. The two primary methods of metadata extraction include the SQL procedure and SAS I/O functions.

For example, consider the common task of needing to extract the list of variables (for some data set) programmatically. Variable names are maintained in the DICTIONARY.Columns table, although this table contains the variable names of *all* variables maintained throughout your entire SAS environment. Thus, key to efficient processing, is the use of a WHERE clause to isolate the specific library and data set that contain the variables of interest.

To extract the list of variables maintained in the Purchases data set (created in Section 12.3), the following SQL procedure creates a one-column data set (Tamale_columns):

```
proc sql noprint;
    create table tamale_columns as
        select name from dictionary.columns
            where libname='WORK' and memname='PURCHASES';
quit;
```

Tamale_columns (not shown) has five observations, each of which represents one of the five variables—item, quantity, units, cost, and store—in the Purchases data set.

More commonly, however, extraction of dictionary metadata initializes macro variables that can be used to write code dynamically. Thus, a similar SQL procedure initializes the &TAMALE_VARS macro variable, a user-defined space-delimited macro list, to the same metadata:

User-defined macro lists are introduced in Section 10.2, and are contrasted with user-defined indexed macro lists in Section 10.3

```
proc sql noprint;
    select name into : tamale_vars separated by ' '
        from dictionary.columns
            where libname='WORK' and memname='PURCHASES';
```

```
quit;
%put &=tamale_vars;
```

The use of a space-delimited macro list is an appropriate data structure in which to maintain SAS variables because variables can contain neither spaces nor other special characters. The log displays the &TAMALE_VARS macro list:

```
TAMALE_VARS=item quantity units cost store
```

For example, consider the discovery of a historic version of the Purchases data set (Purchases_old), an abbreviated version of which can be created with the following DATA step:

```
data purchases_old;
    infile datalines delimiter=',' dsd;
    length number 3 item $35 quantity 8 units $20 cost 8
        store $25 employee $30;
    input number item $ quantity units $ cost store $
        employee $;
    datalines;
5, carne asada, 16.4, pounds, 12.84, Kroger, Bob
;
```

If an analysis of Purchases_old is warranted, but analysts want to inspect only those variables found in the current Purchases data set, they could utilize the &TAMALE_VARS macro variable to programmatically retain only current variables by leveraging the KEEP option:

```
data keep_the_current;
    set purchases_old (keep=&tamale_vars);
run;
```

The resultant data set (Keep_the_current) now contains only the five variables found in Purchases. And if the decision is later made to update Purchases to include more or fewer variables, the SQL procedure that initializes &TAMALE_VARS could be rerun, and the Keep_the_current data set recreated, and the data set would again be synchronized.

In some cases, it is undesirable to run multiple processes to generate the dynamic functionality that &TAMALE_VARS provides, and in these instances, the second method of extracting dictionary metadata—reliance on built-in I/O functions—can assist.

The GET_VARS macro function declares a single parameter (DSN), representing the data set name, and returns a space-delimited list containing all variables in the data set:

User-defined macro
functions are
introduced in
Section 3.6.1

```
%macro get_vars(dsn /* data set name */);
%local dsid vars i close;
%let dsid=%sysfunc(open(&dsn,i));
%let vars=%sysfunc(attrn(&dsid,nvars));
%do i=1 %to &vars;
   %sysfunc(varname(&dsid, &i))
   %end;
%let close=%sysfunc(close(&dsid));
%mend;


%put %get_vars(purchases);
```

The %PUT statement prints the results of the GET_VARS macro function to the log:

```
item quantity units cost store
```

Thus, GET_VARS can be called from inside the KEEP option in the DATA step to retain only those variables found in the Purchases data set:

```
data keep_the_current;
   set purchases_old (keep=%get_vars(purchases));
run;
```

The Keep_the_current data set is identical to the previous Keep_the_current data set created with the &TAMALE_VARS macro variable; however, as no SQL procedure is required in the GET_VARS macro function, all functionality is now contained within one DATA step.

In most cases, the requirement to extract metadata from SAS Dictionary tables will be more complicated than enumerating a list of variables. For example, consider the more complex endeavor of creating a LENGTH statement dynamically that copies the variable names, data types, and lengths for all variables in the Purchases data set.

A static representation of the code (that will be generated dynamically) follows:

```
data purchases_new;
   length item $30 quantity 8 units $20 cost 8
      store $30;
run;
```

The GET_LENGTHS macro function declares a single parameter (DSN), representing the data set name, and returns a list of variables and their associated lengths that can be applied dynamically to a LENGTH statement:

```
%macro get_lengths(dsn /* data set name */);
%local dsid vars i close;
%let dsid=%sysfunc(open(&dsn,i));
%let vars=%sysfunc(attrn(&dsid,nvars));
%do i=1 %to &vars;
   %sysfunc(varname(&dsid, &i))
   %if %sysfunc(vartype(&dsid, &i))=C %then %do;
      $
      %end;
   %sysfunc(varlen(&dsid, &i))
   %end;
%let close=%sysfunc(close(&dsid));
%mend;
```

The DYNO_LENGTH user-defined macro function, shown in Section 10.4.3, generates the LENGTH statement from a user-defined data dictionary

```
%put %get_lengths(purchases);
```

Note that the VARNAME function extracts the variable name; the VARTYPE function extracts the data type; and the VARLEN function extracts the variable length. The %PUT statement displays the results of the GET_LENGTHS invocation to the log:

```
item $ 30 quantity 8 units $ 20 cost 8 store $ 30
```

Thus, the following DATA step recreates the Purchases_new data set, now using data-driven methods that extract variable metadata:

```
data purchases_new;
   length %get_lengths(purchases);
run;
```

Reusable macro functions such as GET_VARS and GET_LENGTHS are invaluable to data-driven design because they can evaluate data set metadata in real-time. Moreover, these metadata can be extracted, transformed, and used in the DATA steps or SAS procedures in which the functions are called.

12.4.2 Programmatically Comparing Data Sets

User-defined macro *procedures* are introduced in Section 3.5.1, and can contain step boundaries, unlike macro functions and subroutines

In Section 12.4.1, a legacy copy of the Purchases data set (Purchases_old) was discovered that had two gratuitous variables (Number and Employee), and the GET_VARS macro function was invoked to retain only current variables. Although this ancillary data validation is useful in certain circumstances, data validation can be the *primary* objective of other processes. And in these cases, it is often more appropriate to perform this validation in macro *procedures* than in macro *functions*—because there is no requirement that the validation functionality be run from inside a DATA step or SAS procedure.

For example, consider the requirement to validate not only the variables within the Purchases_old data set, but also the data types, variable lengths, and formats. Furthermore, all discrepancies discovered between any of these elements should be printed to a color-coded HTML report that is dynamically generated. The built-in COMPARE procedure provides some, but not all, of this functionality, so it will not be explored.

Instead, the DICTIONARY.Columns table can be queried, its metadata extracted (for both tamale data sets), and compared for discrepancies. And because this seems like useful functionality that could come in handy in the future, a reusable macro should be developed so that *any* two data sets can be compared for similar discrepancies.

The first step is realizing that extracting metadata represents discrete functionality that should be captured within a single macro. Thus, the PULL_DICT macro uses the SQL procedure to pull the variable name, data type, length, and format from the DICTIONARY.Columns table:

```
%macro pull_dict(dsn /* data set as DSN or LIB.DSN */,
    dsnout /* data set created with metadata */);
%local lib;
* default to WORK library if only DSN provided;
%if %length(%scan(&dsn,2,.))>0 %then %do;
    %let lib=%upcase(%scan(&dsn,1,.));
```

```
    %let dsn=%scan(&dsn,2,.);
    %end;
%else %let lib=WORK;
%let dsn=%upcase(&dsn);
* pull metadata;
proc sql noprint;
    create table &dsnout as
        select upcase(name) as name label 'Column Name',
            type, length, format
        from dictionary.columns
            where libname="&lib" and memname="&dsn"
                order by name;
quit;
%mend;
```

Note that as the library and data set must be specified separately (within the WHERE clause), the &LIB macro variable must be dynamically initialized to the value preceding the period (if LIB.DSN format is passed) or to WORK (if DSN format is passed). This enables SAS practitioners to call the macro while specifying the data set name using either of two common formats—explicitly including the particular SAS library name, or omitting the library name to imply the WORK library.

Also note that because variable names are case-sensitive within DICTIONARY.Columns, the UPCASE function is applied to ensure that variable case does not adversely affect later table joins. Finally, the table is sorted (operationalized by the ORDER statement) to prepare for the subsequent DATA step in which the validation is performed.

The PULL_DICT invocation on the Purchases data set denotes that the Purchases_dict data set will be created:

```
%pull_dict(dsn=purchases, dsnout=purchases_dict);
```

Purchases_dict, shown in Table 12.3, represents a local copy of the relevant observations and fields in DICTIONARY.Columns. Thus, by calling PULL_DICT twice (which occurs in the subsequent macro implementation), two metadata data sets are created, and can be subsequently compared for discrepancies.

The COMPARE_DICTS macro declares three parameters—DSN1, representing the baseline data set, DSN2, representing the data set being

	Column Name	Column Type	Column Length	Column Format
1	COST	num	8	DOLLAR8.2
2	ITEM	char	30	$30.
3	QUANTITY	num	8	8.
4	STORE	char	30	$30.
5	UNITS	char	20	$20.

Table 12.3 Purchases_dict Data Set (from DICTIONARY.Colums Table)

compared, and DSNOUT, the validation data set that is created. After the first two data sets have been created, logical operations compare each of their respective values, and flag all inconsistencies:

```
* Note that DSN1 represents the Baseline data set;
* ERRNAME=1 if variable missing in new DSN;
* ERRNAME=2 if extra variable in new DSN;
* ERRTYPE=1 if data types are not equal;
* ERRLEN=1 if new variable is too short;
* ERRLEN=2 if new variable is too long;
* ERRFMT=1 if formats are not equal;
%macro compare_dicts(
    dsn1 /* 1st data set as DSN or LIB.DSN */,
    dsn2 /* 2nd data set as DSN or LIB.DSN */,
    dsnout /* output data set with validation */);
%pull_dict(&dsn1, zzztemp1);
%pull_dict(&dsn2, zzztemp2);
data &dsnout;
    length errname errtype errlen errfmt 8;
    merge zzztemp1 (in=a) zzztemp2 (in=b rename=
        (type=type1 length=length1 format=format1));
    by name;
    if a and ^b then errname=1;
    else if ^a and b then errname=2;
    else do;
        if type^=type1 then errtype=1;
        if length1<length then errlen=1;
        else if length1>length then errlen=2;
```

```
      if format^=format1 then errfmt=1;
      end;
run;
%mend;
```

Note that DSN1 represents the baseline data set, which is known to be correct, whereas DSN2 represents the transactional data set (or the data set being validated). The ordering here is critical, as it affects the subsequent business rules. For example, the following logic initializes the Errlen variable, establishing that a longer baseline variable length evaluates to an error code of 1 (i.e., an error), whereas a shorter baseline variable length evaluates to an error code of 2 (i.e., a warning):

```
      if length1<length then errlen=1;
      else if length1>length then errlen=2;
```

This logic establishes two exception levels (e.g., warning vs. error) because a shorter variable length may truncate data, whereas a longer variable length may signal cause for concern, yet not necessarily risk the integrity of the data the variable contains.

The following invocation calls COMPARE_DICTS, and generates the Validation data set that can be used to drive subsequent exception reporting:

```
%compare_dicts(purchases, purchases_old, validation);
```

The RPT macro creates an exception report that demonstrates discrepancies found in the historical tamale data set:

```
%macro rpt(dsn_validate /* validation data set */);
title;
proc report data=&dsn_validate nocenter nowindows;
   column name errname type1 errtype length1 errlen
      format1 errfmt dummy;
   define name / display;
   define errname / display noprint;
   define type1 / display;
   define errtype / display noprint;
   define length1 / display;
   define errlen / display noprint;
   define format1 / display;
```

The DICT_INGEST macro in Section 12.5.3 shows a more dynamic method to associate specific error variables with input variables

```
define errfmt / display noprint;
define dummy / computed noprint;
compute dummy;
    %do i=1 %to 7 %by 2;
        if _c%eval(&i+1)_=1 then call define
            ("_c&i._",'style','style=
            [backgroundcolor=very light red]');
        if _c%eval(&i+1)_=2 then call define
            ("_c&i._",'style','style=
            [backgroundcolor=yellow]');
    %end;
endcomp;
run;
%mend;
```

Dynamic color-coding can also be achieved through user-defined formats, as demonstrated in Sections 16.5.1 and 16.5.2

The Dummy variable is created in the REPORT procedure, and is subsequently used to assign dynamic color-coding within the COMPUTE block. The macro counter (&I) loops through each attribute (i.e., variable name, data type, length, and format) and highlights warnings (error codes of 2) in yellow and errors (error codes of 1) in red.

The following invocation calls RPT, and uses the validation output (Validation data set) created by the preceding COMPARE_DICTS call:

```
%rpt(validation);
```

The resultant HTML exception report, depicted in Figure 12.1, identifies several errors and several warnings. In the first column, depicting variable name, the Employee and Number variables are highlighted as warnings because these variables do not appear in the baseline data set but do appear in the comparison data set. This is indicated as a warning in lieu of an error because a gratuitous variable is often of less concern than a missing variable.

In the third column, depicting variable length, Item is highlighted as a warning because Item length is shorter in the baseline data set than in the comparison data set—declared as $30 in the baseline and $35 in the comparison. The Store variable is highlighted as an error because its length is longer in the baseline data set than in the comparison data set—declared as $30 in the baseline and $25 in the comparison.

Column Name	Column Type	Column Length	Column Format
COST	num	8	
EMPLOYEE	char	30	
ITEM	char	35	
NUMBER	num	3	
QUANTITY	num	8	
STORE	char	25	
UNITS	char	20	

Figure 12.1 Exception Report Generated by RPT Macro

In the fourth column, five variables are highlighted as errors—all variables in the baseline data set. This occurs because the baseline data set defines formats whereas the comparison data set does not. For example, when the Purchases data set was created in Section 12.4, the FORMAT statement assigned formats for all variables, yet when Purchases_old was created in Section 12.4.1, the FORMAT statement was omitted.

In more advanced exception reporting, additional dynamic elements can be incorporated, such as flyover/popup windows that display information about a warning or error when a user hovers over a cell. Nevertheless, the exception report demonstrates a reliable, reusable, scalable artifact that can be generated automatically when data sets need to be compared against a trusted baseline. Moreover, if the data structure of the Purchases data set (i.e., the baseline) is modified in the future, these repeatable macro processes can be rerun to generate new reporting that compares data sets against the updated baseline.

The FLYOVER option is demonstrated within the REPORT procedure in Sections 12.5.2 and 12.5.3

12.5 USER-DEFINED DATA DICTIONARIES

User-defined data dictionaries are those created by developers and other stakeholders to describe or prescribe data sets and other data objects. Whereas built-in data dictionaries are nearly always *prescriptive*, in that their rules enforce the data structures they describe, user-defined data dictionaries can be *descriptive*, in that they represent only static documentation. For example, a data dictionary defined within a Word document or a data dictionary defined with a spreadsheet (yet not interpreted by software) each embodies a less desirable descriptive data dictionary. Prescriptive user-defined data dictionaries, introduced in Section 12.2, are preferred to descriptive data dictionaries because they can dynamically control software. Moreover, well designed and documented prescriptive data dictionaries can often suffice as a single artifact that communicates to both stakeholders and software.

As discussed in Section 12.1, only built-in data dictionaries can be *active*, in which dictionary metadata are synchronized with the data objects they model, and in which dictionary metadata must be queried before data objects can be accessed. Although user-defined data dictionaries lack true synchronization (in the sense of real-time integration with the data objects they model), SAS practitioners should still aim to "synchronize" data dictionaries (to the extent possible) by ensuring that data dictionaries reflect the current state, structure, and content of data objects.

Data dictionary design and formulation can (and often should) precede development of code, and especially within a data-driven design paradigm, user-defined data dictionaries commonly model control tables and other control files used by data-driven processes. User-defined data structures benefit from being conceptualized early in the SDLC because developers will understand the input that data-driven processes will receive, and the output or objects they must return or produce. Only with an understanding of these control data structures can functional interpreters and operations be built.

One of the benefits of data-driven design is the ability of developers to build programs while analysts and other subject matter experts (SMEs) create and maintain data models, business rules, and other control data within control data structures. This specialization empowers all stakeholders to work in their respective areas of expertise, and in some cases, to build programs and control data *in parallel* to fast-track software development. To ensure data structures and the code that interprets them can communicate, precise specifications must rigidly describe control data; these specs often comprise user-defined data dictionaries.

In Section 12.2, Rey's Tamales documented a descriptive data dictionary—a few bullet points aimed at improving and standardizing entry of data into the Purchases data set. A more robust solution would describe not only the broad context or content of the data being entered, but also the precise data rules that define each variable. Thus, whereas descriptive data dictionaries can sometimes be recorded in plain English, prescriptive

	A	B	C	D	E	F	G	H
1	var	pos	type	len	infmt	fmt	lab	canbemiss
2	item	1	char	30	$30	$30	Item	n
3	quantity	2	num	8	8	8	Quantity	n
4	units	3	char	20	20	20	Units	y
5	cost	4	num	8	8.2	dollar8.2	Cost	n
6	store	5	char	30	$30	$30	Store	n

Table 12.4 Shopping_dict Data Dictionary for Purchases Data Set

data dictionaries can comprise math, symbols, equations, and other more exacting content that can be programmatically leveraged.

Still formatted as bullet points, the descriptive data dictionary can be redefined to include more specificity:

- **Item** – The variable has a character data type with a length of 30; it is categorical and cannot be missing.
- **Quantity** – The variable has a numeric data type with a length of 8; it can represent an integer or have decimals (e.g., 2.5), and cannot be missing.
- **Unit** – The variable has a character data type with a length of 20; it is categorical and cannot be missing.
- **Cost** – The variable has a numeric data type with a length of 8; it cannot be missing.
- **Store** – The variable has a character data type with a length of 30; it is categorical and cannot be missing.

These data rules are codified within the user-defined data dictionary, a spreadsheet (shown in Table 12.4) that should be exported to a CSV file (shopping_dict.csv).

The data dictionary can be saved as shopping_dict.csv:

```
var,pos,type,len,infmt,fmt,lab,canbemiss
item,1,char,30,$30,$30,Item,n
quantity,2,num,8,8,8,Quantity,n
units,3,char,20,20,20,Units,y
cost,4,num,8,8.2,dollar8.2,Cost,n
store,5,char,30,$30,$30,Store,n
```

The following DATA step ingests the data dictionary:

```
%let loc=d:\sas\;       * USER MUST CHANGE LOCATION *;
data dict;
    infile "&loc.shopping_dict.csv" truncover dsd
        delimiter=',' firstobs=2;
    length var $32 pos 8 type $6 len 8 infmt $32
        fmt $32 lab $100 canbemiss $3;
    input var $ pos type $ len infmt $ fmt $ lab $
        canbemiss $;
    format var $32. pos 8. type $6. len 8. infmt $32.
        fmt $32. lab $100. canbemiss $3.;
    label var='Variable' pos='Variable Position'
        type='Data Type' len='Length' infmt='Informat'
        fmt='Format' lab='Label'
        canbemiss='Can Be Missing';
run;
```

The CSV file (shopping_dict.csv) represents an *external* data dictionary, whereas the derivative data set (Dict) represents an *internal* data dictionary—the distinction being that the former *indirectly* drives software functionality, whereas the latter *directly* drives software functionality. These pairs are common whenever the original source of control data is maintained outside of the SAS application within a more interoperable data structure than proprietary SAS data sets.

Thus, external data sets facilitate MDM objectives, by enabling one control table (like shopping_dict.csv) to drive both SAS and non-SAS applications and processes. However, it is essential that the external and internal data dictionaries remain *aligned*—that is, synchronized through manual or user-automated processes—to ensure they contain and convey identical information at all times.

12.5.1 Applying User-Defined Informats

Lookup tables and methods to operationalize them are demonstrated throughout Chapter 13

Before tackling the metadata of an entire data object (like the Purchases data set), it is often beneficial to decompose the object into elements that can be singly defined and validated. This subsection demonstrates how a lookup table can be constructed to facilitate entity resolution—that is, not only identifying invalid values, as *validation* often implies, but also mapping those invalid values to the valid entities they should represent.

	A	B
1	Ingredient	Variation
2	tomato	tomato
3		tomatoes
4		tomate
5		tomates
6	corn husk	corn husk
7		corn husks
8		husk
9		husks
10		hojas de maiz
11	cilantro	cilantro
12	onion	onion
13		onions
14		cebolla
15		cebollas

Table 12.5 Ingredients Lookup Table (Ingredients.csv)

For example, the Purchases data set, shown in Table 12.1, contains three variations of "tomato":

```
tomato,3,lbs,5.6,Ralph's
tomatos,100,,10.2,
tomatoes,5,lbs,6.32,Target
```

A many-to-one data mapping (i.e., a *multimap*) can model these invalid values of *tomato*, and redirect (transform) them to the valid value—tomato. A spreadsheet (shown in Table 12.5) maps a partial list of tamale ingredients. The first column denotes the valid ingredient name, and the second column lists spelling variations thereof.

Data mappings and *multimaps* are discussed in Section 4.3.3*

The spreadsheet should be exported from Excel, and saved as a CSV file (ingredients.csv):

```
Ingredient,Variation
tomato,tomato
,tomatoes
,tomate
,tomates
```

```
lard,corn husk
,corn husks
,husk
,husks
,hojas de maiz
cilantro,cilantro
onion,onion
,onions
,cebolla
,cebollas
```

The CSV file can be subsequently ingested into a SAS data set, and used to create a SAS informat using the CNTLIN option:

The BUILD_FORMAT macro, demonstrated in Section 15.3, provides a more flexible method to create data-driven formats and informats than the CNTLIN option

```
%let loc=d:\sas\;        * USER MUST CHANGE LOCATION *;
data ingredients (drop=oldingredient);
    infile "&loc.ingredients.csv" truncover dsd
        delimiter=',' firstobs=2;
    length ingredient $30 raw $30;
    input ingredient $ raw $;
    format ingredient $30. raw $30.;
    label ingredient='Ingredient';
    if _n_>1 then do;
        if missing(ingredient)
            then ingredient=oldingredient;
        end;
    oldingredient=ingredient;
    retain oldingredient;
run;

data ingredients_fmt;
    set ingredients (rename=(ingredient=label
        raw=start)) end=eof;
    length fmtname $32 type $1 hlo $1;
    fmtname='ingredients';
    type='j';            * J denotes a character informat;
    hlo='';
    output;
```

```
if eof then do;
   start='';
   label='_error_';
   hlo='o';      * O denotes other value;
   output;
   end;
run;


proc format cntlin=ingredients_fmt;
run;
```

The FORMAT procedure CNTLIN option provides a data-driven approach for creating user-defined formats and informats, and is preferred to hardcoded methods that instead enumerate values within the code itself. Thus, CNTLIN empowers stakeholders to modify user-defined formats and informats without altering code—we only have to modify the control data contained within the data set specified by CNTLIN.

The Purchases data set is created by ingesting purchases.csv, and relies on the user-defined INGREDIENTS informat to ingest the Item variable:

```
data purchases;
   infile "&loc.purchases.csv" truncover dsd
      delimiter=',' firstobs=2;
   length item $30 quantity 8 units $20 cost 8
      store $30 err 3;
   input item : $ingredients. quantity units $
      cost store $;
   format item $30. quantity 8. units $20.
      cost dollar8.2 store $30.;
   label item='Item' quantity='Quantity' units='Units'
      cost='Cost' store='Store';
   if _error_ then err=1;
run;
```

The SAS log demonstrates that the INGREDIENTS informat bins both "tomato" and "tomatoes" into the "tomato" entity. However, because "tomatos" is not included in the second column of the lookup table (shown in Table 12.5), the DATA step interprets "tomatos" as an invalid value,

denotes this with a "NOTE: Invalid data" in the log, and sets the automatic
ERROR value to 1 for the observation:

```
NOTE: The infile "d:\sas\purchases.csv" is:
      Filename=d:\sas\purchases.csv,
      RECFM=V,LRECL=32767,File Size (bytes)=160,

NOTE: Invalid data for item in line 3 1-7.
RULE:       ----+----1----+----2----+----3----+----4----+-
---5----+----6----+----7----+----8----+----
3            tomatos,100,,10.2, 18
item=  quantity=100 units=  cost=$10.20 store=  err=1
_ERROR_=1 _N_=2
NOTE: Invalid data for cost in line 5 15-19.
5            cilantro,1,lb,$2.23 ,Costco 27
item=cilantro quantity=1 units=lb cost=. store=Costco
err=1 _ERROR_=1 _N_=4
NOTE: 5 records were read from the infile
"d:\sas\purchases.csv".
      The minimum record length was 18.
      The maximum record length was 27.
NOTE: The data set WORK.PURCHASES has 5 observations and
6 variables.
```

The log also demonstrates that the $2.23 Cost value was flagged
because it contains a dollar sign. Thus, the Err variable is set to 1 for the
second and fourth observations, in which the Item and Cost values do not
conform to their respective informats. Additional informats (not shown)
could be defined in separate lookup tables to overcome unwanted
variability in the Units and Store variables.

Two limitations exist, however, in that Err does not denote the specific
variable (or its value) that triggered _ERROR_, nor is the invalid value
"tomatos" saved in the Purchases data that is created. Unfortunately, these
limitations require SAS practitioners to rely on the log to obtain this
information, whereas a best practice is to collect these metadata
programmatically, and include them within exception reports. The two next
subsections overcome these limitations.

12.5.2 Applying Informats and Saving the Scraps

Data can be validated and cleaned using user-defined informats, such as INGREDIENTS (created in Section 12.5.1), and built-in informats, such as the numeric informat (8) used to input the Cost variable (within purchases.csv). To identify invalid values programmatically, however, the _ERROR_ value must be saved as an independent error variable (e.g., Item_e, Quantity_e) for each data set variable (e.g., Item, Quantity), after which _ERROR_ must be reset to 0 so that subsequent invalid values (occurring in the same observation) can be detected if they exist.

Moreover, to identify programmatically what specific invalid values are encountered, shadow variables (e.g., Item_r, Quantity_r) must be created for each variable (e.g., Item, Quantity) so that invalid values can be saved as character variables. These shadow variables do not become part of the final data product, but are used in exception reporting. To minimize file size, shadow variable values are only initialized for invalid values (i.e., _ERROR_=1); the remaining shadow variable values will be missing.

The following refactored DATA step recreates the Purchases data set, and creates five error variables that denote invalid values (i.e., Item_e, Quantity_e, Units_e, Cost_e, Store_e) and five shadow variables that denote raw input (i.e., Item_r, Quantity_r, Units_r, Cost_r, Store_r):

```
data purchases;
    infile "&loc.purchases.csv" truncover dsd
        delimiter=',' firstobs=2;
    length item $30 quantity 8 units $20 cost 8
        store $30
        item_e 3 quantity_e 3 units_e 3 cost_e 3
            store_e 3
        item_r $30 quantity_r $30 units_r $30 cost_r $30
            store_r $30;
    input item : $ingredients. @;
    if _error_=1 then do;
        item_e=1;
        _error_=0;
        end;
    input quantity @;
    if _error_=1 then do;
```

```
      quantity_e=1;
      _error_=0;
      end;
  input units $ @;
  if _error_=1 then do;
     units_e=1;
     _error_=0;
     end;
  input cost : dollar8.2 @;
  if _error_=1 then do;
     cost_e=1;
     _error_=0;
     end;
  input store $ @;
  if _error_=1 then do;
     store_e=1;
     _error_=0;
     end;
  input @1 item_r $ quantity_r $ units_r $ cost_r $
     store_r $;
  if missing(item_e) then item_r='';
  if missing(quantity_e) then quantity_r='';
  if missing(units_e) then units_r='';
  if missing(cost_e) then cost_r='';
  if missing(store_e) then store_r='';
  format item $30. quantity 8. units $20. cost
     dollar8.2 store $30.;
  label item='Item' quantity='Quantity' units='Units'
     cost='Cost' store='Store';
run;
```

The log again shows some inscrutable note about "invalid data" detected during data ingestion:

```
NOTE: Invalid data for item in line 3 1-7.
NOTE: 5 records were read from the infile
"d:\sas\purchases.csv".
      The minimum record length was 18.
```

	Item	Quantity	Units	Cost	Store	item_e	item_r
1	tomato	3	lbs	$5.60	Ralph's		
2		100		$10.20		1	tomatos
3	tomatoes	5	lbs	$6.32	Target		
4	cilantro	1	lb	$2.23	Costco		
5	onion	2	lbs	$3.41	Cosco		

Table 12.6 Purchases Data Set with Error Variables

The maximum record length was 27.

NOTE: The data set WORK.PURCHASES has 5 observations and 15 variables.

Despite the minimally helpful log, the Purchases data set has now been created with columns that describe the "invalid data" in explicit detail! You no longer have to guess what invalid data have been encountered!

Shown in Table 12.6, Purchases contains one error variable (Item_e), which is initialized to 1 to denote that "tomatos" does not appear in the INGREDIENTS informat (created from the ingredients.csv control table). Correspondingly, Item_r is initialized to "tomatos" to denote the raw (but invalid) value for Item. The unacceptably formatted Cost ($2.23) is now successfully ingested using the DOLLAR8.2 informat (rather than the 8.0 informat), which ingests values irrespective of a leading dollar sign.

With invalid values now individually identified (and raw values retained), SAS practitioners can quickly query the data set to understand the "invalid value" message displayed in the log. Moreover, automated, data-driven processes can rely on these error variables to communicate invalid data to stakeholders, or to initiate other dynamic actions.

For example, the EXCEPTION macro uses the REPORT procedure to generate an exception report that highlights data quality issues:

```
%macro exception;
%local i;
proc report data=purchases nocenter nowindows
      nocompletecols
      style(report)=[foreground=black
      backgroundcolor=grey background=black]
      style(header)=[font_size=2 background=black
      backgroundcolor=black foreground=white]
      style(column)=[backgroundcolor=white
```

```
          foreground=black];
      column item item_e item_r quantity quantity_e
          quantity_r units units_e units_r cost cost_e
          cost_r store store_e store_r dummy;
      define item / display;
      define item_e / display noprint;
      define item_r / display noprint;
      define quantity / display;
      define quantity_e / display noprint;
      define quantity_r / display noprint;
      define units / display;
      define units_e / display noprint;
      define units_r / display noprint;
      define cost / display;
      define cost_e / display noprint;
      define cost_r / display noprint;
      define store / display;
      define store_e / display noprint;
      define store_r / display noprint;
      define dummy / computed noprint;
      compute dummy;
      %do i=1 %to 5;
         if _c%eval(((&i-1)*3)+2)_=1 then do;
            call define ("_c%eval(((&i-1)*3)+1)_",
               'style','style=
               [backgroundcolor=very light red]');
            call define ("_c%eval(((&i-1)*3)+1)_",
               'style/merge','style=[flyover=
               "' || _c%eval(((&i-1)*3)+3)_ || '"]');
            end;
         %end;
         endcomp;
   run;
   %mend;

   %exception;
```

The NOPRINT option in the DEFINE statements denotes columns that are not printed; thus, the HTML report (shown in Figure 12.2) contains only five columns. The counter (&I) iterates over these columns to detect invalid values (denoted by an error value of 1), in which case the cell is colored red and a flyover/popup is generated that contains the raw (i.e., invalid) value (e.g., "tomatos"). When viewing the report, users can hover over any red cell to open a popup window that displays the raw value (operationalized through the FLYOVER element), thus enabling them to identify and troubleshoot invalid data without reliance on the log.

Also note that the INGREDIENTS user-defined informat transformed "tomatoes" to "tomato" in the third observation, and "cebolla" to "onion" in the fifth observation. Although not demonstrated, user-defined informats could be similarly created to standardize spelling variations (such as mapping values from Spanish to English) within the remaining two categorical variables, Units and Store. Thus, the user-defined informats provide the dual functionality of excluding invalid values and mapping spelling variations to their respective entities.

Notwithstanding the functionality of the exception report, including its reliance on the INGREDIENTS informat (which espouses data-driven design), the ingestion, validation, and visualization of Purchases is a primarily concrete process—built for a single purpose and a single data set. This hardcoded design lacks data independence, and commingles data and code.

One test of this unwanted dependence (and coupling) is to count the tamale terminology in the REPORT procedure, including references in the DEFINE statements to Item, Cost, and Unit. A more dynamic process could

Loose coupling is a design objective within OOP (and data-driven design), as discussed in Section 1.3, yet the design of this ETL process and exception report is tightly coupled with tamales

Item	Quantity	Units	Cost	Store
tomato	3	lbs	$5.60	Ralph's
	100		$10.20	
tomatos				
tomato	5	lbs	$6.32	Target
cilantro	1	lb	$2.23	Costco
onion	2	lbs	$3.41	Cosco

Figure 12.2 Data Quality (Exception) Report

instead abstract this functionality so it could run on *any* data set having equivalent error variables.

The final subsection demonstrates a more abstract solution, in which the updated data dictionary (shown in Table 12.7) is used to dynamically ingest, validate, and clean data, and to generate exception reporting.

12.5.3 User-Defined Data Dictionaries Implemented

Sections 12.5.1 and 12.5.2 demonstrate how informats can be used to validate and clean data, and to visualize data integrity issues. These processes can be streamlined through data-driven design that achieves equivalent functionality by relying on a data dictionary that prescribes the variable names, positions, types, lengths, informats, formats, and other attributes for a data set.

The data dictionary, shown in Table 12.4, is updated in Table 12.7, in which the INGREDIENTS informat is specified for the Item variable, and the DOLLAR8.2 informat is specified for the Cost variable.

The following data should be saved as purchases_dict.csv to update the data dictionary:

```
var,pos,type,len,infmt,fmt,lab,canbemiss
item,1,char,30,ingredients,$30,Item,n
quantity,2,num,8,8,8,Quantity,n
units,3,char,20,20,20,Units,y
cost,4,num,8,dollar8.2,dollar8.2,Cost,n
store,5,char,30,$30,$30,Store,n
```

The DICT_INGEST macro ingests purchases_dict.csv, and dynamically builds a series of global macro variables that contain SAS statements to be executed within a subsequent DATA step:

```
%macro dict_ingest(dict= /* path and CSV file name for
```

	A	B	C	D	E	F	G	H
1	var	pos	type	len	infmt	fmt	lab	canbemiss
2	item	1	char	30	ingredients	30	Item	n
3	quantity	2	num	8	8	8	Quantity	n
4	units	3	char	20	20	20	Units	y
5	cost	4	num	8	dollar8.2	dollar8.2	Cost	n
6	store	5	char	30	30	30	Store	n

Table 12.7 Updated Data Dictionary (Purchases_dict.csv)

```
      data dictionary*/);
data tempdict;
   infile "&dict" truncover dsd delimiter=','
      firstobs=2;
   length var $32 pos 8 type $6 len 8 infmt $32
      fmt $32 lab $100 canbemiss $3;
   input var $ pos type $ len infmt $ fmt $ lab $
      canbemiss $;
   format var $32. pos 8. type $6. len 8.
      infmt $32. fmt $32. lab $100. canbemiss $3.;
   label var='Variable' pos='Variable Position'
      type='Data Type' len='Length' infmt='Informat'
      fmt='Format' lab='Label'
      canbemiss='Can Be Missing';
run;
proc sort data=tempdict;
   by pos;
run;
data _null_;
   length varlist lenlist inputlist inputlist2
      formlist lablist misslist canbemisslist $1000;
   retain varlist lenlist inputlist inputlist2
      formlist lablist misslist canbemisslist '';
   if _n_=1 then do;
      lenlist='length';
      inputlist2='input @1';
      formlist='format';
      lablist='label';
      end;
   set tempdict end=eof;
   * evaluates invalid values that violate informats;
   if find(fmt,'.')=0 then fmt=strip(fmt) || '.';
   if find(infmt,'.')=0 then infmt=strip(infmt)
      || '.';
   varlist=strip(varlist) || ' ' || strip(var);
   lenlist=strip(lenlist) || ' ' || strip(var) || ' '
```

```
       || ifc(strip(upcase(type))='CHAR','$','')
       || strip(put(len,8.)) || ' ' || strip(var)
       || '_e 3 ' || strip(var) || '_r $100';
    inputlist=strip(inputlist) || 'input '
       || strip(var) || ' : ' || strip(infmt) || ' @;';
    inputlist=strip(inputlist)
       || 'if _error_=1 then do; ' || strip(var)
       || '_e=1; _error_=0; end;';
    inputlist2=strip(inputlist2) || ' ' || strip(var)
       || '_r $';
    misslist=strip(misslist) || ' if missing('
       || strip(var) || '_e) then ' || strip(var)
       || '_r="";';
    formlist=strip(formlist) || ' ' || strip(var)
       || ifc(strip(upcase(type))=' CHAR','$','')
       || strip(fmt);
    lablist=strip(lablist) || ' ' || strip(var)
       || '="' || strip(lab) || '"';
    * evaluates missing variables;
    if upcase(canbemiss)='N' then do;
       canbemisslist=strip(canbemisslist) || ' '
          || 'if missing(' || strip(var)
          || ') and missing (' || strip(var)
          || '_e) then do; ' || strip(var) || '_e=2; '
          || strip(var) || '_r="' || upcase(strip(var))
          || ' cannot be missing"; end;';
       end;
    * initializes macro variables;
    if eof then do;
       lenlist=strip(lenlist) || ';';
       inputlist2=strip(inputlist2) || ';';
       formlist=strip(formlist) || ';';
       lablist=strip(lablist) || ';';
       call symputx('varlist',strip(varlist),'g');
       call symputx('lenlist',strip(lenlist),'g');
       call symputx('inputlist',strip(inputlist),'g');
```

```
         call symputx('inputlist2',
             strip(inputlist2),'g');
         call symputx('formlist',strip(formlist),'g');
         call symputx('lablist',strip(lablist),'g');
         * deletes raw values if no error detected;
         call symputx('misslist',
             strip(misslist),'g');
         * evaluates missing value errors;
         call symputx('canbemisslist',
             strip(canbemisslist),'g');
         end;
    run;
    %mend;


    %let loc=d:\sas\;       * USER MUST CHANGE LOCATION *;
    %dict_ingest(dict=&loc.purchases_dict.csv);
```

The DATA step contains no explicit references to tamales, tomatoes, or to other variables or values contained within the purchase history spreadsheet (purchases.csv). Thus, this more abstract data-driven design enables *any* data set to be ingested, validated, and cleaned, as long as the data structure is first defined within an equivalently structured data dictionary. The DICT parameter passes the data dictionary CSV file, and provides flexibility to ensure the DICT_INGEST macro can be reused to process unrelated data sets.

The DATA step (within DICT_INGEST) dynamically creates several global macro variables that comprise SAS statements to be executed. For example, &LENLIST writes the LENGTH statement, &INPUTLIST writes the INPUT statement, and &INPUTLIST2 writes the second INPUT statement, which initializes character variables (e.g., Item_r) when an invalid value is detected (e.g., when Item is "tomatos").

Note that the FIND function (within the DATA step) detects whether each format or informat contains a trailing period, and if it does not, appends a trailing period. This functionality ensures that data dictionaries maintained within Excel (which deletes trailing periods unless the cell format is changed to "text") can be used to maintain formats and informats, irrespective of whether they have a trailing period.

The Canbemiss variable within the Purchases_dict data dictionary is also now evaluated, and creates the &CANBEMISSLIST global macro variable, which contains conditional logic that denotes an error when a required variable (e.g., Canbemiss=Y) is missing. The following DATA step executes the dynamic statements (contained within the global macro variables) to validate and clean the purchases.csv data set:

```
data purchases;
    infile "&loc.purchases.csv" truncover dsd
        delimiter=',' firstobs=2;
    &lenlist;
    &inputlist;
    &inputlist2;
    &misslist;
    &formlist;
    &lablist;
    &canbemisslist;
run;
```

The log again provides little detail about the dynamic processes (codified within the macro variables) that have been run, indicating again the single invalid value detected by the INGREDIENTS informat:

```
NOTE: Invalid data for item in line 3 1-7.
NOTE: 5 records were read from the infile
"d:\sas\purchases.csv".
      The minimum record length was 18.
      The maximum record length was 27.
NOTE: The data set WORK.PURCHASES has 5 observations and
15 variables.
NOTE: DATA statement used (Total process time):
```

The dynamic processes can be understood more clearly when the SYMBOLGEN system option is activated prior to running the DATA step:

```
options symbolgen;
data purchases;
    infile "&loc.purchases.csv" truncover dsd
        delimiter=',' firstobs=2;
    &lenlist;
```

```
    &inputlist;

    &inputlist2;

    &misslist;

    &formlist;

    &lablist;

    &canbemisslist;

run;

options nosymbolgen;
```

The log now details the dynamic statements that were executed via the various global macro variables:

```
1778   data purchases;
SYMBOLGEN:   Macro variable LOC resolves to d:\sas\
1779       infile "&loc.purchases.csv" truncover dsd
1780         delimiter=',' firstobs=2;
1781       &lenlist;
SYMBOLGEN:   Macro variable LENLIST resolves to length
item $30 item_e 3 item_r $100 quantity  8
           quantity_e 3 quantity_r $100 units $20
units_e 3 units_r $100 cost  8 cost_e 3
           cost_r $100 store $30 store_e 3 store_r
$100;
1782       &inputlist;
SYMBOLGEN:   Macro variable INPUTLIST resolves to input
item : ingredients. @;if _error_=1 then
           do; item_e=1; _error_=0; end;input quantity
: 8. @;if _error_=1 then do;
           quantity_e=1; _error_=0; end;input units :
20. @;if _error_=1 then do; units_e=1;
           _error_=0; end;input cost : dollar8.2 @;if
_error_=1 then do; cost_e=1; _error_=0;
           end;input store : $30. @;if _error_=1 then
do; store_e=1; _error_=0; end;
1783       &inputlist2;
SYMBOLGEN:   Macro variable INPUTLIST2 resolves to input
@1 item_r $ quantity_r $ units_r $
           cost_r $ store_r $;
```

```
1784      &misslist;
SYMBOLGEN:  Macro variable MISSLIST resolves to if
missing(item_e) then item_r=""; if
             missing(quantity_e) then quantity_r=""; if
missing(units_e) then units_r=""; if
             missing(cost_e) then cost_r=""; if
missing(store_e) then store_r="";
1785      &formlist;
SYMBOLGEN:  Macro variable FORMLIST resolves to format
item $30. quantity 8. units 20. cost
             dollar8.2 store $30.;
1786      &lablist;
SYMBOLGEN:  Macro variable LABLIST resolves to label
item="Item" quantity="Quantity"
             units="Units" cost="Cost" store="Store";
1787      &canbemisslist;
SYMBOLGEN:  Macro variable CANBEMISSLIST resolves to if
missing(item) and missing (item_e) then
             do; item_e=2; item_r="ITEM cannot be
missing"; end; if missing(quantity) and
             missing (quantity_e) then do; quantity_e=2;
quantity_r="QUANTITY cannot be
             missing"; end; if missing(cost) and missing
(cost_e) then do; cost_e=2;
             cost_r="COST cannot be missing"; end; if
missing(store) and missing (store_e) then
             do; store_e=2; store_r="STORE cannot be
missing"; end;
1788   run;
```

Thus, in showcasing data-driven design, the DATA step no longer statically references any variables within purchases.csv, and instead relies on the DICT_INGEST macro to read and interpret the data dictionary, and to transform these control data into dynamic instructions—statements to be run in the subsequent DATA step.

Finally, the EXCEPTION macro is refactored into the DYNO_EXCEPTION macro, which espouses configurable, data-driven design in that it can be run on *any* data set, so long as that data set is defined by a comparable data dictionary. Thus, as with the DICT_INGEST macro, DYNO_EXCEPTION references neither variables nor values from purchases.csv; instead, it relies on the dynamically generated &VARLIST global macro variable, which lists all variables defined in the data dictionary:

```
* requires DICT_INGEST macro to have first been run;
%macro dyno_exception(dsn= /* data set name */,
   varlist= /* space-delim list of variables */);
%local cnt i;
%let cnt=%sysfunc(countw(&varlist));
title;
proc report data=&dsn nocenter nowindows
      nocompletecols
      style(report)=[foreground=black
      backgroundcolor=grey background=black]
      style(header)=[font_size=2 background=black
      backgroundcolor=black foreground=white]
      style(column)=[backgroundcolor=white
      foreground=black];
   column
   %do i=1 %to &cnt;
      %scan(&varlist,&i,,S) %scan(&varlist,
         &i,,S)_e %scan(&varlist,&i,,S)_r
      %end;
      dummy;
%do i=1 %to &cnt;
   define %scan(&varlist,&i,,S) / display;
   define %scan(&varlist,&i,,S)_e / display noprint;
   define %scan(&varlist,&i,,S)_r / display noprint;
   %end;
   define dummy / computed noprint;
   compute dummy;
   %do i=1 %to &cnt;
      if _c%eval(((&i-1)*3)+2)_>0 then do;
         call define ("_c%eval(((&i-1)*3)+1)_",
```

```
                   'style','style=
                   [backgroundcolor=very light red]');
                call define ("_c%eval(((&i-1)*3)+1)_",
                   'style/merge','style=[flyover="' ||
                   strip(_c%eval(((&i-1)*3)+3)_) || '"]');
                end;
             %end;
             endcomp;
         run;
         %mend;


         %dyno_exception(dsn=purchases, varlist=&varlist);
```

The HTML output for the REPORT procedure, shown in Figure 12.3, demonstrates the "invalid data" note from the log, in which "tomatos" is evaluated (by the INGREDIENTS user-defined character informat) to be an invalid value for Item. The report also demonstrates a new error that denotes that Store is missing in the second observation, and the text of each error is displayed when a cursor hovers over it (as depicted in Figure 12.3). The Units and Store values could be further standardized (not shown) by creating two additional user-defined informats that could clean these variables.

Most importantly, the DICT_INGEST and DYNO_EXCEPTION macros can be saved as separate files, and reused in future software to evaluate unrelated data sets. Notwithstanding this software modularity, note the inevitable coupling between the DICT_INGEST and DYNO_EXCEPTION

Item	Quantity	Units	Cost	Store
tomato	3	lbs	$5.60	Ralph's
tomatos	100		$10.20	STORE cannot be missing
tomato	5	lbs	$6.32	Target
cilantro	1	lb	$2.23	Costco
onion	2	lbs	$3.41	Cosco

Figure 12.3 Updated Data Quality Exception Report

macros, in that the former must be run prior to the latter to create the error variables, the raw variables, and the &VARLIST global macro variable.

The data dictionary, representing a user-defined data structure, can be extended over time to prescribe and evaluate other aspects of data quality, such as whether a variable must be sorted or whether a value must be unique. This configurability enables users to clean and validate data sets by modifying only control tables—in this example, the single spreadsheet containing the prescriptive data dictionary and the multiple spreadsheets containing informat data mappings.

12.6 SUMMARY

This chapter introduced data dictionaries, and underscored the importance of leveraging them within data-driven design. Several aspects of data dictionaries were contrasted, including the *active-passive* distinction, the *prescription-description* distinction, and the *internal-external* distinction. Data dictionaries abstract and model data sets and other data objects, communicating metadata to both processes and stakeholders.

Active data dictionaries are those integrated with software, in which access to data objects cannot be granted (or data cannot be operationalized) without querying the governing data dictionary. The *SAS Dictionary tables* were introduced as the built-in (active) data dictionaries automatically created for all SAS data sets. Although SAS practitioners cannot build active data dictionaries, we can model their structure, content, and functionality when designing user-defined data dictionaries.

Prescriptive data dictionaries are those user-defined data dictionaries that drive dynamic processes, and which must be rigorously designed so they can be reliably and unambiguously interpreted. Once a sufficiently abstract user-defined dictionary structure has been designed, it can be reused to ingest, validate, standardize, and visualize even unrelated data—as long as their metadata are maintained within an identically structured data dictionary.

User-defined data dictionaries are often maintained in interoperable formats, such as spreadsheets or CSV files, to facilitate non-SAS applications and processes that rely on their data. This interoperability also facilitates MDM objectives because a single, trusted source of these control data—the data dictionary—can be maintained. Thus, *external data dictionaries* are maintained outside of SAS, and are modified directly by end users, whereas *internal data dictionaries* are the SAS data sets that represent (and mirror) their external data dictionary counterparts. Many SAS processes employ only internal data dictionaries maintained within SAS data sets, but where external data dictionaries are leveraged, care must be exercised to ensure internal and external data dictionaries remain synchronized and maintain consistent information at all times.

Chapter 13.

Control Tables: Lookup Tables

This chapter has the following objectives:

- ❖ Define and introduce *lookup tables*, which uniquely represent data elements.

- ❖ Discuss three common use cases for querying lookup tables, including data validation, data cleaning, and data classification.

- ❖ Demonstrate the two common approaches for querying SAS lookup tables, including *procedural* and *functional* querying, and discuss the advantages of the latter.

- ❖ Demonstrate various *procedural* methods to access a lookup table, including with the DATA step MERGE, SQL procedure JOIN, SAS array, and DATA step hash object.

- ❖ Demonstrate various *functional* methods to access a lookup table, including the creation of user-defined functions, user-defined subroutines, and user-defined formats.

Lookup tables catalog unique data (or series of data) through an index that defines one or more *key variables*, and which may reference one or more additional *non-key variables*, sometimes called *data variables*. SAS processes can leverage a lookup table using a range of operations to evaluate whether one or more values appear in the table; for some use cases, non-key variables can also be returned. Lookup tables are commonly used to validate, transform, clean, or classify (*categorize*) data, and some lookup tables can perform each of these operations simultaneously.

Lookup tables come in all shapes and sizes—well, they are all table shaped—but all different sizes, at least. Single-column lookup tables always will include a list of unique values because the only column is also the primary key. For example, the list of U.S. state abbreviations might be maintained within a single-column table. *Non-key columns* can juxtapose key columns, and in many lookup operations, the objective is to return the value(s) held in the non-key column(s). For example, a two-column lookup table might include a key column with each U.S. state abbreviation and a non-key column with the associated state's name. *Composite primary keys* contain two or more key variables but are not discussed in this text.

Master data are discussed within master data management (MDM) objectives in Section 8.2

Lookup tables, which often maintain *master data*, constitute *master tables*—that is, they facilitate data governance, and should be considered to be the authoritative source for the information they contain. As a master table, a lookup table also should not be redundantly duplicated across a team or organization; one will suffice. For example, a lookup table that includes all unique employee IDs and corresponding employee names is commonly maintained within organizations. And although various derivative data sets and data products might be produced from this lookup table, multiple versions of the table itself need not exist.

Data validation operations query a lookup table for a specific value, and effectively return True if the value appears in the key and False if it does not. Data cleaning operations can query a lookup table, and additionally return a transformed (i.e. cleaned) representation of the value. Other transformations can query a lookup table to return an equivalent

Data mappings, including multimaps, are introduced in Section 4.3.3

value appearing in a different format, such as transforming a state abbreviation into the associated state name. Finally, data classification operations can query a lookup table to bin values into groups based on a many-to-one multimap model that the lookup table describes, in which multiple keys map to the same value.

Just as lookup table operations can have various objectives, they can also be operationalized through various SAS programming techniques. *Functional* methods broadly capture lookup queries effected by a single line of code, with user-defined functions, subroutines, and formats demonstrated in this chapter. Functional methods are desired, especially in data-driven design, because discrete, callable modules can be invoked to transform data while the complexities of the transformation logic remain concealed in the user-defined module's implementation. Functional methods are highly readable and reusable.

Procedural methods, conversely, may query the same lookup table, but do so through multiple steps, statements, or procedures, and thus are typically less reusable than functionally equivalent functional methods. Notwithstanding, procedural methods can still represent data-driven design when the lookup table prescribes the logic that transforms data.

Despite the clear design advantages of functional lookup methods, software performance, including runtime and efficient resource utilization, also must be considered in real-world usage. Thus, although this chapter focuses on design considerations, the performance of procedural methods can, in some cases, warrant selection of those methods in lieu of equivalent functional methods.

Lookup tables inherently represent data-driven design because control data are maintained within external control tables, and thus embody control data independence. In some cases, the control table will be the only source of flexibility or configurability afforded the program, but this should not diminish its "data-driven" status.

Within the SAS language, many-to-one joins can be performed through several techniques, including DATA step merges, SQL joins, DOW loops, SAS arrays, SAS indexes, multiple SET statements, SAS formats, hash objects, FCMP functions, and the IN operator, to name several. That is, once the lookup table data structure has been defined, procedural abstraction enables SAS practitioners to select how best to engineer and implement lookup operations.

Moreover, where lookup techniques leverage user-defined functions or subroutines, if a faster method is later designed (by a team of SAS users) or engineered (by SAS Institute developers), the function or subroutine *implementation* can be upgraded while its *invocation* remains unchanged. This refactoring can provide increased performance over time while not

---

Hiding complexity in the implementation is introduced in Section 1.4 as a principle of data-driven design, and embodies information hiding, as discussed in Section 8.4.1

Data independence, the third pillar of data-driven design, is introduced in Section 1.3, and described in Section 1.3.3

The procedural *implementation* and *invocation* are introduced in Sections 3.3 and 3.4, respectively

disrupting the usage and reusage of the user-defined functions and subroutines being upgraded.

13.1 WINTER IS COMING!

HBO's *Game of Thrones* premiered in 2011, captivating the hearts and souls of adoring fans the world round. An adaptation of George R.R. Martin's series, *A Song of Ice and Fire*, Game of Thrones showcases warring regions, clans, and families amid a fantastical medieval backdrop. With so much fandom and online commentary, a wealth of Game of Thrones data has no doubt been generated, and some of those data can be explored through simulated examples.

The primary data source for this chapter mimics an online survey posted to a Game of Thrones fan website, in which users were asked a series of questions about their favorite aspects of the series. The CSV file (GOT_favorites.csv) contains two columns, denoting each user's favorite character and favorite season:

```
Jaime Lannister,2
Cersei Lannister,7
Daenerys,4
Daneris,7
Daenerys Targaryen,2
Jaime,1
Kit Harington,2
Aria Stark,7
Tyrion Lannister,3
Sansa Stark,5
```

No fan was foolish enough to select the heretically disappointing Season 8, but the web designers seem to have made equally poor decisions as the script writers! For example, users were allowed to enter their favorite character in a text field, rather than selecting the character from a lookup field (of categorical values). This oversight has contributed to significant, unwanted variability in the data, with several spelling variations immediately observed.

The following DATA step ingests the CSV file into the GOT_Favorites data set:

```
%let loc=d:\sas\;       * USER MUST CHANGE LOCATION *;
```

```
data got_favorites;
   infile "&loc.got_favorites.csv" dsd delimiter=','
      truncover;
   length favcharacter $30 favseason 8;
   input favcharacter $ favseason ;
   format favcharacter $30. favseason 8.;
   label favcharacter='Favorite Character'
      favseason='Favorite Season';
run;
```

Throughout this chapter, the Favcharacter value (in the GOT_favorites data set) will be analyzed repeatedly to determine if it exists in various lookup tables. Successive examples explore various lookup objectives (demonstrated in chapter sections) utilizing various lookup methods (demonstrated in chapter subsections) to deliver functionally equivalent solutions. Not all methods are shown for all objectives.

13.2 DATA VALIDATION: PROCEDURAL APPROACH

One of the most common data analytic objectives is the evaluation of whether some categorical value is valid, with *validity* conferred by that value's membership (or lack thereof) within some pile of data.

A very abridged Game of Thrones character list should be saved to a CSV file (GOT_characters.csv):

```
Jaime Lannister
Cersei Lannister
Tyrion Lannister
Tywin Lannister
Daenerys Targaryen
Jon Snow
Sansa Stark
Arya Stark
Robb Stark
Bran Stark
```

Despite having only a single column of data, this table of unique characters constitutes a lookup table, as it contains unique master data. The following DATA step ingests the lookup table into the GOT_characters data set:

```
%let loc=d:\sas\;        * USER MUST CHANGE LOCATION *;
data got_characters;
    infile "&loc.got_characters.csv" truncover dsd
        delimiter=',';
    length charactername $30;
    format charactername $30.;
    input charactername $;
run;
```

In each of the subsequent examples in this section, the GOT_validation data set will be created, which includes all observations in the GOT_characters data set, and defines the Err variable, denoting whether the character's name is valid.

13.2.1 Hardcoded Validation

The following hardcoded DATA step is undesirable because the entire lookup table must be encoded statically after the IN operator:

```
data got_validation;
    length err 3;
    label err='Error';
    set got_favorites;
    if favcharacter ^in('Jaime Lannister',
        'Cersei Lannister','Tyrion Lannister',
        'Tywin Lannister','Daenerys Targaryen',
        'Jon Snow','Sansa Stark',
        'Arya Stark','Robb Stark','Bran Stark')
        then err=1;
run;
```

The DATA step creates the GOT_validation data set, shown in Table 13.1, in which the Err variable is initialized to 1 when the character name (Favcharacter variable) does not appear in the comma-delimited list. Note that an error is indicated in five observations. For example, some character names were entered only as a first name (e.g., Daenerys, Jaime), and other names were misspelled (e.g., Daneris, Aria). The actor Kit Harington was also listed erroneously rather than his character, Jon Snow.

	Error	Favorite Character	Favorite Season
1	.	Jaime Lannister	2
2	.	Cersei Lannister	7
3	1	Daenerys	4
4	1	Daneris	7
5	.	Daenerys Targaryen	2
6	1	Jaime	1
7	1	Kit Harington	2
8	1	Aria Stark	7
9	.	Tyrion Lannister	3
10	.	Sansa Stark	5

Table 13.1 GOT_validation Data Set

Although the solution is functional and the data set is accurate, the hardcoded methodology is not considered scalable, given the large number of characters who would need to be added to the code to represent the entire Game of Thrones cast. Moreover, changes to the list of characters, although unlikely after the series' conclusion, would require modification directly in the code. Thus, all subsequent solutions leverage the GOT_characters lookup table to facilitate this evaluation.

13.2.2 Validation with a DATA Step MERGE

If not already apparent, the relationship of the Favcharacter variable (in the GOT_favorites data set) and the GOT_characters lookup table represents a many-to-one relationship. That is, although multiple fans will have indicated the same Game of Thrones character is their favorite (within the GOT_favorites data set), each character will appear only once in the lookup table. And when SAS practitioners envision many-to-one relationships among tables, we instinctively turn to the trusted twosome—the DATA step MERGE and the SQL procedure JOIN.

The MERGE statement requires that the data sets being joined are either sorted or indexed by the BY variable(s). Thus, the following two SORT procedures and single DATA step generate the GOT_validation data set:

```
proc sort data=got_characters out=got_characters_sorted;
   by charactername;
run;
```

```
proc sort data=got_favorites out=got_favorites_sorted;
    by favcharacter;
run;

data got_validation;
    length err 3;
    label err='Error';
    merge got_favorites_sorted (in=a)
        got_characters_sorted (in=b
        rename=(charactername=favcharacter));
    by favcharacter;
    if a;
    if ^b then err=1;
run;
```

GOT_validation is identical to the data set shown in Table 13.1, with the exception that it is now sorted alphabetically by the Favcharacter variable. If this reordering is not desired, the original order will need to be preserved in the GOT_favorites data set. Although still common, these SORT-SORT-JOIN dalliances have fallen from favor in the past decades where comparable SQL statement joins, hash object lookups, and other methods can elicit the same functionality sans sorting. Indexing presents another viable alternative, as it can eliminate the need to sort data sets prior to the MERGE statement.

The indexing of a lookup table is demonstrated in Section 13.5

13.2.3 Validation with a SQL Procedure JOIN

As discussed in the previous subsection, the SQL procedure is commonly utilized to join data sets, including when data from a lookup table must be accessed. The following SQL procedure generates the GOT_validation data set:

```
proc sql;
    create table got_validation (drop=charactername) as
    select input(coalesce(got_characters.charactername,
            '1'), 3.) as err label 'Error', * from
            got_favorites
        left join got_characters on
```

```
      got_favorites.favcharacter =
      got_characters.charactername;
quit;
```

GOT_validation is identical to the data set shown in Table 13.1, with the exception that it is now sorted alphabetically by the Favcharacter variable, as also occurred with the previous DATA step MERGE method.

Comparisons are often drawn between the SQL JOIN and the DATA step MERGE, with many SAS practitioners firmly advocating for one over the other. For example, although some users may view the single SQL procedure as a slicker alternative, others criticize that readability can suffer where complex joins and other transformations are jumbled. In the end, the decision to use one method over the other often comes down to a mix of performance and personal preference.

13.2.4 Validation with a Macro List

The prior methods to validate a data set (using a lookup table) have not relied on the SAS macro language. However, a SAS practitioner with basic macro familiarity might see an opportunity in which the comma-delimited list of names (in Section 13.2.1) could be replaced with a macro variable.

This technique is inadvisable because it unnecessarily converts a SAS data set, a built-in data structure, into a macro list, a less desirable user-defined data structure. Notwithstanding, this ubiquitous technique is demonstrated solely so it can be avoided like the anathema it is.

User-defined macro lists are introduced in Section 10.2, and Section 11.1 demonstrates the successful weaning off macro lists in favor of control tables

The SQL procedure can be used to initialize &CHARACTERLIST to a comma-delimited list of Charactername values, after which the character list is interpolated into the DATA step after the IN operator:

```
proc sql noprint;
   select quote(strip(charactername)) into :
      character_list separated by ','
   from got_characters;
quit;
data got_validation;
   length err 3;
   label err='Error';
   set got_favorites;
   if favcharacter^in(&character_list) then err=1;
run;
```

The DATA step creates the identical GOT_validation data set shown in Table 13.1, and the original order of GOT_favorites is preserved. However, because of the unnecessary reliance on the macro list, this method is not recommended for most lookup tables, given the variability of data that could exist within data set values, such as unmatched quotes and other special characters. Moreover, far superior lookup methods exist.

13.2.5 Validation with a SAS Array

SAS arrays are introduced in Section 10.1, and temporary arrays are repeatedly demonstrated throughout Section 11.2

SAS arrays offer an efficient method to query a lookup table, in which the entire lookup table is *preloaded* into the array before the primary data set is read. This method requires two SET statements, and a DO loop must initialize the array. SAS temporary arrays (denoted with the _TEMPORARY_ option) are especially well-suited for lookup operations because they are automatically retained across all observations, and are automatically deleted when the DATA step terminates.

Temporary arrays must be dimensioned with a constant, so the number of observations in the lookup table must be assessed prior to the DATA step that declares an array. Thus, the following SQL procedure initializes the &NOBS macro variable to the number of observations in GOT_characters, after which the DATA step performs the lookup:

```
proc sql noprint;
    select count(*) into : nobs
        from got_characters;
quit;

data got_validation (drop=i charactername);
    length err 3;
    label err='Error';
    if _n_=1 then do;
        i=0;
        array arrkey[&nobs] $30 _temporary_;
        do until(eof);
            i=i+1;
            set got_characters end=eof;
            arrkey[i]=charactername;
            end;
        end;
```

```
    set got_favorites;
    if favcharacter ^in arrkey then err=1;
    output;
run;
```

The DATA step creates the identical GOT_validation data set shown in Table 13.1, and the original order of GOT_favorites is preserved. Readability is one potential downside to this method, given the complexity of having to declare and initialize the array through *external iteration* mechanics. The bulk of this DATA step is consumed with array functionality while the evaluation (of Favcharacter against the lookup table) occupies only one line:

External iteration is introduced in Section 5.2.2, and *internal iteration* in Section 5.2.1

```
    if favcharacter ^in arrkey then err=1;
```

Moreover, reusability is diminished because one array must be declared for each lookup table variable that needs to be either evaluated or returned. So, once your lookup objective extends beyond only validation and begins to encompass cleaning, transformation, or categorization, multiple arrays will need to be declared and initialized. This is by no means a poor solution, as it performs well, but it is neither a flexible nor especially readable solution. Finally, note that the array is destroyed when the DATA step terminates, so it must be recreated within each successive DATA step.

13.2.6 Validation with a DATA Step Hash Object

Hash objects also support the validation of data within a lookup table, and offer somewhat sleeker syntax than the preceding array-based approach. Hash leverages in-memory processing, and because the hash object inherently iterates the lookup table being loaded into memory, no loop or external iteration is required (as is the case with array initialization).

The DATASET option in the DECLARE statement indicates that the GOT_characters data set is being loaded into memory (as the lookup table). In general, hash objects store key-value pairs, and are used to lookup a key and return an associated non-key value; however, as discussed, a hash object can also store *only* a list of keys, in which case it only evaluates whether some value is found in those keys. Thus, the DEFINEKEY method denotes Charactername as the key, but no DEFINEDATA method is required. This pattern is common when either validating or counting keys.

The following DATA step instantiates a hash object that is subsequently queried using the CHECK method to evaluate value validity:

```
data got_validation (drop = rc charactername);
   length err 3 charactername $30;
   label err='Error';
   set got_favorites;
   if _n_ = 1 then do;
      declare hash h(dataset: 'got_characters');
      rc = h.defineKey('charactername');
      rc = h.defineDone();
      call missing(charactername);
      end;
   err=ifn(h.check(key: favcharacter)=0,.,1);
run;
```

Some OOP concepts are discussed in relation to data-driven design in Section 8.4, but OOP *methods* lie beyond the scope of this text

Some disadvantages of instantiating a hash object within the DATA step are overcome in Section 13.3.3, in which FCMP hash objects are demonstrated

The DATA step creates the identical GOT_validation data set shown in Table 13.1, and the original order of GOT_favorites is preserved. Hash objects are favored as an extremely efficient, in-memory lookup solution—after all, they live to lookup. Notwithstanding their stellar credentials, hash adoption by SAS practitioners has been measured at best. After all, many even skilled SAS users may be unfamiliar with *methods* as they are defined and utilized throughout the object-oriented programming (OOP) world. Despite the subtle complexity (or novelty, to some), hash and her indefatigable methods should not be overlooked.

One of the only performance drawbacks to hash can occur when large lookup tables need to be loaded, and when lookups must recur across multiple DATA steps. The hash object, as instantiated within a DATA step, is but chaff in the wind, and like SAS arrays, is deleted when the DATA step terminates. Thus, albeit running efficiently for a single usage, multiple successive calls to the same hash object across multiple DATA steps will require the hash object to be built, destroyed, and rebuilt repeatedly—and for sufficiently large lookup tables, this can unnecessarily delay processing.

13.3 DATA VALIDATION: FUNCTIONAL APPROACH

Validation methods thus far have demonstrated a *procedural* as opposed to a *functional* approach, in that the lookup functionality was generated through multiple statements, and in the case of the DATA step MERGE, even multiple procedures. This is not to say that the array and hash solutions do not demonstrate data-driven design; however, where complex code is required to perform some operation, that operation is inherently less flexible and less likely to be reused, and this can diminish the quality of the software being developed.

Thus, the remaining three solutions also demonstrate data-driven design, but additionally take a *functional* approach, in which the entire validity operation occurs within a single statement and line of code. Not only does this embody simpler, more readable syntax, but these callable operations are more likely to persist than to be discarded.

13.3.1 Validation with a User-Defined Format

User-defined formats and informats can be used to validate data, in which case a lookup table is loaded into memory and accessed by applying the format or informat. The creation of user-defined formats requires a preliminary DATA step followed by the FORMAT procedure. However, these steps must be run only once, after which the user-defined format can operate in perpetuity.

The following DATA step reads the lookup table (GOT_characters, defined in Section 13.2), after which the FORMAT procedure creates the CHARNAME format using the CNTLIN option:

```
data charformat;
   set got_characters (rename=(charactername=start))
      end=eof;
   length label 8 fmtname $32 type $1 hlo $1;
   label=.;
   fmtname='charname';
   type='c';    * denotes a character format;
   hlo='';
   output;
   if eof then do;
      start='';
      label=1;
      hlo='o'; * denotes other value;
      output;
      end;
run;


proc format library=work cntlin=charformat;
run;
```

The key variable (in the lookup table) must be represented by the Start variable. The Label variable specifies that all values found in the lookup table will return a missing value, whereas all values not found in the lookup table will return a value of 1. The Type value "C" denotes the character format. Start, Label, and Type are required by the subsequent CNTLIN option (in the FORMAT procedure), and thus cannot be renamed.

With the CHARNAME format now defined, the following DATA step evaluates the GOT_favorites data set, and initializes Err by applying the CHARNAME format:

```
data got_validation;
    length err 3;
    label err='Error';
    set got_favorites;
    err=input(put(favcharacter,$charname.),3.);
run;
```

The DATA step creates the identical GOT_validation data set shown in Table 13.1, and the original order of GOT_favorites is preserved. Note the advantage in that the single line of code in which Err is initialized performs the entire lookup! No need to sort data sets, or join data sets, or write a dozen lines of array-based loops and other statements. Thus, pivotal to data-driven design, the user-defined format hides all complexity within the format definition.

And because all logic that evaluates validity is contained within the GOT_characters lookup table, if new characters need to be added, removed, or modified, the lookup table can be changed, after which the FORMAT procedure can be rerun, and the user-defined format will have been updated and be synchronized with the lookup table it represents. User-defined formats also have the advantage that they can be reused *across* DATA steps, unlike both SAS arrays and hash objects, which are discarded.

13.3.2 Validation Missteps with a User-Defined Function

User-defined functions, created with PROC FCMP, are introduced in Section 3.6.2

User-defined functions are a versatile solution for transforming data while hiding complexity in the function's definition. This benefits the end user (calling the function) because no complex code must be scoured, and it benefits the developers (designing and maintaining the function) because they can make modifications when necessary to either improve the function's performance or extend its functionality. That is, user-defined functions beautifully model procedural abstraction, and are a win-win-win where they additionally espouse data-driven design.

But...and this is a big *but*...perhaps the biggest *but* of all...not all procedural abstraction incorporates data-driven design, and moreover, the performance of a function will be hideous if it be hideously designed and implemented.

Consider the contemptuously craptastic user-defined function CHARACTER_VALID_BAD, which similarly evaluates the validity of a character's name against the Game of Thrones lookup table:

Section 6.1 describes how procedural abstraction does not, in and of itself, denote data-driven design

```
* returns . if valid, 1 if invalid;
proc fcmp outlib=sasuser.myfuncs.got;
    function character_valid_bad(character $);
        if character in('Jaime Lannister',
            'Cersei Lannister','Tyrion Lannister',
            'Tywin Lannister','Daenerys Targaryen',
            'Jon Snow','Sansa Stark',
            'Arya Stark','Robb Stark','Bran Stark')
        then return(.);
        else return(1);
        endfunc;
quit;
```

Lies! The function does *not* reference the GOT_character lookup table! Instead, it statically enumerates the characters contained within the lookup table, mimicking the poor, hardcoded logic shown in Section 13.2.1.

The OPTIONS statement tells SAS where to find this abominable function, after which it is called in the following DATA step:

```
options cmplib=sasuser.myfuncs;


data got_validation;
    length err 3;
    label err='Error';
    set got_favorites;
    err=character_valid_bad(favcharacter);
run;
```

The DATA step creates the identical GOT_validation data set shown in Table 13.1, and the original order of GOT_favorites is preserved. And the invocation even looks slick—like the CHARACTER_VALID_BAD developer might have known what he was doing—and owing to this slickness, you might decide to continue using and reusing this user-defined function while never peeking under the covers to see if you really ought to be in bed with CHARACTER_VALID_BAD in the first place!

And herein lies perhaps the greatest albatross of procedural abstraction—that poorly designed logic can be stowed away behind the shiny trappings of a user-defined macro, function, or subroutine, only to vex users with subpar performance or faulty functionality. Careful inspection of a user-defined function's implementation is often warranted before usage, and especially where the function's origins or originators are questionable or unknown.

> The *procedural implementation* is introduced in Section 3.3, including the importance of aptly documenting functionality

13.3.3 Validation with an FCMP Function Hash Object

Section 13.2.6 lauded over the implementation of the hash object within the DATA step as an efficient lookup method, but noted the unfortunate complexity that it added to the DATA step. This complexity can be hidden, however, by encasing the hash object instantiation and logic within a user-defined function, which yields the best of both data-driven design and procedural abstraction.

For reference, the previous DATA step defines the hash object directly:

```
data got_validation (drop = rc charactername);
    length err 3 charactername $30;
    label err='Error';
    set got_favorites;
    if _n_ = 1 then do;
        declare hash h(dataset: 'got_characters');
        rc = h.defineKey('charactername');
        rc = h.defineDone();
        call missing(charactername);
        end;
    err=ifn(h.check(key: favcharacter)=0,.,1);
run;
```

A preferred solution hides hash complexity, and the following FCMP procedure now defines the CHARACTER_VALID function, which instantiates the hash object to perform the validity check:

```
proc fcmp outlib=sasuser.myfuncs.got;
   function character_valid(charactername $);
      declare hash h(dataset: 'got_characters');
      rc = h.defineKey('charactername');
      rc = h.defineDone();
      err=h.check();
      return(ifn(h.check()=0,.,1));
      endfunc;
quit;
```

Note that the hash declaration, hash key definition, and CHECK method are virtually unchanged. Moreover, the DO block is no longer required because the instantiation occurs inside FCMP.

The function is called in the following DATA step:

```
options cmplib=sasuser.myfuncs;


data got_validation;
   length err 3;
   label err='Error';
   set got_favorites;
   err=character_valid(favcharacter);
run;
```

The DATA step creates the identical GOT_validation data set shown in Table 13.1, and the original order of GOT_favorites is preserved. The entire lookup operation is executed through this single function call, which is dwarfed by the prodigious code required for procedural methods like the DATA step MERGE or the SQL JOIN, demonstrated in Sections 13.2.2 and 13.2.3, respectively.

Note the caveat that the full functionality of the hash object is currently not supported by the FCMP procedure, with only 13 of 27 SAS hash methods (available in the DATA step) supported by FCMP. Thus, although simple hash functionality can be abstracted and converted to user-defined functions, a significant portion of hash functionality remains unsupported.

For example, the DATA step hash object supports the SUMINC option (in the DECLARE statement) and the SUM method, which in combination generate counts of key values, and can produce a frequency table. However, as the FCMP hash object supports neither SUMINC nor SUM, this functionality cannot be ported to a user-defined function or subroutine.

13.3.4 Validation with a Format Calling a Function

One final approach to data-driven validation is offered by a user-defined format, which can be designed to call a function—to include a user-defined function. Formats are far more syntactically promiscuous than functions, as they fit just about anywhere within SAS syntax. For example, you can format data in real-time within PRINT, MEANS, and FREQ procedures, where user-defined functions cannot operate.

With the CHARACTER_VALID user-defined function created in Section 13.3.3, a user-defined format can be designed to call this function. The FORMAT procedure defines the CHARNAME_HASH format, and the OTHER option directs all unformatted values (i.e., all values) to be processed by the CHARACTER_VALID user-defined function:

```
proc format;
   value $ charname_hash other=[character_valid()];
run;
```

Thereafter, the user-defined format can be saved and used in perpetuity. The following DATA step applies the format to the Favcharacter variable to evaluate its validity and initialize the Err variable:

```
data got_validation;
   length err 3;
   label err='Error';
   set got_favorites;
   err=input(put(favcharacter,$charname_hash.),3.);
run;
```

The DATA step creates the identical GOT_validation data set shown in Table 13.1, and the original order of GOT_favorites is preserved. At first glance, it may seem that this user-defined format poses no advantage over the hash-based method demonstrated in Section 13.3.3—after all, the CHARNAME_HASH format directly calls the CHARACTER_VALID function, so why not just skip the middleman?

As one example, consider the requirement to apply a temporary format to a variable specified by a SAS procedure like PRINT. The following PRINT procedure applies the CHARNAME_HASH format to Favcharacter only for the duration of the procedure, thus skipping a gratuitous DATA step that otherwise would have been required to apply the CHARACTER_VALID function directly to the Favcharacter variable:

```
proc print data=got_favorites;
   format favcharacter $charname_hash.;
   var favcharacter;
run;
```

Thus, the PRINT procedure can temporarily leverage the CHARNAME_HASH format to produce more readable or desirable output, yet the underlying GOT_favorites data set does not need to have this format permanently applied to its data.

Other incredulous users might contemplate whether the CHARNAME_HASH format is different than the user-defined format already demonstrated in Section 13.3.1—in fact, it is. More precisely, in this straightforward case of a one-to-one mapping, the two user-defined formats are identical. However, the advantage of user-defined formats that call user-defined functions is the power of the function—not just to perform table lookups, but also to evaluate complex logic statements. Thus, entire decision tables could be abstracted within a user-defined function, yet effortlessly called and applied using an associated user-defined format.

13.4 DATA CLEANING

Data validation, in the strictest sense, often evaluates only whether data are valid—it does not necessarily act to replace, update, or correct invalid data. Thus, in Sections 13.2 and 13.3, the validation of categorical values seeks to determine only whether those values appear in a list or lookup table containing the set of all valid values. Correspondingly, the result or return value of a validation operation is often a *return code*—a Boolean representing either validity or invalidity.

Data cleaning, however, may also validate data, but moreover transforms those data, where prescribed, into valid values. Thus, whereas data validation evaluates data to elicit a status, data cleaning aims to transform data. Especially where numeric data are being cleaned, data quality rules and business rules may drive complex logic that cleans data algorithmically, and where numeric data are missing or invalid, data imputation can generate replacement data to be used in their stead.

Character data are sometimes cleaned through natural language processing (NLP) and other veins of artificial intelligence (AI) that seek to automate and replace complex cleaning and standardization models that once could only have been built by hand. Notwithstanding these technological advances, significant quantities of data are still cleaned through logic that leverages key-value indexing to detect the presence of a key and return the transformed, standardized, or valid representation thereof. These methods remain practical for categorical data, and especially where data models need to prescribe precisely what values should be used to replace specific invalid values.

For example, within the GOT_favorites data set created in Section 13.1, Daenerys Targaryen (i.e., one entity) is represented three different ways, with the first two values representing invalid data:

```
Daenerys,4
Daneris,7
Daenerys Targaryen,2
```

Data mappings and *multimaps* are defined and introduced in the context of SAS formats in Section 4.3.1

The correct spelling (Daenerys Targaryen) already appears in the GOT_characters lookup table, created in Section 13.2, and can be used to validate that the first two values are incorrect. However, by adding the two invalid values to the lookup table, and mapping them to the correct spelling, a *data mapping*—a many-to-one *multimap*—can be created to drive *entity resolution*. That is, when a cleaning function encounters an invalid value, it can query a lookup table, and return the standardized or valid spelling of Daenerys Targaryen.

An updated data model (GOT_characters_model.csv) now includes two columns—the first representing the valid character names, and the second representing known spelling variations thereof:

```
Jaime Lannister,Jaime Lannister
,Jaime
Cersei Lannister,Cersei Lannister
Tyrion Lannister,Tyrion Lannister
,Tyrion
Tywin Lannister,Tywin Lannister
Daenerys Targaryen,Daenerys Targaryen
```

```
,Daenerys
,Daneris
Jon Snow,Jon Snow
Sansa Stark,Sansa Stark
Arya Stark,Arya Stark
,Aria Stark
Robb Stark,Robb Stark
Bran Stark,Bran Stark
```

Note that where values in the first column are missing, this represents a continuation from the previous non-missing value. For example, in the second observation, Jaime is mapped to Jaime Lannister, who is listed in the first observation as a valid entry. This data structure is sometimes referred to as a *multimap*—a many-to-one relationship between entity variations and the unique entities they represent.

The following DATA step ingests GOT_characters_model.csv to create the GOT_characters_model data set:

```
%let loc=d:\sas\;        * USER MUST CHANGE LOCATION *;
data GOT_characters_model;
    infile "&loc.GOT_characters_model.csv" truncover dsd
        delimiter=',';
    length charactername $30 name_raw $40;
    format charactername $30. name_raw $40.;
    label charactername='GOT Character'
        name_raw='Raw Character';
    input charactername $ name_raw;
run;
```

The GOT_characters_model lookup table is shown in Table 13.2, with unique *valid* character names appearing in the GOT Character column, and unique *raw* character names appearing in the Raw Character column. This format, in which keys are not displayed where they represent a carryover from the previous non-missing observation, is arguably more readable, but is more commonly applied when displaying relational data—for example, those linked between or among tables—or hierarchical data.

In a relational sense, when columns are displayed in this format, some columns could be represented as the primary key of their own tables. For example, the Charactername value (in the GOT Character column) could

	GOT Character	Raw Character
1	Jaime Lannister	Jaime Lannister
2		Jaime
3	Cersei Lannister	Cersei Lannister
4	Tyrion Lannister	Tyrion Lannister
5		Tyrion
6	Tywin Lannister	Tywin Lannister
7	Daenerys Targaryen	Daenerys Targaryen
8		Daenerys
9		Daneris
10	Jon Snow	Jon Snow
11	Sansa Stark	Sansa Stark
12	Arya Stark	Arya Stark
13		Aria Stark
14	Robb Stark	Robb Stark
15	Bran Stark	Bran Stark

Table 13.2 GOT_characters_model Data Model

represent a lookup table queried by the Name_raw value (in the Raw Character column) to determine whether Name_raw values were valid.

Normalization describes this process of segmenting columns of data into separate tables, with tables indexed by primary keys and referenced via foreign keys held in other tables or by processes. A typical objective of normalization reduces data redundancy by enforcing unique primary keys, and thus minimizes the volume of data that must be maintained and stored.

Normalization also can eliminate invalid data that result from data entry errors or computational errors. For example, the intentionally missing values in Table 13.2 are incorruptible so long as they remain missing. However, if the end user maintaining the CSV file instead were required to duplicate Jaime Lannister across both the first and second observations, this duplication would increase not only data storage but also risk, with the potential for the second Jaime Lannister to be misspelled.

Denormalization, on the other hand, describes the process of representing inter-table relationships within a single table, and may logically aggregate multiple tables (that had been previously normalized into separate tables). Denormalization is commonly required for analytic purposes, in which multiple characteristics, attributes, or columns must appear in a single row to support some multivariate evaluation.

With respect to lookup tables and data-driven design, denormalization can also be required to construct key-value pairs that facilitate data cleaning, classification, and other data transformation. For example, I can infer from Table 13.2 that the value Jamie should map to Jaime Lannister because I can readily visualize this connection. However, a process evaluating only the second observation in this data set would find only a missing value in the Charactername variable, and the key-value pair between Jamie and Jaime Lannister could not be defined.

For this reason, a more *denormalized* representation of GOT_characters_model can be created by retaining (and thus duplicating) the values for Charactername across observations. The following DATA step ingests and denormalizes GOT_characters_model.csv:

```
data GOT_characters_lookup (drop=oldname);
   retain oldname;
   infile "&loc.GOT_characters_model.csv" truncover dsd
      delimiter=',';
   length charactername $30 name_raw $40;
   format charactername $30. name_raw $40.;
   label charactername='GOT Character'
      name_raw='Raw Character';
   input charactername $ name_raw;
   if missing(charactername) then charactername=oldname;
   else oldname=charactername;
run;
```

Note that the RETAIN statement retains the value of Charactername from one observation to the next, and is used to initialize Charactername to the last non-missing value (observed in preceding observations).

The denormalized lookup table is demonstrated in Table 13.3, with Charactername no longer missing from any observations. Thus, Charactername can no longer be used as a key (unless first deduplicated), so Name_raw becomes the *key*, and Charactername the *value* to be leveraged (or returned) by data cleaning lookup operations.

In the next few subsections, various methods for cleaning and transforming data are demonstrated, each of which leverages GOT_characters_lookup. Only *functional* data-driven approaches are

	GOT Character	Raw Character
1	Jaime Lannister	Jaime Lannister
2	Jaime Lannister	Jaime
3	Cersei Lannister	Cersei Lannister
4	Tyrion Lannister	Tyrion Lannister
5	Tyrion Lannister	Tyrion
6	Tywin Lannister	Tywin Lannister
7	Daenerys Targaryen	Daenerys Targaryen
8	Daenerys Targaryen	Daenerys
9	Daenerys Targaryen	Daneris
10	Jon Snow	Jon Snow
11	Sansa Stark	Sansa Stark
12	Arya Stark	Arya Stark
13	Arya Stark	Aria Stark
14	Robb Stark	Robb Stark
15	Bran Stark	Bran Stark

Table 13.3 GOT_characters_lookup Denormalized Lookup Table

represented, as contrasted with the slew of *procedural* approaches demonstrated under Section 13.2. However, a single hardcoded method first demonstrates the functional data cleaning objectives being pursued.

13.4.1 Hardcoded Cleaning

Although undesirable, values can be cleaned and transformed through hardcoded logic. For example, the following DATA step applies the logic implied in the GOT_characters_lookup table (demonstrated in Table 13.3), albeit operationalized through IF-THEN conditional statements, to clean the Favcharacter variable in the GOT_favorites data set:

```
data got_cleaning;
   set got_favorites;
   if favcharacter in('Jaime Lannister','Jaime')
      then favcharacter='Jaime Lannister';
   else if favcharacter in('Cersei Lannister')
      then favcharacter='Cersei Lannister';
   else if favcharacter in('Tyrion Lannister','Tyrion')
      then favcharacter='Tyrion Lannister';
   else if favcharacter in('Tywin Lannister')
```

```
   then favcharacter='Tywin Lannister';
else if favcharacter
   in('Daenerys Targaryen','Daenerys','Daneris')
   then favcharacter='Daenerys Targaryen';
else if favcharacter in('Jon Snow')
   then favcharacter='Jon Snow';
else if favcharacter in('Sansa Stark')
   then favcharacter='Sansa Stark';
else if favcharacter in('Arya Stark','Aria Stark')
   then favcharacter='Arya Stark';
else if favcharacter in('Robb Stark')
   then favcharacter='Robb Stark';
else if favcharacter in('Bran Stark')
   then favcharacter='Bran Stark';
run;
```

Note that although all values within GOT_characters_lookup are represented in the logic statements, not all need to be. For example, a statement that "transforms" Cersei Lannister into Cersei Lannister is doing nothing, save showcasing her vanity.

Thus, with these extraneous statements removed, the preceding DATA step can be refactored to be more concise, yet provide identical functionality:

```
data got_cleaning;
   set got_favorites;
   if favcharacter in('Jaime')
      then favcharacter='Jaime Lannister';
   else if favcharacter in('Tyrion')
      then favcharacter='Tyrion Lannister';
   else if favcharacter in('Daenerys','Daneris')
      then favcharacter='Daenerys Targaryen';
   else if favcharacter in('Aria Stark')
      then favcharacter='Arya Stark';
run;
```

Each of the functionally equivalent DATA steps creates the identical GOT_cleaning data set, shown in Table 13.4. Although the second method is both faster and more efficient, owing to the loss of useless logic

	Favorite Character	Favorite Season
1	Jaime Lannister	2
2	Cersei Lannister	7
3	Daenerys Targaryen	4
4	Daenerys Targaryen	7
5	Daenerys Targaryen	2
6	Jaime Lannister	1
7	Kit Harington	2
8	Arya Stark	7
9	Tyrion Lannister	3
10	Sansa Stark	5

Table 13.4 GOT_cleaning Data Set

statements, only the first method can be extended to perform data validation in addition to cleaning.

For example, the following DATA step again lists all values of Favcharacter—both valid and invalid—and in doing so, can utilize a terminal ELSE statement to initialize the Err variable to denote when a rogue value (occurring outside of the data model) is encountered:

```
data got_cleaning_and_validation;
   length err 3;
   label err='Error';
   set got_favorites;
   if favcharacter in('Jaime Lannister','Jaime')
      then favcharacter='Jaime Lannister';
   else if favcharacter in('Cersei Lannister')
      then favcharacter='Cersei Lannister';
   else if favcharacter in('Tyrion Lannister','Tyrion')
      then favcharacter='Tyrion Lannister';
   else if favcharacter in('Tywin Lannister')
      then favcharacter='Tywin Lannister';
   else if favcharacter
      in('Daenerys Targaryen','Daenerys','Daneris')
      then favcharacter='Daenerys Targaryen';
   else if favcharacter in('Jon Snow')
      then favcharacter='Jon Snow';
```

```
    else if favcharacter in('Sansa Stark')
       then favcharacter='Sansa Stark';
    else if favcharacter in('Arya Stark','Aria Stark')
       then favcharacter='Arya Stark';
    else if favcharacter in('Robb Stark')
       then favcharacter='Robb Stark';
    else if favcharacter in('Bran Stark')
       then favcharacter='Bran Stark';
    else err=1;
run;
```

The GOT_cleaning_and_validation data set is demonstrated in Table 13.5, and additionally demonstrates the Err variable. Thus, when Kit Harington, who does not appear in the GOT_characters_lookup lookup table, is evaluated, the invalid value is unchanged, although the Err variable is set to 1 to denote invalid data that could not be cleaned. This two-in-one cleaning and validation functionality is efficient because it requires only one pass through the lookup table to both clean and validate.

Also note that the data are being cleaned *in situ*, in which the Favcharacter value itself is being overwritten. This saves storage space because the invalid value is permanently deleted; however, overwriting also eliminates the possibility to recover the original value, where the transformation modified the raw value. Thus, for many purposes, rather

In Section 13.5, rather than cleaning Favcharacter *in situ*, a new variable is initialized with the cleaned value to preserve the raw value

	Error	Favorite Character	Favorite Season
1	.	Jaime Lannister	2
2	.	Cersei Lannister	7
3	.	Daenerys Targaryen	4
4	.	Daenerys Targaryen	7
5	.	Daenerys Targaryen	2
6	.	Jaime Lannister	1
7	1	Kit Harington	2
8	.	Arya Stark	7
9	.	Tyrion Lannister	3
10	.	Sansa Stark	5

Table 13.5 GOT_cleaning_and_validation Data Set

than overwriting Favcharacter, the conditional logic would need to initialize a new variable to the cleaned value.

The next few subsections demonstrate various data-driven methods that leverage the GOT_characters_lookup table to recreate the GOT_cleaning data set. One of the advantages of these more dynamic methods is the ability to clean data either by overwriting the original value or by initializing a new variable to the transformed value. That is, not only are these methods reusable, but their invocation is far more flexible than the undesirable hardcoded methods demonstrated in this subsection.

13.4.2 Cleaning Rogue and Missing Values

When transforming data with a multimap lookup table, *rogue* values (i.e., values not appearing as keys within the lookup table) will often be encountered in a data set being analyzed. When this occurs, the operation leveraging the lookup table must return or generate *some* value—even a missing or Null value—and this choice represents a common design consideration for data cleaning and other transformation functionality.

For example, throughout Sections 13.2 and 13.3, invalid data were represented consistently as a 1, and valid data as a missing value. However, each of the functionally equivalent validation solutions instead could have been designed to return a 1 to represent valid data and a 0 to represent invalid data. SAS practitioners can select whatever symbology makes sense, including whether to return character or numeric data.

Throughout Section 13.4, Kit Harington is "cleaned" by retaining this value, whereas throughout Section 13.5, this rogue value is "cleaned" by deleting it

However, when the lookup table objective shifts from validation to transformation, the design of return values for missing and rogue input is more critical and has a greater impact on how transformation operations can be called. For example, when encountering a rogue value like Kit Harington, who appears in the GOT_favorites data set (created in Section 13.1), SAS practitioners must decide whether to retain the rogue value or to initialize the new transformed variable to a missing value.

If rogue values are retained after some cleaning operation has occurred, then care must be exercised to communicate that the results of the cleaning operation are not necessarily *clean* data, but only *cleaner* data—that is, the sentiment representing "We've done all we can do at this point." In other cases, the rogue value is deleted (or its new variable initialized to missing) to ensure that subsequent, dependent operations do not accidentally attempt to transform an invalid value. And especially where user-defined functions may be daisy-chained in series, where a cleaning function might precede a transformation function, each function must understand the specific input and output criteria of the others.

13.4.3 Cleaning with a User-Defined Format

Leveraging a lookup table to create a user-defined format is demonstrated in Section 13.3.1, in which a format is used to validate whether a value appears in the lookup table. User-defined formats can also be constructed to clean data, in which case they do not return a Boolean representing validity, but rather a transformed version of the value itself. That is, cleaning functions more typically generate a *return value* than a *return code*.

Return values and *return codes* are defined in Sections 6.8.1 and 6.8.2, respectively

The following DATA step creates the Charclean data set from the GOT_characters_lookup table (created in Section 13.4), which the FORMAT procedure converts to a user-defined format using CNTLIN:

```
data charclean;
   set got_characters_lookup (rename=
      (name_raw=start charactername=label));
   fmtname='charclean';
   type='c';          * denotes character format
run;


proc format library=work cntlin=charclean;
run;
```

Thereafter, the DATA step applies the CHARCLEAN format to transform the Favcharacter variable:

```
data got_cleaning;
   set got_favorites;
   favcharacter=put(favcharacter,$charclean.);
run;
```

The GOT_cleaning data set that is created is identical to the data set shown in Table 13.4. However, now improved by data-driven design, the DATA step is uncluttered because the complex logic that transforms Favcharacter has been hidden inside the format's definition.

Moreover, CHARCLEAN can be applied to initialize a new variable:

```
data got_cleaning;
   length new_var $30;
```

```
    set got_favorites;
    new_var=put(favcharacter,$charclean.);
run;
```

This alternative GOT_cleaning data set (not shown) now depicts both the original (raw) and transformed (cleaned) versions of the Favcharacter variable, thus demonstrating the flexibility in which user-defined formats and user-defined functions can be applied.

13.4.4 Cleaning with an FCMP Function Hash Object

Leveraging a lookup table to create a user-defined function using the FCMP procedure is demonstrated in Section 13.3.2, in which a hash object is used to validate whether a value appears in the lookup table. In this section, the user-defined function is modified to instead return the transformed value rather than a Boolean representing validity or lack thereof.

The CHARACTER_CLEAN function reads GOT_characters_lookup (created in Section 13.4) into the hash object, and now requires the DEFINEKEY method to define Name_raw as the *key*, and the DEFINEDATA method to define Charactername as the *value* in the key-value pair.

The FIND method returns the cleaned value of the Game of Thrones character name, and if a rogue value is encountered (that does not appear within the data model, either as a valid or invalid value), then the raw value is returned. This necessitates the two RETURN statements within the FCMP procedure.

The following FCMP procedure defines the CHARACTER_CLEAN user-defined function:

```
proc fcmp outlib=sasuser.myfuncs.got;
    function character_clean(name_raw $) $;
        length charactername $30;
        declare hash h(dataset: 'got_characters_lookup');
        rc = h.defineKey('name_raw');
        rc = h.defineData('charactername');
        rc = h.defineDone();
        rc = h.find();
        if rc=0 then return(charactername);
        else return(name_raw);
        endfunc;
    quit;
```

Thereafter, the DATA step invokes CHARACTER_CLEAN to transform the Favcharacter variable:

```
data got_cleaning;
   set got_favorites;
   favcharacter=character_clean(favcharacter);
run;
```

The GOT_cleaning data set that is created is identical to the data set shown in Table 13.4.

13.4.5 Cleaning with a Format Calling a Function

Leveraging a lookup table to create a user-defined format (derived from a function) is demonstrated in Section 13.3.4, in which the FORMAT procedure uses the OTHER option to call a user-defined format. This method can be expanded to create a user-defined format that cleans—rather than validates—some value.

The CHARCLEAN_HASH format is defined using the FORMAT procedure, and calls the CHARACTER_CLEAN function, created in Section 13.4.4:

```
proc format;
   value $ charclean_hash other=[character_clean()];
run;
```

Thereafter, CHARCLEAN_HASH can be applied, either *in situ* or to initialize a new variable, to transform the raw Game of Thrones characters to cleaned values:

```
data got_cleaning;
   set got_favorites;
   favcharacter=put(favcharacter, $charclean_hash.);
run;
```

Thus, despite its modest appearance, the CHARCLEAN_HASH format boasts the stellar functionality of the CHARACTER_CLEAN function, which leverages a hash object for in-memory lookup.

Moreover, because formats can be applied in ways that functions cannot, CHARCLEAN_HASH can be applied inside SAS procedures. For example, the following PRINT procedure temporarily transforms the Favcharacter variable by relying on CHARCLEAN_HASH:

```
proc print data=got_favorites;
    format favcharacter $charclean_hash30.;
    var favcharacter;
run;
```

Thus, for some use cases, a user-defined format may have more flexibility and utility than the functionally equivalent user-defined function that it calls. This flexibility does come at a cost, however, as user-defined formats that call user-defined functions can run several times slower than calling those functions directly.

13.5 DATA CLASSIFICATION (CATEGORIZATION)

A third objective of lookup tables facilitates the classification, categorization, or "binning" of data, in which values are aggregated into higher-level groups. Data cleaning (discussed throughout Section 13.4) and data classification both represent data transformation that abstracts data to a higher level; however, *cleaning* performs entity resolution by standardizing variations of a single entity, whereas *classification* aggregates separate entities based on some superordinate characteristic they share. Despite the subtle shift in focus, both cleaning and classification often can rely on identical transformation methods.

Within the Game of Thrones empire, seven kingdoms (or regions) are described from which all characters originate. For example, the Lannister family hails from the Westerlands, as does the Targaryen family. Thus, an analysis of character region could group the Lannister and Targaryen families together in a "Westerlands" category. Classifying does not imply that Game of Thrones characters lose their individual identities, but rather that a region's name or attributes can be assigned to each character.

Data cleaning operations always should precede data classification operations. For example, Table 13.4 and Table 13.5 demonstrate that Arya Stark (originally misspelled Aria within the GOT_favorites data set) is now spelled correctly, thanks to the lookup table data model. Because the character names have already been corrected, the action of binning them into regions is simplified; only one spelling of Arya—the correct one—must be mapped to her region, the North. Had this initial cleaning not occurred, the misspelled Aria would not have been mapped to her region.

Table 13.6 demonstrates an updated data model in which a new variable (Region) has been added. Note that where multiple characters hail

	A	B	C
1	The Westerlands	Jaime Lannister	Jaime Lannister
2			Jaime
3		Cersei Lannister	Cersei Lannister
4		Tyrion Lannister	Tyrion Lannister
5			Tyrion
6		Tywin Lannister	Tywin Lannister
7		Daenerys Targaryen	Daenerys Targaryen
8			Daenerys
9			Daneris
10	The North	Jon Snow	Jon Snow
11		Sansa Stark	Sansa Stark
12		Arya Stark	Arya Stark
13			Aria Stark
14		Robb Stark	Robb Stark
15		Bran Stark	Bran Stark

Table 13.6 Game of Thrones Lookup Table (GOT_regions_model.csv)

This hierarchical data model is updated in Table 15.1, in which actor name is added

from the same region, the Region variable persists (implied by empty cells) rather than being repeated. This is a common method used to represent hierarchical or relational data structures and is discussed in Section 13.4.

The Game of Thrones data model facilities entity resolution. Where character names are misspelled, truncated, or are otherwise varied but can still be identified, these variations are subsumed into a single character entity. And where characters need to be represented by their respective regions, the character entities can also be categorized into region entities. In maintaining a single lookup table to prescribe these relationships, end users need only modify one master data source, and developers writing software need only interact with one control table.

Master data are introduced in Section 8.2, in which the principle of maintaining only one copy of master data is described as the *golden record*

The following data (shown in Table 13.6) should be saved as a CSV file (GOT_regions_model.csv):

```
The Westerlands,Jaime Lannister,Jaime Lannister
,,Jaime
,Cersei Lannister,Cersei Lannister
,Tyrion Lannister,Tyrion Lannister
,,Tyrion
,Tywin Lannister,Tywin Lannister
```

```
,Daenerys Targaryen,Daenerys Targaryen
,,Daenerys
,,Daneris
The North,Jon Snow,Jon Snow
,Sansa Stark,Sansa Stark
,Arya Stark,Arya Stark
,,Aria Stark
,Robb Stark,Robb Stark
,Bran Stark,Bran Stark
```

The following DATA step ingests GOT_regions_model.csv, and creates the GOT_regions_lookup table, representing a denormalized version of the CSV file:

```
%let loc=d:\sas\;        * USER MUST CHANGE LOCATION *;
data GOT_regions_lookup (drop=oldregion oldname
        index=(region_name=(region charactername)));
    retain oldname oldregion;
    infile "&loc.GOT_regions_model.csv" truncover dsd
        delimiter=',';
    length region $30 charactername $30 name_raw $40;
    format region $30. charactername $30. name_raw $40.;
    label region='Region' charactername='GOT Character'
        name_raw='Raw Character';
    input region $ charactername $ name_raw;
    if missing(region) then region=oldregion;
    else oldregion=region;
    if missing(charactername) then
        charactername=oldname;
    else oldname=charactername;
run;
```

Note that a composite index (Region_name) is created by the DATA step INDEX option, and is required to build data maps. For example, in reviewing Table 13.6, a map from the cleaned character name to geographic region would require an unduplicated list of character names as key values. The index is later used to ensure that all keys are unique, by selecting only the first key when a key is duplicated across multiple observations. SAS indexes (including composite indexes) lie outside the scope of this text, but in this scenario, obviate having to sort the lookup table, which otherwise would have been required.

The following subsections leverage the GOT_regions_lookup table to classify the GOT_favorites data set by geographic region. Note that because the data model has been updated to include the Region variable, all previous user-defined functions and formats should be redefined to query this new model. Thereafter, so long as the model remains consistent, it can expand and contract—with greater or fewer observations—and yet require no further code modifications.

13.5.1 Hardcoded Classification

In Section 13.5, the Game of Thrones data model was updated to include the geographic origin of each character, either the Westerlands or the North, denoted by the Region variable. Section 13.1 also introduced the GOT_favorites data set, which records Game of Thrones fans' favorite character from the show. Thus, consider the requirement to map the character's region onto the GOT_favorites data set for each character.

But because the GOT_favorites data set encodes the character name as free text, the values of the Favcharacter variable first must be cleaned—with spelling variations standardized into valid character names. Thereafter, rogue values that cannot be cleaned should be expunged as invalid. Finally, cleaned character names should be mapped to their respective geographic regions. Thus, as is often the case, classifying or categorizing data is best accomplished after the data have been cleaned and validated.

The following DATA step represents a painfully hardcoded approach that cleans, validates, and classifies the GOT_favorites data set:

```
data got_class;
    length err 3 region $30 character_cleaned $30;
    label err='Error' region='Region'
        character_cleaned='GOT Character'
        favcharacter='Raw Character';
    set got_favorites;
    if favcharacter in('Jaime Lannister','Jaime')
        then do;
            character_cleaned='Jaime Lannister';
            region='The Westerlands';
```

```
        end;
    else if favcharacter in('Cersei Lannister')
        then do;
            character_cleaned='Cersei Lannister';
            region='The Westerlands';
            end;
    else if favcharacter in('Tyrion Lannister','Tyrion')
        then do;
            character_cleaned='Tyrion Lannister';
            region='The Westerlands';
            end;
    else if favcharacter in('Tywin Lannister')
        then do;
            character_cleaned='Tywin Lannister';
            region='The Westerlands';
            end;
    else if favcharacter
        in('Daenerys Targaryen','Daenerys','Daneris')
        then do;
            character_cleaned='Daenerys Targaryen';
            region='The Westerlands';
            end;
    else if favcharacter in('Jon Snow')
        then do;
            character_cleaned='Jon Snow';
            region='The North';
            end;
    else if favcharacter in('Sansa Stark')
        then do;
            character_cleaned='Sansa Stark';
            region='The North';
            end;
    else if favcharacter in('Arya Stark','Aria Stark')
        then do;
            character_cleaned='Arya Stark';
            region='The North';
```

```
        end;
    else if favcharacter in('Robb Stark')
        then do;
            character_cleaned='Robb Stark';
            region='The North';
            end;
    else if favcharacter in('Bran Stark')
        then do;
            character_cleaned='Bran Stark';
            region='The North';
            end;
        else err=1;
    run;
```

The DATA step creates the GOT_class data set, shown in Table 13.7. Note that whereas the original GOT_favorites data set only included Raw Character (Favcharacter variable) and Favorite Season (Favseason variable), not only have the character names been standardized but their respective regions have been added. Moreover, Kit Harington, who falls outside the model—because he is the *actor* who plays Jon Snow—is now shown as invalid data.

Note that GOT_class differs from GOT_cleaning_and_validation (shown in Table 13.5) in two important ways. First, the uncorrected, raw version of the character's name is now retained, whereas previously the raw data were overwritten (*in situ*) with the cleaned version; this retention can be required for auditing, or to run subsequent operations or exception

	Error	Region	GOT Character	Raw Character	Favorite Season
1	.	The Westerlands	Jaime Lannister	Jaime Lannister	2
2	.	The Westerlands	Cersei Lannister	Cersei Lannister	7
3	.	The Westerlands	Daenerys Targaryen	Daenerys	4
4	.	The Westerlands	Daenerys Targaryen	Daneris	7
5	.	The Westerlands	Daenerys Targaryen	Daenerys Targaryen	2
6	.	The Westerlands	Jaime Lannister	Jaime	1
7	1			Kit Harington	2
8	.	The North	Arya Stark	Aria Stark	7
9	.	The Westerlands	Tyrion Lannister	Tyrion Lannister	3
10	.	The North	Sansa Stark	Sansa Stark	5

Table 13.7 GOT_class Data Set

reporting. Second, because a new, cleaned version of the character's name (Character_cleaned) is initialized, where invalid data are detected (as with Kit Harington), the Character_cleaned variable will be initialized to missing.

The following subsections each recreate the GOT_class data set using data-driven design methods, including user-defined formats and user-defined functions. Both methods enable SAS practitioners to alter functionality by interacting only with this lookup table, thus obviating changes to the underlying code that interprets and operationalizes the model.

13.5.2 Classification with a User-Defined Format

Section 9.3 discusses control data persistence and the objective for only a single version of control data to be maintained as the "active" version

Now that the Game of Thrones data model has been redefined to include the Region variable, the existing definitions for the CHARNAME and CHARCLEAN user-defined formats, created in Sections 13.3.1 and 13.4.3, respectively, should be redefined to map to the updated model. This ensures that the new model remains the single source of truth, and enables the retirement of the two previous models—the GOT_characters and GOT_characters_lookup data sets.

The following DATA step and FORMAT procedure recreate the CHARCLEAN user-defined format, now leveraging the GOT_regions_lookup table:

```
data charclean;
    set got_regions_lookup (rename=
        (name_raw=start charactername=label)) end=eof;
    length fmtname $32 type $1 hlo $1;
    fmtname='charclean';
    type='c';    * denotes character format;
    hlo='';
    output;
    if eof then do;
        start='';
        label='';
        hlo='o'; *denotes other value;
        output;
        end;
    run;
```

```
proc format library=work cntlin=charclean;
run;
```

The CHARCLEAN format cleans character names by standardizing spelling discrepancies. Note that the END option (in the SET statement) is utilized to capture values that lie outside the data model, which will be assigned a missing value by the format.

The following DATA step and FORMAT procedure recreate the CHARNAME user-defined format, now leveraging the GOT_regions_lookup table:

```
data charformat(rename=(charactername=start));
    set got_regions_lookup end=eof;
    by region charactername;
    length label 8 fmtname $32 type $1 hlo $1;
    if first.charactername;
    label=.;
    fmtname='charname';
    type='c';    * denote character format;
    hlo='';
    output;
    if eof then do;
        charactername='';
        label=1;
        hlo='o'; * denotes other value;
        output;
        end;
run;


proc format library=work cntlin=charformat;
run;
```

The CHARNAME format validates character names, and can be used after the cleaning operation to detect values that appear outside the GOT_regions_lookup data model. Thus, CHARNAME returns a 1 when it detects a rogue name in the data model (such as Kit Harington).

With both the CHARCLEAN and CHARNAME user-defined formats redefined and mapped to the new lookup table (GOT_regions_lookup), the final step is to create the user-defined function to map Game of Thrones cleaned character names to their respective regions.

The following DATA step and FORMAT procedure create the CHARREGION user-defined format:

```
data charregion(rename=(charactername=start
      region=label));
   set got_regions_lookup;
   by region charactername;
   if first.charactername;
   fmtname='charregion';
   type='c';          * denotes character format;
run;


proc format library=work cntlin=charregion;
run;
```

Note that this format represents a many-to-one multimap from unique character names to their regions, and because the Charactername variable is not unique within the GOT_regions_lookup data set, the FIRST method must be utilized to select only unique character names. The FIRST method requires the BY statement, which requires the data set either be indexed or sorted, thus leveraging the index that was defined in Section 13.5 for the GOT_regions_lookup lookup table.

With the three user-defined formats now created, the following DATA step first cleans, then validates, and finally classifies Game of Thrones raw character names:

```
data got_class;
   length err 3 region $30 character_cleaned $30;
   label err='Error' region='Region'
      character_cleaned='GOT Character'
      favcharacter='Raw Character';
   set got_favorites;
   character_cleaned=put(favcharacter, $charclean.);
   err=input(put(character_cleaned, $charname.),3.);
   region=put(character_cleaned, $charregion.);
run;
```

The GOT_class data set that is created is identical to the data set shown in Table 13.7. However, it can now be updated dynamically by modifying only the lookup table (GOT_regions_lookup) from which the three user-defined formats are created. Thereafter, the code to define these formats can be rerun—requiring no modifications to the code itself—and GOT_class will be updated to reflect the revised data model.

The data-driven solution is simple and straightforward while maximizing flexibility, configurability, and maintainability—but does it do so at a performance cost? This will ultimately depend on the size and complexity of both the data set being evaluated and the lookup table representing the data model.

For example, the functionally equivalent hardcoded DATA step demonstrated in Section 13.5.1 is ugly, error-prone, compromises readability, and would be difficult to maintain; however, it requires only a single pass through the data model. Conversely, the previous DATA step effectively accesses the lookup table three times because three separate user-defined formats are applied in sequence.

Thus, when representing more complex data models, one limitation of user-defined formats is their ability to return (or resolve) only one value. A user-defined format could not, for example, evaluate the raw character name and return the cleaned name, the character's region, and a variable representing validity or lack thereof for the raw or cleaned character name.

For smaller data sets, three successive format applications will not cause performance degradation. However, if performance does become a concern where ginormous data are being processed, bear in mind that a user-defined subroutine can be engineered to update multiple variables at once—while accessing the data model only once—as demonstrated in Section 13.5.5. Also consider that procedural methods to operationalize lookup tables, as demonstrated under Section 13.2, may offer performance advantages in certain circumstances.

13.5.3 Classification with an FCMP Function Hash Object

In lieu of classifying data using user-defined formats, user-defined functions often can demonstrate equivalent—or even expanded—functionality. The CHARACTER_VALID and CHARACTER_CLEAN functions, defined in Sections 13.3.3 and 13.4.4, respectively, should be recreated so that all user-defined functions will rely on the same lookup table—GOT_regions_lookup, created in Section 13.5.

The following FCMP procedure redefines the CHARACTER_CLEAN function, which now returns a missing value when an invalid character name is detected (that does not appear as a key value in the hash object):

```
proc fcmp outlib=sasuser.myfuncs.got;
    function character_clean(name_raw $) $;
        length charactername $30;
        declare hash h(dataset: 'got_regions_lookup');
        rc = h.defineKey('name_raw');
        rc = h.defineData('charactername');
        rc = h.defineDone();
        rc = h.find();
        if rc=0 then return(charactername);
        else return('');
        endfunc;
quit;
```

Once CHARACTER_CLEAN has been used to standardize the raw character names (within the GOT_favorites data set), those cleaned values can be used as input for the subsequent two functions that validate and classify character names.

Thus, the following FCMP procedure redefines the CHARACTER_VALID function, which again returns a 1 when an invalid character name is detected:

```
proc fcmp outlib=sasuser.myfuncs.got;
    function character_valid(charactername $);
        declare hash h(dataset: 'got_regions_lookup');
        rc = h.defineKey('charactername');
        rc = h.defineDone();
        err=h.check();
        return(ifn(h.check()=0,.,1));
        endfunc;
quit;
```

The equivalent user-defined format (CHARNAME, defined in Section 13.5.2) required GOT_regions_lookup to be indexed because only unique values of the cleaned character name could be used as key values; thus, the BY statement and the FIRST method were also required in the DATA step that defined the format (for use with the CNTLIN option).

By default, however, the hash object populates the hash table with only the first unique value of each key, and discards all subsequent duplicate key values. Thus, it more readily accommodates the complexities of the GOT_regions_lookup data model, and does not require manual deduplication.

Finally, the following FCMP procedure defines a new function (CHARACTER_REGION) that returns the region of a character when passed the character's cleaned name:

```
proc fcmp outlib=sasuser.myfuncs.got;
    function character_region(charactername $) $;
        length region $30;
        declare hash h(dataset: 'got_regions_lookup');
        rc = h.defineKey('charactername');
        rc = h.defineData('region');
        rc = h.defineDone();
        rc = h.find();
        if rc=0 then return(region);
        else return('');
        endfunc;
quit;
```

Note that if the FIND method does not locate the character name in the lookup table, CHARACTER_REGION returns a missing value; in all other cases, the Region variable is returned.

The following DATA step now leverages these three user-defined functions to clean and transform the GOT_favorites data set:

```
options cmplib=sasuser.myfuncs;

data got_class;
    length err 3 region $30 character_cleaned $30;
    label err='Error' region='Region'
        character_cleaned='GOT Character'
        favcharacter='Raw Character';
    set got_favorites;
    character_cleaned=character_clean(favcharacter);
```

```
    err=character_valid(character_cleaned);
    region=character_region(character_cleaned);
run;
```

The GOT_class data set that is created is identical to the data set shown in Table 13.7; however, the DATA step performing these transformations represents flexible, maintainable data-driven design.

13.5.4 Classification with a Format Calling a Function

Leveraging a lookup table to create a user-defined format (derived from a function) is demonstrated in Section 13.3.4, in which the FORMAT procedure uses the OTHER option to call a user-defined format. This method can be replicated to create user-defined formats that clean, validate, and classify data.

The CHARCLEAN_HASH format is redefined using the FORMAT procedure, and calls the CHARACTER_CLEAN function, created in Section 13.5.3:

```
proc format;
    value $ charclean_hash other=[character_clean()];
run;
```

The CHARNAME_HASH format is redefined using the FORMAT procedure, and calls the CHARACTER_VALID function, created in Section 13.5.3:

```
proc format;
    value $ charname_hash other=[character_valid()];
run;
```

A new format (CHARREGION_HASH) is defined using the FORMAT procedure, and calls the CHARACTER_REGION function, created in Section 13.5.3:

```
proc format;
    value $ charregion_hash other=[character_region()];
run;
```

With three user-defined formats created, they can be applied similar to the usage shown in Section 13.5.2. The following DATA step applies

CHARCLEAN_HASH,   CHARNAME_HASH,   and   CHARREGION_HASH
formats to clean, validate, and classify the character name:

```
data got_class;
   length err 3 region $30 character_cleaned $30;
   label err='Error' region='Region'
      character_cleaned='GOT Character'
      favcharacter='Raw Character';
   set got_favorites;
   character_cleaned=put(favcharacter,
      $charclean_hash30.);
   err=input(put(character_cleaned,
      $charname_hash.),3.);
   region=put(character_cleaned, $charregion_hash30.);
run;
```

The GOT_class data set that is created is identical to the data set shown in Table 13.7; however, the DATA step performing these transformations represents flexible, maintainable data-driven design. Moreover, these formats, as compared with the equivalent formats created in Section 13.5.2, could have supported more complex logic, as they are derived indirectly from user-defined functions rather than directly from a lookup table (referenced by the CNTLIN option in the FORMAT procedure).

13.5.5 Classification with a User-Defined Subroutine

Although the solutions demonstrated in Sections 13.5.3, 13.5.4, and 13.5.5 represent preferred data-driven design, as discussed in Section 13.5.2, the reliance on multiple, successive calls to evaluate the same lookup table could—given sufficiently sized data—diminish performance. This occurs because each operation—cleaning, validation, and classification—requires a separate evaluation of the lookup table.

A user-defined format can only return or resolve a single value, and a user-defined function similarly only returns one value. Thus, neither method supports an operation that could query a lookup table *only once*, yet simultaneously clean the character name, assess the validity thereof, and assign the character's region as an attribute.

However, a user-defined subroutine—leveraging the *call-by-reference* (rather than *call-by-value*) argument passing method—can provide a functionally equivalent solution that combines multiple operations into one

Call by reference and *call by value* are introduced in Sections 6.5.2 and 6.5.1, respectively

callable module. Although this combination does commingle different operations, which diminishes their flexibility (because they are no longer *functionally discrete*), it nevertheless embodies data-driven design, and has the potential to improve performance.

The CHARACTER_CLEAN_VALID_REGION user-defined subroutine is created in the following FCMP procedure, which now cleans, validates, and classifies data within one callable module:

```
proc fcmp outlib=sasuser.myfuncs.got;
    subroutine character_clean_valid_region(name_raw $,
            charactername $, region $, err);
        outargs name_raw, charactername, region, err;
        length charactername $30 region $30 err 3;
        declare hash h(dataset: 'got_regions_lookup');
        rc = h.defineKey('name_raw');
        rc = h.defineData('charactername', 'region');
        rc = h.defineDone();
        rc = h.find();
        if rc^=0 then do;
            charactername='';
            region='';
            err=1;
            end;
        endsub;
    quit;
```

The OUTARGS statement denotes that all four parameters are declared as *call by reference*, representing that these arguments can be modified in the calling program. Also note that the hash object is queried only once by the FIND method, which simplifies previous mechanics in which it was queried three times—once for each separate cleaning, validation, and classification operation.

Thus, when the Name_raw key is found within the lookup table (i.e., the H hash object), the values of Charactername and Region (within the DATA step) are initialized to the non-key variables Charactername and Region (maintained within the hash object). And when a rogue value is detected (that lies outside of the hash object), FIND returns a value other than 0. The subsequent conditional block initializes Charactername and Region to missing values, and Err is initialized to 1 to represent an error.

The following DATA step calls CHARACTER_CLEAN_VALID_REGION to transform the GOT_favorites data set:

```
options cmplib=sasuser.myfuncs;
data got_class;
    length err 3 region $30 character_cleaned $30;
    label err='Error' region='Region'
        character_cleaned='GOT Character'
        favcharacter='Raw Character';
    set got_favorites;
    call missing(err, region, character_cleaned);
    call character_clean_valid_region(favcharacter,
        character_cleaned, region, err);
run;
```

The GOT_class data set that is created is identical to the data set shown in Table 13.7; however, all three operations are now performed through a single user-defined subroutine. This represents a very effective method where these operations are tightly coupled and always performed together; however, it diminishes the ability to perform these operations separately, as was demonstrated in the previous subsections.

In the end, requirements should drive the degree to which separate operations (and functionality) are bundled together, but this proof of concept demonstrates how performance could be improved through a user-defined subroutine that can alter or initialize multiple variables in one pass.

13.6 SUMMARY

Lookup tables broadly represent uniquely indexed tables that can be queried to determine whether a given value matches a key value within the table. Moreover, lookup tables can define key-value pairs, and thus facilitate the return of one or more data values (i.e., non-key attributes) when a key value is found in the table.

Given these characteristics, lookup tables are commonly used to validate data by evaluating whether a value appears in a lookup table. Other objectives instead transform data, and can be used to clean or standardize data, or to classify data into categories. Variables are sometimes transformed *in situ*, in which the raw value is overwritten, but in many cases, new variables are initialized to the non-key values returned by a lookup table, thus preserving raw data.

This chapter demonstrated both *procedural* and *functional* approaches to leveraging lookup tables, with the advantages of the latter demonstrated through more flexible, reusable, readable, maintainable data-driven operations. Both user-defined formats and user-defined functions (that leverage the hash object) were created that clean, validate, and classify data. The advantages of each method were demonstrated, with functions providing more expansive functionality, and formats having the ability to be applied within SAS procedures.

A final solution demonstrated a user-defined subroutine that simultaneously cleans, validates, and classifies data by passing multiple arguments *by reference*. This efficient approach can provide a more concise invocation, but lacks functional discretion within the subroutine's implementation because several operations are juxtaposed into a single callable module.

Chapter 14.

CONTROL TABLES: OTHER NAMED TABLES

This chapter has the following objectives:

❖ Introduce decision tables, and demonstrate how they can model conditional logic statements.

❖ Define a reusable decision table data structure, and document the formatting rules that prescribe its usage.

❖ Demonstrate the design of an interpreter that transforms decision table control data into dynamic, conditional logic.

❖ Introduce checkpoint tables, and demonstrate how they can support software recoverability objectives, including more autonomous, efficient recovery after software failure.

Some control tables are so ubiquitous or specialized that they are more commonly referenced by their specific names than generically as "control tables." Data dictionaries, discussed in Chapter 12, and lookup tables, discussed in Chapter 13, represent two such control tables. This chapter continues the focus on control tables, and introduces two final named control tables—decision tables and checkpoint tables.

Decision tables provide a matrix of evaluation criteria with which business rules or other decision rules can be evaluated. Both input criteria and the outcomes they produce are described within these tables. Decision tables provide a tabular, user-friendly data structure in which to modify decision rules without having to interact with the underlying code that interprets them.

Checkpoint tables record process completion status and statistics, including for successful completion of processes and for failed attempts thereof. Checkpoint tables inform dependent processes and users of completion status, thus validating when prerequisite processes have finished, and signaling that dependent processes can commence. Thus, checkpoint tables can be queried to determine what process should be run next within a serialized workflow, or whether to abort after some failure has been detected.

At a high level, control tables share a common objective—driving dynamic functionality. They also share a common design pattern, in which hardcoded, conditional logic is replaced with abstract instructions that are dynamically derived from control data. Thus, data quality rules, business rules, decision rules, data models, and other malleable inputs are stored outside of code within external data structures. This data independence facilitates ease of access to control data, enabling end users to modify functionality without altering code. In the case of checkpoint tables, processes (rather than people) modify control tables to achieve autonomy.

Control tables also facilitate procedural abstraction because the interpretation and operationalization of control data are hidden from end users executing callable processes. As long as the definition of a user-defined data structure remains consistent, developers can design and implement various operations to interpret and act upon those data, thus improving performance or extending functionality over time. Moreover, stable data structures facilitate reuse of those structures by SAS practitioners in support of subsequent, unrelated software products and projects.

Data independence is introduced as a pillar of data-driven design in Section 1.3.3, and is further described in Section 4.6

Procedural abstraction is discussed throughout Chapter 3, and *information hiding* in Section 8.4.1

14.1 DECISION TABLES

The International Organization for Standardization (ISO) defines a *decision table* as a "table of all contingencies that are to be considered in the description of a problem together with the action to be taken."[92] For example, a coworker may wash his hands after using the restroom *only* when the restroom has other occupants, but when he is alone, the dirty bird does not wash his hands. In this example, he has only one contingency—whether other occupants are present. This single contingency drives his dichotomous outcome, the decision of whether to wash or not to wash his hands. ISO defines a *decision outcome* as the "result of a decision (which therefore determines the control flow alternative taken)."[93]

Decision outcomes are driven by decision rules, the conditional logic statements that prescribe some predetermined outcome based on inputs. ISO defines a *decision rule* as a "combination of conditions (also known as causes) and actions (also known as effects) that produce a specific outcome in decision table testing and cause-effect graphing."[94] In a code-driven design paradigm, decision rules are hardcoded, whereas data-driven design extracts decision rules from code, and maintains them within external data structures.

Thus, although some decision tables are just pretty pictures that *describe* decision rules, other operational decision tables *prescribe* rules that are interpreted by code to produce dynamic outcomes. Decision tables can represent any knowledge domain, and as long as they can be codified within a data structure, can drive dynamic functionality. Like other control tables, the primary benefit of decision tables is the ability to modify their contents (i.e., decision rules and outcomes) without altering the underlying code that interprets these control data. Decision tables are especially useful where constraints can be identified, contingencies defined, and respective outcomes clearly stated.

14.1.1 Designing a User-Defined Decision Table

When contemplating the design of a new user-defined data structure, one of the first assessments should be what built-in file types, built-in data structures, and built-in operations can be leveraged to reduce unnecessary

	A	B	C	D	E	F
1	Game of Thrones		Last Week Tonight			Action
2	GOT		LWT			Action
3	ON	OFF	NEW	RERUN	OFF	Action
4	yes	no	yes	no	no	Viewing Party
5	yes	no	no	yes	no	Viewing Party
6	yes	no	no	no	yes	Viewing Party
7	no	yes	yes	no	no	Watch at home
8	no	yes	no	yes	no	Workout at the gym
9	no	yes	no	no	no	Cancel HBO

Table 14.1 Decision Table for HBO Subscription and Viewing

development. Decision tables are tables, after all, so they can be constructed within SAS data sets to take advantage of all the built-in functionality of this built-in data structure.

The *prescription-description gap* is described in Section 9.6, and Sections 9.5 and 9.6 describe the importance of the selection of the superordinate file type and data structure

However, a user-defined data structure representing the decision table construct must be designed on top of a superordinate data set substrate. And this user-defined data structure requires apt design and documentation to ensure it can be interpreted reliably and reused consistently. It can help to populate a sample data structure and document the rules thereafter, and Table 14.1 introduces a sample user-defined data structure representing a decision table.

For example, a critical decision that vexed millions of Americans in 2019 was whether to cancel our HBO subscriptions following the Game of Thrones series finale on May 19, 2019. Even HBO's John Oliver, host of the Sunday evening satirical comedy show, Last Week Tonight, joked about the "impending finale"—as his show would no longer be preceded by Game of Thrones, and no longer benefit from its legion of loyal viewers.

When the eighth (and final) season of Game of Thrones was still underway, I distilled my own contemplations about HBO viewership and subscribership into the following decision rules:

- If Game of Thrones has a new episode, I will host a viewing party.
- If Game of Thrones is not on and Last Week Tonight has a new episode, I will watch at home.
- If Game of Thrones is not on and Last Week Tonight is a rerun, I will work out instead.

- If Game of Thrones is not on and Last Week Tonight is not on, I will cancel my HBO subscription.

These decision rules are captured in the HBO decision table in Table 14.1. Each observation represents a unique pairing of all contingencies, leading to an outcome which may or may not be unique. For example, three separate pathways lead to having a "Viewing Party," although the other three outcomes are unique. This spreadsheet can be exported as a CSV file, ingested by SAS, and used to support data-driven design.

The decision table, shown in Table 14.1, can be exported to HBO_decision.csv:

```
Game of Thrones,,Last Week Tonight,,,Action
GOT,,LWT,,,Action
ON,OFF,NEW,RERUN,OFF,Action
yes,no,yes,no,no,Viewing Party
yes,no,no,yes,no,Viewing Party
yes,no,no,no,yes,Viewing Party
no,yes,yes,no,no,Watch at home
no,yes,no,yes,no,Workout at the gym
no,yes,no,no,no,Cancel HBO
```

Decision tables can be represented myriad ways, with this table demonstrating only one method. However, as the table also represents a user-defined data structure, it is essential that data rules be defined for this data structure, which increases the likelihood that the data structure will be reused as a template for future decision tables of unrelated content:

- The decision table is stored in tabular format (e.g., Excel, CSV).
- Each row must have the same number of columns.
- Each column must have the same number of rows.
- The first row contains labels that can be optionally applied, with each label appearing in the column of its first option; the rightmost column must be ACTION.
- The second row contains variable names, with each name appearing in the column of its first option; the rightmost column must be ACTION.
- The third row contains a list of options (i.e., case-insensitive values) that correspond to the labels/variables above; the rightmost column must be ACTION.

> User-defined data structures should have data rules defined and documented, as demonstrated in Section 1.2

- The fourth and subsequent rows contain case-insensitive values of YES or NO, depicting whether the above option is active or inactive for a specific rule.
- Data types for all cells are character.
- All column widths have a maximum number of 32 characters.
- A total number of 50 columns (across all variables and their respective options) can be evaluated.

Note that the rules speak only to the data structure and its contents; they do not allude to how the data are interpreted by user-defined operations, nor the subject matter (i.e., knowledge domain) of the data contained in the decision table. This separation ensures that end users or subject matter experts (SMEs) who are maintaining the decision table are focused on entering accurate data in the correct format, whereas developers are focused on understanding the structure so they can implement an appropriate solution to interpret and operationalize the control data within the data structure. This procedural abstraction (and information hiding) facilitated the creation of the decision table (demonstrated in Table 14.1), even *before* the DATA step (that interprets the table) was designed or developed.

Procedural abstraction is the focus of Chapter 3, and *information hiding* is discussed in Section 8.4.1

14.1.2 Developing a Decision Table Interpreter

Having designed the user-defined decision table data structure in the previous subsection, development can commence on the underlying program that will interpret the control data maintained within decision tables. Note that the underlying interpreter must be flexible enough to read not only *this* decision table demonstrated in Table 14.1, but *any* decision table that follows the data structure formatting rules enumerated in the previous subsection.

One dynamic, array-based method to interpret the decision table follows, and should be saved as decision_tables.sas:

```
* saved as d:\sas\decision_table.sas;
%macro decision_table(csv= /* CSV file name */);
data _null_;
   infile "&csv" truncover end=eof;
   length line $10000 tot 8 i 8 rule $30000;
   format line $10000.;
   input line & $;
```

```
array contlabel[50] $32 _temporary_;
array contlist[50] $32 _temporary_;
array vallist[50] $32 _temporary_;
retain tot;
retain rule '';
* get contingency labels;
if _n_=1 then do;
   do tot=1 to countw(line,',','m');
      contlabel[tot]=scan(line,tot,',','m');
      end;
   tot=tot-1;
   end;
* get contingency groups/variables;
if _n_=2 then do;
   do i=1 to tot;
      contlist[i]=scan(line,i,',','m');
      if missing(contlist[i]) then
         contlist[i]=contlist[i-1];
      end;
   end;
* get contingency values;
if _n_=3 then do;
   do i=1 to tot;
      vallist[i]=upcase(scan(line,i,',','m'));
      end;
   end;
* get decision rules;
if _n_>3 then do;
   do i=1 to tot;
      if i=tot then do;
         rule=strip(rule) || ' then action="' ||
            strip(scan(line,i,',')) || '";';
         end;
      else do;
         if i=1 then rule=strip(rule) ||
            ifc(_n_=4,' if',' else if');
```

```
        else rule=strip(rule) || ' and ';
        rule=strip(rule) || ' upcase(' ||
            strip(contlist[i]) || ')' ||
            ifc(upcase(scan(line,i,','))='YES',
            '=','^=') || '"' ||
            strip(vallist[i]) || '"';
        end;
    end;
end;
if eof then call
symputx('decisionrules',strip(rule),'g');
run;
%mend;
```

The DATA step first dynamically assesses the number of variables—in this example, GOT and LWT—after which it assesses how many options are subsumed under each variable. Thereafter, each observation is parsed, and the Rule variable is incrementally filled with IF-THEN-ELSE conditional logic statements that are dynamically built. When the DATA step reaches the last observation, it initializes the &DECISIONRULES global macro variable to the final value of Rule.

The following invocation runs the DECISION_TABLE macro to generate the &DECISIONRULES rules that describe the HBO business rules:

```
%let loc=d:\sas\;       * USER MUST CHANGE LOCATION *;
%include "&loc.decision_table.sas";


%decision_table(csv=&loc.hbo_decision.csv);
```

The &DECISIONRULES global macro variable contains an unformatted text string that can be dynamically called from within a subsequent DATA step to execute all decision rules contained within the table. The %BQUOTE function facilitates writing &DECISIONRULES to the log:

```
%put %bquote(&decisionrules);
```

```
if upcase(GOT)="ON" and upcase(GOT)^="OFF" and
upcase(LWT)="NEW" and
upcase(LWT)^="RERUN" and upcase(LWT)^="OFF" then
action="Viewing Party"; else if upcase(GOT)="ON"
and upcase(GOT)^="OFF" and upcase(LWT)^="NEW" and
upcase(LWT)="RERUN" and upcase(LWT)^="OFF" then
action="Viewing Party"; else if upcase(GOT)="ON" and
upcase(GOT)^="OFF" and upcase(LWT)^="NEW" and
upcase(LWT)^="RERUN" and upcase(LWT)="OFF" then
action="Viewing Party"; else if upcase(GOT)^="ON"
and upcase(GOT)="OFF" and upcase(LWT)="NEW" and
upcase(LWT)^="RERUN" and upcase(LWT)^="OFF" then
action="Watch at home"; else if upcase(GOT)^="ON" and
upcase(GOT)="OFF" and
upcase(LWT)^="NEW" and upcase(LWT)="RERUN" and
upcase(LWT)^="OFF" then action="Workout at the
gym"; else if upcase(GOT)^="ON" and upcase(GOT)="OFF"
and upcase(LWT)^="NEW" and
upcase(LWT)^="RERUN" and upcase(LWT)^="OFF" then
action="Cancel HBO";
```

To test the rules, a CSV file containing an abridged version of HBO's 2019 schedule is created, including all Sundays from March 24 through June 2. The schedule depicts whether Game of Thrones was on or not, and whether Last Week Tonight was new, a rerun, or off the air. The CSV file (hbo_schedule.csv) follows:

```
Date,Game of Thrones,Last Week Tonight
3/24/2019,off,rerun
3/31/2019,off,new
4/7/2019,off,new
4/14/2019,on,new
4/21/2019,on,new
4/28/2019,on,rerun
5/5/2019,on,new
5/12/2019,on,new
5/19/2019,on,new
6/2/2019,off,new
```

The following DATA step ingests hbo_schedule.csv, and applies the decision rules (codified in the &DECISIONRULES global macro variable) to create the HBO_schedule data set (demonstrated in Table 14.2):

```
data hbo_schedule;
    infile "&loc.hbo_schedule.csv" dsd delimiter=','
        truncover firstobs=2;
    length date 8 got $6 lwt $6 action $30;
    input date : mmddyy10.  got $ lwt $ action $;
    format date mmddyy10. got $6. lwt $6. action $30.;
    &decisionrules;
run;
```

In abstracting the decision rules into a single macro variable, code readability (within the DATA step) is improved, and developers need not understand the business rules defined within the decision table; these rules are instead maintained by business analysts or other knowledge domain SMEs. SAS practitioners are also free to refactor the code, if necessary, to improve performance or increase functionality. For example, SAS practitioners could refactor the DECISION_TABLE macro to read and evaluate the same decision table structure using a hash object lookup.

Most importantly, the DATA step that parses the decision table relies on array processing to facilitate extreme data abstraction and iteration abstraction. Thus, any future decision table of unrelated content and disparate size can be ingested by the same DECISION_TABLE macro to generate dynamic rules, as long as the decision table structure follows the data rules previously enumerated.

	Date	GOT	LWT	Action
1	3/24/2019	off	rerun	Workout at the gym
2	3/31/2019	off	new	Watch at home
3	4/7/2019	off	new	Watch at home
4	4/14/2019	on	new	Viewing Party
5	4/21/2019	on	new	Viewing Party
6	4/28/2019	on	rerun	Viewing Party
7	5/5/2019	on	new	Viewing Party
8	5/12/2019	on	new	Viewing Party
9	5/19/2019	on	new	Viewing Party
10	6/2/2019	off	new	Watch at home

Table 14.2 Decision Outcomes for HBO Subscription and Viewing

And about that HBO subscription—it turns out that Last Week Tonight is available on YouTube, so I amended my decision table, and bid the Home Box Office adieu.

14.2 CHECKPOINT TABLES

Reliability and robustness are two of the most touted performance objectives in software development, and considerable effort is made to deliver software that will not fail of its own accord. But even the most reliable software can fail when blackouts, network bottlenecks, operating system (OS) issues, or other events occur. In planning for this reality, SAS practitioners should prioritize *recoverability*—the ability to restore functionality when software stumbles or falls.

Checkpoints provide one method to facilitate autonomous and efficient software recovery; they record which processes have completed correctly, and in so doing, allow software to recover from the point of last known success. ISO defines a *checkpoint* as a "point in a computer program at which program state, status, or results are checked or recorded."[95] Checkpoint tables commonly record not only successful process completions but also failed attempts, thus facilitating programmatic, real-time evaluation of process status.

Checkpoint tables vary widely in their structure and content, although some common attributes include:

- Process Name – uniquely differentiate a process from others
- Start Date/Time – timestamp for process start
- Stop Date/Time – timestamp for process termination (for either success or failure)
- Warning/Error Code – codes or notes that denote exceptions, warnings, runtime errors, or other process status information

Some checkpoint tables contain a single entry (i.e., observation) for each process, and this observation is continually updated (i.e., overwritten) when a process is rerun. In other cases, checkpoint tables maintain a running history of all successful and failed attempts, and thus can be used for historical evaluation of process performance trends, in addition to real-time evaluation. The checkpoint table in this section demonstrates this latter method in which all process attempts are recorded.

Checkpoint tables are commonly implemented when independent processes run on a recurrent basis. For example, a batch job might attempt to run a set of SAS extract-transform-load (ETL) processes once per hour; however, processes that had completed successfully within the previous three hours could be skipped because their data was considered to be "current enough." In this example, developers could restart failed processes while subsequent, independent processes continued to execute.

This autonomous recovery is especially beneficial in environments that rely on third-party data sources, and especially where those data sources or their connectivity may fail. Thus, when one connection drops, the software can autonomously transfer its resources to accessing another data source, and can autonomously reattempt the dropped connection every hour until those data are retrieved or received.

Checkpoint tables can be difficult to test because they inherently rely on testing *exceptional* functionality—that is, dynamic program flow triggered by exceptions. However, with clever finagling, a checkpoint table as well as its operations can be tested.

The following example relies on the GOT_favorites data set, created in Section 13.1, which simulates comments that adoring Game of Thrones fans might have submitted through an online forum.

The BUILD_FAVS macro creates ten identical copies of GOT_favorites, named Favorites1 through Favorites10, simulating ten online fan tables that a SAS program might periodically query to retrieve updated data from various web databases:

```
%macro build_favs();
%do i=1 %to 10;
   data favorites&i;
      set got_favorites;
   run;
   %end;
%mend;
```

```
%build_favs;
```

The MAKE_CTRL macro creates the user-specified checkpoint table if it does not exist:

```
%macro make_ctrl(ctrl /* control table (DSN) */);
%if %sysfunc(exist(&ctrl))=0 %then %do;
   data &ctrl;
```

```
        length process $32 dtgstart 8 dtgstop 8
            errcode 8;
        format process $32. dtgstart datetime17.
            dtgstop datetime17. errcode 8.;
    run;
    %end;
%mend;
```

Because control tables can become corrupted, especially during development and testing, they often need to be deleted and re-instantiated. A reusable macro procedure that creates an empty control table is an essential tool because it allows developers to delete a current control table with the confidence that a new one will be spawned automatically when the software is run again.

The MAKE_CTRL macro is also essential when software (that relies on checkpoint tables) is run for the first time, including when software is promoted between SDLC regions, such as from a development to a test or production environment.

The UPDATE_CTRL macro opens the control table and appends an observation that denotes process completion status:

```
%macro update_ctrl(ctrl= /* control table (DSN) */,
    process= /* process name (<32 char) */,
    dtgstart= /* start time in SAS dtg */,
    dtgstop= /* stop time in SAS dtg */,
    errcode= /* SYSCC error code */);
data &ctrl;
    set &ctrl end=eof;
    if ^missing(process) then output;
    if eof then do;
        process="&process";
        dtgstart=&dtgstart;
        dtgstop=&dtgstop;
        errcode=&errcode;
        output;
        end;
run;
%mend;
```

UPDATE_CTRL appends a new observation to the checkpoint table after both successful and failed processes. However, whereas every instance of success will be listed, not all failed processes will be indicated, especially where external failures may have crippled the SAS application itself, the network, or the infrastructure. For example, if a SAS server itself takes a nosedive, the macro will stop running, and the failure will not be recorded in the checkpoint table.

For this reason, checkpoint tables can be used to validate successful process completion, but cannot be used to validate *all* process failures—because many failures may not be demonstrated in the checkpoint table. However, because the "last successful completion" will always be documented in the checkpoint table, querying the table during software recovery enables software to resume without unnecessarily rerunning processes that had previously completed without failure.

In this example, processes are run recurrently after a parameterized amount of time (i.e., codified in the HRS parameter) has passed. The TEST_COMPLETION macro evaluates the checkpoint table to determine if some specific process should be run (or rerun):

```
* returns global macro test_RC: 1 if if needs to run;
* returns 0 if the process has been freshly run;
* within the HRS number of hours indicated;
%macro test_completion(ctrl= /* ctrl table (DSN) */,
    process= /* process name (<32 char) */,
    hrs= /* integer or decimal number of hours */);
%global test_RC;
%let test_RC=1;
data _null_;
    set &ctrl end=eof;
    retain rc 1;
    if upcase(process)="%upcase(&process)"
        and errcode=0 and dtgstop+(&hrs*3600)>datetime()
        then rc=0;
    if eof then call symputx('test_rc',
        strip(put(rc,8.)),'g');
run;
%mend;
```

The TEST_COMPLETION macro parameterizes the number of hours (in integer or decimal notation), after which a successful process should be rerun. That is, TEST_COMPLETION will *always* attempt to rerun a process if the checkpoint table contains only instances of that process failing; however, it will also attempt to rerun any process that has completed successfully—if the most recent successful completion had occurred prior to the number of hours specified &HRS.

For example, if TEST_COMPLETION is invoked and &HRS is 3, the macro will attempt to rerun all processes that have never succeeded, as well as processes that had previously succeeded but had completed more than three hours before the current time. The &TEST_RC return code of 1 indicates a process should be run (or rerun), and 0 indicates a process does not need to be rerun (because it has executed successfully within the parameterized amount of time, &HRS).

Finally, the RUN_SOME_PROCESSES macro simulates ten independent processes—sorting the various Favorites1 through Favorites10 data sets. The MAKE_CTRL macro first evaluates whether the checkpoint table exists, and if it does not, creates the control table. The TEST_COMPLETION macro then evaluates whether each specific process needs to be completed, and initializes the &TEST_RC global macro variable to 1 if a process should be rerun.

Failure can be difficult to mimic when testing any system, but failure within RUN_SOME_PROCESSES is simulated using the RAND function, which initializes the &RAND macro variable to a value between 1 and 100. The &RAND macro variable is subsequently compared to the parameterized &PCT_SUCCESS macro variable, enabling software testers to specify the success rate as a percentage. For example, passing the PCT_SUCCESS argument of 70 will simulate failures (represented by an &ERRCODE of 4) approximately 30 percent of the time.

After the SORT procedure has succeeded (or alternatively "failed"), the UPDATE_CTRL macro passes these process metrics to the checkpoint table and updates it. Each invocation of RUN_SOME_PROCESSES attempts to sort each Favorites data set only once, so setting a lower PCT_SUCCESS argument (e.g., 50 percent), and invoking RUN_SOME_PROCESSES two or three times will best demonstrate the iterative and incremental nature of software recovery, facilitated by checkpoint tables.

The RUN_SOME_PROCESSES macro follows:

```
%macro run_some_processes(ctrl= /* ctrl tab (DSN) */,
```

```
      pct_success=50 /* integer from 10 to 90 percent */,
      hrs = /* integer or decimal number of hours */);
%local i rand process ercode dtgstart dtgstop;
%make_ctrl(&ctrl);
%do i=1 %to 10;
   %let process=sorting&i;
   %test_completion(ctrl=&ctrl, process=&process,
      hrs=&hrs);
   %if &test_RC %then %do;
      %let rand=%eval(%sysfunc(int(
         %sysfunc(rand(uniform))*100))+1);
      %let dtgstart=%sysfunc(datetime());
      %if %eval(&rand<&pct_success) %then %do;
         proc sort data=favorites&i;
            by favcharacter;
         run;
         %let errcode=0;
         %end;
      %else %let errcode=4;
      %let dtgstop=%sysfunc(datetime());
      %update_ctrl(ctrl=&ctrl, process=&process,
         dtgstart=&dtgstart, dtgstop=&dtgstop,
         errcode=&errcode);
      %end;
   %end;
%mend;
```

RUN_SOME_PROCESSES can be invoked using the following macro call, in which the HRS argument is set to 0.1 hours (i.e., six minutes):

```
%run_some_processes(ctrl=ctrl_table, pct_success=70,
   hrs=.1);
```

When the macro completes, the checkpoint table will have been updated, showing the successful and failed statuses of each attempted SORT. These results will vary due to randomization, but will look similar to Table 14.3, with a success rate (on average) of 70 percent. Successful process execution is denoted by an Errcode of 0.

	Process	DTGStart	DTGStop	Errcode
1	sorting1 01JAN22:22:00:00	01JAN22:22:00:01		0
2	sorting2 01JAN22:22:00:00	01JAN22:22:00:01		4
3	sorting3 01JAN22:22:00:00	01JAN22:22:00:01		0
4	sorting4 01JAN22:22:00:00	01JAN22:22:00:01		0
5	sorting5 01JAN22:22:00:00	01JAN22:22:00:01		0
6	sorting6 01JAN22:22:00:00	01JAN22:22:00:01		0
7	sorting7 01JAN22:22:00:00	01JAN22:22:00:01		4
8	sorting8 01JAN22:22:00:00	01JAN22:22:00:01		0
9	sorting9 01JAN22:22:00:00	01JAN22:22:00:01		0
10	sorting10 01JAN22:22:00:00	01JAN22:22:00:01		0

Table 14.3 Checkpoint Table – First Run

Note that on the first run (at **01JAN22:22:00:01**), all processes will be attempted because the checkpoint table does not exist, and thus contains no control data. In all subsequent attempts, as long as those attempts occur within the parameterized amount of time (HRS), fewer observations will be added because the macro will be rerunning only failed—not successful—processes. This efficiency savings can be substantial, as processes that have previously succeeded do not need to be inefficiently run again.

If the RUN_SOME_PROCESSES macro is immediately rerun (within the six-minute threshold specified by the 0.1 HRS argument), only the failed processes—SORTING2 and SORTING7—will be reattempted.

	Process	DTGStart	DTGStop	Errcode
1	sorting1 01JAN22:22:00:00	01JAN22:22:00:01		0
2	sorting2 01JAN22:22:00:00	01JAN22:22:00:01		4
3	sorting3 01JAN22:22:00:00	01JAN22:22:00:01		0
4	sorting4 01JAN22:22:00:00	01JAN22:22:00:01		0
5	sorting5 01JAN22:22:00:00	01JAN22:22:00:01		0
6	sorting6 01JAN22:22:00:00	01JAN22:22:00:01		0
7	sorting7 01JAN22:22:00:00	01JAN22:22:00:01		4
8	sorting8 01JAN22:22:00:00	01JAN22:22:00:01		0
9	sorting9 01JAN22:22:00:00	01JAN22:22:00:01		0
10	sorting10 01JAN22:22:00:00	01JAN22:22:00:01		0
11	sorting2 01JAN22:22:04:00	01JAN22:22:04:01		0
12	sorting7 01JAN22:22:04:00	01JAN22:22:04:01		0

Table 14.4 Checkpoint Table – Second Run

Whether they succeed or fail, the checkpoint table is again updated, and Table 14.4 demonstrates that both processes succeeded the second time they were run (at 01JAN22:22:04:01), four minutes after their first run.

At this point, if the RUN_SOME_PROCESSES macro is run a third time (before the six-minute threshold), the macro will determine that no further processing is necessary, and exit without updating the control table. However, once the six-minute threshold has passed (for any of the previously successful processes), those processes will be reattempted.

Checkpoint tables are essential where software recoverability objectives demand a recovery that is efficient and autonomous, as they allow software to skip processes that have completed successfully. Checkpoint tables also represent control tables that operate independently of end users, as they are evaluated and modified only by software processes. Finally, checkpoint tables demonstrate bidirectional communication of control data, as they are both read from and updated by software processes.

Bidirectional communication is discussed in Section 9.8, and demonstrated through subroutines in Sections 3.7.2 and 3.7.3

14.3 SUMMARY

This chapter introduced two named control tables that serve specialized roles, including *decision tables* and *checkpoint tables*, both of which were operationalized within the SAS data set built-in data structure. Control tables that rely on built-in data structures, such as the SAS data set, facilitate the greatest functionality and flexibility because of the endless built-in operations that developers can utilize to interact with control data.

Decision tables model conditional logic through a tabular structure that lists contingencies, decision rules, and their respective outcomes. This chapter introduced a user-defined data structure in which decision tables of varying size, complexity and content can be maintained and operationalized, thus maximizing the reuse of both this user-defined data structure and its associated user-defined operations.

Checkpoint tables record process metrics and can be used to validate and demonstrate successful process completion. They also can facilitate autonomous and efficient software recovery when processes have failed, and can be used to run recurrent processes at parameterized intervals. In all cases, these control tables facilitate data independence by enabling end users and software processes to modify control data without altering the underlying code.

Chapter 15.

HIERARCHICAL DATA MODELS

This chapter has the following objectives:

❖ Introduce hierarchical data models, and demonstrate how they can be denormalized and represented within tabular data structures.

❖ Demonstrate the use of spreadsheets in representing hierarchical data models.

❖ Demonstrate the use of XML files in representing hierarchical data structures.

❖ Introduce operations that can create SAS user-defined formats that represent complex, multilevel, hierarchical data models.

H ierarchical data models expand the complexity of tabular data structures by representing structures such as data trees and relational data. As described within this chapter, hierarchical data models have two or more variables, in which at least one variable is subsumed under another. These more complex data structures often must be interpreted and operationalized by commensurately more complex techniques than those used for tabular data.

The realization that hierarchical relationships exist is the first step in hierarchical data modeling. Too often, separate control tables may be maintained independently, despite representing different facets of the same data model. In joining disparate control tables into a single, cohesive data structure, master data management (MDM) objectives are supported because a single, trusted version of the data model can be maintained.

Master data management (MDM) is discussed in Section 8.2

The second step is deciding how to represent a hierarchical model. A relational database can be a preferred method, but falls outside the scope of this text. Other options include spreadsheets, XML files, and SAS data sets, all of which are demonstrated in this chapter. With a data structure selected, end users—and especially knowledge domain subject matter experts (SMEs)—can begin to populate external hierarchical data models.

The final step belongs to SAS practitioners, as we design and develop operations that will interact with hierarchical models while trying not to force models to conform to the two-dimensional tables with which we are arguably more comfortable. For example, the FORMAT procedure, a formidable soldier whose reputation should not be sullied, nevertheless has limitations in modeling hierarchical data. With savvy design, however, FORMAT and other methods can be re-envisioned to operate on hierarchical data models, and thus promote their use as master data.

This chapter extends the Game of Thrones data model, demonstrated in Table 13.6, by adding actor name as an attribute ascribed to character name. Two equivalent control files are created—a spreadsheet, and an XML file and associated XML map—to demonstrate functionally equivalent methods of reading and operationalizing hierarchical data.

15.1 DATA MODELS AS SPREADSHEETS

Excel is a preferred tool for representing hierarchical data models, if for no other reason than the application's ubiquity across industries and organizations, as well as the ease with which it facilitates data entry, modification, and maintenance—including by nontechnical end users.

	A	B	C	D
1	The Westerlands	Nikolaj Coster-Waldau	Jaime Lannister	Jaime Lannister
2				Jaime
3		Lena Headey	Cersei Lannister	Cersei Lannister
4		Peter Dinklage	Tyrion Lannister	Tyrion Lannister
5				Tyrion
6		Charles Dance	Tywin Lannister	Tywin Lannister
7		Emilia Clarke	Daenerys Targaryen	Daenerys Targaryen
8				Daenerys
9				Daneris
10	The North	Kit Harington	Jon Snow	Jon Snow
11		Sophie Turner	Sansa Stark	Sansa Stark
12		Maisie Williams	Arya Stark	Arya Stark
13				Aria Stark
14		Richard Madden	Robb Stark	Robb Stark
15		Isaac Hempstead Wright	Bran Stark	Bran Stark

The general structure and columns of Table 15.1 are explained in Section 13.5, in which the data model defines columns as Region, Actor, Character Name, and Raw Name

Table 15.1 Game of Thrones Hierarchical Data Model (Spreadsheet)

Spreadsheets can be readily exported to comma-separated values (CSV) files, a canonical, interoperable data structure that facilitates data transfer.

Table 15.1 demonstrates an abridged version of the Game of Thrones hierarchical data model maintained within a spreadsheet. The spreadsheet can be exported to a CSV file (GOT_model.csv):

```
The Westerlands,Nikolaj Coster-Waldau,Jaime
Lannister,Jaime Lannister
,,,Jaime
,Lena Headey,Cersei Lannister,Cersei Lannister
,Peter Dinklage,Tyrion Lannister,Tyrion Lannister
,,,Tyrion
,Charles Dance,Tywin Lannister,Tywin Lannister
,Emilia Clarke,Daenerys Targaryen,Daenerys Targaryen
,,,Daenerys
,,,Daneris
The North,Kit Harington,Jon Snow,Jon Snow
,Sophie Turner,Sansa Stark,Sansa Stark
,Maisie Williams,Arya Stark,Arya Stark
,,,Aria Stark
,Richard Madden,Robb Stark,Robb Stark
,Isaac Hempstead Wright,Bran Stark,Bran Stark
```

Note that as is typical within hierarchical or relational data structures (represented in tabular form), unique entities are shown only once. For example, the first column, representing the Region variable, lists the Westerlands and the North only once each, with empty cells implying the continuation of the previous non-missing value. This construction facilitates readability because an end user can visually identify demarcations among groups or characteristics.

The MDM principle of maintaining a single version of the truth is also facilitated by hierarchical data models because entities are not unnecessarily repeated. For example, were "Westerlands" typed repeatedly in rows one through nine (rather than appearing only once in the first row), this would not alter the data model, but it would introduce the risk of some of those "Westerlands" being misspelled. Moreover, if the "Westerlands" entity required modification, those changes would (unnecessarily) need to be performed across all rows that explicitly (rather than implicitly) referenced "Westerlands."

15.1.1 Importing Spreadsheets into SAS

The data model shown in Table 15.1, having been exported to GOT_model.csv, is imported into the GOT_model data set using the following DATA step:

```
%let loc=d:\sas\;      * USER MUST CHANGE LOCATION *;
data GOT_model;
    infile "&loc.got_model.csv" truncover
       dsd delimiter=',' end=eof;
    length region $50 actor $50 character $50
       variation $50;
    format region $50. actor $50. character $50.
       variation $50.;
    label region='Region' actor='Actor'
       character='GOT Character'
       variation='Raw Character';
    input region $ actor $ character $ variation $;
run;
```

Note that the GOT_model data set retains the hierarchical structure from the spreadsheet, as demonstrated in Table 15.2, in which observations inherit higher-level attributes from preceding observations.

	Region	Actor	GOT Character	Raw Character
1	The Westerlands	Nikolaj Coster-Waldau	Jaime Lannister	Jaime Lannister
2				Jaime
3		Lena Headey	Cersei Lannister	Cersei Lannister
4		Peter Dinklage	Tyrion Lannister	Tyrion Lannister
5				Tyrion
6		Charles Dance	Tywin Lannister	Tywin Lannister
7		Emilia Clarke	Daenerys Targaryen	Daenerys Targaryen
8				Daenerys
9				Daneris
10	The North	Kit Harington	Jon Snow	Jon Snow
11		Sophie Turner	Sansa Stark	Sansa Stark
12		Maisie Williams	Arya Stark	Arya Stark
13				Aria Stark
14		Richard Madden	Robb Stark	Robb Stark
15		Isaac Hempstead Wright	Bran Stark	Bran Stark

Table 15.2 Game of Thrones Hierarchical Data Model (SAS Data Set)

Data analysis, however, generally requires all relevant attributes to be represented within each observation. Thus, in the same light in which normalized tables (that might exist within a relational database) are often denormalized before analysis, the higher-level attributes within the data set also must be distributed across all observations to which they apply.

To create an equivalent denormalized data structure, the following revised DATA step now ingests and denormalizes the CSV file, creating the GOT_model_tabular data set, aided by the RETAIN statement:

```
%let loc=d:\sas\;        * USER MUST CHANGE LOCATION *;
data GOT_model_tabular (drop=region1 actor1
     character1);
   infile "&loc.got_model.csv" truncover
      dsd delimiter=',' end=eof;
   length region $50 actor $50 character $50
      variation $50 region1 $50 actor1 $50
      character1 $50;
   format region $50. actor $50. character $50.
      variation $50. region1 $50. actor1 $50.
      character1 $50.;
   label region='Region' actor='Actor'
      character='GOT Character'
```

```
        variation='Raw Character';
    input region $ actor $ character $ variation $;
    if missing(region) then region=region1;
    if missing(actor) then actor=actor1;
    if missing(character) then character=character1;
    region1=region;
    actor1=actor;
    character1=character;
    retain region1 actor1 character1;
run;
```

The hierarchical data are ingested and now more clearly represent a tabular structure, as demonstrated in Table 15.3. The data have not abandoned their hierarchical nature; however, multitiered relationships can now be evaluated by inspecting a single observation.

For example, within Table 15.3, it is clear that Aria Stark represents a spelling variation (i.e., misspelling) of Arya Stark, a member of the Westerlands region. Conversely, this multi-tiered assessment cannot be made from viewing a single observation within the hierarchical data model (Table 15.2) because the misspelled Aria Stark observation contains no values for the Region, Actor, or Character variables; thus, they must be imputed from previous observations.

	Region	Actor	GOT Character	Raw Character
1	The Westerlands	Nikolaj Coster-Waldau	Jaime Lannister	Jaime Lannister
2	The Westerlands	Nikolaj Coster-Waldau	Jaime Lannister	Jaime
3	The Westerlands	Lena Headey	Cersei Lannister	Cersei Lannister
4	The Westerlands	Peter Dinklage	Tyrion Lannister	Tyrion Lannister
5	The Westerlands	Peter Dinklage	Tyrion Lannister	Tyrion
6	The Westerlands	Charles Dance	Tywin Lannister	Tywin Lannister
7	The Westerlands	Emilia Clarke	Daenerys Targaryen	Daenerys Targaryen
8	The Westerlands	Emilia Clarke	Daenerys Targaryen	Daenerys
9	The Westerlands	Emilia Clarke	Daenerys Targaryen	Daneris
10	The North	Kit Harington	Jon Snow	Jon Snow
11	The North	Sophie Turner	Sansa Stark	Sansa Stark
12	The North	Maisie Williams	Arya Stark	Arya Stark
13	The North	Maisie Williams	Arya Stark	Aria Stark
14	The North	Richard Madden	Robb Stark	Robb Stark
15	The North	Isaac Hempstead Wright	Bran Stark	Bran Stark

Table 15.3 Denormalized Game of Thrones Data Model (SAS Data Set)

15.2 DATA MODELS AS XML FILES

The Extensible Markup Language (XML) is a canonical file type in which hierarchical data models can be represented within text files. As a markup language, elements and attributes are individually marked with tags that facilitate keyword identification of variables. Values are mapped to their respective variables, similar to key-value pairs and keyword parameters.

XML files can represent hierarchical data, but within SAS, an additional XML map is required, which defines the relationships among variables, including identifying hierarchical relationships. An XML map instructs SAS how to process an XML file to ensure that its data structure and data are interpreted correctly.

Keyword parameters are introduced in support of procedural abstraction in Section 6.4.2, and *key-value pairs* are introduced in support of configuration files in Section 16.3.5

The Game of Thrones hierarchical data model, demonstrated in Table 15.1, is represented by the following XML file (GOT_model.xml):

```xml
<?xml version="1.0" encoding="utf-8" ?>
<TABLE>
    <REGION> The Westerlands
            <CHARACTER ACTOR="Nikolaj Coster-
Waldau">Jaime Lannister
                    <VAR VARIATION="Jaime Lannister"/>
                    <VAR VARIATION="Jaime"/>
            </CHARACTER>
            <CHARACTER ACTOR="Lena Headey">Cersei
Lannister
                    <VAR VARIATION="Cersei Lannister"/>
            </CHARACTER>
            <CHARACTER ACTOR="Peter Dinklage">Tyrion
Lannister
                    <VAR VARIATION="Tyrion Lannister"/>
                    <VAR VARIATION="Tyrion"/>
            </CHARACTER>
            <CHARACTER ACTOR="Charles Dance">Tywin
Lannister
                    <VAR VARIATION="Tywin Lannister"/>
            </CHARACTER>
            <CHARACTER ACTOR="Emilia Clarke">Daenerys
Targaryen
```

```
                    <VAR VARIATION="Daenerys Targaryen"/>
                    <VAR VARIATION="Daenerys"/>
                    <VAR VARIATION="Daneris"/>
          </CHARACTER>
     </REGION>
     <REGION> The North
          <CHARACTER ACTOR="Kit Harington">Jon Snow
                    <VAR VARIATION="Jon Snow"/>
          </CHARACTER>
          <CHARACTER ACTOR="Sophie Turner">Sansa Stark
                    <VAR VARIATION="Sansa Stark"/>
          </CHARACTER>
          <CHARACTER ACTOR="Maisie Williams">Arya
Stark
                    <VAR VARIATION="Arya Stark"/>
                    <VAR VARIATION="Aria Stark"/>
          </CHARACTER>
          <CHARACTER ACTOR="Richard Madden">Robb Stark
                    <VAR VARIATION="Robb Stark"/>
          </CHARACTER>
          <CHARACTER ACTOR="Isaac Hempstead
Wright">Bran Stark
                    <VAR VARIATION="Bran Stark"/>
          </CHARACTER>
     </REGION>
</TABLE>
```

The intricacies of XML files and XML map files are not further
described in this text, as end users will rarely be required to interact with
these raw data structures. More commonly, XML control data are managed
through graphical user interfaces (GUIs) or applications. For example, the
SAS XML Mapper provides XML management capabilities, as well as
applications such as Excel, and web browsers like Chrome and Firefox.

The XML map file (GOT_map.xml) defines the structure and entity
relationships of the XML file to be imported:

```
<?xml version="1.0" ?>
<SXLEMAP version="2.1">
```

```
<TABLE name="GOT">
<TABLE-PATH
 syntax="XPath">/TABLE/REGION/CHARACTER/VAR
        </TABLE-PATH>
<COLUMN name="REGION">
        <PATH>/TABLE/REGION </PATH>
        <TYPE>character</TYPE>
        <DATATYPE>string</DATATYPE>
        <LENGTH>50</LENGTH>
</COLUMN>
<COLUMN name="ACTOR">
        <PATH>/TABLE/REGION/CHARACTER/@ACTOR </PATH>
        <TYPE>character</TYPE>
        <DATATYPE>string</DATATYPE>
        <LENGTH>50</LENGTH>
</COLUMN>
<COLUMN name="CHARACTER">
        <PATH>/TABLE/REGION/CHARACTER </PATH>
        <TYPE>character</TYPE>
        <DATATYPE>string</DATATYPE>
        <LENGTH>50</LENGTH>
</COLUMN>
<COLUMN name="VARIATION">
        <PATH>/TABLE/REGION/CHARACTER/VAR/@VARIATION
</PATH>
        <TYPE>character</TYPE>
        <DATATYPE>string</DATATYPE>
        <LENGTH>50</LENGTH>
</COLUMN>
</TABLE>
</SXLEMAP>
```

The interoperable structure of XML facilitates data transfer among environments, platforms, and systems—including native ingestion of data into the SAS application, as demonstrated in the next section.

15.2.1 Importing XML Files into SAS

XML files and their respective XML maps are processed in SAS by the XML LIBNAME Engine. The following FILENAME statements define the XML file and its map, after which the DATA step imports the XML file to create the GOT_xml data set:

```
%let loc=d:\sas\;       * USER MUST CHANGE LOCATION *;
filename myxml "&loc.got_model.xml";
filename xmlmap "&loc.got_map.xml";
libname myxml xmlv2 xmlmap=xmlmap;
data got_xml;
   set myxml.got;
run;
```

The resultant data set is identical to the GOT_model data set demonstrated in Table 15.2. Note that as before, the data set retains its hierarchical structure; thus, higher-level attributes are not inherited to lower tiers. For example, the (misspelled) Aria Stark observation does not include the corresponding Region, Actor, or Character attributes.

To translate the hierarchical structure into a denormalized, analytic-friendly structure, the RETAIN attribute (with YES specified) can be added to the COLUMN elements for Region, Actor, and Character within the XML map file. The following GOT_map_tabular.xml file includes these three changes:

```
<?xml version="1.0" ?>
<SXLEMAP version="2.1">
    <TABLE name="GOT">
    <TABLE-PATH
syntax="XPath">/TABLE/REGION/CHARACTER/VAR
            </TABLE-PATH>
    <COLUMN name="REGION" retain="YES">
            <PATH>/TABLE/REGION </PATH>
            <TYPE>character</TYPE>
            <DATATYPE>string</DATATYPE>
            <LENGTH>50</LENGTH>
    </COLUMN>
    <COLUMN name="ACTOR" retain="YES">
```

```
            <PATH>/TABLE/REGION/CHARACTER/@ACTOR </PATH>
            <TYPE>character</TYPE>
            <DATATYPE>string</DATATYPE>
            <LENGTH>50</LENGTH>
        </COLUMN>
        <COLUMN name="CHARACTER" retain="YES">
            <PATH>/TABLE/REGION/CHARACTER </PATH>
            <TYPE>character</TYPE>
            <DATATYPE>string</DATATYPE>
            <LENGTH>50</LENGTH>
        </COLUMN>
        <COLUMN name="VARIATION">
            <PATH>/TABLE/REGION/CHARACTER/VAR/@VARIATION
</PATH>
            <TYPE>character</TYPE>
            <DATATYPE>string</DATATYPE>
            <LENGTH>50</LENGTH>
        </COLUMN>
    </TABLE>
</SXLEMAP>
```

The XML file is imported again; the SAS code is identical, except it now references the revised XML map file (GOT_map_tabular.xml) in which attributes are retained across observations:

```
%let loc=d:\sas\;        * USER MUST CHANGE LOCATION *;
filename myxml "&loc.got_model.xml";
filename xmlmap "&loc.got_map_tabular.xml";
libname myxml xmlv2 xmlmap=xmlmap;
data got_xml_tabular;
    set myxml.got;
run;
```

The resultant data set (GOT_xml_tabular) is identical to the data set shown in Table 15.3. The underlying hierarchical relationships of the data are maintained; however, all attributes are now represented across all observations, so observation-level analysis is again facilitated.

15.3 OVERCOMING SAS FORMAT LIMITATIONS

This chapter demonstrates the simplicity of maintaining hierarchical data models within external data structures, as well as the relative ease with which these models can be imported from spreadsheets and XML files into SAS. Once hierarchical data structures are maintained within SAS data sets, however, developers may find them difficult to wrangle into meaningful data (or data transformations). For example, operations that are straightforward with two levels of data (such as data mapping) may not readily scale when three or more data levels exist.

Within the SAS language, SAS formats and informats (or equivalent two-column lookup tables) are often relied upon to model and transform data. The true nature of the Game of Thrones hierarchical data model, however, demonstrates complexity beyond the one-to-one and many-to-one relationships that SAS formats and informats can model.

For example, mapping Variation to Character represents a many-to-one relationship, and mapping Character to Region represents a second many-to-one relationship, with these nested relationships performing two levels of transformation. Adding complexity to this model, mapping Variation to Actor also represents a many-to-one relationship, as does mapping Actor to Region. Finally, mapping Actor to Character (or vice versa) represents a one-to-one relationship.

The Game of Thrones hierarchical data model, whether maintained within XML or Excel, accurately portrays each of these relationships. Moreover, when the model must be modified, a change can be made in one file only. Conversely, representing the hierarchical data model using SAS formats would require a separate format for each mapping (each with a CNTLIN option specifying a different control table), and one change to the data model could require modifying numerous SAS formats individually.

One method to overcome the limitations of SAS formats is to build formats dynamically from a single hierarchical data model, rather than from multiple two-column control tables.

The BUILD_FORMAT macro, published separately by the author, represents a scalable, reusable method to create formats dynamically from hierarchical and relational data models:[96]

```
%macro build_format(fmtname= /* name of SAS format
        to be generated */,
    dsnmodel= /* data set in LIB.DSN or DSN format
```

```
              containing the data model */,
       var1= /* variable (within the model) being
           transformed or categorized */,
       var2= /* variable (within the model) to which VAR1
           is transformed */,
       invalid=DROP /* KEEP or DROP indicates how to handle
           values found that are outside data model */);
%global build_format_RC;
%let build_format_RC=FAILURE;
%let syscc=0;
%local lib dsn len1 type1 len2 type1 type2 obs1 obs2;
* parse LIB and DSN if both provided, otherwise assign
WORK to library;
%if %length(%scan(&dsnmodel,2,.))=0 %then %do;
    %let lib=WORK;
    %let dsn=%upcase(&dsnmodel);
    %end;
%else %do;
    %let lib=%upcase(%scan(&dsnmodel,1,.));
    %let dsn=%upcase(%scan(&dsnmodel,2,.));
    %end;
* determine the formats and lengths of VAR1 and VAR2;
proc sql noprint;
    select length, lowcase(substr(type,1,1)) into
        : len1, : type1
    from dictionary.columns
    where upcase(libname)="&lib" and upcase(memname)=
        "&dsn" and upcase(name)="%upcase(&var1)";
    select length, lowcase(substr(type,1,1)) into
        : len2, : type2
    from dictionary.columns
    where upcase(libname)="&lib" and upcase(memname)=
        "&dsn" and upcase(name)="%upcase(&var2)";
quit;
* delete temp data sets if they already exist;
%if %sysfunc(exist(format_temp1)) %then %do;
```

```
      proc delete data=format_temp1;
      %end;
%if %sysfunc(exist(format_temp2)) %then %do;
      proc delete data=format_temp2;
      %end;
* extract values from model for dynamic format;
data format_temp1;
      length fmtname $32 type $2 hlo $1;
      length start %sysfunc(ifc(%substr(&type1,
          1,1)=c,$,)) &len1 label
          %sysfunc(ifc(%substr(&type2,
          1,1)=c,$,)) &len2;
      set &dsnmodel (keep=&var1 &var2 rename=
          (&var1=start &var2=label));
      fmtname="&fmtname";
      type="&type1";
      hlo='';
run;
* remove duplicate values if created during binning;
proc sort data=format_temp1 nodupkey;
      by start label;
run;
* fail if LABEL variable is duplicate (invalid SQL or
      invalid format);
proc sort data=format_temp1 out=format_temp2 nodupkey;
      by start;
run;
proc sql noprint;
      select count(*)
      into : obs1
      from format_temp1;
      select count(*)
      into : obs2
      from format_temp2;
quit;
* create OTHER option for format if DROP is specified;
```

```
%if %upcase(&invalid)=DROP %then %do;
   data format_temp1;
      set format_temp1 end=eof;
      output;
      if eof then do;
         start='';
         label=.;
         hlo='o';  * denotes other value;
         output;
         end;
   %end;
%if &syscc=0 %then %do;
   %if &obs1=&obs2 %then %do;
      * create format;
      proc format cntlin=format_temp1;
      run;
      %if &syscc=0 %then %let build_format_RC=;
      %else %let build_format_RC=FAILURE DURING FORMAT;
      %end;
   %else %let build_format_RC=
      FAILURE ON VARIABLE ORDER OR XML DATA;
   %end;
%else %let build_format_RC=FAILURE BEFORE FORMAT;
%mend;
```

The FMTNAME parameter defines the name of the format to be dynamically created. As the macro essentially transforms any column in a hierarchical model to any equivalent level or superordinate-level column, passing a FMTNAME argument that references the two columns can be helpful. For example, if transforming the Variation variable into the Character variable (to standardize and clean the raw values for Game of Thrones character names), VARIATION_TO_CHARACTER would be an appropriately named format.

The DSNMODEL parameter defines the denormalized data model from which dynamic formats will be created. It is essential that only a denormalized data model (such as Table 15.3) is utilized, as normalized models (such as Table 15.2) will fail.

The VAR1 and VAR2 parameters respectively represent the starting format and ending format of the data being transformed. For example, when transforming the Raw Name column (Variation variable) into the Character Name column (Character variable), VAR1 and VAR2 should be Variation and Character, respectively.

Finally, the INVALID parameter denotes whether values that lie outside the data model should be maintained or dropped. For example, Kit Harington appears in the GOT_favorites data set (created in 13.5.2) as a raw character name that is incorrect, and which falls outside the Game of Thrones data model. Thus, setting the INVALID argument to DROP prevents Kit from being retained after a transformation that seeks to format his column, whereas specifying KEEP will retain the unformatted Kit Harington—even in the newly formatted column.

The following DATA step reprises code in Section 13.5, in which user-defined formats clean, validate, and classify (i.e., categorize) the GOT_favorites data set (created in 13.5.2):

```
data got_class;
   length err 3 region $30 character_cleaned $30;
   label err='Error' region='Region'
      character_cleaned='GOT Character'
      favcharacter='Raw Character';
   set got_favorites;
   character_cleaned=put(favcharacter, $charclean.);
   err=input(put(character_cleaned, $charname.),3.);
   region=put(character_cleaned, $charregion.);
run;
```

The user-defined formats CHARCLEAN and CHARREGION both transform values, and were created using the CNTLIN option of the FORMAT procedure. However, by adding a level of abstraction, BUILD_FORMAT dynamically creates these formats directly from the Game of Thrones denormalized data model. BUILD_FORMAT eliminates the need to prepare data for CNTLIN ingestion; thus, the Start, Label, Fmtname, and Type variables are dynamically created.

For example, to map the Game of Thrones raw character names (i.e., Variation variable) to corrected character names (i.e., Character variable), the following BUILD_FORMAT invocation dynamically creates the VARIATION_TO_CHARACTER format:

```
%build_format(fmtname=variation_to_character,
   dsnmodel=GOT_model_tabular,
   var1=variation,
   var2=character,
   invalid=DROP);
```

With the VARIATION_TO_CHARACTER user-defined format now defined, it can be applied to transform raw character names into cleaned names. The following DATA step applies VARIATION_TO_CHARACTER to the Favcharacter variable in the GOT_favorites data set:

```
data got_cleaned;
   length character_cleaned $30;
   label character_cleaned='GOT Character'
      favcharacter='Raw Character';
   set got_favorites;
   character_cleaned=
      put(favcharacter, $variation_to_character.);
run;
```

The GOT_cleaned data set is demonstrated in Table 15.4, in which the Raw Character column (Favcharacter variable) has been transformed into the GOT Character column (Character_cleaned variable). Note that as Kit Harington does not appear in the Game of Thrones data model (GOT_model_tabular data set), and as the INVALID argument specified DROP (in the BUILD_FORMAT invocation), this invalid value is dropped in lieu of being included in its raw form.

The BUILD_FORMAT macro can be invoked a second time to create the CHARACTER_TO_REGION format, which bins cleaned character names into their respective geographic regions:

```
%build_format(fmtname=character_to_region,
   dsnmodel=GOT_model_tabular,
   var1=character,
   var2=region,
   invalid=DROP);
```

Once again, DROP is specified in the INVALID argument to prevent invalid values from being retained in the transformed variable. For example, if the first BUILD_FORMAT invocation had instead specified KEEP for the

	GOT Character	Raw Character	Favorite Season
1	Jaime Lannister	Jaime Lannister	2
2	Cersei Lannister	Cersei Lannister	7
3	Daenerys Targaryen	Daenerys	4
4	Daenerys Targaryen	Daneris	7
5	Daenerys Targaryen	Daenerys Targaryen	2
6	Jaime Lannister	Jaime	1
7		Kit Harington	2
8	Arya Stark	Aria Stark	7
9	Tyrion Lannister	Tyrion Lannister	3
10	Sansa Stark	Sansa Stark	5

Table 15.4 GOT_cleaned Data Set after Dynamic Data Cleaning

INVALID argument, Kit Harington would have appeared in both the raw and cleaned character columns. Thereafter, if the second BUILD_FORMAT invocation had also specified KEEP for the INVALID argument, Kit Harington would have appeared in the Region column! For some use cases, retention of invalid values (after transformation) is desired, but this is definitely not one of those cases, so DROP is specified for both BUILD_FORMAT invocations.

With the CHARACTER_TO_REGION user-defined format now defined, it can be applied to transform character names into their respective regions. The following DATA step applies both user-defined formats to first clean and subsequently classify two variables:

```
data got_cleaned_classified;
    length region $30 character_cleaned $30;
    label region='Region'
        character_cleaned='GOT Character'
        favcharacter='Raw Character';
    set got_favorites;
    character_cleaned=put(favcharacter,
        $variation_to_character.);
    region=put(character_cleaned,
        $character_to_region.);
run;
```

	Region	GOT Character	Raw Character	Favorite Season
1	The Westerlands	Jaime Lannister	Jaime Lannister	2
2	The Westerlands	Cersei Lannister	Cersei Lannister	7
3	The Westerlands	Daenerys Targaryen	Daenerys	4
4	The Westerlands	Daenerys Targaryen	Daneris	7
5	The Westerlands	Daenerys Targaryen	Daenerys Targaryen	2
6	The Westerlands	Jaime Lannister	Jaime	1
7			Kit Harington	2
8	The North	Arya Stark	Aria Stark	7
9	The Westerlands	Tyrion Lannister	Tyrion Lannister	3
10	The North	Sansa Stark	Sansa Stark	5

Table 15.5 GOT_cleaned_classified Data Set

The GOT_cleaned_classified data set is demonstrated in Table 15.5, in which the Raw Character column is cleaned and transformed into the GOT Character column (using the VARIATION_TO_CHARACTER format), and in which the GOT Character column is subsequently categorized and transformed into Region (using the CHARACTER_TO_REGION format).

The GOT_cleaned_classified data set is identical to the GOT_class data set shown in Table 13.7—with the exception that the Err variable is not displayed. However, the user-defined formats applied to create GOT_class were defined through multiple, convoluted DATA steps and subsequent FORMAT procedures. Conversely, the equivalent user-defined formats created using the BUILD_FORMAT macro required only a few arguments that referenced the underlying (denormalized) hierarchical data model. Moreover, any format referencing two columns in the data model can be created by calling the reusable BUILD_FORMAT macro.

BUILD_FORMAT adds a level of procedural abstraction, and eliminates the need to interact directly with the finicky CNTLIN option. Moreover, as the data model is modified over time, all dependent formats are modified automatically (by calling BUILD_FORMAT), which eliminates the chaos of trying to maintain multiple data mappings and their respective formats. Finally, the BUILD_FORMAT macro embodies data-driven design because its extreme abstraction facilitates commensurate flexibility and reusability, with a straightforward invocation that conceals complexity within the macro implementation.

Procedural implementation and invocation are discussed in Sections 3.3 and 3.4, respectively

Abstraction levels are introduced in Section 2.2, and are contrasted with flexibility in Section 2.2.1

15.4 SUMMARY

Hierarchical and relational data models are often a more appropriate representation of complex data than tabular structures; however, denormalized hierarchical data often can be represented in tabular form. This chapter demonstrated how to represent hierarchical data within spreadsheets and XML files, as well as how to ingest hierarchical data models into SAS data sets.

This chapter demonstrated the BUILD_FORMAT macro, which dynamically creates user-defined formats from hierarchical and relational data models. Dynamically created formats overcome many limitations of the FORMAT procedure, by expanding beyond one-to-one and many-to-one mapping relationships. BUILD_FORMAT increases the efficiency with which user-defined formats can be developed, and ensures that related formats (subsumed within the same data model) remain synchronized, and can be collectively modified when necessary.

The use of hierarchical data models, when appropriate, improves data-driven design through data independence, in which external data structures can be modified without the use of hardcoded FORMAT procedures or the CNTLIN option. Espousing MDM principles, hierarchical data models also promote data integrity because a single, trusted version of a data model can be maintained.

Chapter 16.

CONFIGURATION FILES

This chapter has the following objectives:

- ❖ Introduce configuration files as a mechanism to maintain control data.

- ❖ Demonstrate two methods of attribute identification, including *positional* and *nominal* (i.e., keyword) identification.

- ❖ Demonstrate how user-defined SAS formats can facilitate color-coded "traffic light" reporting.

- ❖ Introduce cascading style sheets (CSS) and their role in maintaining stylistic attributes.

- ❖ Demonstrate how the CSSSTYLE option within the REPORT procedure can apply stylistic elements maintained in a CSS file.

C onfiguration files maintain the options, arguments, configuration items, and other control data that are interpreted by software to elicit dynamic functionality. Configuration files, a type of control file, are typically read during software or process initialization, after which their effects persist throughout software execution. Most configuration files are maintained within text files (using key-value pairs, XML, or other canonical data structures), although spreadsheets and other file formats are sometimes utilized.

Configuration files often contain the same control data that can be passed as arguments through procedural parameterization. Configuration files differ primarily because their control data *persist* (to support control data versioning, auditing, and other data archival objectives), not because their control data *differ*. Thus, their control data are often more similar to arguments than dissimilar, as both arguments and configuration items facilitate procedural abstraction.

Procedural abstraction is the focus of Chapter 3

Built-in configuration files are those produced for commercial software applications. For example, the SAS application configuration file (sasv9.cfg) drives SAS functionality and includes a repository of SAS system options that are initialized at startup. In some SAS environments, all instances of SAS rely on the same SAS configuration file, thus ensuring options are standardized for all users. In other environments, however, SAS practitioners can maintain personal copies of the SAS configuration file to individualize and save SAS application settings.

User-defined configuration files, conversely, represent configuration files developed by SAS practitioners. User-defined configuration files are especially useful where a process defines many parameters, or where complex arguments representing linear, tabular, or other data structures must be passed. Thus, the data-driven design objective of *configurability*, as the name suggests, is often facilitated through configuration files that maintain and pass control data.

Control data persistence is introduced and discussed in Section 9.3

One of the principal benefits of configuration files is their persistence. Control data can be saved within a configuration file to facilitate their archival for testing and validation purposes, or to support software versioning or auditing. Because data-driven design dictates that software comprises both code and control data, whenever a snapshot of software functionality must be taken, it must include not only code but also the control data that supply dynamic inputs, including configuration files.

This chapter introduces built-in and user-defined configuration files, and demonstrates how they can be implemented within SAS software. It demonstrates how control data can be maintained and identified within configuration files, as well as extracted and operationalized by SAS processes. Cascading style sheets (CSS) are introduced as a canonical configuration file data structure that facilitates the configuration of stylistic elements within SAS reports and other data products.

16.1 CONFIGURATION VS. CUSTOMIZATION

Software *configuration* and software *customization* are often conflated, if not interchanged intentionally, despite describing distinct methods, objectives, and outcomes. Software *configuration* describes everything you can do to affect software functionality and performance without modifying code, whereas *customization* always requires code modification. Software configuration often can be performed by nontechnical end users, whereas customization is performed by developers. Configuration is *customers-*focused, satisfying the multitudes, whereas customization is *customer-*focused, narrowly satisfying a single set of requirements for one user or user base.

This differentiation is critical within a data-driven design paradigm because the principal objectives of data-driven design include increased flexibility, configurability, and reusability, all of which convey the ability of software to adapt. Software is not adaptive when it must be continually rewritten for each new purpose, data source, customer, or other source of anticipated variability. Thus, *configuration* and the performance objective of *software configurability* are aptly discussed throughout this text, whereas *customization* is not.

The International Organization for Standardization (ISO) defines *configuration* as the "manner in which the hardware and software of an information processing system are organized and interconnected."[97] Configuration should be pursued early in the software development life cycle (SDLC), including the identification of *configuration items*—the articulation points at which software flexes. In subsequent SDLC phases, configurability is often achieved through procedural abstraction, in which end users and processes supply control data (passed through parameterization, configuration files, or other control files) to software.

ISO defines *customization* as the "adaptation of a software or documentation product to the needs of a particular audience."[98] Software

> Articulation points are discussed in relationship to flexibility and abstraction in Section 2.2.1

customization occurs through the release of software updates, in which increased or modified functionality is delivered to meet specific requirements. Customization is not inherently a bad thing, as it is customer-focused, but where equivalent software flexibility can be supplied instead through configuration, data-driven design can reduce the amount of redesign and rework that customization inherently requires.

For example, consider the nontechnical analysts who require modifications to the color or other style attributes of their SAS reports. Within a code-driven design paradigm, where color selection is hardcoded, nontechnical stakeholders must solicit the assistance of developers to modify (i.e., *customize*) color schemes—a seemingly simple task. However, by extracting stylistic elements from code, and instead maintaining these control data within configuration files, data-driven design can empower nontechnical end users themselves to *configure* the look and feel of their data products. Moreover, developers are freed to do more technical or imaginative work.

16.2 SAS APPLICATION CONFIGURATION FILE

The SAS application's primary configuration file is sasv9.cfg, where the "V" denotes the SAS version. A valid SAS configuration file is required to launch the SAS application, and works in coordination with the optional autoexec.sas file, if present. Autoexec.sas (not discussed in this text) is a great location to initialize SAS libraries, and to run other scripts that are systemic or environmental in nature, whereas sasv9.cfg is the sanctum sanctorum that maintains SAS system option settings.

The SAS configuration file can be located using the SASROOT environmental variable:

```
%put %sysget(SASROOT);
C:\Program Files\SASHome\SASFoundation\9.4
```

Section 6.4.2 demonstrates an alternative initialization of SAS system options from the OS command prompt

In some cases, this initial configuration file is only a shell that redirects to the actual configuration file:

```
-config "C:\Program
Files\SASHome\SASFoundation\9.4\nls\en\sasv9.cfg"
```

Among other contents, the SAS configuration file enumerates SAS system options that are initialized when the SAS application starts:

```
-FONTSLOC C:\windows\Fonts
-SET MYSASFILES "?FOLDERID_Documents\My SAS Files\9.4"
-SASUSER "?FOLDERID_Documents\My SAS Files\9.4"
-WORK "!TEMP\SAS Temporary Files"
-MEMSIZE 24G
-SORTSIZE 22G
-SET SASCFG "C:\Program
Files\SASHome\SASFoundation\9.4\nls\en"
-LOCALE en_US
-ENCODING wlatin1
-TEXTURELOC !SASROOT\common\textures
-SET SAS_NO_RANDOM_ACCESS "1"
```

Modifying the SAS configuration file is risky, as invalid or corrupt data can cause the SAS application to fail to initialize. A safer alternative, in many instances, is to create a local copy of sasv9.cfg, to make all modifications within this copy, and to specify this local configuration file (using the CONFIG parameter) during initialization of the SAS application.

For example, tired of having to specify the CPUCOUNT=ACTUAL option (which maximizes the number of CPUs the SAS application utilizes) each time I open the SAS application, I can instead include this option within a local SAS configuration file. The GETOPTION function displays the default CPUCOUNT value, which may be fewer than the maximum number of available CPUs:

```
%put %sysfunc(getoption(cpucount));
4
```

This limitation can be quickly remedied, however, by copying the configuration file (sasv9.cfg) to D:\sas\mysasconfig.cfg, and by appending the following line to the preceding list of options:

```
-CPUCOUNT actual
```

When the SAS application is subsequently restarted (from the command line or from a batch file), the local configuration file must be specified using the CONFIG parameter:

```
C:\Progra~1\SASHome\SASFoundation\9.4\sas.exe -config
"d:\sas\mysasconfig.cfg"
```

When the SAS application initializes, the GETOPTION function reveals that the CPUCOUNT has been increased from 4 to 8 (where 8 represents the maximum number of available CPUs on the system):

```
%put %sysfunc(getoption(cpucount));
8
```

As long as the mysasconfig.cfg file is referenced by the CONFIG parameter, SAS will retain this system option setting for future initializations. The risk of corrupting the actual SAS application configuration file has also been eliminated because only a local copy has been edited. Moreover, where local policy does not prohibit or restrict the use of local SAS configuration files, maintaining a local copy enables SAS practitioners to configure individual system options irrespective of the options selected by their team or organization.

Like so many aspects of data-driven design, developers often can create the most reliable, robust user-defined data structures by mimicking the built-in data structures (and their respective operations) with which we are familiar. The SAS application configuration file is no exception, and provides an excellent archetype for SAS practitioners to model when designing user-defined configuration files.

16.3 USER-DEFINED CONFIGURATION FILES

Section 2.2.3 introduces the *least privilege* concept, which minimizes stakeholder interaction with control data (or code) to mitigate risk, and Section 9.2 discusses control data stewardship

User-defined configuration files are most commonly maintained within text files. Configuration files are always intended to be modified by *someone*, but nontechnical stakeholders are not always their intended custodians. Many software applications may have layers of configuration files, enabling lower-risk attributes to be modified by end users, whereas system or higher-risk configuration items are maintained separately by developers or administrators. This separation facilitates integrity of both the control data within configuration files and the processes they direct.

Configuration files commonly comprise key-value pairs that map arguments to parameters (or attributes to elements). More complex configuration file data structures exist, however, including those that support hierarchical grouping of control data. Configuration file design considerations also include how to represent comments, how missing or invalid values should be handled, and what input validation should occur when a configuration file is ingested.

The design and documentation of configuration file data structures are generally straightforward because configuration files are typically read-only. Thus, although *codeless* software adds a user interface (i.e., a level of abstraction through which software can modify configuration control data), this design pattern is uncommon within SAS development. Within this read-only paradigm, only one user-defined operation—configuration file ingestion—typically must be developed.

Codeless software is described in Section 7.1.3

For this reason, teams and organizations often strive to standardize a configuration file data structure so that its template can be reused for disparate configuration files across SAS programs. This reuse of a consistent data structure supports software productivity because new data structures and their respective operations do not need to be repeatedly developed. End users also grow accustomed to a consistent data structure, and grow confident with updating control data within that structure. Given this standardization objective, data structure design considerations are discussed in the following subsections.

16.3.1 Design Considerations

Numerous design considerations should be evaluated when conceptualizing a user-defined configuration file data structure:

Several of these design considerations are introduced in Section 9.1, including data stewardship, file type, and element decomposition

- **Stakeholders** – For whom is the configuration file intended—SAS administrators, developers, subject matter experts (SMEs), or nontechnical end users? This decision should influence the amount and detail of data structure documentation, and the extent of control data validation required when reading the configuration file.
- **Scope** – Will the configuration file affect all SAS software, some programs, or a single program or process? Attributes with far-reaching scope, like SAS library definitions or some system options, are often more appropriately placed in the sasv9.cfg or autoexec.sas files than in user-defined configuration files.
- **File Type** – Should the configuration file be maintained as a simple text file, or should a spreadsheet, XML file, or other file type or data structure be used?
- **Data Structure Rules** – Every user-defined data structure has explicit or implicit rules that define the structure, format, and content of the control data they can maintain. What are these rules,

and to what extent are they documented (as comments) within the configuration file template?

- **Element Decomposition** – How are unique values or elements differentiated? As with all user-defined data structures, when built-in constructs (such as SAS variable boundaries, or spreadsheet cell boundaries) do not demarcate the end of one element and the beginning of another, user-defined methods must be engineered to ensure elements can be unambiguously identified.

- **Attribute Identification** – How are attributes ascribed to a specific element, or values to a specific key? Similar to procedural parameterization, values within a configuration file must be able to be identified through either file *position* (e.g., line number) or *keyword* (e.g., key-value pair).

- **Validation** – A configuration file can have the ability to make sweeping, functional changes across software. This power should be checked through data quality controls that validate the format and content of control data. If an element or attribute is invalid, exception handling can prescribe that the software does not initialize, or that it initializes with imputed or default values for all invalid attributes.

- **Data Independence** – Can data independence be achieved, in which control data are maintained within the configuration file apart from other explicit functionality? For example, the value BLUE can be listed, if identified positionally, or COLOR1=BLUE, if identified as part of a key-value pair; however, configuration files should be free of other statements, functions, or references that specify *how* BLUE is to be implemented.

- **Data Abstraction Level** – The data abstraction level will dictate in part how flexibly a configuration file data structure will support future reuse. For example, some configuration files define a set of parameters—specific keys, apart from which no other attributes can be maintained. Other configuration files more liberally define only the way in which keys must be structured, and thus can support any attributes—irrespective of key name—that are included.

Element decomposition is introduced in Section 9.6, and is a primary rationale for selecting built-in data structures over their user-defined counterparts

Section 4.7 discusses various ways that *blue* can be maintained and interpreted as control data

Section 16.3.6 shows the tiered_config.cfg configuration file in which *any* LIBRARY elements can be specified, yet *only* two STOPLIGHT elements can be defined

16.3.2 File Type and Data Structure Inheritance

In contrast with built-in data structures, most user-defined data structures—including configuration files—must be parsed to be decomposed into their constituent elements. Notwithstanding this effort, user-defined data structures are often necessary because they extend built-in software functionality—and where they can be built to be reliable, robust, and flexible, their reuse will be maximized.

Inheritance is discussed in Section 8.4.3

Configuration files are typically constructed within text files, and thus are subordinate to this file type. Text file rules might prescribe file characteristics such maximum line length, allowable characters, and automatic end-of-line (EOL) and end-of-file (EOF) markers—all of which are inherited by configuration files and other control files that are built within text files (e.g., CSS, CSV).

For example, a configuration file (colorconfig.txt) is parsed by separating variables (to the left of the equal sign) from values (to the right of the equal sign):

```
absinthe=25F95B
zaya=DE9421
fireball=DE8721
blue=38508F
black=0D1F4F
```

The following DATA step ingests the configuration file, relying on the implied data structure of key-value pairs:

```
%let loc=d:\sas\;       * USER MUST CHANGE LOCATION *;
data colorconfig;
    infile "&loc.colorconfig.txt" truncover
        delimiter='=';
    length color $32 hex $10;
    input color $ hex $;
    color=upcase(color);
    hex=upcase(hex);
run;
```

This configuration file ingestion process is updated in Section 16.3.3 so that comments can be incorporated into the file

Within the DATA step, the INPUT statement (coupled with the INFILE statement DELIMITER option) reads each line of the configuration file, and initializes the Color variable and corresponding hexadecimal values.

However, the internal iteration within the DATA step recognizes the text file's EOL marker, and advances to the next line. Because the text file's file type always contains EOL markers, user-defined methods do not have to be developed to advance to the next line of the configuration file as it is ingested.

Other user-defined data structures define both row and column elements, similar to the SAS data set, enabling individual elements to be readily identified and extracted from the data structure. For example, configuration files defined within spreadsheets not only have EOL and EOF markers, but also have cell delimiters. For this reason, a delimiter like the equal sign (required to separate key-value pairs in the colorconfig.txt configuration file) may not be required in spreadsheets—because cell barriers intrinsically provide this separation.

Thus, user-defined configuration files constructed in spreadsheets will typically be structured differently than those constructed in text files—because the user-defined data structures inherit characteristics from these superordinate built-in file types and data structures. An understanding of these nuances facilitates the selection of the superordinate data structure and file type that will best support a specific user-defined configuration file that is being designed.

16.3.3 Comments and Rules

Defining a commenting methodology is often one of the first objectives in configuration file design—because comments can convey concise rules that describe how the configuration file and its control data must be structured. The SAS language denotes comments with asterisks, and this symbology can be adopted when designing user-defined configuration files.

For example, the configuration file (colorconfig.txt) demonstrated in Section 16.3.2 can be updated to include comments:

```
* comments appear with preceding asterisks
* file saved as colorconfig.txt, used by Read_Colors
* KEY-VALUE pairs are separated by =
* KEYs represent named colors
* VALUEs represent hexadecimal values
* neither KEYs nor VALUEs should have special chars

***** DO NOT EDIT ABOVE THIS LINE *****
```

```
black=0D1F4F
blue=38508F
absinthe=25F95B
zaya=DE9421
fireball=DE8721
```

The configuration file data structure represents a common key-value pairing, so verbose explanations are unnecessary. Stakeholders will understand how to modify and maintain the control data, and the "DO NOT EDIT" caveat further distinguishes (and helps protect from unruly modification) the configuration file's data rules.

In a separate publication, the author documents instructions for how to not only structure a configuration file, but also implement its tags:[99]

```
***** IN THIS CONFIGURATION FILE *****

* <bracketed> terms represent user-defined tags that are
parsed into comma-delimited variables
* tags cannot contain spaces and must conform to SAS
variable naming conventions
* tag metadata must conform to SAS variable labeling
conventions
* tag metadata cannot contain asterisks, commas, or
other special characters

<desc>Program Description
<ver>Program Version
<auth>Author
<crdt>Create Date
<updt>Last Update
<test>Test Date
<vadt>Validation Date
<prdt>Production Date
<reqver>Required SAS Version
<vuln>Vulnerabilities
```

```
***** WHEN THESE TAGS ARE USED IN SAS PROGRAMS *****

* the final character (i.e., the semicolon) of all
metadata is removed

* an asterisk must precede each tag so Author would
appear as *<auth>Art Carpenter;
* all metadata are ingested as 100 character text fields
and saved as 500 character variables
* for example, five <desc> tags could be used to create
a longer description

* in the data set that is created, TAG_ precedes all
variables to avoid collision
* for example, the <auth> tag is saved as the 500
character variable TAG_AUTH
```

Regardless of the quantity and detail of commenting that initially exists within a user-defined configuration file, commenting should be considered part of software continuous quality improvement (CQI), in that as new software failure patterns are detected (and traced back to faulty configuration file control data), configuration file comments should be updated to help guard against similar failures in the future.

Especially where communal configuration files are maintained by stakeholders, these configuration files will become corrupted by stakeholders in accidental (yet ingenuous) methods never anticipated by developers. Accurate configuration file commenting can help mitigate this risk, and can be further buttressed by programmatic validation of configuration file structure and control data.

16.3.4 Positional Attribute Identification

Section 6.4.1 demonstrates the equivalent positional parameters defined within procedural abstraction

Positionally identified attributes are extremely uncommon in configuration files because they can more easily become corrupted, and because they can be impossible to comprehend visually. To illustrate these deficiencies, consider the wayward configuration file (two_colors.txt):

```
blue
green
```

The following DATA step reads the configuration file and, because the configuration file contains no keys or tags by which to identify attributes, must identify attributes by line number:

```
%let loc=d:\sas\;       * USER MUST CHANGE LOCATION *;
data _null_;
   infile "&loc.two_colors.txt" truncover;
   length color $32;
   input color $;
   if _n_=1 then call symputx('color1',
      strip(color),'g');
   else if _n_=2 then call symputx('color2',
      strip(color),'g');
run;


%put &=color1;
%put &=color2;
```

That is, &COLOR1 must appear in the first line, and &COLOR2 must appear in the second line. The somewhat eccentric (and risky) solution is functional, and the log demonstrates the initialization of the macro variables:

```
%put &=color1;
COLOR1=blue
%put &=color2;
COLOR2=green
```

However, were the number of attributes to increase, readability would be decreased because the attributes could not be distinguished visually. Moreover, if attribute order were accidentally shifted, this corruption might not be detected, but would cause attributes to be assigned to the wrong elements. The next subsection demonstrates the preferred key-value pairing method of attribute identification within configuration files.

16.3.5 Key-Value Pairs

Key-value pairs identify attributes *nominally*—based on named element tags, similar to keyword parameters that are declared within procedures and other callable modules. Where configuration files are maintained within unstructured text files (as opposed to canonical structures like XML

Section 6.4.2 demonstrates keyword parameters defined within procedural abstraction

files), keys are typically identified as the text *preceding* some delimiter, such as an equal sign or colon, or as the text surrounded by symbols, like open and closed brackets. For example, the following configuration file (three_colors.txt) defines three keys—COLOR1, COLOR2, and COLOR3:

```
* comments start with asterisks


***** DO NOT EDIT ABOVE THIS LINE *****
color1=red
color2=white
color3=blue
```

The DATA step ingests the configuration file, and reads each line into a single variable (Line):

```
%let loc=d:\sas\;        * USER MUST CHANGE LOCATION *;
data color_config (drop=line);
    infile "&loc.three_colors.txt" truncover dsd
        delimiter='=';
    length line $1000 color $32 value $32;
    input line & $ @;
    if lengthn(line)>0 and
            substr(strip(line),1,1)^='*' then do;
        input @1 color $ value $;
        call symputx(strip(color),strip(value),'g');
        output;
        end;
run;
%put &=color1;
%put &=color2;
%put &=color3;
```

The Line variable is first parsed to determine if it contains a comment (i.e., begins with an asterisk), and the @ operator holds the observation open after this initial input. When comments are not detected, a second INPUT statement rereads each line (specifying @1), and ingests delimited values into the Color and Value variables, respectively. The Color_config data set is created, and contains all key-value pairs of color mappings.

Finally, the SYMPUTX subroutine declares global macro variables (&COLOR1, &COLOR2, and &COLOR3) that are initialized to red, white, and blue, respectively, as shown in the log:

```
%put &=color1;
COLOR1=red
%put &=color2;
COLOR2=white
%put &=color3;
COLOR3=blue
```

Subsequent operations (not shown) could utilize either the Color_config data set or the color macro variables to drive dynamic functionality. Especially where arguments are numerous or complex, key-value pairs are the preferred method for identifying attributes.

16.3.6 Hierarchical Configuration Files

Given that arguments can pass linear, tabular, and hierarchical control data, configuration files, too, can be designed to represent more complex data structures than key-value pairs. Thus, the same methods that can parse complex user-defined arguments (during invocations) can be implemented to parse user-defined configuration files.

> Section 10.4 demonstrates passing tabular arguments to modules, and Chapter 15 demonstrates hierarchical control data maintained in spreadsheets and XML files

For example, one publication by the author defines a hierarchical configuration file (tiered_config.txt) and demonstrates how to extract its control data, which comprise categories, elements, and attributes:[100]

```
* comments start with asterisks
* headings appear in <BRACKETS>
* required headings include <LIBRARY> and <STOPLIGHT>
* elements and attributes are delimited by colons
* STOPLIGHT elements must be either LEV1 or LEV2


***** DO NOT EDIT ABOVE THIS LINE *****


<LIBRARY>
reports: d:\sas\lilweezie\procrastination\overduepapers\
<STOPLIGHT>
lev1: green
lev2: very light red
```

The subsequent DATA step ingests the configuration file, initializes the REPORTS library using the LIBNAME function, and initializes the global macro variables &LEV1 and &LEV2. Note that because the Category variable (representing either LIBRARY or STOPLIGHT) is retained across observations, the subsequent key-value pairs are subsumed under one of these hierarchical headings. For example, once <LIBRARY> is detected in the configuration file, all subsequent lines will inherit the LIBRARY attribute (in the Category variable) until a new bracketed term (like <STOPLIGHT>) is detected.

The following DATA step ingests the configuration file, whose control data initializes a SAS library and several macro variables:

```
data _null_;
    length line $100 category $8 lib $8 loc $32;
    infile "&loc.tiered_config.txt" truncover;
    input line $100.;
    if lengthn(line)>0 and substr(strip(line),1,1)^='*'
        then do;
        if upcase(line)="<LIBRARY>"
            then category="library";
        else if upcase(line)="<STOPLIGHT>" then
            category="stoplight";
        else do;
            if category="library" then do;
                lib=scan(line,1,":");
                loc=scan(line,2,":");
                rc=libname(lib,loc);
                end;
            else if category="stoplight" then do;
                if strip(lowcase(scan(line,1,":")))="lev1"
                    then call symputx("lev1",
                    strip(scan(line,2,":")),'g');
                if strip(lowcase(scan(line,1,":")))="lev2"
                    then call symputx("lev2",
                    strip(scan(line,2,":")),'g');
                end;
            end;
```

```
        end;
    retain category;
run;
```

All elements and attributes are interpreted through key-value pairs; however, they are operationalized differently based on their superordinate category. For example, key-value pairs listed under LIBRARY are ingested irrespective of their element name; however, key-value pairs listed under STOPLIGHT must correspond to either the LEV1 or LEV2 elements—a much more restrictive requirement, but one which promotes validation of control data.

A balance always must be struck between flexibility and focus, with less restrictive methods like LIBNAME supporting greater flexibility, and more restrictive methods like STOPLIGHT supporting focus. Regardless of the level of flexibility desired, validation of control data should be prioritized.

16.4 CONFIGURATION FILE VALIDATION AND REUSE

The DATA step in Section 16.3.5 ingests a single configuration file, and initializes color names to named color values contained in key-value pairs within the configuration file (three_colors.txt). Realizing that this functionality could be reused, a SAS practitioner might create a macro subroutine (CONFIG) that declares and initializes global macro variables for all key-value pairs maintained within a parameterized configuration file:

CONFIG is considered to be a *user-defined macro subroutine,* discussed in Section 3.7.2, because it does not contain a step boundary and does not resolve to a value

```
* CONFIG initializes a global macro var for each key;
* comments in the config file begin with asterisks;
* key-value pairs are delimited by an equal sign;
* elements/keys must conform to SAS variable naming;
* no masking/validation of attributes/values is done;
%macro config(cfg= /* configuration file name */);
%local fil rc fid eq var val close;
%let fil=ref;
%let rc=%sysfunc(filename(fil,&cfg));
%let fid=%sysfunc(fopen(&fil,i));
%if &fid>0 %then %do %while(%sysfunc(fread(&fid))=0);
    %let rc=%sysfunc(fget(&fid,line,500));
    %if %length(&line)>0 %then %do;
        %if "%substr(&line,1,1)"^="*" %then %do;
```

```
            %let eq=%index(&line,=);
            %if &eq>1 %then %do;
                %let var=%scan(&line,1,=);
                %let val=%substr(&line,%eval(&eq+1));
                %if %sysfunc(nvalid(&var))=1 %then %do;
                    %global &var;
                    %let &var=&val;
                    %end;
                %else %do;
                    %let syscc=1;
                    %put WARNING: Variable name (&var) does
not conform to SAS naming conventions. Config file will
continue processing;
                    %end;
                %end;
            %end;
        %end;
    %end;
%if &fid>0 %then %let close=%sysfunc(fclose(&fid));
%mend;
```

The CONFIG macro uses SAS input/output (I/O) functions to open a parameterized configuration file, and to read and iterate across its observations (i.e., key-value pairs). Lines beginning with an asterisk are defined as comments and skipped. The NVALID function validates that elements/keys conform to SAS variable-naming conventions, and all invalid variable names both set the &SYSCC global macro variable to 1 (a warning condition) and print a color-coded warning to the log.

The more_than_colors.txt configuration file is intended to be read by the CONFIG macro:

```
color1=red
color2=white
color3=blue
123nonvar=orange
toolong01234567890123456789012345678=green
blank space=gray
```

Because CONFIG is a macro subroutine that contains no step boundaries, it can be executed from inside a DATA step or SAS procedure. For example, the following DATA step calls CONFIG, which ingests More_than_colors, validates that the elements/keys are valid SAS variable names, and initializes the &COLOR1, &COLOR2, and &COLOR3 global macro variables:

```
%let loc=d:\sas\;        * USER MUST CHANGE LOCATION *;
data test_values;
   length c1 c2 c3 $10;
   %config(cfg=&loc.more_than_colors.txt);
   c1="&color1";
   c2="&color2";
   c3="&color3";
run;
```

The SAS log demonstrates that the last three elements in the configuration file could not be initialized as macro variables—one element starts with a number; one element exceeds 32 characters; and one element contains a space:

```
%let loc=d:\sas\;        * USER MUST CHANGE LOCATION *;
data test_values;
   length c1 c2 c3 $10;
   %config(cfg=&loc.more_than_colors.txt);
WARNING: Variable name (123nonvar) does not conform to
SAS naming conventions. Config file will
continue processing
WARNING: Variable name
(toolong012345678901234567890123456789) does not conform
to SAS naming
conventions. Config file will continue processing
WARNING: Variable name (blank space) does not conform to
SAS naming conventions. Config file will
continue processing
   c1="&color1";
   c2="&color2";
   c3="&color3";
   run;
```

```
NOTE: The data set WORK.TEST_VALUES has 1 observations
and 3 variables.
NOTE: DATA statement used (Total process time):
      real time            0.00 seconds
      cpu time             0.01 seconds
```

This example demonstrates basic validation of element (key) names to ensure they conform to SAS variable-naming conventions. However, substantially more validation could be warranted based on the need for robustness as well as the anticipated reuse cases for the configuration file data structure.

For example, SYSCC and SYSERR are both valid SAS variable names, so the NVALID function will not flag them; however, you would not want to allow a configuration file to pass these elements, as &SYSCC and &SYSERR are automatic macro variables, and thus could not be redeclared. Additionally, any attempt to assign a value to &SYSERR would fail because the automatic macro variable is read-only.

Additional validation also might be necessary to ensure that values or attributes do not contain special characters, or that special characters are appropriately masked. With these improvements, however, a more robust, reliable configuration file ingestion engine could be constructed, thus supporting reuse of both this ingestion operation and the configuration file data structure.

16.5 CASCADING STYLE SHEETS (CSS)

Chazz Michaels Michaels IS figure skating—and cascading style sheets (CSS) ARE data-driven design! CSS files embody an excellent way to conclude chapters on control data because they capture a historical paradigm shift from code-driven web design to data-driven web design. CSS files were born out of a necessity to separate webpage substance from style—maintaining the content of an HTML page apart from the attributes that prescribe how that content should be rendered. Thus, CSS files replace the outmoded practice of embedding attribute tags (i.e., control data) within domain data.

CSS files define stylistic elements within documents such as HTML web pages. CSS files are preferred because they are interoperable and can be read and rendered by countless software applications (including SAS).

Moreover, the maintenance of a single, trusted repository for these stylish control data supports master data management (MDM) objectives. Thus, the integrity of a single CSS file is greater because a single golden record is being maintained. MDM principles also facilitate greater maintainability; when a style must be changed, it can be modified in one file to alter stylistic elements in all derivative data products and documents that rely on that CSS file.

> MDM is introduced in Section 8.2, and stresses the importance of maintaining unique master data

The following subsections introduce stylistic elements within SAS data products, using both concrete and data-driven design methods. The cast of J.K Rowling's inimitable *Harry Potter* series provides a backdrop to produce stylized data products.

The Students data set, comprising young wizards and witches attending the Hogwarts School of Wizardry and Witchcraft, is created and represents data that SAS practitioners might want to stylize:

```
data students;
    infile datalines delimiter=',';
    length student $30 house $20;
    input student $ house $;
    label student='Students' house='House';
    datalines;
Neville Longbottom, Gryffindor
Draco Malfoy, Slytherin
Ginny Weasley, Gryffindor
Hannah Abbott, Hufflepuff
Tom Marvolo Riddle, Slytherin
Harry Potter, Gryffindor
;
```

The PRINT procedure prints the data set to the Output Delivery System (ODS), as illustrated in Figure 16.1:

```
proc print data=students noobs label;
run;
```

The *substance* of the report is accurate; however, the *style* leaves much to be desired, as it represents only hackneyed, default style settings. But *default* is only the beginning, and SAS provides ample opportunity to configure every aspect of its reports and other output.

Students	House
Neville Longbottom	Gryffindor
Draco Malfoy	Slytherin
Ginny Weasley	Gryffindor
Hannah Abbott	Hufflepuff
Tom Marvolo Riddle	Slytherin
Harry Potter	Gryffindor

Figure 16.1 Abridged Hogwarts Student Roster with House Affiliation

For example, if a customer requested that the "house colors" (i.e., the two colors that represent each Hogwarts house) be applied to the house names, this could be accomplished through the STYLE option within the REPORT procedure. This initial method is demonstrated in the next subsection, after which it is refactored to support data-driven design through CSS styles.

16.5.1 Style without CSS

The FORMAT procedure can generate formats that provide color and other stylistic elements dynamically based on values maintained in a data set (and operationalized with the CNTLIN option). For example, if a Hogwarts student belongs to the Gryffindor house, the Gryffindor color scheme can be dynamically applied to text or other components. Each Hogwarts house has two colors, differentiated as HOUSEBACK and HOUSEFORE, representing background and foreground, respectively:

```
proc format;
value $ houseback
    'Gryffindor'='#7F0909'
    'Slytherin'='#0D6217'
    'Hufflepuff'='#EEE117'
    'Ravenclaw'='#000A90';
run;
```

```
proc format;
value $ housefore
   'Gryffindor'='#FFC500'
   'Slytherin'='#AAAAAA'
   'Hufflepuff'='#000000'
   'Ravenclaw'='#946B2D';
run;
```

The REPORT procedure now relies on these user-defined formats to color the Hogwarts house names programmatically, avoiding the conditional logic nightmare that too often plagues REPORT and other procedures when styles are conditionally applied through hardcoded logic statements:

```
proc report data=students nocenter nowindows
       nocompletecols style(header)=[fontfamily=
       "engravers mt" fontsize=4 color=#FFFFFF
       backgroundcolor=#696969]
       style(column)=[fontfamily="century gothic"
       fontsize=3];
   column house student;
   define house / order 'Hogwarts House'
   style(column)=[backgroundcolor=$houseback.
       color=$housefore.];
   define student / display 'Student';
run;
```

The output is demonstrated in Figure 16.2, in which Hogwarts house names are printed in two-color highlighting. The REPORT procedure is concise, but half of its content is dedicated to stylistic instruction. If even more prescriptive requirements about the report style were added, the structure of the report would be further obfuscated—hidden beneath layers of fonts and colors and shading and cell margins and flyover text and all of the other configurable aspects of ODS.

The data-driven solution is to extract stylistic elements from the REPORT procedure, and to maintain these control data within an external data structure like a CSS file.

HOGWARTS HOUSE	STUDENT
Gryffindor	Neville Longbottom
	Ginny Weasley
	Harry Potter
Hufflepuff	Hannah Abbott
Slytherin	Draco Malfoy
	Tom Marvolo Riddle

Figure 16.2 Hogwarts Students Displayed in House Colors

16.5.2 Style with CSS

The Hogwarts data set was created in Section 16.5, and a basic report was produced. The report style was updated in Section 16.5.1 using user-defined formats that define two-color highlighting schemes and stylistic elements hardcoded in the REPORT procedure. Unfortunately, the hardcoding of stylistic elements commingles report style with report substance, decreasing the maintainability of each.

This jumbling can also threaten report integrity; report substance could be unintentionally modified when someone is attempting to modify only stylistic elements. Moreover, when stylistic elements are contained wholly within the report definition, they cannot be inherited from external sources.

For example, a team or organization might want to brand its report styles, which under a code-driven design paradigm would require separately modifying each REPORT procedure as well as other SAS procedures that generate output. CSS offers a solution by maintaining style elements in a single file that can be accessed by SAS and other applications.

The style elements can be removed from the REPORT procedure, and placed in a CSS file (Hogwarts_style.css):

```
.Header
{
    font-family: engravers mt;
    font-size: 4;
```

```
   color: #FFFFFF;
   background-color: #696969;
   border: 1px #C0C0C0 solid;
   padding: 10px;
}
.Data
{
   font-family: century gothic;
   font-size: 3;
   color: #000000;
   background-color: #FFFFFF;
   border: 1px #C0C0C0 solid;
}
.Table
{
   border-collapse: collapse;
}
td, td
{
   padding: 10px;
}
```

The CSSSTYLE option (within the REPORT procedure) specifies a style sheet from which to import stylistic control data. Note the reduced scope of the refactored REPORT procedure now that stylistic elements are abstracted to the CSS control file:

```
ods html path="&loc" file="hogwarts.html"
   cssstyle="&loc.hogwarts_style.css";
proc report data=students nocenter nowindows
       nocompletecols;
   column house student;
   define house / order 'Hogwarts House'
   style(column)=[backgroundcolor=$houseback.
      color=$housefore.];
   define student / display 'Student';
run;
ods html close;
```

The report output is identical to Figure 16.2, demonstrating the successful extraction of stylistic elements from the code to an external control file. However, not only *this* report but *all* reports now can rely on this CSS file, thus supporting MDM objectives of maintaining a single source of the truth. When global stylistic updates are required, they no longer must be feared because they can be made within a single CSS file to modify all derivative data products—without modification of any code.

Moreover, as CSS files are highly interoperable, these same stylistic definitions can drive non-SAS data products, such as HTML webpages or reports produced in other programming languages or applications. In so doing, data-driven design facilitates increased maintainability far beyond the SAS landscape to include the entire enterprise.

16.6 SUMMARY

This chapter demonstrated the critical role that configuration files play in data-driven design, in facilitating the interpretation, modification, and retention of control data. Configuration files are especially useful where control data must be versioned during software development, where they must be archived, and where stakeholders want to maintain and modify individualized instances of control data.

The SAS application configuration file (sasv9.cfg) was introduced, including methods that allow SAS practitioners to maintain local copies of this file. User-defined configuration files were also demonstrated, including the commonly implemented key-value pair method of identifying control data attributes within (and extracting them from) configuration files. The importance of configuration file data rules was discussed, including the benefits of incorporating rules into configuration file comments so they can guide stakeholder interaction with configuration items.

CSS files were introduced, which facilitate data independence of stylistic elements, allowing them to be maintained in external data structures rather than statically in code. Both code-driven and data-driven design paradigms were demonstrated for producing SAS reports, showing the clear advantages of the latter.

Finally, configuration files and their dynamic interpretation, like other control data, embody the pillars of data-driven design—abstraction, software modularity, and control data independence. Their fervent embrace can deliver the software flexibility, configurability, maintainability, and reusability for which data-driven design is sought.

Index

References

1   "biweekly." *Merriam-Webster.com*. 2019. https://www.merriam-webster.com/dictionary/biweekly.

2   Raymond, Eric. 2003. *The Art of Unix Programming*. Boston, Massachusetts: Addison-Wesley Professional.

3   Mitchell, Shaun. 2013. *SDL Game Development*. Birmingham, England: Packt Publishing.

4   Tan, Caitlin, Rochelle King, Elizabeth Churchill. 2017. *Designing with Data: Improving the User Experience with A/B Testing*. Boston, Massachusetts: O'Reilly Media, Inc.

5   ISO/IEC/IEEE 24765:2017. *Systems and software engineering—Vocabulary*. Geneva, Switzerland: International Organization for Standardization and Institute of Electrical and Electronics Engineers.

6   ISO/IEC 25010:2011. *System and software engineering—Systems and software Quality Requirements and Evaluation (SQuaRE)—System and software quality models*. Geneva, Switzerland: International Organization for Standardization and International Electrotechnical Commission.

7   Social Security Administration. *Age to Receive Full Social Security Benefits*. https://www.ssa.gov/planners/retire/retirechart.html.

8   In-N-Out Burger® Nutritional Facts. 2010. http://www.in-n-out.com/pdf/nutrition_2010.pdf.

9   ISO/IEC 19506:2012. *Information technology—Object Management Group Architecture-Driven Modernization (ADM)—Knowledge Discovery Meta-Model (KDM)*. Geneva, Switzerland: International Organization for Standardization and International Electrotechnical Commission.

10 "abstraction." 1916. *New Standard Dictionary of the English Language upon Original Plans Designed to Give, in Complete and Accurate Statement, in the Light of the Most Recent Advances in Knowledge, in the Readiest Form for Popular Use, the Orthography, Pronunciation, Meaning, and Etymology of All the Words, and the Meaning of Idiomatic Phrases, in the Speech and Literature of the English-Speaking Peoples, Together with Proper Names of All Kinds,*

the Whole Arranged in One Alphabetical Order. New York and London: Funk and Wagnalls.

11 Ellis, Rod. 1996. *Data Abstraction and Program Design: From Object-Based to Object-Oriented Programming, 2ed.* London, England: UCL Press.

12 Liskov, Barbara, and John Guttag. 1986. *Abstraction and Specification in Program Development.* The MIT Press. Cambridge, Massachusetts. Page 3.

13 Martin, Robert. 2017. *Clean Architecture: A Craftsman's Guide to Software Structure and Design.* Boston: Pearson Education.

14 Garbutt, David J. 2012. "Re-programming a many-to-many merge with Hash Objects." *Pharmaceutical Users Software Exchange (PHuse).* Budapest, Hugary.
https://www.lexjansen.com/phuse/2012/cs/CS05.pdf.

15 Liskov, Barbara, and John Guttag. 1986.

16 *SAS® 9.4 and SAS® Viya® 3.4 Programming Documentation / Base SAS Procedures Guide: SORT Procedure.* Cary, North Carolina: SAS Institute.
https://documentation.sas.com/?cdcId=pgmsascdc&cdcVersion=9.4_3.4&docsetId=proc&docsetTarget=p1nd17xr6wof4sn19zkmid81p926.htm&locale=en.

17 ISO/IEC/IEEE 29148:2011. *Systems and Software Engineering—Life cycle processes—Requirements engineering.* Geneva, Switzerland: International Organization for Standardization and International Electrotechnical Commission.

18 *CISSP Glossary—Student Guide.* International Information System Security Certification Consortium.
https://www.isc2.org/Certifications/CISSP/CISSP-Student-Glossary#

19 ISO/IEC 19500-2:2012. *Information technology—Object Management Group—Common Object Request Broker Architecture (COBRA)—Part 2: Interoperability.* Geneva, Switzerland: International Organization for Standardization and International Electrotechnical Commission.

20 ISO/IEC/IEEE 24765:2010. *Systems and software engineering—Vocabulary.* Geneva, Switzerland: International Organization for Standardization and Institute of Electrical and Electronics Engineers.

21 SAS® 9.4 Functions and CALL Routines: Reference, Fifth Edition: ANYDIGIT Function. Cary, North Carolina: SAS Institute.
https://documentation.sas.com/api/collections/pgmsascdc/9.4_3.5/docsets/lefunctionsref/content/lefunctionsref.pdf

22 ISO/IEC 19500-2:2012.

23 ISO/IEC 19770:2012. *Information technology—Software asset management—Part 1: Processes and tiered assessment of conformance.* Geneva, Switzerland: International Organization for Standardization and International Electrotechnical Commission.

24 Friedman, Linda Weiser. 1991. *Comparative Programming Languages: Generalizing the Programming Function.* Englewood Cliffs, New Jersey: Prentice Hall.

25 ISO/IEC/IEEE 24765:2017.

26 ISO/IEC/IEEE 24765:2017.

27 Hughes, Joan K. 1986. *PL/I Structured Programming, Third Edition.* New York, New York: John Wiley and Sons.

28 Hughes, Joan K. 1986

29 Pollack, Seymour V. and Sterling, Theodor D. 1980. *A Guide to Structured Programming and PL/I, Third Edition.* New York, New York: Holt, Rinehart and Winston.

30 SAS Institute Inc. 1982. *SAS User's Guide: Basics, 1982 Edition.* Cary, North Carolina: SAS Institute Inc.

31 SAS Institute Inc. 1988. *SAS Language Guide for Personal Computers, Release 6.03 Edition.* Cary North Carolina: SAS Institute Inc.

32 SAS Institute Inc. 1990. *SAS Language: Reference, Version 6, First Edition.* Cary, North Carolina: SAS Institute Inc.

33 SAS Institute Inc. 1997. *SAS Macro Language: Reference, First Edition.* Cary, North Carolina: SAS Institute Inc.

34 SAS Institute Inc. 1991. *SAS/Toolkit Software: Usage and Reference, Version 6, First Edition.* Cary, North Carolina: SAS Institute Inc.

35 SAS Institute Inc. 2003. *The FCMP Procedure.* Cary, North Carolina: SAS Institute Inc.

36 SAS Institute Inc. 2016. *SAS 9.4 Functions and CALL Routines: Reference, Fifth Edition.* Cary, North Carolina: SAS Institute Inc.

37 ISO/IEC/IEEE 24765:2017.

38 Liskov, Barbara, and John Guttag. 1986.

39 Zimmer, J.A. 1985. *Abstraction for Programmers.* New York, New York: McGraw-Hill.

40 ISO/IEC/IEEE 24765:2017.

41 IEEE Std 1320.2-1998 (R2004). *IEEE Standard for Conceptual Modeling Language - Syntax and Semantics for IDEF1X97 (IDEFobject).* New York, New York: Institute of Electrical and Electronics Engineers.

42 ISO/IEC/IEEE 24765:2017.

43 ISO/IEC/IEEE 24765:2017.

44 IEEE Std 1320.2-1998 (R2004).

45 SAS® 9.4 Language Reference: Concepts, Sixth Edition. 2019. *Definitions for Array Processing*. Cary, North Carolina: SAS Institute. https://documentation.sas.com/?docsetId=lrcon&docsetTarget=n1d z2m2a92evwwn15vaikevup5pr.htm&docsetVersion=9.4&locale=en.

46 ISO/IEC/IEEE 24765:2017.

47 IEEE Std 1320.2-1998 (R2004).

48 ISO/IEC/IEEE 24765:2017.

49 ISO/IEC/IEEE 24765:2017.

50 ISO/IEC/IEEE 24765:2017.

51 ISO/IEC/IEEE 24765:2017.

52 ISO/IEC/IEEE 24765:2017.

53 ISO/IEC/IEEE 24765:2017.

54 ISO/IEC/IEEE 24765:2017.

55 SAS Institute Inc. 2016. *SAS 9.4 Macro Language: Reference, Fifth Edition*. Cary, North Carolina: SAS Institute Inc.

56 ISO/IEC/IEEE 24765:2017.

57 ISO/IEC/IEEE 24765:2017.

58 ISO/IEC/IEEE 24765:2017.

59 ISO/IEC/IEEE 24765:2017.

60 Hughes, Troy. 2016. *SAS® Data Analytic Development: Dimensions of Software Quality*. Hoboken, New Jersey: John Wiley and Sons.

61 ISO/IEC/IEEE 24765:2017.

62 Kolosova, Tanya, and Samuel Berestizhevsky. 1995. *Table-Driven Strategies for Rapid SAS® Application Development*. Cary, North Carolina: SAS Institute.

63 Kolosova, Tanya, and Samuel Berestizhevsky. 1995.

64 ISO/IEC 25024:2015. *Systems and software engineering—Systems and software Quality Requirements and Evaluation (SQuaRE)— Measurement of data*. Geneva, Switzerland: International Organization for Standardization and International Electrotechnical Commission.

65 Berson, Alex, and Larry Dubov. 2007. *Master Data Management and Customer Data Integration for a Global Enterprise*. New York, New York: McGraw-Hill.

66   Loshin, David. 2009. *Master Data Management.* Boston, Massachusetts: Morgan Kaufmann Publishers.

67   Martin, Robert C. 2018.

68   James Taylor. 2011. *Decision Management Systems: A Practical Guide to Using Business Rules and Predictive Analytics.* Upper Saddle River, New Jersey: IBM Press.

69   Taylor, James. 2011. *Decision Management Systems: A Practical Guide to Using Business Rules and Predictive Analysis.* Upper Saddle River, NJ: IBM Press.

70   Bhansali, Neera. 2013. *Data Governance: Creating Value from Information Assets.* New York, New York: Auerbach Publications.

71   Chisholm, Malcolm. 2004. *How to Build a Business Rules System.* Boston, Massachusetts: Morgan Kaufmann Publishers.

72   Miller, Robert. 2015. *Patterns, Principles, and Practices of Domain-Driven Design.* Birmingham, England: Wrox.

73   Rad, Reza. 2014. *Microsoft SQL Server 2014: Business Intelligence Development: A Beginner's Guide.* Birmingham, England: Packt Publishing.

74   Loshin, David. 2012. *Business Intelligence: The Savvy Manager's Guide, 2nd Edition.* David Loshin. Boston, Massachusetts: Morgan Kaufmann Publishers.

75   ISO/IEC 10746-2:2009. *Information technology — Open Distributed Processing — Reference Model: Foundations.* Geneva, Switzerland: International Organization for Standardization and International Electrotechnical Commission.

76   ISO/IEC 19500-1:2012. *Information technology—Object Management Group—Common Object Request Broker Architecture (CORBA)—Part 1: Interfaces.* Geneva, Switzerland: International Organization for Standardization and International Electrotechnical Commission.

77   Pree, Wolfgang. 1995. *Design Patterns for Object-Oriented Software Development.* Reading, Massachusetts: Addison-Wesley.

78   IEEE Std 1320.2-1998 (R2004).

79   ISO/IEC/IEEE 24765:2017.

80   Marvin, Ryan, Mark Nga, and Amos Omondi. 2018. *Python Fundamentals.* Birmingham, England: Packt Publishing.

81   ISO/IEC 25010:2011.

82   IEEE Std 1320.2-1998 (R2004).

83   ISO/IEC/IEEE 24765:2017.

84   IEEE Std 1320.2-1998 (R2004).

85 IEEE 1701-2011. *IEEE Standard for Optical Port Communication Protocol to Complement the Utility Industry End Device Data Tables.* New York, New York: Institute of Electrical and Electronics Engineers. https://ieeexplore.ieee.org/document/5716536.

86 ISO/IEC 10746-2:2009. *Information technology—Open Distributed Processing—Reference Model: Foundations.* Geneva, Switzerland: International Organization for Standardization and International Electrotechnical Commission.

87 ISO/IEC/IEEE 15289:2015. *Systems and software engineering—Content of life-cycle information products (documentation).* Geneva, Switzerland: International Organization for Standardization and International Electrotechnical Commission.

88 ISO/IEC 25024:2015.

89 Narayan, Rom. 1988. *Data Dictionary Implementation, Use, and Maintenance.* Englewood Cliffs, New Jersey: Prentice-Hall, Inc.

90 Leong-Hong, Belkis W. and Plagman, Bernard K. 1982. *Data Dictionary/Directory Systems: Administration, Implementation and Usage.* New York, New York: John Wiley and Sons.

91 Wertz, Charles J. 1989. *The Data Dictionary Concepts and Uses, Second Edition.* Wellesley, Massachusetts: QED Information Sciences, Inc.

92 ISO 5806:1984. *Information processing—Specification of single-hit decision tables.* Geneva, Switzerland: International Organization for Standardization.

93 ISO/IEC/IEEE 29119-4:2015. *Software and systems engineering—Software testing—Part 4: Test techniques.*

94 ISO/IEC/IEEE 29119-4:2015. *Software and systems engineering—Software testing—Part 4: Test techniques.* Geneva, Switzerland: International Organization for Standardization and International Electrotechnical Commission.

95 ISO/IEC/IEEE 24765:2017.

96 Hughes, Troy M. 2018. "Abstracting and Automating Hierarchical Data Models: Leveraging the SAS® FORMAT Procedure CNTLIN Option To Build Dynamic Formats That Clean, Convert, and Categorize Data." *PharmaSUG.* Seattle, Washington. https://www.pharmasug.org/proceedings/2018/QT/PharmaSUG-2018-QT04.pdf

97 ISO/IEC 2382:2015. *Information Technology—Vocabulary.* Geneva, Switzerland: International Organization for Standardization and International Electrotechnical Commission.

98 ISO/IEC 26514:2008. *Systems and software engineering—requirements for designers and developers of user documentation.* Geneva, Switzerland: International Organization for Standardization and International Electrotechnical Commission.

99 Hughes, Troy M. 2016. "Your Local Fire Engine Has an Apparatus Inventory Sheet and So Should Your Software: Automatically Generating Software Use and Reuse Libraries and Catalogs from Standardized SAS® Code." *Western Users of SAS Software (WUSS).* Long Beach, California. https://www.lexjansen.com/wuss/2017/118_Final_Paper_PDF.pdf.

100 Hughes, Troy M. 2015. SAS® Spontaneous Combustion: Securing Software Portability through Self-Extracting Code. *Western Users of SAS Software (WUSS).* San Diego, California. https://www.lexjansen.com/wuss/2015/78_Final_Paper_PDF.pdf.

Made in the USA
Middletown, DE
10 September 2024

60043971R00316